AF755331

EU Law Enforcement
The Evolution of Sanctioning Powers

Routledge Research in EU Law

Available titles in this series include:

The Evolving EU Counter-terrorism Legal Framework
Maria O'Neill

The Early Warning System for the Principle of Subsidiarity
Constitutional Theory and Empirical Reality
Philipp Kiiver
The European Constitution, Welfare States and Democracy
The Four Freedoms vs. National Administrative Discretion
Christoffer C. Eriksen

New Governance and the European Strategy for Employment
Samantha Velluti

Human Rights and Minority Rights in the European Union
Kirsten Shoraka

Centralized Enforcement, Legitimacy and Good Governance in the EU
Melanie Smith

EU External Relations and Systems of Governance
The CFSP, Euro-Mediterranean Partnership and migration
Paul James Cardwell

The EU Social Market Economy and the Law
Theoretical Perspectives and Practical Challenges for the EU
Delia Ferri and Fulvio Cortese

Gender and the Court of Justice of the EU
Jessica Guth and Sanna Elfving

The EU and the Proliferation of Integration Principles under the Lisbon Treaty
Francesca. Ippolito, Maria Eugenia Bartoloni, Massimo Condinanzi

Migration Law and the Externalization of Border Controls
European State Responsibility
Anna Liguori

Member States Interests and European Union Law
Revisiting the Foundations of Member State Obligations
Marton Varju

https://www.routledge.com/Routledge-Research-in-EU-Law/book-series/ROUTEULAW

Edited by
Stefano Montaldo, Francesco Costamagna, Alberto Miglio

EU Law Enforcement
The Evolution of Sanctioning Powers

Routledge
Taylor & Francis Group
LONDON AND NEW YORK

G. Giappichelli Editore

First published 2021
by Routledge
2 Park Square, Milton Park, Abingdon, Oxon OX14 4RN

and by Routledge
605 Third Avenue, New York, NY 10158

Routledge is an imprint of the Taylor & Francis Group, an informa business

British Library Cataloguing-in-Publication Data
A catalogue record for this book is available from the British Library

Library of Congress Cataloging-in-Publication Data
A catalog record has been requested for this book

ISBN: 978-88-921-3454-6 (hbk-G. Giappichelli Editore)
ISBN: 978-0-367-18640-1 (hbk-Routledge)
ISBN: 978-0-367-76566-8 (pbk)
ISBN: 978-0-429-19781-9 (ebk-Routledge)

Typeset in Simoncini Garamond
by G. Giappichelli Editore, Turin, Italy

The manuscript has been subjected to the double blind peer review process prior to publication.

The publication of this book was funded by Fondazione Compagnia di San Paolo, in the framework of the research project of the University of Turin "Offenders' Rehabilitation in the European Union", coordinated by Prof. Stefano Montaldo.

Compagnia
di San Paolo

CONTENTS

Chapter 1
INTRODUCTION

In 1992, Advocate General Giuseppe Tesauro noted that the issue of sanctions in the EU (then Community) legal order raised some concern, as sanctioning powers were considered to be lacking.[1] These words highlighted the shortcomings deriving from the limited sanctioning powers conferred upon the then European Community. At the time, three main factors contributed to scaling down the EC's role in this domain. Firstly, the lack of legal bases in the Treaty and the Member States' unwillingness to strengthen the sanctioning powers of the EC institutions, with limited exceptions. Secondly, according to some commentators, the European institutions were themselves focused on developing the Community legal order and policies, rather than on securing the implementation of relevant legislation at domestic level. Thirdly, the exercise of *jus puniendi* was still perceived as a primary task of the national authorities, due to its close connection with the idea of sovereignty over a given territory and a group of people. Consequently, the EC sanctioning system was originally confined to those limited provisions of secondary legislation expressly conferring such a task to the Community institutions.

In less than thirty years, the scenario has steadily changed.

Following the *Amsterdam Bulb* and *Greek Maize* case law,[2] EU law may require the Member States to impose proportionate, appropriate and effective sanctions as a corollary to their general obligation to ensure the effectiveness of EU law. This duty stems from the principle of loyal cooperation and has been considered *a contrario* as evidence of the existence of a structured EU-driven repressive system. Indeed, it provides a legal basis for the imposition of a sanction even in the absence of specific provisions of EC law.[3] However, *Greek Maize* situations merely reflect the multi-layered structure of the European legal order and the general rule according to which the Member States are tasked with implementing and executing EU law. Although national authorities have the duty to punish certain conduct under Article 4(3) TEU, the Union's *jus puniendi* is blurred by the allocation of the choice regarding the type and extent of a sanctioning measure at domestic level. Certainly, recent practice indicates that the margin of discretion left to the Member States is gradual-

---

[1] G. Tesauro, La sanction des infractions au droit communautaire, General Report, XV FIDE Congress, Lisbon, 1992, 425.

[2] Case 50/76, *Amsterdam Bulb*, ECLI:EU:C:1977:13; case C-68/88, *Commission v. Greece (Greek Maize)*, ECLI:EU:C:1989:339.

[3] This can be inferred from Advocate General Capotorti's opinion as expressed in *Amsterdam Bulb*, para. 4.

ly being eroded, as the European legislature increasingly sets out the nature of the sanctions to be enacted at domestic level and the basic criteria of their intensity.

Yet, this is just one of the developments affecting the EU's ability to exercise sanctioning powers. Indeed, EU institutions and bodies are increasingly endowed with direct sanctioning powers. The reach of the integration process has instigated a transformation process of the Union's law enforcement powers and responsibilities, prompting the centralisation of enforcement powers into the hands of EU institutions and bodies.

On one hand, ever since the first cases in which the Court of Justice acknowledged that the then Community was entitled to impose sanctions, European institutions have fully exploited broadly worded primary legal bases – such as provisions enabling them to take all necessary measures to ensure the functioning of a given mechanism or system – to strengthen their direct enforcement powers. The common agricultural policy is a case in point. Neither the original version of Article 40 EEC (subsequently re-numbered as Article 34) nor the current wording of Article 40 TFEU expressly codifies such a power. Nonetheless, the Union legislature has relied on this legal basis to enact a vast array of measures to enrich its sanctioning toolbox. The compatibility of these instruments with the Treaties has been confirmed *in abstracto* by the Court of Justice.[4] As a consequence, the recourse to sanctioning powers (and to the broad definition of the very notion of sanction) has expanded to other domains, such as the environment policy. Interestingly, the Court of Justice has resorted to a similar approach in relation to its own powers pursuant to Article 279 TFEU, which entitles the Court to prescribe "any necessary interim measures".[5]

On the other hand, over the last two decades, Treaty reforms and new legislation have led either to the formal attribution to EU institutions and bodies of the power to impose sanctions directly or to the strengthening of previously granted competences, for instance with regard to restrictive measures and country sanctions, in infringement proceedings, in the framework of the EMU and of the Banking Union.

Moreover, in the absence of a formal definition, the very notion of sanction has been construed broadly. The EU toolbox has been gradually equipped with an array of both punitive and restorative measures. The former are intended to place burdens on those who affect European interests or more generally infringe EU law, be they Member States, third countries, natural or legal persons. These include traditional monetary sanctions – e.g. competition fines, sanctions for breaches of data protection rules, fines issued in the framework of the banking supervision rules, and lump sums and penalties pursuant to Article 260 TFEU – but also much more diversified measures, such as the suspension from the enjoyment of certain rights, the prohibition

---

[4] See for instance 354/95, *National Farmers' Union*, ECLI:EU:C:1997:379.

[5] Case C-441/17 R, *Commission v. Poland*, paras 103 and 104, ECLI:EU:C:2017:877.

on receiving EU funding for a given period or on performing a given activity, seizure and confiscation. The latter are basically intended to restore the situation prior to a violation of EU law occurring and are mainly represented by restitutions of unduly obtained sums and revocations of decisions, awards and statuses. Even though both categories of measures contribute to shaping the EU system of repression, punitive sanctions pose particular challenges and call into question the scope and breadth of the Union's powers. Therefore, they represent the principal focus of this book.

Although the development of EU law enforcement schemes and methods has recently triggered insightful studies, the advances of the EU's direct sanctioning power are still largely under-examined among legal scholars. Against this background, the book aims to provide a comprehensive picture of this phenomenon and its evolution, including its systemic implications for the European legal order and the relationship between EU and national law. For this purpose, the book is structured as follows.

Firstly, the trend towards the expansion and strengthening of EU sanctioning powers is reflected in the growing complexity of the EU's institutional setting and a variety of agencies has been or is expected to be endowed with law enforcement responsibilities. When considered from a more general perspective, the emergence of an articulated repressive machinery at supranational level is a sign of the degree of complexity and maturity reached by the EU legal order. In the opening chapter, Miroslava Scholten assesses this intricacy and categorises the models of EU law enforcement, highlighting the role played by sanctions in this regard. Her analysis is complemented by the chapter written by Jacopo Alberti, which focuses on the growing diversification of entities endowed with sanctioning powers at EU level by concentrating on the role of EU agencies. The chapter argues that the vague legal status of these bodies and their diversified structures and tasks have contributed to the fragmentation of EU law enforcement models into as many bits and pieces as the relevant stakeholders that are involved.

In addition to mapping models and stakeholders, the book identifies the main triggers and rationales of the evolution of EU sanctioning power. As is generally recognised, *jus puniendi* pursues the well-established goals of fostering the effectiveness of Union policies and overseeing the proper implementation of EU law at domestic level. This is further confirmed by the fact that the strengthening of the EU's sanctioning capabilities is often a reaction to a perceived lack of effectiveness of the relevant legal framework. The economic and financial crisis and the rule of law backsliding taking place in certain Member States provide apt examples in this regard.

In this context, the book investigates the rationale behind the EU sanctioning power also with regard to traditional enforcement mechanisms. The chapter by Luca Prete does just this, focusing on the infringement procedure and discussing its most recent developments. The problem of effectiveness also lies at the core of the debate on the recourse to sanctions in order to protect the values of the Union.

Matteo Bonelli, in his chapter, focuses on the EU sanctioning toolbox and its suitability for protecting the rule of law, illustrating the interplay between preventive mechanisms and hard sanctions, and between political and judicial enforcement tools.

The teleological approach to sanctioning powers unveils an inherent tension between the quest for the effectiveness of EU law and policies with the general principles of the EU legal order. The further the EU sanctioning authority expands, the greater the need becomes to establish appropriate limits on the use of punitive powers by EU institutions and bodies. From this perspective, Nicole Lazzerini addresses the relevance of the Charter of Fundamental Rights, while Stefano Montaldo looks at EU sanctions through the lens of the principle of proportionality, which underpins the whole sanctioning cycle, from the abstract pre-determination of the form and amount of a sanction to its actual imposition in an individual case.

Beyond this general institutional layer, the evolution of EU sanctioning powers follows diversified paths depending on the specific policy domain involved. Here, the blurring of enforcement models reaches its peak, in parallel with the scope and breadth of the EU's competence to impose sanctions. The book depicts this complex and diversified scenario by providing insights into key areas where the Union is entitled to issue repressive measures to safeguard compliance with its interests and policies.

Alberto Miglio and Francesco Costamagna look at the enforcement machinery in the EMU economic pillar and observe that, despite the prominence of sanctioning mechanisms and the emphasis on fiscal discipline, recourse to formal sanctions has been negligible due to the presence of alternative enforcement tools. This chapter is complemented by Frédéric Allemand's analysis of the new sanctioning toolbox given to the European Central Bank in the framework of prudential supervision on the banking system.

Two chapters focus on EU restrictive measures in the context of the CFSP. Charlotte Beaucillon discusses the normative power of the Union to use these sanctions as tools of value exportation. She outlines the possible future developments of the EU's practice and critically addresses the political conditionality of partnership agreements, illustrated by human rights clauses, which have led some third countries to prioritise the establishment of commercial relationships with other areas of the world. Andrea Spagnolo provides a complementary perspective on CFSP sanctions by looking at the topic through the lens of international law, discussing the legality of EU autonomous CFSP sanctions in light of recent complaints raised before the International Court of Justice and the WTO against similar sanctions imposed by the United States.

The concluding set of chapters covers EU policies where the Union's repressive powers are either particularly deeply rooted and developed or stand out due to their peculiar features. Luca Calzolari looks at competition law fines pursuant to Articles 101 and 102 TFEU and the respective secondary legislation, examining the legal nature of sanctions, their rationale, and the calculation methods. Francesco Munari outlines the main features of EU environmental law enforcement, affecting not only Member States with infringement procedures and interim measures, but also individuals under the Environmental Liability Directive and the Environmental Crime Directive. Lastly, Paul de Hert's chapter provides a detailed analysis of law enforcement tools in the context of EU data protection law, mapping the sweeping changes brought about by the GDPR.

Stefano Montaldo – Francesco Costamagna – Alberto Miglio
(University of Turin)

Chapter 2

EU (SHARED) LAW ENFORCEMENT: WHO DOES WHAT AND HOW?

Miroslava Scholten *-**

ABSTRACT: *Enforcement of EU law has changed considerably in the last decades. By bringing the recent developments together, this chapter offers a 'bird's-eye view' of the 'what, who and how' concerning enforcement of EU law. It discusses the many ways of enforcement under the three scenarios and zooms in on the most intrusive enforcement power, i.e., the sanctioning power. All in all, it shows that enforcement of EU law has been done differently in different policy areas, which demonstrates an ongoing search for the conditions and factors of when EU law enforcement can be enforced more effectively and what role there is for sanctions to play.*

KEYWORDS: *enforcement – models – sanctions – EU*

2.1. Introduction

The European Union (EU) has rapidly evolved from being an international organization to become a supranational polity with autonomous regulatory and enforcement powers. Its regulatory power, which is derived from hard, case and soft law, has expanded from pure 'economic' areas, such as the original coal and steel sector, to include other policy fields like environmental policy. What is more, in recent decades, the enforcement power of the EU has increased drastically in various ways, including direct enforcement powers by EU enforcement authorities (EEAs)

---

* Associate Professor of EU Law, RENFORCE, Utrecht University.

** This chapter is a part of the ongoing research project of the author 'Shared tasks, but separated controls in the EU – how to make it work for democracy and the rule of law', funded by the Dutch Research Council (NWO) under the 'veni' scheme of M. Scholten. I would like to thank Tom Huisjes, Maurits Munck, Giancarlo Pistelli and Leander Stähler for their assistance. A first draft was presented before the scholars and students at the conference 'European Union Law Enforcement: The Evolution of Sanctioning Powers', Turin, 28-29 March 2019, for which I am grateful to the organisors-editors of this volume.

vis-à-vis private parties.[1] Enforcement implies monitoring compliance with laws, investigating an alleged violation of a law and the sanctioning for a violation.[2] It is essential for the implementation of any policy as it can rectify non-compliance and promote the attainment of policy goals.[3] At the same time, enforcement power, and especially its sanctioning stage, implies interfering in activities and with rights and freedoms of the affected parties. Therefore, it is essential that the enforcement power is exercised in accordance with the rule of law ideals – legitimacy and necessary controls to prevent the abuse of power and arbitrary interferences – which is challenging in a multi-jurisdictional legal order of the EU.

Enforcement of EU law has been experiencing many changes in recent years. Many actors have appeared at the EU and national levels to prescribe enforcement standards, by being involved in direct enforcement and sanctioning and supervising the direct enforcers. The differences between enforcement processes in different policy areas are not that easy to explain and it seems that the development has occurred quite sporadically and in different forms and speeds in different sectors.[4] This is alongside the fact that there are different ways as to how law can be enforced in general and EU law in particular, also as to whether sanctioning takes part (or should take part) in the enforcement process or not and of what type.[5] So, who does what in EU (shared) law enforcement and what sanctions can be involved? I will start with defining enforcement (section 2). On these premises, I will discuss different enforcement scenarios that have emerged in varied sectors (section 3). Then, I will zoom in on the most far reaching enforcement power, namely the sanctioning power (section 4). In section 5, I present some conclusions. Overall, this chapter aims to show who does what in the enforcement of EU law, building on existing literature[6] and information presented in other chapters of this book.

---

[1] M. Scholten, M. Luchtman, *Law Enforcement by EU Authorities: Implications for Political and Judicial Accountability* (Edward Elgar Publishing 2017).

[2] J. Vervaele, 'Shared Governance and Enforcement of European Law: From Comitology to a Multi-level Agency Structure?', in C. Joerges, E. Vos (eds), *EU Committees: Social Regulation, Law and Politics* (Hart Publishing 1999) 131.

[3] C. Knill, and J. Tosun, *Public Policy: A New Introduction* (NY Palgrave Macmillan 2012); G. Falkner, O. Treib, M. Hartlapp, S. Leiber, *Complying with Europe: EU Harmonisation and Soft Law in the Member States* (Cambridge University Press 2005).

[4] M. Scholten, 'Mind the Trend! Enforcement of EU law has been moving to 'Brussels'' (2017) 24 *Journal of European Public Policy* 9, 1348.

[5] In this light, it is important to note that the differences in enforcement mechanisms, types of sanctions and institutional characteristics of enforcers in different jurisdictions in the EU is an additional concern for ensuring enforcement of EU law in a consistent manner, especially where cross-jurisdictional cooperation is necessary.

[6] This chapter is also informed by useful insights gained from semi-structured interviews and meetings during a number of research projects supporting the 'veni' project (fn **) that I have

2.2. Defining EU law enforcement and its types

Since the very beginning, the EU has been set up to make rules. These rules can relate to the entire breadth of Union law – from the free movement of goods, services, capital, and people to environmental law and cooperation in criminal law matters. Once these norms have been set, they will then need to be 'enforced' so as to prevent a violation or to respond to an existing violation of the norm. But what is law enforcement? Enforcement is a process that aims at "preventing or responding to the violation of a norm" in order to promote the implementation of the set laws and policies.[7] According to Vervaele, "[L]aw enforcement comprises monitoring, investigating and sanctioning violations of substantive norms".[8] These stages in turn can be exercised by different enforcement powers such as the power to request information for monitoring and/or investigating stages and the power to impose fine (of administrative and/or criminal nature) and/or publish a public notice. These powers can be granted to an enforcement authority by EU and/or national law and may vary from sector to sector and member state to member state, which may make cooperation in shared enforcement more challenging.

Enforcement of EU law can be understood broadly and narrowly.

In a board way, it can even include the stage of registration of specific entities at a supervising-enforcement authority to be supervised, such as the case with the credit ranking agencies at the European Securities and Markets Authority.[9] After registration, the stage of monitoring takes place, relevant authorities check whether natural and/or legal persons are adhering to the law. If the monitoring of persons leads to a certain degree of suspicion, the competent authority can then start an administrative and/or criminal investigation during which it gathers further information. If the investigation concludes that there has been a violation of the law, the competent authority can then sanction the natural and/or legal person in question. The decision of the competent authority may be then enforced by another institutions, such as the court, or appealed by the affected person before a Board of Ap-

---

been part of: 'verticalization of enforcement' at the Utrecht Centre for Regulation and Enforcement in Europe (RENFORCE), two projects for the European Commission upon the 'Hercule' funding schemes and the 'the rule of law' project organized with Prof. Alex Brenninkmeijer at RENFORCE.

[7] V. Röben, 'The enforcement authority of international institutions' in A. von Bogdandy *et al* (eds), *The Exercise of Public Authority by International Institutions: Advancing International Institutional Law* (Springer 2009) 819-42.

[8] Vervaele (fn 3) 131.

[9] See for instance, M. van Rijsbergen, M. Scholten, 'ESMA Inspecting: The Implications for Judicial Control under Shared Enforcement' (2016) 7 *European Journal of Risk Regulation* 3, 569; J. Foster, M. van Rijsbergen, 'Rating' ESMA's accountability: 'AAA' status', in M. Scholten, M. Luchtman (eds), *Law Enforcement by EU Authorities* (Edward Elgar Publishing 2017).

peal or the court. The grounds for appeal could include procedural and/or substantive arguments, depending on relevant laws.

In a narrow sense, enforcement can be pictured as actions of police and judicial authorities of the investigative and sanctioning stages.

Scholars have delineated direct and indirect administration in the EU.[10] In light with these terms, one could classify direct enforcement as monitoring, investigating and sanctioning vis-à-vis those subjects that are subject to substantive norms, e.g. companies and citizens.[11] In light of concerns about national sovereignty, direct enforcement of EU law has been largely kept at the national level, with the only exception of EU competition law where the EU Commission has played traditionally a great role in enforcing EU competition rules vis-à-vis undertakings. What the EU has been doing in enforcement in other sectors can therefore be called indirect enforcement, i.e. "the supervision of the application of the law by public authorities – and foremost of the Member States – but not directly over whether citizens as such obey it."[12] The EU Commission (e.g. the Food and Veterinary Office) and later also EU agencies such as the European Maritime Safety Agency (EMSA)[13] and the European Court of Auditors have been among the key actors in checking upon EU member states. As I investigated elsewhere, next to late transposition, there are different procedural and substantive reasons for non-implementation.[14] Procedurally, the member states could be late in transposing EU legislation at home and could lack financial and human resources to apply and enforce EU law properly. Substantively, an incorrect transposition (whether or not this is on purpose) and (political) unwillingness could lead to non-implementation.[15] In addition, differences in national laws and procedures could result in disparities in the uniform application of EU law and the ineffectiveness of EU policies.[16]

The growing number of infringements and the variety of sources causing those infringements have led to modifications of the strategies that the Commission would

---

[10] J.H. Jans, S. Prechal, R.J.G.M. Widdershoven, *Europeanisation of Public Law* (Europa Law Publishing 2015), H.C.H. Hofmann, A.H. Türk, *Legal Challenges in EU Administrative Law: Towards an Integrated Administration* (Edward Elagar Publishing 2009).

[11] Vervaele (fn 3) 129-50; W. Duk, *Recht en Slecht: Beginselen van Algemene Rechtsleer* (Ars Aequi Libri 1999); G. Rowe, 'Administrative supervision of administrative action in the European Union', in H. Hofmann, A. Tűrk (eds), *Legal Challenges in EU Administrative Law: Towards an Integrated Administration* (Edward Elgar Publishing 2009) 136-67.

[12] Rowe (fn. 11).

[13] Please, see chapter by Alberti in this volume.

[14] Scholten (fn 4).

[15] *Ibidem*; E. Thomann, A. Zhelyazkova, 'Moving beyond (non-)compliance: the customization of European Union policies in 27 countries' (2017) 24 *Journal of European Public Policy* 9, 1269.

[16] Scholten (fn 4), see also M. Scholten, A. Ottow, 'Institutional design of enforcement in the EU: the case of financial markets' (2014) 10 *Utrecht Law Review* 5, 80.

employ in indirect enforcement and the proliferation of EU direct enforcement power.[17] The growth of the EU's authority in regulating matters of national enforcement and establishing various new modes of enforcement are among the most recent developments in this respect. Generally, enforcement of EU law has become more and more 'shared', though, as this book also shows, what is shared, how it is shared and among whom it is shared have found different formulas in different policy areas. This expansion of the EU competences from one (regulatory) step in the policy cycle to another (enforcement) can be explained from a functional spillover perspective: if the implementation of EU law is facing difficulties at the national level, enforcement at the EU level is likely to follow.[18]

2.3. EU (shared) law enforcement in different policy areas

Vervaele observes that "it is not a secret that the European Communities founding fathers underestimated the importance of the enforcement of Community law. Apart from a few exceptions in primary Treaty law, such as the obligation for Member States to criminalize violations of Euratom confidentiality or perjury in front of the European Court of Justice, they maintained a resolved silence concerning Community law enforcement."[19] The situation has changed with the years. Who does what and what is exactly shared, between whom and how? As this section and this edited volume show, this varies greatly in different sectors and even within the same categories of actors, such as EU agencies. My initial search for 'models of enforcements' have faced a challenge of distinguishing 'models', including the search for an appropriate term for various enforcement processes and procedures that have appeared in the EU recently.[20] It seems to depend on a particular departing point of what kinds of, to use this term for the sake of example, 'models' can be distinguished. This in turn may depend on the overall purpose of why such 'modelling' exercise has been undertaken in the first place. One could determine models in relation to what rules are being enforced, including for instance, primary or treaty obligations against national governments or private actors. They could be determined by departing from the question of 'who' – which institution, such as the Commission, the European Central Bank or the Court of Justice – undertakes an enforcement action and at what level. The fact remains that using different departing points is likely to lead to different numbers and

---

[17] Scholten and Luchtman (fn 1); see also Scholten (fn 4).

[18] Scholten (fn 4); M. Scholten, D. Scholten, 'From regulation to enforcement in the EU policy cycle: A new type of functional spillover?' (2017) 55 *Journal of Common Market Studies* 4, 925.

[19] J. Vervaele, *European Criminal Justice in the Post-Lisbon Area of Freedom, Security and Justice* (University of Trento 2014), p. 11, available at: http://eprints.biblio.unitn.it/4399/1/COLLANA_QUADERNI__VOLUME_5__VERVAELE_FORNASARI_SARTORI__02.09.2015.pdf.

[20] I am grateful for our continuous debate on this issue with Prof. Michiel Luchtman.

types of such models, bringing into question the usefulness of such an exercise.[21] Moreover, the term 'model' can lead to misleading considerations, especially for experts with different scientific backgrounds. Therefore, I leave the 'modelling' exercise and the question about its usefulness for future research and debate. In this section, I describe three scenarios as to how EU law can be enforced, which seem to accommodate various actors and policy areas, also included in this book. The question of whether this is an attempt for 'modelling' I leave up to the reader to assess and for future research to finetune. These scenarios are being distinguished based on two considerations: 1. interrelations between relevant actors and 2. material scope of laws to be enforced.

Scenario 1

EU laws set up norms for different actors, primarily national governments and private actors.[22] Therefore, the first scenario concerns enforcement of EU legislation and policies by EU and/or national authorities vis-à-vis public and/or private actors in the EU. Starting from the Treaties, Article 2 TEU, for instance, promotes the core values of the Union, such as democracy and the rule of law and, next to the Treaties, secondary law imposes various standards and procedures to adhere to in order to achieve the aims of the Treaties. For instance, in accordance with Article 191 TFEU 'a high level of protection' is required for the purposes of EU environmental policy, which is then supported further by more than 200 pieces of EU secondary legislation (mainly directives) to be further implemented and enforced at the national level.[23]

First, the most typical case here is that the Member States must implement particular primary and secondary legislation adopted by the EU legislator. They are oftentimes free to choose which type of enforcement to use in order to enforce substantive norms. For example, Member States can choose to enforce a substantive norm regarding environmental law by creating an agency or delegating the task to a ministry, also through sanctions derived from administrative, criminal, or private law. In most cases, it is up to the Member States to choose a sanction or combination of sanctions. This derives from the principle of national institutional autonomy,[24] with some limitations. Enforcement sanctions must be equivalent,

---

[21] See, for instance, an interesting 'modeling' for the purpose of a specific study on the interactions between EU and national levels: M. Luchtman, J. Vervaele, 'Comparison of the legal frameworks', in M. Luchtman, J. Vervaele, *Investigatory powers and procedural safeguards: Improving OLAF's legislative framework through a comparison with other EU law enforcement authorities (ECN/ESMA/ECB)* (Utrecht University 2017) 248-253.

[22] P Craig, G de Brca, *EU Law: Text, Cases and Materials* (Oxford University Press 2015).

[23] See chapter by Munari in this volume.

[24] Jans, Prechal, Widdershoven (fn 10).

effective, dissuasive, and proportional.[25] Also, the Member States must observe fundamental rights, general principles of Union law, and the Treaty freedoms.[26] The large margin of discretion in the choice of sanctions has, since the mid-1980s, decreased and the EU has increasingly prescribed which (type of) sanctions the Member States ought to impose.[27] From the beginning of the 21st century, this has also led to the EU no longer limiting itself to prescribing administrative sanctions, but also punitive sanctions for violations of substantive norms in fields such as environmental law.

When enforcement is entrusted in national authorities, the EU executive actors, such as the Commission, EU agencies and networks, largely monitor the implementation of EU laws by national governments and private actors. In other words, they identify if the policy goals and core values are adhered to. As Alberti mentions in this volume, the number of such monitoring EU agencies has been increasing. This is the case, for instance, for the European Chemicals Agency, European Fisheries Control Agency, the newly established European Labour Agency, to name but a few, where information gathered by such agencies may lead to further actions, including sanctioning at the national or EU levels. Next to monitoring, the 'infringement procedure'[28] is available to ensure that the national governments comply with the implementation of EU secondary laws. In short, if a Member State does not live up to its obligations under the EU law, the EU Commission or other Member States can start an infringement procedure in order to force the Member State to enforce the specific norm (Articles 258-260 TFEU).[29] As Prete mentions in this volume, this possibility has not been there since the outset but came about later with the Treaty of Maastricht.[30] This procedure has two pre-judicial and judicial phases and both the Commission or the Member States can initiate it. First, the Member State of the perceived failure is informed about the breach, which the Member State can then counter. Subsequently, the Commission can issue a 'reasoned opinion' on the issue. This reasoned opinion will include a time limit for the breach of EU law to be ended.[31] If the breach of EU law is not resolved by the end of the time limit, the Commission can bring the case to

---

[25] 68/88, *Commission v Greece (Greek Maize)*, ECLI:EU:C:1989:339.

[26] See the chapter by Lazzerini in this volume.

[27] Jans, Prechal, Widdershoven (fn 10) 281.

[28] Craig, de Búrca (fn 23) 429 and on the functioning of the infringement procedure under Article 258 TFEU, see 431.

[29] *Ibidem.*

[30] See Prete's contribution to this volume.

[31] Craig, de Búrca (fn 22) 431 and 435. See also: E. Korkea-Aho, 'Watering Down the Court of Justice: The Dynamics between Network Implementation and Article 258 TFEU Litigation' (2014) 20 *European Law Journal* 649.

the Court of Justice of the EU. If the Commission considers that the Member State does not comply with the conclusion of the Court, it can bring the case before the Court once more. During these proceedings the Court can impose a fine (lump sum) as punishment for the continued breach of EU law. An interesting development in the recent years has been the establishment of 'EU pilots' mechanism, which promotes resolving possible non-implementation by the Member States without opting for a lengthy and costly infringement procedure.[32]

Two separate specific procedures that can be brought under this scenario are the enforcement procedures under Article 7 TEU and for the Economic Monetary Union (EMU). These procedures involve the Member States being in charge of enforcing specific primary and secondary EU laws, whereas the EU institutions monitor and can sanction violations, yet in procedures established specifically for these cases. As Bonelli describes in this volume, "Article 7(1) TEU allows the Council to determine, after obtaining the European Parliament's consent, the existence of a 'clear risk of a serious breach' of EU values in a Member State of the EU" (section 4.1.). The Commission or the European Parliament can initiate this 'preventive' procedure to set a dialogue between EU institutions and the Member State in question. The sanctions can be imposed under Article 7(2-4) TEU if the European Council determines 'a serious and persistent breach' of values of Article 2 TEU.[33] As Costamagna and Miglio discuss in this volume, Article 126 TFEU and the Stability and Growth Pact lays down the powers to monitor the decision taken by national authorities concerning their budgets and impose fines if they deviate from the agreed benchmarks.[34]

At the same time, since recently, we witness the proliferation of the so-called EU enforcement authorities, which can be involved in enforcing EU law together with national authorities or even do this on their own. Some use the term 'shared enforcement' to describe this situation,[35] although this term may be misleading in consideration of the processes where different – EU and national – actors are being involved. This brings us to the second scenario.

Scenario 2

This scenario can be characterized by the establishing of a more direct link between EU authorities and private actors, although this happens with the involvement of

---

[32] On the EU pilot schemes, Craig, de Búrca (fn 22) 435. See also: D. Hadrousek, 'Speeding up Infringement Procedures: Recent Developments Designed to Make Infringement Procedures More Effective' (2012) 9 *Journal for European Environmental and Planning Law* 235.

[33] See the chapter by Bonelli in this volume.

[34] See the chapter by Costamagna and Miglio in this volume.

[35] M. Scholten, M. Luchtman, E. Schmidt, 'The proliferation of EU enforcement authorities: a new development in law enforcement in the EU' in M. Scholten, M. Luchtman (eds), *Law Enforcement by EU Authorities: Implications for Political and Judicial Accountability* (Edward Elgar Publishing 2017).

relevant national authorities in the process of enforcement. The monitoring function of the Commission is then altered as relevant courts, parliaments and other controlling actors become overseers of such enforcement processes. This so-called 'direct shared enforcement' by an EU authority has been known in the area of EU competition law for a long time.[36] The Commission has had enforcement powers to investigate and sanction private actors almost from the outset of EU integration. For the protection of the financial interests of the EU and the fight against fraud a specific office – the European Anti-fraud Office (OLAF) – was set up in 1999. It can conduct administrative investigations within the EU institutions and the Member States.[37] Since the beginning of the 21st century, more and more of such authorities started to be created. The reasons why some authorities are created in the shape of an agency or a body or why the enforcement of EU law by national authorities should be helped by an EU coordinating network are yet to be better explored.[38] It is also unclear why some of such authorities have more enforcement powers than others, and to what extent they truly share enforcement with national authorities. The following observations stand out here.

First, from the functional perspective, these authorities can be subdivided into two groups: those, which enjoy powers to realize all the enforcement stages (monitoring, investigation and sanctioning) and those, which do not have all those powers and have to rely upon national authorities. The former includes, for instance, the EU Commission in the area of competition law, European Securities and Markets Authority and European Central Bank within the Single Supervisory Mechanism (SSM). The latter includes the Anti-Fraud Office, European Medicines Agency, European Aviation Safety Agency and European Fisheries Control Agency.[39] In addition, the European Public Prosecutor's Office (EPPO) will be soon operational as an independent and decentralized prosecution office of the European Union, with the competence to investigate, prosecute and bring to judgment crimes against the

---

[36] *Ibidem*, 6.; see also Calzolari in this volume.

[37] Regulation 883/2013 concerning investigations conducted by the European Anti-Fraud Office (OLAF) [2013], OJ 2013 L248/1. See, also See, also M. Luchtman, M. Wassmeier, 'The political and judicial accountability of OLAF' in M. Scholten, M. Luchtman (eds), *Law Enforcement by EU Authorities: Implications for Political and Judicial Accountability* (Edward Elgar Publishing 2017).

[38] L. Van Kreij, 'Towards a Comprehensive Framework for Understanding EU Enforcement Regimes' (2019) 10 *European Journal of Risk Regulation* 3, 439; M. Scholten, 'Shared Tasks, but Separated Controls: Building the System of Control for Shared Administration in an EU Multi-Jurisdictional Setting' (2019) 10 *European Journal of Risk Regulation* 3, 538. See also the respective blog: M. Scholten, 'Shared Tasks, but Separated Controls. How to build a system of control for EU shared administration?', in *EU Law Enforcement blog*, available at: https://eulawenforcement.com/?author=2.

[39] Scholten (fn 4).

EU budget, such as fraud, corruption or serious cross-border VAT fraud.[40]

Secondly, these EU enforcement authorities do not replace relevant national authorities. This has led to using of the term 'shared' enforcement to such cases.[41] A closer look at these authorities[42] reveals the many facets of such sharedness and what it can mean. This sharedness does not seem to follow a particular logic, such as for instance the functional subdivisions considered in the previous paragraph. The European Securities and Markets Authority is, for instance, an agency enjoying the powers to monitor the performance of specific financial market participants, such as credit rating agencies, or to investigate the cases of suspicion and sanction for violation of EU laws. In this particular function, it may delegate certain tasks to be performed by its national counterparts, but it would remain in charge of the enforcement process, including the sanctioning stage.[43] In this case, reliance upon national counterparts is at ESMA's discretion and would take place only for a particular part of the enforcement process, such as when making an online inspection.[44] The case of the European Aviation Safety Agency sheds a different light upon the term 'shared enforcement'. Here, it can be observed that the task of enforcement of the aviation safety laws is shared between EU and national relevant agencies but with a clear division of competences and procedures. The EASA is in charge of ensuring the safety of a particular type of an aircraft, whereas the national authorities look after the individual units of that type.[45] The term 'shared' in the case of the

---

[40] *Council Regulation (EU) 2017/1939 of 12 October 2017 implementing enhanced cooperation on the establishment of the European Public Prosecutor's Office ('the EPPO')* [2017], J. Vervaele, 'Judicial and political accountability for criminal investigations and prosecutions by a European Public Prosecutor's Office in the EU: the dissymmetry of shared enforcement', in M. Scholten, M. Luchtman (eds), *Law Enforcement by EU Authorities: Implications for Political and Judicial Accountability* (Edward Elgar Publishing 2017).

[41] See also M. Scholten, M. Maggetti, E. Versluis, 'Political and Judicial Accountability in Shared Enforcement in the EU' in M. Scholten, M. Luchtman (eds), *Law Enforcement by EU Authorities: Implications for Political and Judicial Accountability* (Edward Elgar Publishing 2017).

[42] Scholten and Luchtman (fn 1).

[43] *Van Rijsbergen and Scholten (fn 9); see also: Van Rijsbergen and Foster (fn 9). A. Karagianni, M. Scholten, M. Simonato, 'EU 'vertical' report 'The exchange of information between national and EU authorities'',* in M. Simonato, M. Luchtman, J. Vervaele (eds) *Exchange of information with EU and national enforcement authorities: Improving OLAF legislative framework through a comparison with other EU authorities (ECN/ESMA/ECB)* (Utrecht University 2018) 7-32.

[44] I have conducted a number of interviews and held talks with experts from and on ESMA, which revealed that ESMA did not seem to use this function that often and may be unlikely to be using it due to a number of considerations. This includes, for instance, the fact that ESMA registers the entities to be supervised where its national authorities do not normally have any supervision over those entities, which may diminish the necessity and useful of the help from their side.

[45] L. Mustert, M. Scholten, 'Controls in the case of the EU civil aviation safety rules' in M. Scholten, A. Brenninkmeijer, *Controlling EU Agencies. The Rule of Law in a Multi-jurisdictional Legal Order* (Edward Elgar Publishing 2020) and Luchtman and Scholten (fn 1).

European Central Bank reflects also on the shared enforcement but more on the shared structures used in enforcement. For instance, the monitoring stage over the 'big banks' is organized by the so-called joint supervisory teams, where both ECB and relevant national staff work together and employ both relevant EU and national law for substance and procedure.[46] Finally, for example, to ensure effective enforcement of authorization and supervision of medicinal products (Regulation 726/2004), the European Medicines Agency (EMA) has come to share enforcement stages of monitoring, investigating suspicious cases via national authorities, and imposing fines via the Commission.[47] While the EMA has no authority to investigate the premises of authorization holders directly, it can, for example, order the initiation of such investigations by national investigators, who may be accompanied by an expert appointed by the Agency (Article 8 of Regulation No. 726/2004).

These observations are important as they make it clear that enforcement takes place in different settings in all the above cases. It also shows that these differences will have different implications for other pertinent questions, such as legitimacy, controls and legal protection for the shared enforcement.[48] The clearer the division of tasks between EU and national authorities is, the clearer the rules for controls (political, judicial, etc.) are likely to be. In any case, however, the new complex interactions between EU and national enforcement actors results in complex enforcement procedures, which in turn may lead to decisions, which can be checked only by appropriate, sophisticated systems of controls.[49]

Scenario 3

A peculiar situation exists in the area of EU Common Foreign and Security Policy (CFSP)[50] in which sanctions have been imposed against other states and individuals.[51] Thus, this scenario features other types of actors and procedures and interaction with International law. Beaucillon captures this in the beginning of her chapter

---

[46] A. Karagianni, M. Scholten, 'Accountability Gaps in the Single Supervisory Mechanism (SSM) Framework' (2018) 34 *Utrecht Journal of International and European Law* 2, 185; see also Allemand in this volume.

[47] M. Chamon, S. Wirtz, 'Complex procedures as hurdle to accountability: verticalization of pharmaceutical enforcement' in M. Scholten, M. Luchtman (eds), *Law Enforcement by EU Authorities: Implications for Political and Judicial Accountability* (Edward Elgar Publishing 2017).

[48] Scholten, Maggetti, Versluis (fn 41); T. Binder, A. Karagianni, M. Scholten, 'Emergency! But What about Legal Protection in the EU?' (2018) 9 *European Journal of Risk Regulation* 1, 99.

[49] Scholten (fn 35). M. Scholten, A Brenninkmeijer *Controlling EU Agencies. The Rule of Law in a Multi-jurisdictional Legal Order* (Edward Elgar Publishing 2020).

[50] European Commission - *Service for Foreign Policy Instruments (FPI)* available at: https://ec.europa.eu/fpi/what-we-do/sanctions_en.

[51] *Ibidem* See also Craig, de Búrca (Fn 22) 344 on the Common Foreign and Security Policy (CFSP).

in this volume, "to what extent does respect for human rights in Syria, the Iranian nuclear crisis or the international fight against terrorism fall within the scope of the enforcement of European Union law?" And as both Beaucillon and Spagnolo show in this volume, the EU seems to promote its values and laws also beyond its territory via instruments of restrictive measures and sanctions against third countries and individuals. According to Spagnolo, "as of today, more than thirty unilateral sanctions adopted by the EU against third countries are in force, demonstrating the vitality of the instrument and the frequency of its use. Within them, a large number of sanctioning regimes are 'autonomous', namely adopted outside – or in addition to – the framework of a resolution of the UN Security Council. In other words, the EU adopts sanctions without any authorization from the UN" (*section 1*); Title IV TFEU governs the procedure on the adoption of 'restrictive measures'.[52]

The number of countries under CFSP sanctions has increased dramatically, from six in 1991 to almost thirty in 2018.[53] As of February 2018, the EU has ten sanction programs implementing UN measures, eight cases in which it applies its own additional sanctions in parallel to UN sanctions, and 24 autonomous sanction programs.[54] The composition of sanction programs in place by April 2018 was as follows: 30 asset freezes, 27 visa bans, 21 arms embargoes, 9 commodity trade restrictions, 7 bans on exports of equipment for internal repression, 7 financing, banking and investment restrictions, 3 bans on dual-use exports, 3 flight bans and 2 shipping bans.[55]

The measures and sanctions adopted under the CFSP serve several objectives, including: safeguarding the EU's values, preserving peace, consolidating and supporting democracy, and preventing conflicts and strengthening international security.[56] They can be aimed at governments, entities, groups, or individuals.[57] There is a wide range of possible restrictive measures that could be imposed by the EU. These include: arms embargoes, economic and financial sanctions, diplomatic sanctions, suspensions of cooperation, boycotts of events, and restrictions on admission (such as visa and travel bans).[58] Individual sanctions within the EU amongst others form a

---

[52] See also Craig, de Búrca (Fn 22) 348.

[53] M. Russell, *EU sanctions: A key foreign and security policy instrument* (Briefing, European Parliamentary Research Service 2018) 2, available at https://www.europarl.europa.eu/RegData/etudes/BRIE/2018/621870/EPRS_BRI(2018)621870_EN.pdf.

[54] *Ibidem*, 4.

[55] *Ibidem*.

[56] Council of the European Union - *Sanctions: how and when the EU adopts restrictive measures* (2019) available at: https://www.consilium.europa.eu/en/policies/sanctions/.

[57] Council of the European Union, *Guidelines on Implementation and Evaluation of Restrictive Measures (Sanctions) in the Framework of the EU Common and Foreign Security Policy* (2018) 5.

[58] European Commission, *Restrictive Measures* (2008) 3-5. See also, notably, joined cases C-402 and 415/05 P *Kadi v Council and Commission*, ECLI:EU:C:2008:461.

part of the broader counterterrorism strategy, mainly pursuing objectives of the European Arrest Warrant [59] and the European Security Strategy. [60] After all, terrorism has been identified as the first of five key threats to European interests. [61]

2.4. EU enforcement and sanctions

An important element of any enforcement process is the sanctioning stage. Not necessarily the imposition of the sanction as such but the possibility thereof may have the necessary deterrent effect and enhance compliance. [62] The possibility to impose sanctions puts even stronger emphasis on the necessity of relevant mechanisms of controls for enforcement, such as access to the courts to challenge a fine, political controls over sanctioning policy of a supervisor and the existence of other safeguards and principles, such as the principle of proportionality and fundamental rights. [63] This is because the sanctioning stage has an intrusive effect upon the rights and freedoms of the parties subject to sanctions. [64] As Montaldo mentions in this volume on the principle of proportionality, "the more intense a public power and its effects on individuals are, the more demanding this principle becomes. This is why proportionality is of a particular significance in the domain of sanctions, where the magnitude of public coercive powers reaches its peak" (section 7.1).

Sanction can be defined as "a strong action taken in order to make people obey a law or rule, or a punishment given when they do not obey." [65] A strong action can be corrective (in order to make people obey a law) and penalizing (to punish). Irrespective of the scenarios of shared enforcement outlined before, the EU sanctioning

---

[59] Council Framework Decision 2002/475/JHA of 13 June 2002 on combating terrorism OJ 2002, L 164/3 and Council Framework Decision 2002/584/JHA of 13 June 2002 on the European arrest warrant and the surrender procedures between Member States [2002] OJ L 190/1. For a more extensive discussion on the European Arrest Warrant (EAW) see: Craig, de Búrca (fn 22) 990-996.

[60] C. Eckes, 'Test Case for the Resilience of the EU's Constitutional Foundations' (2009) 15 *European Public Law* 3, 351.

[61] C. Eckes, 'Sanctions against Individuals. Fighting Terrorism within the European Legal Order' (2008) 4 *European Constitutional Law Review* 2, 205, 208. See also: Craig, de Búrca (fn 22) 347.

[62] See M. Bovens, 'Analysing and Assessing Accountability: A Conceptual Framework' (2007) 13 *European Law Journal* 4, explaining this logic behind the sanctioning stage for accountability process. See also: C.E. Koops, *Contemplating Compliance: European compliance mechanisms in international perspective* (2014) PhD thesis, University of Amsterdam.

[63] See Lazzerini in this volume.

[64] Craig, de Búrca (fn 22) 348-349.

[65] See, for instance, an online Cambridge dictionary: https://dictionary.cambridge.org/dictionary/english/strong.

power can be categorized in different ways and perspectives. Who has the power to impose sanctions? Who is the subject to the sanction? Who has the power to determine which type of sanctioning (if at all) should be used for violation of EU law? As seen from the scenarios above as well as in the chapters of this book, the sanctioning power for violation of EU law has been oftentimes entrusted in an EU or a national authority (courts and public executive entities). In the past decade, the number and type of EU authorities that have acquired a sanctioning power has increased. In addition to the Commission and the Court of Justice, the list now includes the European Council, the Council of the European Union, the European Central Bank, and a growing number of EU agencies. Sanctions could be used vis-à-vis the Member States and EU authorities, private actors, states and individuals. Finally, who has the authority to determine which type of sanction? Via-à-vis the Member States, other states and individuals, it is the EU institutions who play the key role here. Vis-à-vis private actors, the EU enforcement authorities as mentioned above and national authorities are largely in charge of implementing relevant statutes, which *inter alia* regulate the type of sanctions, their amount and the discretion given to those enforcement authorities in determining the sanctions.

What is important to mention is that the legislative authority to establish specific types, amounts and other peculiarities of sanctions has become shared between the EU and national levels. Since the 1980s, the EU legislator has increased its legislative authority on the matters of institutional, procedural and operational issues of enforcement by national authorities, including sanctions. [66] Along with that, the executive actors, including the Commission and EU agencies, have been issuing 'guidance' as to how enforcement should or can take place, for instance by issuing documents such as fining guidelines in the area of EU competition law (see Calzolari in this volume) or ESMA soft law. [67]

Furthermore, the Court of Justice has contributed to the shaping of the sanctioning power of the EU via a number of landmark judgments. Among the key judgments are the following. In the *Greek Maize* case (Case 68/88), [68] the Court held that the penalties that the Member States impose for violation of EU law must be effective, dissuasive, and proportionate. The fact that penalties must be effective and dissuasive can ensure that the goal of enforcement is achieved in practice and the principle of proportionality ensures that the sanction does not go beyond what is reasonable given the gravity of the offence. In *Commission v Council* (Case 176/03), [69] the possibility to prescribe criminal sanctions for the breaches of EU law

---

[66] Jans, Prechal, Widdershoven (fn 10).

[67] M. van Rijsbergen, *EU agencies' soft rule-making Lessons Learnt from the European Securities and Markets Authority* (PhD dissertation Utrecht University, 2018).

[68] *Greek Maize* (fn 25).

[69] C-176/03 *Commission v Council*, ECLI:EU:C:2005:542.

by the EU legislator was discussed. Criminal sanctions used to be the prerogative of national administrations, yet the Commission launched the development of criminal sanctions at the EU level.[70] The Court supported the 'initiative' though with a reservation: "a general rule, neither criminal law nor the rules of criminal procedure fall within the Community's competence [...]. However, this finding does not prevent the Community legislature, when the application of effective, proportionate and dissuasive criminal penalties by the competent national authorities is an essential measure for combatting serious environmental offences, from taking measures which relate to the criminal law of the Member States which it considers necessary in order to ensure that the rules which it lays down on environmental protection are fully effective" (para. 47 and 48). Thanks to this 'blessing' from the Court, the Commission issued in 2011 its communication about the possibility to prescribe criminal sanctions also in other sectors if necessary.[71] Furthermore, in *Bonda*,[72] the Court of Justice concluded that if the investigation concludes that there has been violation of the law, the competent authority can then sanction the natural or legal person in question. Such a sanction can have a restorative character or a punitive character depending on the *Bonda*-criteria, which build upon the *Engel* criteria established by the European Court of Human Rights.[73]

There is a great variety of sanctions that have been used across sectors. At the EU level, these include fines, periodical penalties and interim measures by the Commission: suspension of rights (including the voting right in the Council) warnings, (public) recommendations and fines by the Commission and Council within the Stability and Growth Pact, penalties and fines by the ECB within the SSM, public notices and fines by ESMA and sanctions against third countries and individuals within the CFSP. This is next to sanctions available at the national level where some EU actors, including the Commission and EU agencies, may monitor their imposition. For instance, ESMA supervises the imposition of administrative and criminal sanctions and other types of administrative measures by national competent authorities. In accordance with the Market Abuse Regulation,[74] ESMA publishes an An-

---

[70] Concerning the administrative sanctions, since 1980s, starting with the Common Agricultural Policy (CAP), "the Community increasingly required Member States to impose sanctions that went further than simple reparation" Jans, Prechal, Widdershoven (fn 10).

[71] European Commission Communication, 'Towards an EU Criminal Policy: Ensuring the effective implementation of EU policies through criminal law' (Brussels COM2011) available at: file:///C:/Users/gian9/Downloads/1.2_COM%20(2011)573_final_EU_en.pdf, the Commission proposed to consider criminal law "as an element to ensure the effective enforcement of EU policies." ; J. Vervaele, 'The European community and harmonization of the criminal law enforcement of community policy. A Cessio Bonorum from the Third to the First Pillar?' in K. Nuotio (ed.), *Festschrift in honour of R. Lahti* (University of Helsinki 2007) 119-42.

[72] C-489/10 *Bonda* [2012] ECLI: EU: C: 2012: 319.

[73] *Engel and Others v. the Netherlands*, application no. 5100/71; 5101/71; 5102/71; 5354/72.

[74] Regulation No 596/2014 on Market Abuse [2014] OJ L173/1.

nual Report on the sanctions imposed by national authorities.[75] At the same time, various enforcement procedures do show that the sanctioning stage can be a process of a number of steps, in which the seriousness of a sanction grows with each step, though the sanctioning authority may have discretion as to follow the 'pre-sanctioning' steps or not. For instance, for an Article 7 procedure, next to the sanctions as the suspension of the voting rights, there exists the possibility of a preventive measure and a dialogue with the Member State in question. "The "soft" coordination mechanisms are backed by "hard" sanctions under the Stability and Growth Pact and the Macroeconomic Imbalances Procedure."[76] The area of EU competition law has experienced the development of taking commitment and settlement decisions instead of imposing sanctions.[77] De Hert in this volume mentions the possibility to use deterrence and persuasion that can enhance compliance with the data protection rules.

2.5. Conclusion

All in all, enforcement of EU law has seen many changes, especially in recent decades.

First, the scope of EU law (the 'what') that needs to be enforced has been expanding considerably over the years. Roughly speaking, today it is not 'only' about the rules governing the internal market and competition law, even though the enforcement of internal market regulation is an area that is still in search of an appropriate enforcement mechanism.[78] It is also about how national governments adopt their budgets and go about data protection. It is also about regulation and supervision of major financial actors in the financial markets, such as banks, and the adherence of the Member States to the key values of democracy and the rules of law (Article 2 TEU), including adherence beyond the border of the European Union.

Second, we should note the proliferation of actors ('who') that can enforce EU law, at both the EU and national levels as well as transnationally.[79] We witness a rapid growth of enforcement of powers of the EU institutions as such – EU Commission (different DGs) and the European Central Bank (SSM) – and those of EU and national agencies. Also, various new enforcement structures have appeared, such as joint supervisory teams of the European Central Bank. The interactions

[75] ESMA, Annual Reports, available at: https://www.esma.europa.eu/document-types/annual-report.

[76] See the chapter by Costamagna and Miglio in this volume.

[77] See the chapter by Calzolari in this volume.

[78] From my inform talks with public servants working at the moment of writing on a reform on enforcement for the internal market.

[79] G.J. Brandsma, 'Transnational executive bodies: very effective but hardly accountable?', in *EU Law Enforcement blog*, available at: https://eulawenforcement.com/?author=52.

among those actors – EU and national, private and public – have resulted in complex, 'composite'[80] procedures raising challenging legal questions, such as the choice of jurisdiction, applicable laws and standards to govern and review,[81] which are yet to be investigated and which bring us to the last point.

Finally, there have been changes in 'how' enforcement has or should take place. Here, one sees the growth of laws and principles that shape – facilitate and limit – the process of enforcement. The Charter of Fundamental Rights has affected enforcement as to the way it should be done (for instance, in accordance with the principles of good administration, due process, etc.) and the purpose of why it should be done (for instance, Article 37 to ensure environmental protection).

An important development here has been the growth in both 'quantity and quality' of the sanctioning power for violating EU law. Two trends can be distinguished in this respect as shown in the coming chapters. On the one hand, in light of the proliferating (shared) enforcement, especially by EU authorities, one can talk about the growth of 'hard' sanctioning power of the EU. The EU legislator can prescribe, for instance, not only administrative but also criminal sanctions to be employed for violation of EU law. Also, EU authorities such as ESMA, have received direct sanctioning powers, including imposing fines upon private actors. On the other hand, there seems to be a growing realization of the importance of preventive mechanisms. Among these are pre-judicial stages in the infringement procedure, solid monitoring of compliance before any investigation or sanctioning and correcting via monitoring via dialogue, rather than opting for 'hard' mechanisms, such as lengthy and expensive court proceedings. At the end of the day, enforcement of law is there to ensure the attainment of policy goals and promoting core values, which could be more effective to achieve at the earlier (monitoring) stages of enforcement and by preventive measures, rather than sanctioning.

---

[80] P. Craig, 'Shared Administration, Disbursement of Community Funds and the Regulatory State', in H. Hofmann, A. Türk (eds), *Legal Challenges in EU Administrative Law: Towards an Integrated Administration* (Edward Elgar Publishing 2009) 34; G. Della Cananea, 'The European Union's Mixed Administrative Proceedings' (2004) *Law and Contemporary Problems* 68, 197; H. Hofmann *et. Al.*, *Administrative Law and Policy of the European Union* (Oxford University Press 2011).

[81] These issues seem to stand high on (research) agenda where a number of PhD projects have been conducted. See, for instance: H. Andersson, *Dawn Raids under Challenge. A Study of the European Commission's Dawn Raid Practices in Competition Cases from a Fundamental Rights Perspective* (Stokholm University 2017), available at: https://www.diva-portal.org/smash/get/diva2:1051228/FULLTEXT01.pdf. At this moment, I am involved in co-supervising a PhD project of A. Karagianni (together with Prof. Michiel Luchtman and Prof. Rob Widdershoven), investigating these questions for the case of the European Central Bank (Utrecht University). This project runs in parallel with the PhD project of K. Bovend'Eerdt investigating the protection of fundamental rights in the case of OLAF (supervised by Prof. Michiel Luchtman, Prof. John Vervaele and Dr. Stanislaw Tosza). Both projects are funded by the Dutch Research Council (NWO) upon the 'vidi' scheme of Prof. Luchtman.

Chapter 3

NEW ACTORS ON THE STAGE: THE EMERGING ROLE OF EU AGENCIES IN EXERCISING SANCTIONING POWERS

Jacopo Alberti *-**

ABSTRACT: *The well-known fragmentation of EU executive has brought to the emersion of new bodies endowed with sanctioning powers or with auxiliary functions within the sactioning procedure: the EU agencies. After a brief overview of these bodies, this chapter discusses how EU agencies have enhanced the capability of the EU to impose sanctions. In particular, it highlights EU agencies' role as bridge between the EU and the Member States and as 'legislative laboratories' where new enforcement practices are negotiated and tested in practice. Moreover, this chapter provide a detailed taxonomy of the sanctioning powers exercised by EU agencies, pointing out in particular their auxiliary (yet fundamental) role vis-à-vis the Commission and national authorities; how they are silently eroding the Commission's prerogatives in the infringement procedure; their powers to impose fees to market operators and the relevance of granting unlimited jurisdiction to the Court of justice for scrutinising those powers. By way of conclusion, the chapter presents and discuss the main driving forces according to which the EU legislator decides to grant sanctioning powers to EU agencies.*

KEYWORDS: *EU agencies – taxonomy – infringement proceedings – unlimited jurisdiction – delegation of powers*

3.1. Introduction

Since the beginning of the '90s, the European Union (EU) has been witnessing a growing proliferation of quasi-independent administrative bodies, dealing with virtually every policy field conferred to the EU. [1]

These bodies, made up of representatives of national administrations and mainly entrusted with technical and scientific functions, have gained over the years a significant role in EU decision-making, despite the lack of a clear legislative framework concerning their functions. Thanks to this institutional flexibility, they have also been able to perform – sometimes only indirectly, often together with other EU institutions – almost every type of EU law enforcement: monitoring activities, collection of evidences, technical and scientific evaluations, infringements and, most importantly, sanctions.

Therefore, even though endowing EU agencies with sanctioning powers has not changed the theoretical underpinnings of sanctioning, [2] it has brought several innovations not only in terms of actors involved, but also with regards to procedures to be follow for sanctioning, legitimacy of sanctions, legal acts used for these purposes and judicial protection.

This chapter aims at shedding some light on how the rise of agencies has been affecting the EU sanctioning power and how the latter could, or should, evolve in light of the former. After a brief overview of EU agencies (Section 3.2) and the features of these bodies that are most relevant for the topic to which this book is devoted (Section 3.3), a taxonomy of their sanctioning functions will be provided (Section 3.4). In the end, some conclusive remarks on their contribution to EU sanctioning will be given (Section 3.5).

---

* Associate Professor of EU Law, University of Ferrara.

** The A. thanks Francesco Costamagna, Stefano Montaldo and Alberto Miglio for their comments and suggestions on the draft version of this chapter. A further acknowledgement goes to Chiara Giussani, SRB Policy Officer. Errors and horrors remain solely mine.

[1] On the mushrooming of specialized bodies at European level see E. Chiti, 'The emergence of a community administration: the case of European agencies', (2000) *Common Market Law Review* 341; R. Dehousse, 'Misfits: EU law and the transformation of European governance', (2002) 2 *Jean Monnet Working Papers*. Please note that two agencies had already been established in the 70ies: the European Centre for the Development of Vocational Training (CEDEFOP, pursuant to Council Regulation of 10 February 1975 No 337/75, OJ 1975, L 39/1 (as subsequently amended) and the European Foundation for the Improvement of Living and Working Conditions (EUROFOUND, pursuant to Council Regulation (EEC) of 26 May 1975 No 1365/75, OJ 1975, L 139/1 (as subsequently amended).

[2] For taking stock of the established debates on this point mainly with regards to the international legal order, see M.L. Picchio Forlati, *La sanzione nel diritto internazionale* (1974, CEDAM) 29-47 (for some general reflection on sanctions within the general legal theory, also p. 9-28); with regards to the administrative legal doctrine, see G. Pagliari, *Profili teorici della sanzione amministrativa* (1988, CEDAM) *passim* (for a specific overview on the Italian debate, 45-145). As for the established literature on sanctions in EU, EEC and EC Law, see below mainly at Section 3.3.

3.2. EU agencies: a brief overview

3.2.1. EU agencies: what's in a name? Some methodological caveats for assessing the bodies under scrutiny…

In a nutshell, EU agencies are bodies established through secondary law (usually, EU Regulations) to assist EU institutions (mainly, the Commission) in the regulation of almost every EU policy. Even though they all have a clear common root, both in legal and political terms, their functions, role, powers, composition and independence vis-à-vis EU institutions may well vary, going from a mere auxiliary role in sharing best practices among the Member States to the regulation of markets through binding acts (and sanctions).

It is quite complex to define EU agencies and frame this institutional category in a precise manner.[3] Even though the general budget of the EU has a specific part devoted to 'EU decentralised agencies'[4] and the EU official website dedicates a specific page to these bodies,[5] there is actually neither an official definition of 'EU decentralised agencies', nor a common understanding of the bodies that could be subsumed under this label.

This definitional problem is, however, largely irrelevant for the purpose of the present research. Only two points deserve to be made, for the sake of methodological accuracy.

First, this study covers only EU *decentralised* agencies, and therefore it does not deal with EU *executive* agencies. These latter bodies are internal – albeit quite autonomous – offices of the European Commission; their acts can always be ascribed to the Commission and, in any case, they have extremely limited sanctioning pow-

---

[3] Several attempts have been made at both an institutional and academic level. As for the former, see Commission Communication of 11 December 2002, The operating framework for the European Regulatory Agencies, COM(2002)718 final, p. 4; Draft Interinstitutional Agreement on the operating framework for the European regulatory agencies, presented by the Commission on 25.2.2005, COM(2005)59 final, p. 11; and, by way of demonstration of the failure of these attempts, see the Joint Statement of the European Parliament, the Council of the EU and the European Commission on decentralised agencies, adopted on 19 July 2012, where no definition is given (indeed, in the *travaux préparatoires* of the Joint Statement is written that 'there is no outstanding need to have a uniform definition of 'agency'': see Analytical Fiche No 1, *Definition and classification of "Agency"*, 3, available at https://europa.eu/european-union/about-eu/agencies/overhaul_en. As for the latter, see, *ex multis* and only among studies that propose a definition, D. Fischer-Appelt, *Agenturen der Europäischen Gemeinschaft* (1999, Duncker & Humblot) 38; S. Griller, A. Orator, 'Everything under control? The "way forward" for European agencies in the footsteps of the *Meroni* doctrine', (2010) *European Law Review* 3; M. Groenleer, *The Autonomy of European Union Agencies* (2009, Eburon) 18-19; J. Alberti, *Le agenzie dell'Unione europea* (2018, Giuffrè) 14.

[4] Definitive adoption (EU, Euratom) 2019/333 of the European Union's general budget for the financial year 2019, OJ 2019, L 67/1, 1955.

[5] See https://europa.eu/european-union/about-eu/agencies_en.

ers.[6] According to the common (though imprecise) synecdoche, this chapter will refer to 'EU agencies' as synonym of 'EU decentralised agencies'.

Second, the bodies that will be subsumed under this label are a sum of those listed in the above-mentioned general budget of the Union, plus those that are mentioned in the *travaux préparatoires* of the 2012 Joint Declaration on EU decentralised agencies,[7] and those mentioned in the official website of the EU dedicated to EU agencies.[8] This approach has pros and cons, which cannot be discussed in detail here and which, in a nutshell, are related to the fact that some bodies are excluded from this categorization;[9] however, in the context of the present book, cons are largely drowned out thanks to the specific chapters dedicated to these other 'agency-like' bodies.[10]

3.2.2 ... and some key-features particularly relevant for understanding their limits and potentialities in issuing sanctions

Among the common features that all EU agencies share,[11] two deserve to be discussed in detail.

First and foremost, EU agencies are hubs of national administrations. They are made up of representatives of each national administration (or, sometimes, independent national authority). Usually these members sit in the decision-making body of the agency; rarely, on an advisory board which, however, typically exercises a strong influence over the agency's decisions.[12]

---

[6] Executive agencies find a common legal framework in Council Regulation (EC) No 58/2003 of 19 December 2002, OJ 2003, L 11/1. Fully outside the attention of legal scholars, some reflections on these bodies can be found in European Court of Auditors, 'Delegating Implementing Tasks to Executive Agencies: A Successful Option?', Special Report No 13/2009.

[7] See Analytical Fiche No 1, *Definition and classification of "Agency"*, *supra*, note 3, 4-6.

[8] *Supra*, note 5. Even though legal scholars traditionally struggle to recognise a legal relevance to (albeit official) websites and other means of communication, this approach seems nowadays to deserve a re-evaluation, aimed at taking those sources into account, at least for auxiliary purposes. For an interesting analysis on central banks' communication, see Opinion of AG Cruz-Villalón, case C-62/14, *Gauweiler*, ECLI:EU:C:2015:7, paras 86-88.

[9] See J. Alberti, *supra* note 3, 6-14.

[10] See, for instance, Chapters 8, 9, 14.

[11] A detailed analysis of EU agencies' homo- and heterogeneity fall outside the scope of this study; see, *ex multis*, C. Tovo, *Le agenzie decentrate dell'Unione europea* (2016, Editoriale Scientifica), 31-66; M. Chamon, *EU Agencies. Legal and political limits to the transformation of the EU administration* (2016, OUP) 5-15.

[12] For general references on EU agencies' management boards, see C. Tovo, *supra*, note 11, 193-214; M. Chamon, *supra*, note 11, 65 et seq; J. Alberti, *supra*, note 3, 171-177; for specific references on some outdated, but still interesting, practices in some agencies, see M. Busuioc, *The accountability of European agencies: legal provisions and ongoing practices* (2010, Utrecht University Repository-Dissertation).

Therefore, EU agencies are able to merge the European and national levels of regulation: [13] their acts clearly belong to the EU legal order, despite being absolutely atypical; [14] however, they also maintain a strong connection with the national ones. This is also due to their very technical and scientific nature: unlike the acts of the Council, which are similarly taken by an assembly of national representatives, EU agencies' acts are not the outcome of political compromises, but of the evaluation of different administrative practices, scientific evaluations, technical operations. Moreover, in several cases EU agencies' acts are simply recommendations to national administrations, which thence have to (or, sometimes, are more-or-less 'free' to choose whether and how to) implement them. [15] Thus, as seen from EU agencies, the boundaries between EU and national regulation become quite blurred; as will be discussed below, this has significant implications on sanctioning. [16]

Secondly, EU agencies suffer a very scant recognition in primary law. [17] Despite almost three decades of agencification, over 37 bodies established so far and several amendments to the EU treaties, there is still no explicit legal basis to establish agencies and to delegate powers to them. An attempt to introduce such a clause had been made at the time of the European Convention; however, former Commission President Prodi clearly took an opposite stance, arguing that fully recognising agencies in the treaties would have enhanced their powers to the detriment of the Commission. [18] Therefore, over the years EU agencies have never been fully acknowledged in primary law, being established firstly through the flexibility clause, and subsequently on the basis of the provisions of the treaties dealing with the policy field in which the agency operates. In the last decade, Art. 114 TFEU (i.e. the clause for the approximation of national legislation) has also been used as a (controversial) legal basis. [19]

The Lisbon Treaty brought only a subtle, albeit interesting, innovation (which, however, as often happens is slightly more than a codification of a principle previ-

---

[13] The literature on this point is extremely rich. See, *ex multis*, A. Kreher, 'Agencies in the European Community – A step towards administrative integration in Europe' (1997) *Journal of European Public Policy* 225; S. Cassese, 'European Administrative Proceedings', (2004) 68 *Law & Contemporary Problems* 21; D. Geradin, R. Muñoz, N. Petit, *Regulation through Agencies in the EU – A new Paradigm of European Governance* (2005, Elgar).

[14] C. Tovo, *supra* note 11, 268 *et seq.*

[15] J. Alberti, 'L'utilisation d'actes de soft law par les agences de l'Union européenne', (2014) *Revue de l'Union européenne* 161.

[16] See below at Section 3.3.1.

[17] EUROPOL (art. 88 TFEU), EUROJUST (Articles 85 and 86 TFEU) and the European Defence Agency (Articles 42 and 45 TEU) are interesting exceptions, despite irrelevant from a general perspective.

[18] See E. Vos, 'Agencies and the European Union', in T. Zwart, L. Verhay (eds), *Agencies in European and Comparative Law* (2003, Intersentia) 128-129.

[19] On EU agencies' legal basis see, *ex multis*, J. Alberti, *supra*, note 3, 122-137.

ously stated by the Court of Justice of the EU).[20] EU agencies are now mentioned in relation to some of the competences of the Court, namely the action for annulment, for failure to act, the preliminary ruling and the plea of illegality.[21]

In the landmark *Short Selling* judgment,[22] the Court legitimised the practice of delegating sanctioning powers to agencies, fostering their evolution in this domain. Consequently, there may exist in the EU legal order acts adopted by agencies, both addressed to individuals (like the imposition of fines) and having general application (thanks to the explicit mention in Art. 277 TFEU). Therefore, the doubts on the possibility of granting sanctioning powers to agencies now seems to have found quite a safe answer in positive terms.[23]

However, many questions are still open.

Who are these agencies, since they are currently named so differently (centre, foundation, office, authority, body, agency…)? How can these non-defined-agencies be established, by whom and for doing what? Which type of powers can be entrusted to them and under which condition? Which kind of acts can they adopt and under which procedures? The treaties do not offer consistent arguments to address those queries,[24] which are tackled by each piece of secondary legislation establishing agencies in a similar, albeit never identical, manner.

Paradoxically enough, this weak constitutional basis has been both a blessing and a curse for EU agencies.

On the one hand, it has clearly limited (and, to some extent, it is still limiting, because of the just mentioned uncertainties) EU agencies' ability to issue sanctions. Sanctioning powers have been delegated only in few circumstances and under specific conditions. As it will be analytically discussed below (Section 3.4), EU agencies perform mainly an auxiliary function, supporting other institutions (usually, the Commission; sometimes, national administrations) with the technical and scientific

[20] Case T-411/06, *Sogelma*, ECLI:EU:C:2009:518. However, this case stated the need to fully recognise EU agencies' acts among those reviewable under Article 263(1) TFEU; the Lisbon Treaty pushed this approach slightly further, recognising agencies' acts also under other actions.

[21] See P. Craig, 'Legal control of regulatory bodies: principle, policy and teleology', in P. Birkinshaw, M. Varney (eds), *The European Union Legal Order after Lisbon* (2010, Wolters Kluwer) 93.

[22] Case C-270/12, *UK v. Parliament and Council (Short selling)*, ECLI:EU:C:2014:18.

[23] For a short but in-depth analysis of this case law (and its multiple limits), see C. Ohler, 'Anmerkung zu einem Urteil des EuGH vom 22.01.2014 (C-270/12; JZ 2014, 244) – Zur Übertragung von Rechtsetzungsbefugnissen auf die Europäische Wertpapier- und Marktaufsichtbehörde', (2014) *Europarecht* 249.

[24] It bears noting that all the provisions of the treaties dealing with these matters (see, for instance, art. 13 TEU on EU institutions and auxiliary committees; art. 290-291 TFEU for the delegation of powers; art. 288 TFEU for the sources of EU law) do not mention at all agencies. They clearly constitute the legal benchmarks for assessing the agencies' legitimacy; however, they do not explicitly tackle these issues.

assessments that are needed to subsequently issue sanctions. Therefore, their shaky position within the EU institutional architecture has definitely pushed EU agencies towards a supporting, secondary role in EU sanctioning, which has been evolving towards new trends only recently.

On the other hand, the lack of a specific normative framework in the treaties is certainly among the reasons behind the success of EU agencies: they have been replicated over more than 30 years, basically in every field of EU law, also because the Member States have found and are still finding in EU agencies a great platform for cooperation, starting from an almost blank page, without empowering an existing (and potentially hostile) institution,[25] deciding its functions, composition and powers on a case-by-case basis. This flexibility has clearly enhanced the EU agencies' political appeal and, hence, their chance to be endowed with sanctioning powers.

3.3. The agencies' contribution to EU law enforcement. A theoretical perspective

Before looking at the actual role of EU agencies in the exercise of sanctioning powers, their contribution to the enforcement of EU law will be analysed from a theoretical perspective. Two issues deserve to be highlighted in this regard.

3.3.1. EU agencies as a tool to force the 'sanction conundrum' of the EU?

As it is well known, the sanctioning powers of the EU (and, previously, the E(E)C) have traditionally been hindered by national powers and prerogatives.

As Bridge pointed out, 'while the Community constitutes a new and independent legal order (Van Gend), it is also in a sense a dependent legal order in that it relies for its enforcement on the legal orders of the Member States'.[26] During the XV° FIDE Congress, Timmermans (institutional rapporteur) took a similar stance, arguing that 'the Community depends, with few exceptions, on the national legal systems to assure respect for Community law';[27] and the General Report by Tesauro confirmed this point, stating that '*la Communauté [...] ne dispose pas des moyens, contraignants ou administratifs, permettant de faire face à des phénomènes de transgression [...], de sorte*

[25] According to M. Shapiro, 'Independent agencies', in P. Craig, G. De Bùrca (eds), *The evolution of EU Law* (2011 OUP) 113, the creation of agencies enabled Member State 'not to further magnify the Brussels profile'.

[26] J. Bridge, 'Procedural Aspects Of The Enforcement Of European Community Law Through The Legal Systems Of The Member States', (1984) 9 *European Law Review* 28.

[27] The verbatim is reported by J. Biancarelli, 'Does the Community Legal Order Have the Power to Institute Sanctions?', in M. Delmas-Marty (ed.), *What Kind of Criminal Policy for Europe?* (1996, Brill) 249; the whole Institutional Report by C.W.A. Timmermans can be found in the XV FIDE Congress Proceedings, Lisbon, 1992.

qu'elle doit nécessairement compter sur les moyens le cas échéant prévus dans les Etats membres'.[28] Moreover, it is worth noting that, according to the same Author, resorting to national sanctioning was not a discretionary choice of the Community, but, in most cases, '*un choix obligé*'.[29]

Some years later, Biancarelli interestingly noted that current Art. 261 TFEU, granting a full jurisdiction to the Court of Justice over sanctions, confirmed the possibility of theoretically enhancing a direct European sanctioning power through regulations.[30] This approach, however, has not been fully exploited by the Community. On the contrary, at that time the outer reach and most effective tool to improve the Community sanctioning powers could be found in the harmonisation of national control.

Against this settled narrative, one may wonder whether the agencification process – which only revealed its full intensity some years later – could be seen as a tool to force the national prerogatives on sanctioning.

Indeed, EU agencies' capability of merging the European and national level has enabled them to overcome, or at least put in a different perspective, the classical problem that the EU (and, previously, the E(E)C) faced when dealing with this issue: the need to respect the national sovereignty in implementing EU law and, thence, issuing sanctions.[31] Within EU agencies, the European and national level merge one with the other; EU agencies go beyond the principle of subsidiarity, creating a common platform of shared governance, endowed with an autonomous legal personality, that disrupt the classical bilateral relationship between the EU and its Member States.[32] The well-known contrast on which level of authority is entitled to act seem to be overcome, within EU agencies, because that power is actually exercised commonly by the EU and national level.[33]

---

[28] G. Tesauro, 'La sanction des infractions au droit communautaire', (1992) *Rivista di diritto europeo* 504-505.

[29] Ivi, p. 505.

[30] J. Biancarelli, *supra*, note 27, 285.

[31] This issue is highly intertwined with the fragmentation of national administration at a European and global level: see, on this point, *ex multis*, S. Cassese, *La nuova costituzione economica: lezioni* (2012, Laterza) 322-323.

[32] R. Piselli, 'Uno sguardo alle agenzie decentrate attraverso il prisma del principio di sussidiarietà', (2017) *Amministrazione in cammino* 14; V. Salvatore, 'Le Agenzie tra Unione europea e Stati membri. Oltre la sussidiarietà', in V. Salvatore (ed.), *Le Agenzie dell'Unione europea. Profili istituzionali e tendenze evolutive* (2011, Pavia University Press) 20. The literature in English on the relation between EU agencies and the principle of subsidiarity is actually more analytical and quite counterintuitive in its conclusion: see D. Geradin, N. Petit, 'The development of agencies at EU and national levels: conceptual analysis and proposals for reform', (2005) *Yearbook of European Law* 173; M. Chamon, *supra* note 11, 162-164.

[33] See *amplius* J. Alberti, *supra*, note 3, 107-115 and 137-142.

The extent of the twist between these two levels may well vary from sector to sector: it ranges from a bare coordination offered by the agency to national authorities, to an explicit substitution of the latter by the former for adopting binding legal acts vis-à-vis specific addressees or categories of individuals. In any case, even in their weakest forms of involvement, EU agencies seem able to force the secret garden of Member States' sovereignty[34] through the backdoor: providing high-level technical and scientific evaluations, that thence will be used – either by national administrations, by other EU institutions, or by EU agencies themselves – as an unavoidable basis for issuing sanctions.

3.3.2. EU agencies as ever-changing creators of enforcement practices

Moreover, EU agencies stand out in the field of EU enforcement also because of some peculiar institutional abilities.

EU agencies at least take part in (or even directly perform) all those types of enforcement already discussed in the previous chapter, namely the promotion of transnational cooperation, the enforcement's influence via hard and soft law, infringement proceedings and the issue of direct sanctions towards individuals.[35] Usually, they perform two or more of these functions at the same time. Indeed, agencies always constitute a forum for transnational cooperation, because every agency is made up of representatives of all the Member States and has the function to collect and share best practices among national administrations for the implementation of EU law (often interacting with third countries and other international organizations).[36] Moreover, a huge majority of agencies harmonise national legislations through acts with a variable nature and impact: industrial standards, opinions and recommendations, guidelines, or the drafting of delegated and implementing acts. Furthermore, some agencies also assist the Commission in infringement proceedings and, finally, a few of them also have direct sanctioning powers towards private parties.[37]

---

[34] Echoing S. Montaldo, *I limiti della cooperazione in materia penale nell'Unione europea* (2015, Editoriale Scientifica), p. 26, who evocatively refers to the *ius puniendi* as secret garden of the Member States; moreover, it bears noting that, also when exercised by bodies other than agencies, the 'Europeanization' of sanctioning functions is the result of an erosion of settled institutional boundaries: see on this point ivi. p. 27.

[35] See Chapter 2.

[36] This area is largely underexplored by legal and political scientists: see G. Schusterschitz, 'European Agencies as Subjects of International Law', (2004) *International Organizations Law Review* 163; C. Rapoport, 'La participation des Etats tiers aux agences de l'Union européenne', in J. Molinier (ed.), *Les Agences de l'Union européenne* (2011, Bruylant) 145; F. Coman-Kund, 'The international dimension of the EU agencies: framing a growing legal-institutional phenomenon', (2018) *European foreign affairs review* 97; J. Alberti, *supra* note 3, 399-452.

[37] The precise analytical taxonomy of EU agencies' sanctioning (or pre-sanctioning) powers

However, the added value of agencies is not only their 'multitasking nature', but also their flexibility in evolving from performing a simpler type of enforcement to a more complex one (think, for instance, from sharing best practices to issuing harmonising guidelines).

Indeed, agencies can also be seen as *legislative laboratories* at the disposal of the EU (and the Member States) to understand how far they want to go in the common regulation of a specific sector. Even when they face a common problem (e.g. asylum; financial stability; energy or TLC regulation), Member States are not sure *ex ante* to what extent they are ready to cope with this issue at EU level or how to concretely solve their common regulatory problems. Instead of granting powers to old institutions like the Commission, which are already too powerful and to some extent also 'biased' in the approach to the issue, Member States often prefer to create an agency. The new body will be made up by new faces coming from national administrations, with mainly a technical and not political background. It will be the task of the newly established agency to identify the enforcement methods that can better suit each policy field or each political momentum. The Commission accepts this compromise, since it also participates in the agency and, moreover, this latter body attracts at EU level powers that otherwise would remain national.[38] For the same reason, the European Parliament usually well accepts this outcome, pushing for powerful EU regulators yet accountable to the legislator.[39]

From this perspective, agencies can be seen both as a boost for enhancing EU sanctioning powers, or as bodies that slow it down. Indeed, they can both foster a common legal and administrative culture of supervision, which constitutes the fundamental basis for developing a common and efficient sanctioning framework; or they can push the political debate towards solutions that can be very different from sanctioning; for instance, because they manage to solve the enforcement problems on a technical level or simply by sharing best practices and standards.

---

will be provided below, at Section 3.4. For a general evaluation of EU agencies' powers and functions, see *ex multis* the different taxonomies provided R. van Ooik, 'The growing importance of Agencies in the EU: Shifting governance and the institutional balance', in D. Curtin, R. Wessel (eds), *Good Governance and the EU: Reflections on Concepts, Institutions and Substance* (2005, Brill) 139; E. Chiti, 'An important part of EU's institutional machinery: features, problems and perspectives of European agencies', (2009) *Common Market Law Review* 1395; P. Craig, *EU Administrative Law* (2012, OUP) 148.; M. Chamon, *supra*, note 11, 18; C. Tovo, *supra*, note 11, 265; J. Alberti, *supra* note 3, 185-204.

[38] See Communication from the Commission to the European Parliament and the Council, COM(2008) 135 final, 'European agencies – The way forward', 5, where the Commission admits that 'the establishment of agencies can make possible a pooling of powers at EU level which would be resisted if centred on the institutions themselves'.

[39] For a comprehensive analysis of the EU agencies' relationship with the European Parliament, see F.B. Jacobs, 'EU agencies and the European Parliament', in M. Everson, C. Monda, E. Vos (eds), *European Agencies in between Institutions and Member States* (2014, Wolters Kluwer) 201.

Economic and political scientists have analysed this phenomenon describing agencies as bodies for an 'experimentalist governance'.[40] Therefore, enforcement through agencies inevitably creates legal incoherencies; this outcome, however, can be very efficient from an economic and perhaps even diplomatic perspective, exactly because it responds to the need to tackle certain transnational problems even if there is still no consensus among the Member States on the solution. This does not prevent, of course, legal scholars from discussing how EU agencies' hybridity should be harmonised with the established set of rules and principles: this point will be tackled further below, after having evaluated in concrete terms EU agencies' powers and functions in the specific field of sanctioning.

3.4. An analytical taxonomy of EU agencies' direct or indirect sanctioning powers

Even though the legal and political literature framing EU agencies' powers and functions is extremely rich,[41] far less attention has been given to the peculiar power of issuing sanctions. Thus, sanctioning powers are usually mentioned as a single category of the broader taxonomies on EU agencies' powers, but no taxonomy has ever been made – according to our knowledge – to discuss in depth the sanctioning powers as such.

EU agencies' contribution to EU and national sanctioning can be sorted out according to the following categories, which are lined up from the weakest form of involvement to the strongest.

3.4.1. Collection and spread of information and best practices among national administrations

As already mentioned, because of its multilateral composition virtually any agency performs this function. However, when engaging in this form of transnational cooperation, agencies simply build the basis upon which usually national administration may eventually rely upon to sanction market operators.[42] *Legally speaking*,

---

[40] C.F. Sabel, J. Zeitlin, 'Learning from Difference: The New Architecture of Experimentalist Governance in the EU', (2008) *European Law Journal* 271; J. Pollak, P. Slominski, 'Experimentalist but not accountable governance? The role of Frontex in managing the EU external borders', (2009) *West European Politics* 904; V. Termini, 'Dall'armonizzazione al mercato unico: Acer – l'Agenzia europea per la regolazione dell'energia', in P. Bilancia (ed.), *La regolazione dei mercati di settore tra autorità indipendenti nazionali e organismi europei* (2012, Giuffrè) 131.

[41] See *supra* note 37.

[42] It is worth noting that this function should nevertheless not be underestimated: see G. Majone, 'The New European Agencies: Regulation by Information', (1997) *Journal of European Public Policy* 262.

there is no direct link between the agencies' activity and the adoption of sanctions. Therefore, this function deserves only to be mentioned at the weakest side on the spectrum of EU agencies' contribution to the topic under scrutiny.

3.4.2 Monitoring activities and inspections that might bring to sanction issued by national or EU authorities

Slightly more interesting are those functions of monitoring and carrying out inspections that might bring to further sanctions issued by other bodies, at either EU or national level. Indeed, in this case there is a formal legal link between the agencies' activity and the opening of sanctioning proceedings: monitoring and inspections are the first steps of an administrative sanctioning procedure.

However, since the degree of discretion left to the sanctioning authorities is maximum, EU agencies are called upon to provide the factual data on whose basis national administrations or the Commission will take the decision of sanctioning. It is worth noting that, contrary to the categories that will follow below, in this case EU agencies are *not* proposing the adoption of a sanction, but simply collecting data that could be used for issuing sanctions.

This happens in the field of chemicals (namely by the European Chemicals Agency, ECHA[43]), fisheries control (by the European Fisheries Control Agency, EFCA[44], for instance for assessing the respect of fish quotas) and cross-border labour flows and working conditions (by the brand new European Labour Agency, ELA[45]). In these cases, agencies carry out inspections whose results are then given to the *national* authorities in charge of issuing sanctions. It is worth noting that the fragmentation of the sanctioning proceedings between final national acts and preliminary European ones might well create some problems in the field of judicial protection. These problems are still to be fully explored with regard to these bodies, since no relevant litigation has arisen so far; however, this possible lack in judicial protection given by the multi-level fragmentation of regulation is gaining a significant relevance in the context of banking supervision, because of the recent empowerment of the ECB,[46] and it, therefore, deserves to be carefully monitored.

Conversely, inspections can also be carried out in view of potential sanctions is-

[43] Art. 77, par. 4, lit. b) and e) of Regulation (EC) No 1907/2006 of the European Parliament and of the Council of 18 December 2006, OJ 2006, L 396/1 (as subsequently amended).

[44] Art. 3, lit. i) and Art. 19 of Regulation (EU) 2019/473 of the European Parliament and of the Council of 19 March 2019, OJ 2019, L 8/18; Art. 79 of Council Regulation (EC) No 1224/2009 of 20 November 2009, OJ 2009, L 343/1 (as subsequently amended).

[45] Art. 8 of the Regulation (EU) 2019/1149 of the European Parliament and of the Council of 20 June 2019, OJ 2019 L 186/21.

[46] Case C-219/17, *Fininvest*, ECLI:EU:C:2018:1023; see, *ex multis*, S. Demková, 'The Grand Chamber's Take on Composite Procedures under the Single Supervisory Mechanism', (2019) *Review of European Administrative Law* 209 and the chapter by F. Allemand in this Book.

sued by European authorities: for instance, this is the case of the European Maritime Safety Agency (EMSA), which operates essentially for the prevention of pollution by ships and by oil and gas installations.[47]

Moreover, the sanctioning authority (whether European or national) can also be left to the specific circumstances of the procedure. An interesting example in this regard, where the agency's involvement in sanctioning is actually quite close to the category discussed in the following sub-section, is provided by the European Medicines Agency (EMA)[48] in the field of pharmaceutical supervision. In this case, the sanction, consisting in the revocation of a market authorization, is adopted by the Commission only as a last-resort, if there is no consensus among the Member States on the urgent measures recommended by the agency.[49] This means that EMA performs not only a scientific evaluation, but also bears a slightly more political role to build a common trust among the Member States on the need to revoke certain market authorizations. If a unanimity among national authorities is reached, then the sanction is taken at national level; otherwise, is up to the Commission to take the decision.[50] This, by the way, goes as further example of EU agencies as platforms that merge the European and national level of implementation and that create the conditions for a 'Europeanization' of sanctioning.

3.4.3. Power to propose to the Commission to impose fees

A further step in EU agencies' involvement in sanctioning can be identified when these bodies propose the adoption of sanctions against market operators to the Commission. Here EU agencies do not simply take part in the sanctioning proceedings, providing technical and scientific support, but actually push their role a step further: performing their institutional activities, they come across possible infringements of EU law by individuals and propose to the European Commission to issue sanctions against those possible breaches of EU law.

The following are some interesting examples of such a power.

In the field of pharmaceuticals and centrally authorised veterinary medicinal products, the abovementioned EMA, when it is of the opinion that the authorization holder is breaching EU law, may request the Commission to investigate whether to

[47] Art. 2(2), lit. b) and Art. 3 of Regulation (EC) No 1406/2002 of the European Parliament and of the Council of 27 June 2002, OJ 2002, L 208/1 (as subsequently amended).

[48] Regulation (EC) No 726/2004 of the European Parliament and of the Council of 31 March 2004, OJ 2004, L 136/1 (as subsequently amended).

[49] Art. 107i – Art. 107k of the Directive 2001/83/EC of the European Parliament and of the Council of 6 November 2001, OJ 2001, L 311/67 (as subsequently amended).

[50] See on this point M. Chamon, S. Wirtz, 'Complex procedures as hurdle to accountability: verticalization of pharmaceuticals enforcement', in M. Scholten, M. Luchtman (eds), *Law Enforcement by EU Authorities* (2017, Elgar) 152.

impose fines and other financial penalties[51]. Therefore, while for the *revocation* of the same authorizations EMA enjoys only an (influent) technical and scientific power of assessment, as mentioned in the sub-section above, for the imposition of fines the agency expand its power, since the sanctioning procedure starts on its own specific request.[52]

A similar power is also granted to the European Aviation Safety Authority (EASA)[53] for monitoring the respect of the safety certification by air operators; also in this case, the agency is entitled to request to the Commission the imposition of fines to single legal entities infringing EU rules on aviation safety.[54]

It bears noting that in these cases the Commission keeps a discretionary power in deciding whether to impose fines; practitioners have not reported any *de facto* restrictions to the Berlaymont's prerogatives, as conversely noted in the purely regulatory domain, where often the draft decision submitted by the agency is almost mirrored by the Commission.[55]

3.4.4. Assistance in the enforcement of EU law (a silent erosion of the Commission's infringement powers?)

EU agencies bear 'indirect' sanctioning powers not only against individuals, but also vis-à-vis national authorities.

Looking from the perspective of the EU agencies' involvement in sanctioning, this task is similar to those already discussed (monitoring/inspective powers and power to propose sanctions). However, it deserves separate and careful attention because it has broader political implications, encroaching (*de facto*, if not *de iure*)[56] upon the Commis-

---

[51] In the field of pharmaceuticals, see Art. 84a(3) of EMA Regulation (*supra*, note 48) and Art. 11-18 of Commission Regulation (EC) No 658/2007 of 14 June 2007, OJ 2007, L 155/10 (as subsequently amended). In the field of centrally authorised veterinary medicinal products, see Art. 136(3) of the Regulation (EU) 2019/6 of the European Parliament and of the Council of 11 December 2018, OJ 2019, L 4/43.

[52] The same power of initiative is vested also in national authorities: see Art. 84a(3) of the EMA Regulation (*supra* note 48).

[53] Regulation (EU) 2018/1139 of the European Parliament and of the Council of 4 July 2018, OJ 2018, L212/1.

[54] Ibid, Art. 84; see M. Chamon, 'Le recours à la soft law comme moyen d'éluder les obstacles constitutionnels au développement des agences de l'UE', (2014) 576 *Revue de l'Union européenne* 156 (note 38).

[55] T. Gehring, S. Krapohl, 'Supranational regulatory agencies between independence and control: the EMEA and the authorization of pharmaceuticals in the European single market', (2007) *Journal of European Public Policy* 208.

[56] It is worth noting that only in three cases (EBA, EIOPA and ESMA, see below) the legal texts explicitly draw a connection between the procedure in which the agencies are involved and the infringement proceeding (and, when doing so, they explicitly deny that the former may limit the Commission's discretion in the latter). However, the fact that the agencies activities could be

sion's prerogatives in the infringement proceedings. To what extent the powers held by EU agencies in this domain are compatible with the treaties and how and whether they could (or should) further evolve to balance some recent weaknesses shown by the infringement procedure pursuant to Articles 258-260 TFEU is an issue that has already been discussed elsewhere and that cannot be recalled here[57].

For the purposes of this study, it is worth highlighting that the degree of the erosion of the Commission's powers in the public enforcement of EU law may well vary, from very weak forms to quite significant ones.

On the weakest side of the spectrum lies EASA[58], the Agency for the Coordination of Energy Regulator (ACER)[59] and the European Railway Agency (ERA),[60] which can make inspections and monitoring activities in the offices of the national authorities to assess the proper implementation of EU law. After the inspection, those agencies report their findings to the Commission, which keeps full discretion on the further steps to be taken. Leaving aside the peculiar political implication mentioned above, these cases are quite similar to the monitoring activities already discussed above.

A far more significant role is played by the Body of European Regulators for Electronic Communications (BEREC).[61] According to Article 7a of Directive 2002/21/EC,[62] when the Commission considers that a national authority is creating a barrier to the single market by imposing, amending or withdrawing an obligation on an operator in (mis)application of EU secondary law on electronic communication, it notifies its concerns both to the national authority and to BEREC. After the notification, the national authority is prevented from the adoption of such measures for three months. Within this time framework, BEREC is entitled to issue an opinion on the Commission's concerns and make it public.[63] If BEREC disagrees with the Commission, deeming the national draft measures fully compatible with EU law, the Berlaymont can keep preventing the national authority from adopting its

---

used well for the purposes of Articles 258-260 TFEU is rather clear from the specific context of every policy field discussed in this sub-section – as well as the fact that the limit to the Commission's discretion should be evaluated in practice, going beyond a bare formalistic analysis.

[57] J. Alberti, *supra* note 3, 246-253.

[58] Art. 85 EASA Regulation, *supra* note 53.

[59] Originally established in 2009, ACER founding Regulation has recently been amended by Regulation (EU) 2019/942 of the European Parliament and of the Council of 5 June 2019, OJ 2019, L 158/22. See, in particular, Art. 6(6) and Article 4(8).

[60] Article 11(1) of Regulation (EU) 2016/796 of the European Parliament and of the Council of 11 May 2016, OJ 2016, L 138/1.

[61] Regulation (EU) 2018/1971 of the European Parliament and of the Council of 11 December 2018, OJ 2018, L 32/1.

[62] Directive 2002/21/EC of the European Parliament and of the Council of 7 March 2002, OJ 2002, L 108/33 (as subsequently amended).

[63] *Ibidem*, Art. 7a (3).

draft measures only providing reasons justifying why it does so despite the different outcome suggested by the agency.[64]

Thus, in this case the agency plays the role of an 'elder brother' of national authorities: it can support them, and thus impose on the parents (i.e. the Commission) an obligation of enhanced motivation for sanctioning; or it can take a step back, leaving the matter to the bilateral relationship between the Commission and the national authority. These powers are clearly much stronger than bare monitoring and can even be seen as a deeper involvement in sanctions than the proposal of fines: the Commission, in those latter cases, does not have to provide any motivation for its action (or inaction).

However, the maximum degree of erosion of the Commission's role as guardian of the treaties is reached by other three agencies: the European Banking Authority (EBA)[65], the European Insurances and Occupational Pensions Authority (EIOPA)[66] and the European Securities and Markets Authority (ESMA).[67]

These agencies have far more intrusive powers than BEREC's, for three main reasons. First, they enjoy broad supervisory powers, i.e. not related to the control over specific national draft measures but with regards to the whole implementation of EU banking and financial law. Second, their relationship with the Commission is almost the opposite than BEREC's: EBA, EIOPA and ESMA are those entitled to act, only after having heard the Commission's opinion, and not vice versa.[68] Third, if a national authority does not properly implement EU law, despite the agencies' and the Commission's requests for doing so, in extraordinary circumstances the agencies can directly adopt binding decisions vis-à-vis national market operators so as to force them to comply with their obligations under EU law, including the cessation of any practice.[69]

---

[64] *Ibidem*, Art. 7a (5).

[65] Regulation (EU) No 1093/2010 of the European Parliament and of the Council of 24 November 2010, OJ 2010, L 331/12 (as subsequently amended).

[66] Regulation (EU) No 1094/2010 of the European Parliament and of the Council of 24 November 2010, OJ 2010, L 331/48 (as subsequently amended).

[67] Regulation (EU) No 1095/2010 of the European Parliament and of the Council of 24 November 2010, OJ 2010, L 331/84 (as subsequently amended).

[68] For the sake of clarity, it is worth noting that the three agencies cannot act against the opinion of the Commission, neither providing due motivation (in contrast to what the Commission might do with regard to BEREC). Moreover, it bears noting that after the submission of this chapter the establishing Regulations of EBA, EIOPA and ESMA have been amended (Regulation (EU) No 2019/2175 of the European Parliament and of the Council, OJ 2019, L 334/1). This reform cannot be discussed in detail here; since comprehensive analyses of the new framework are still lacking, see, *ex multis*, the Commission proposal COM(2017)536 of 20 September 2017 and A. Magliari, 'La proposta di riforma delle Autorità europee di vigilanza finanziaria. Verso un ulteriore accentramento delle funzioni di vigilanza a livello sovranazionale: prospettive e problemi', (2018) *Rivista Italiana di Diritto Pubblico Comunitario* 391.

[69] See Articles 17, 17a and 18 of either EBA, EIOPA or ESMA Regulations, above at notes 65,

In exercising those powers, EBA, EIOPA and ESMA are not sanctioning national authorities, but simply circumventing their inaction by imposing certain measures directly to single private legal entities to properly implement EU law. Therefore, these powers are slightly different than the exercise of 'classical' sanctioning powers, such as the imposition of fines that will be discussed hereinafter. However, in terms of EU agencies' impact over the enforcement of EU law, both cases seem standing on an equal line.

3.4.5. Power to impose fees (and the not-always-unlimited jurisdiction of the Court of Justice of the EU)

The strongest examples of EU agencies' involvement in sanctioning is provided only by very few bodies that are equipped with the power to impose the payment of fees and penalties.

At the current height of the agencification process, those powers are granted only to ESMA (for two purposes: controlling over-the-counter derivative contracts[70] and credit rating agencies[71]) and to the Single Resolution Board (SRB, for the resolution of credit institutions).[72] It bears noting that, in the latter case, the national authorities keep a general power to implement the SRB's decisions (and, thence, also those including sanctions).[73] Since no sanction has been issued yet, there is no practice to evaluate concretely the degree of involvement of national authorities. However, the room left for these latter bodies seems actually extremely scant and formal, as highlighted – albeit in general terms and with no specific reference to sanctions – by both the legal literature[74] and the jurisprudence.[75]

Each provision granting those direct sanctioning powers belongs to a specific

---

66, 67 (these acts are basically identical on this point; after the recent legislative amendments, see also Article 9c of EBA Regulation). For a comprehensive analysis of the so-called 'breach of Union law procedure', see also P. Schammo, 'Actions and inactions in the investigation of breaches of Union law by the European supervisory authorities', (2018) *Common market law review* 1423.

[70] Articles 65-68 of the Regulation (EU) No 648/2012 of the European Parliament and of the Council of 4 July 2012, OJ 2012, L 201/1 (as subsequently amended).

[71] Articles 36a and 36d of Regulation (EC) No 1060/2009 of the European Parliament and of the Council of 16 September 2009, OJ 2009, L 302/1 (as subsequently amended).

[72] Articles 38-41 of the Regulation (EU) No 806/2014 of the European Parliament and of the Council of 15 July 2014, OJ 2014, L 225/1.

[73] Ivi, Article 29.

[74] See Y. Herinckx, 'Judicial Protection In The Single Resolution Mechanism', in R. Houben, W. Vandenbruwaene (eds), *The Single Resolution Mechanism* (2017, Intersentia) 77, in particular paras 38-39.

[75] The case regards the different issue of the *ex ante* calculation of the contribution to the Single Resolution Fund; see, however, paras 57-59 for some general statements concerning the (limited) impact of national implementation of the SRB decisions, that could well be applied also in the different field of sanctions.

legislative framework and has autonomous purposes and procedures; thence, they cannot be discussed here in detail.[76] However, a general remark deserves to be made.

Almost every time an EU agency is equipped with the power to impose or propose the imposition of penalty payments or fines, the Court is likewise endowed with an unlimited jurisdiction over those penalties, according to Article 261 TFEU and, thence, it can cancel, reduce or increase the amount to be paid. This happen with the sanctioning powers of ESMA,[77] but also when EASA[78] and EMA[79] request to the Commission to impose fines. As it is well known, this approach aims at enhancing judicial protection and is fully in line with the established practice in the field of competition, where Article 261 TFEU has been applied mostly,[80] and also with regard to the European Central Bank's sanctioning activity.[81]

Against this framework, the fact that similar powers have not been granted to the Court with regard to the sanctions imposed by SRB comes out quite surprisingly and, perhaps, it is due to the fact that, in the legislative proposal issued by the Commission, sanctions had to be enacted by national authorities following an 'instruction' by the agency,[82] thus falling under national jurisdiction.

This issue seems not to have attracted legal debates so far.[83] By way of exception, Lamandini, Ramos and Solana implicitly argued that the general rules on sanctions by the ECB should also be applied with regards to the Single Supervisory Mechanism and to the Single Resolution Mechanism (i.e., the SRB's domain).[84]

---

[76] For an in-depth analysis of ESMA sanctioning powers see N. Moloney, *The age of ESMA. Governing EU Financial Markets* (2011, Hart) 260; for SRB, see P.E. Berger, D. Vanderstraeten, 'The Single Resolution Mechanism. Institutional and Financing Arrangements for Bank Resolution in the European Banking Union', in R. Houben, W. Vandenbruwaene (eds), *The Single Resolution Mechanism* (2017, Intersentia) 7-48.

[77] Article 69 of the (EU) Regulation No 648/2012, supra, note 70, for OTC penalties; Article 36e of the Regulation (EC) No 1060/2009, supra, note 71, for credit rating agencies.

[78] Article 84(5) EASA Regulation, *supra* note 53.

[79] Article 84a(9) EMA Regulation, supra, note 48, and Article 136(10) of Regulation (EU) 2019/6 of the European Parliament and of the Council of 11 December 2018, OJ 2019, L 4/43.

[80] See B. Vesterdorf, 'The Court of Justice and Unlimited Jurisdiction: What does it mean in practice' (2009) *Global Competition Policy* 2.

[81] Article 5 of the Council Regulation (EC) No 2532/98 of 23 November 1998, OJ 1998, L 318/4 (as subsequently amended).

[82] See Commission proposal COM (2013) 520 final of 10 July 2013, in particular Articles 36 and 37.

[83] See, for instance, the interesting and detailed analysis by Y. Herinckx, 'Judicial Protection In The Single Resolution Mechanism', in R. Houben, W. Vandenbruwaene (eds), *The Single Resolution Mechanism* (2017, Intersentia) 77.

[84] M. Lamandini, D. Ramos, J. Solana, 'The European Central Bank (ECB) Powers As A Cata-

However, while in the former case there is an explicit legal provision stating so,[85] in the latter case there is none. Thus, also according to those Authors, 'the reference to full judicial review of all sanctions should be more explicit'.[86] Whether the Court of Justice enjoys an unlimited jurisdiction over SRB penalties seems, therefore, a quite complex issue that is left open for discussion and deserves to be tackled. If, as it appears, the answer is negative, this would be a quite unjustified *unicum* in the field of EU agencies' (and not only) sanctioning powers, that might require some legislative intervention to be amended. Indeed, the unlimited jurisdiction of the Court over penalties is one of the elements identified by a settled jurisprudence to withstand challenges in light of the principle of effective judicial protection.[87]

Of course, the lack of such an unlimited jurisdiction does not mean *per se* that the Court is prevented from scrutinising the legality of SRB sanctions and that the SRB establishing regulation clashes with Article 47 of the Charter of Fundamental Rights of the EU. As demonstrated by the recent case law on the calculation of the *ex ante* contribution to the Single Resolution Fund,[88] the Court could well control the decision of the SRB that sets the sum to be paid by each bank even if it does not have the power to increase or reduce the amount. Indeed, the Court can always partly or fully annul the decision and, therefore, ask the agency to calculate the payment according to the principles stated by the same Court.[89]

However, the impossibility to substitute its own appraisal for that of the agency clearly makes the Court's scrutiny weaker and, conversely, the agency's independence stronger. The full respect of the principle of effective judicial protection will, therefore, be evaluated case-by-case; also in this case, the lack of any sanctioning practices hinders any further evaluation. From a general perspective, yet, one may wonder why such a deference is given only to SRB: as mentioned above, with regard to penalties imposed by the ECB, the Commission, or other agencies like ESMA, the Court enjoys an unlimited jurisdiction. This can hardly be explained because of some peculiarities

---

lyst For Change In EU Law. Part 2: SSM, SRM And Fundamental Rights', (2017) *Columbia Journal of European Law* 199, 246-247.

[85] Article 18(4)(7) of the Council Regulation (EU) No 1024/2013 of 15 October 2013, OJ 2013, L 287/63.

[86] M. Lamandini, D. Ramos, J. Solana, *supra* note 84, 247.

[87] Case C-272/09 P, *KME Germany and others*, ECLI:EU:C:2011:810, paras 91-106; C-386/10 P, *Chalkor v. Commission*, ECLI:EU:C:2011:815, paras 45-67; Case C-199/11, *Otis*, ECLI:EU:C:2012:684, paras 47-67. See also, on this point, K. Lenaerts, I. Maselis, K. Gutman, *EU Procedural Law* (2014, OUP) 622-631.

[88] *Ex multis*, Case T-365/16, *Portigon AG*, ECLI:EU:T:2019:824.

[89] On the possibility of an in-depth scrutiny of the Court over technical discretionary choices taken by agencies even without a formally unlimited jurisdiction, see E. Vos, 'The European Court of Justice in the face of scientific uncertainty and complexity', in M. Dawson, B. De Witte, E. Muir (eds), *Judicial activism at the European Court of Justice* (2013, Edward Elgar) 142.

of the former body. On the contrary, the fact that SRB – like any other EU agency – suffers a very scant recognition in primary law seems to call for a greater attention in holding this authority under control and, thus, in improving judicial protection. Indeed, the Court's capability to review EU agencies' acts has always been deemed as being a fundamental tool to enhance EU agencies' legitimacy;[90] granting unlimited jurisdiction over penalties would clearly go in this direction.

3.5. EU agencies' contribution to the exercise of sanctioning power: current and future challenges

The huge ambiguity that still embraces EU agencies when it comes to the limits to their powers, functions, independence and, above all, their mission within the already well crowded and even more fragmented EU executive clearly has an impact also on EU agencies' sanctioning powers. Even though some common features can be highlighted, those powers are currently exercised according to different procedures, depending on the sector involved; they are often shared with several other European or national actors, even within the same policy field; above all, after *Short selling* their legitimacy seems generally accepted, although this sometimes is a bare presumption.

Indeed, the evolution of EU agencies' sanctioning powers has been occurring over the years fully in coherence with the general method according to which EU agencies have enhanced their powers: namely, on a case-by-case basis, through a silent erosion of the attributions of neighbouring authorities (European or national), only in those sectors where it was possible and needed, without any previous, general, institutional project. Such a trend is not *per se* negative: as already discussed above, the rise of agencies in exercising sanctioning powers has enabled to push the process of European integration forward even with regards to highly-sensitive policy fields, such as the banking and financial sectors in the troubled times between 2008 and nowadays. Moreover, even their support to established authorities as the Commission goes not always to the detriment of the latter's prerogatives. For instance, when EU agencies bear only powers to propose sanctions, as EMA in the case of the revocation of market authorizations, they act as bodies who build consensus among the Member States or, if no unanimity is reached, who pave the way for a Europeanization of sanctions through the intervention of the Commission.

Against this framework, legal scholars and political scientists have often called for a treaty reform to fully recognise EU agencies.[91] While this request obviously seems fully embraceable, one may wonder whether, before that, it might be worth-

---

[90] See J. Alberti, *supra* note 3, 301-315.

[91] See, most recently, C. Tovo, supra, note 11, 417; M. Chamon, supra, note 11, 372.

while to open a real debate on EU agencies' role and functions within the EU institutional landscape. Several unsuccessful attempts had been made in the past,[92] but the time might be ripe again for a new try. Indeed, the recognised status that nowadays EU agencies enjoy calls for committing these bodies to a reasoned evolution, and not to a trend imposed by contingencies.

Currently, it is actually quite hard to identify the driving forces according to which agencies are empowered with sanctioning powers. By way of a final assessment on the phenomenon under scrutiny, four elements could nevertheless be highlighted.

First, it is undeniable that this is a favourable timeframe. The *Short selling* case has certainly given new impetus to the possibility to enhance the agencies' role in this regard. Indeed, the two most powerful sanctioning agencies (ESMA and SRB) are among the most recent ones and clearly owe their powers also to the *Short selling* judgment.[93] However, it also holds true that ELA, which has been created only recently and well after the judicial legitimation just mentioned, has been endowed with mainly monitoring and inspective powers.

This is because a far more striking factor should instead be identified in the policy field: ESMA and SRB operates in the banking and financial sector, where powerful regulators have long been operating at the national level and which clearly needed, after the financial crisis, more stringent and cross-border control.[94] Other important examples of EU agencies exercising sanctioning powers (albeit only to propose the imposition of fees) can be seen, as discussed above, in the fields of energy, electronic communication, transports: therefore, policy fields that are quite used to being regulated, also at a national level, through independent authorities.[95]

These latter examples introduce the last two elements that should be taken into account for assessing the key factors that currently shape EU agencies' involvement in sanctioning: national sovereignty and European interest.

Counterintuitively, the policy fields that are the closest to national interests are not always those where EU agencies are less likely to be endowed with sanctioning

---

[92] See *supra* note 3. It bears noting that at a national level, agencification has often been anticipated by deep reflections on their role and functions: see, for a comparison, OCSE Report 'Public Administration after New Public Management' (2010, Paris).

[93] The relation between ESMA and *Short selling* is the closest possible, since this latter case deals exactly on the empowerment of the former; as for SRB, the powers of this agency have been shaped by the EU legislator exactly in view of what the Court stated in *Short selling*: see on this point M. Chamon, 'The Empowerment of Agencies under the Meroni Doctrine and Article 114 TFEU: Comment on UK v Parliament and Council (Short-selling) and the Proposed Single Resolution Mechanism', (2014) *European Law Review* 380.

[94] See the report of the High-Level Group (chaired by Mr J. de Larosière) on Financial Supervision in the EU published on 25 February 2009.

[95] K. Verhoest (ed.), *Government agencies: practices and lessons from 30 countries* (2012, Palgrave).

powers: the rise of agencies' sanctions in financial fields clearly stands for the opposite conclusion.

Indeed, national sovereignty should always be matched with the interest of the Union: and in some circumstances the latter can be better protected through a common sanctioning framework managed by EU agencies. Here, again, the recent financial crisis is quite revealing. As pointed out by Chamon, in the field of financial supervision, the Commission initially proposed to give ESMA only indirect sanctioning powers (with ESMA making monitoring and investigations and the Commission issuing fines).[96] The European Parliament rejected this approach, asking for (and obtaining) a more powerful EU technical regulator.[97] Conversely, in the field of energy the European Parliament tried to give similar sanctioning powers to ACER, and the Commission and the Council this time succeeded in opposing it and establishing a model of more indirect enforcement.[98]

It is pretty clear that the threat to the EU financial stability and its impact on the EU political integration process have played a role in shaping a more powerful regulator in financial matters than in the field of energy, even though the former, over the recent years, has clearly been closest to the heart of national sovereignty. The special twist between national and European level that has been created with this agency has certainly played a role in reaching this outcome; *ça va sans dire* that for future agencies (or for further empowerment of existing ones) the balance between national and European interests may well be struck differently.

At the time being, therefore, the main role in shaping the agencies' involvement in performing sanctioning functions still has to be devoted to political considerations, that may well vary from time to time and with regards to each specific *dossier*. Thus, assessing how EU agencies' contribution to the *ius puniendi* might evolve over the next years seems a quite hard task. Indeed, even though EU agencies are often deemed as performing merely technical functions, the sanctioning powers recently attributed to them show the highly political implications tackled by these bodies in their day-to-day activity.

---

[96] M. Chamon, *supra*, note 11, 38, footnote 222.

[97] *Ibidem*, footnote 223.

[98] M. Chamon, *supra*, note 11, 39, footnote 225-226.

Chapter 4

FROM SANCTIONS TO PREVENTION, AND NOW BACK TO SANCTIONS? ARTICLE 7 TEU AND THE PROTECTION OF THE EU FOUNDING VALUES

Matteo Bonelli *

ABSTRACT: *This chapter analyzes the EU procedures to sanction Member States' breaches of the Union founding values: democracy, the rule of law, and human rights. The key provision in this respect is Article 7 TEU, which allows the Council to impose sanctions against the Member State responsible of a 'serious and persistent breach' of the values. Originally introduced by the Treaty of Amsterdam, Article 7 was then amended in Nice with the addition of a preventive mechanism. Further preventive steps, including the adoption of the Rule of Law Framework, have been added over time by the EU institutions. After offering an overview of the Article 7 system and procedures, reflecting in particular on the type of sanctions that can be adopted by the Council, the chapter describes the shift in emphasis and attention from sanctioning to preventive and monitoring procedures. On the basis of an incorrect reading of the provision, Article 7 began to be considered a nuclear option, and the EU institutions preferred focusing on softer dialogical instruments. Only more recently, due to the constitutional crises in Hungary and Poland, Article 7 returned high on the agenda, and was actually activated for the first time, finally reacquiring its centrality in the EU's values-protection toolkit. Furthermore, the EU has strengthened parallel judicial responses to the challenges and is also developing other tools to sanction values-related breaches, such as the proposed new Regulation on Rule of Law conditionality. The chapter reflects on these recent steps and concludes that, while they can be positively assessed, a more coordinated action is needed, better streamlining institutional efforts in the field and closely linking monitoring and sanctioning efforts.*

KEYWORDS: *Article 7 – sanctions – rule of law – constitutional crisis – montioring*

---

* Assistant Professor, Maastricht University. I thank the editors of this volume for their helpful comments. The usual disclaimer applies.

4.1. Introduction

Along with Article 50 TEU, setting out the procedure to withdraw from the European Union, Article 7 TEU is probably the most often discussed provision of the EU Treaties in recent legal, political, and academic debates on EU affairs. A sleeping giant – or, as it has been put more critically, an 'empty' or 'indifferent gesture'[1] – for almost two decades, Article 7 TEU has now taken the center of the stage as the EU tries to react to the processes of constitutional backsliding in Hungary and Poland.[2] In December 2017, the European Commission activated for the first time ever the procedure of Article 7(1) TEU against Poland, and it was soon followed by the European Parliament, which in September 2018 voted on a resolution triggering a parallel but autonomous procedure against Hungary. Both Article 7(1) procedures are now pending before the Council, which has the responsibility to take the final decision, upon obtaining the European Parliament's consent, on the existence of a 'clear risk of a serious breach' of the founding values of the Union identified by Article 2 TEU: most importantly, democracy, the rule of law and human rights.

This chapter discusses the procedures of Article 7 TEU[3] against the background of the increasing 'sanctioning powers' of the EU and the Union's possible transformation into a 'community of coercion'.[4] It will be argued that the introduction of the Article 7 regime, on the one hand, follows the general pattern of growth of EU sanctioning powers described in this volume; on the other, it presents some peculiar features. The evolution of the Article 7 system is in fact not at all linear. At the origins of the system, with the Amsterdam Treaty, EU institutions alone acquired sanctioning

---

[1] A. Williams, 'The indifferent gesture: Article 7 TEU, the Fundamental Rights Agency and the UK's invasion of Iraq' (2006) *European Law Review* 31, 3.

[2] Literature on the two crises is abundant: on Hungary, see e.g. A. von Bogdandy, P. Sonnevend (eds), *Constitutional Crisis in the European Constitutional Area - Theory, Law and Politics in Hungary and Romania* (Hart Publishing, 2015); on Poland, see most recently W. Sadurski, *Poland's Constitutional Breakdown* (Oxford University Press, 2019).

[3] The plural (procedures) is needed considering that Article 7, as it will be shown later, actually creates two distinct mechanisms.

[4] See A. von Bogdandy, 'Ways to Frame the European Rule of Law: Rechtsgemeinschaft, Trust, Revolution, and Kantian Peace', (2018) *European Constitutional Law Review* 14, 682-683, contrasting the 'old' 'community of law' to the developing 'community of coercion' and noting that 'since the early 1990s, there has been an expansion of instruments of sanction going beyond declaratory rulings of the Court of Justice'. See also M. Scholten's chapter in this volume.

powers. They were formally equipped with preventive and monitoring tools only later, and these tools were then further strengthened over the years. Therefore, soon after the establishment of the sanctioning regime, the attention of the EU institutions and of the Member States shifted from the topic of sanctions to that of monitoring and prevention.[5] However, recent developments and, most notably, the inability to address the Hungarian and Polish crises through dialogue[6] and prevention have forced the EU and the Member States to put the theme of sanctions back on the agenda. Article 7 is thus back on the scene, although the two procedures started against Hungary and Poland have so far remained stuck at the first stage, namely the mere activation of Article 7(1) TEU. Furthermore, both institutional and academic actors have reflected on whether new sanctioning mechanisms should be added to the Union's toolkit, trying to identify alternatives to the cumbersome Article 7 system.

The chapter is structured as follows. The second section offers a brief overview of the procedures of Article 7 TEU, concentrating in particular on paragraph (3) that allows the Council to impose sanctions if it is ascertained that a Member State has breached EU values in a 'serious and persistent' manner. The third section illustrates the origins of the Article 7 system and then the following attempts to anticipate EU intervention in cases of threats to common values, moving, in several steps, from sanctions to prevention. Then, the fourth section looks at the more recent developments: the renewed centrality of Article 7, as well as other attempts to bolster the EU sanctioning capacity in cases of breaches of the common values. The concluding section reflects on possible future evolutions of the Article 7 system and generally of the EU values' oversight scheme.

4.2. Article 7 TEU: an overview of the system

The procedures of Article 7 TEU have been the subject of extensive institutional[7] and academic discussion.[8] A brief summary of the main features of the mechanisms is

---

[5] L. Besselink, 'The Bite, the Bark and the Howl: Article 7 TEU and the Rule of Law Initiatives', in A. Jakab and D. Kochenov (eds), *The Enforcement of EU Law and Values* (Oxford University Press, 2017), 128, described this development as a 'backward shift from the issue of sanctions to their preconditions and of powers under prior procedures'.

[6] Critically, on dialogical approaches: R. Uitz, 'Editorial – The Perils of Defending the Rule of Law Through Dialogue', (2019) *European Constitutional Law Review* 15, 1.

[7] See e.g. European Commission, Communication 'On Article 7 on the Treaty on European Union – Respect for and promotion of the values on which the Union is based', Brussels, 15 October 2003, Doc. COM(2003)606; European Parliament, Resolution on the Commission communication on Article 7 of the Treaty on European Union: Respect for and promotion of the values on which the Union is based, Strasbourg, 20 April 2004, Doc. 2003/2249(INI).

[8] E.g. W. Sadurski, 'Adding Bite to a Bark: the Story of Article 7, E.U. Enlargement, and Jorg Haider', (2010) *Columbia Journal of European Law* 16, 385; Williams, *supra* note 1; Besselink, *supra* note 5.

here sufficient for framing the discussion. In the first place, it may be worth emphasising that, while the recent debate has mostly focused on the value of the rule of law, Article 7 can be used to protect *all* the values declared by Article 2 TEU, and most importantly also democracy and human rights. Secondly and crucially, Article 7 is blind to any distinction between EU and national competences: it applies horizontally, across the board, irrespectively of whether the national measures threatening or breaching the common values fall within the scope of EU law or not.[9]

The next paragraphs of this section clarify that Article 7 actually contains two separate procedures that have a different nature and different aims: the first one has a preventive function and leaves room for dialogue between EU institutions and national authorities; the second is more confrontational and can ultimately lead to the imposition of EU sanctions.

4.2.1. Article 7(1): clear risk of a serious breach

Added by the Treaty of Nice,[10] Article 7(1) TEU allows the Council to determine, after obtaining the European Parliament's consent, the existence of a 'clear risk of a serious breach' of EU values in a Member State of the EU. The procedure can be activated by the European Commission, one-third of the Member States, or the European Parliament. The Council takes the final decision by a four-fifths majority of the Member States. For the EP's consent, the required majority is two-thirds of the votes expressed, which should also represent the majority of the EP members.

The finding of a clear risk of a serious breach cannot lead to the imposition of sanctions or other measures against the Member State in question. The instrument has thus only a preventive function and sets the scene for further dialogue between EU institutions and national authorities. In particular, the need for a hearing before the Council and the possibility to issue recommendations even prior to any substantive determination under Article 7 clearly shows that Article 7(1) still envisages a constructive engagement with national authorities.

4.2.2. Article 7(2): serious and persistent breach

The second paragraph of Article 7 is more confrontational in nature and propaedeutic to the imposition of sanctions. It allows the European Council to determine, with previous consent of the EP, the existence of 'a serious and persistent breach' of the values of Article 2 TEU. The European Council[11] decides by unanimity, while the

---

[9] See Commission Communication, *supra* note 7; Sadurski, *supra* note 8; and also C. Hillion, 'Overseeing the rule of law in the EU: legal mandate and means', in C. Closa, D. Kochenov (eds), *Reinforcing Rule of Law Oversight in the European Union* (Cambridge University Press, 2016), 59.

[10] See Section 4.3.1 of this Chapter.

[11] Note that Article 7(2) requires a decision of the European Council, while it is the Council to vote on Article 7(1) procedures.

Member State concerned does not participate in the vote. Importantly, a decision under Article 7(2) does not require a prior determination under Article 7(1). If they believe that the substantive threshold of a 'serious and persistent breach' is fulfilled, the European Commission and one third of the Member States [12] can immediately have recourse to Article 7(2). [13] This could happen either in the case of a sudden breach of the common values, as in the – admittedly unlikely – case of a military coup d'état, or even when EU institutions and the Member States have not reacted to a serious risk according to paragraph 1, and then the situation has further deteriorated. Here too, the national government is called to take part in a hearing and can submit its observations to the European Council.

4.2.3. Article 7(3) and (4): sanctions

Once the European Council has found that there is a 'serious and persistent breach' of EU values in a Member State, the Council *may* (but is not obliged to do so) decide to adopt sanctions with a qualified majority. Consent of the EP is not required under Article 7(3). Following an identical procedure, established in Article 7(4), the Council can then decide to modify or withdraw the sanctions adopted earlier.

More specifically, Article 7(3) allows the Council to 'suspend certain of the rights deriving from the application of the Treaties to the Member State in question'. The provision then illustrates one concrete type of sanction that can be adopted, namely the suspension 'of the voting rights of the representative of the government of that Member State in the Council'. While very often mentioned in the public discussion, this is merely one of the options available to the Council: the text of Article 7(3) clearly says that 'the Council may decide to suspend certain of the rights (…) *including* the voting rights'. The Council is free to opt for other measures. In the absence on any concrete case until now, what precisely could be done under Article 7(3) is still a matter of speculation, and the formulation of the provision seems to leave a very broad discretion to the Council in deciding what rights can be suspended. [14]

In the first place, it seems reasonable to conclude that the Council may suspend both rights deriving from the Treaties and rights deriving from EU secondary law. To offer some examples, beyond the hypothesis of voting rights' suspension, the Council could limit other political rights at EU level, [15] suspend the application of

---

[12] The EP, in contrast to the previous paragraph, does not have the formal power to activate the Article 7(2) mechanism.

[13] See also Commission Communication, supra note 7.

[14] See also Besselink, *supra* note 5, 129: 'Article 7(3) TEU is unclear as to the substance of the sanctions which can be imposed'…'this issue might be a matter of speculation'.

[15] For an overview, Tomas Dumbrovsky, 'Beyond Voting Rights Suspension - Tailored Sanctions as Democracy Catalyst under Article 7 TEU', EUI Working Papers RSCAS 2018/12. An example

free movement provisions or the state's participation to the internal market, or withhold or reduce EU funding.[16] Other examples of sanctions are foreseeable as long as they can be 'translated' in the suspension of EU membership rights, while other types of economic sanctions (financial penalties?) might be harder to reconcile with the text of the norm. In any case, as argued above, the discretion of the Council is very broad, and Article 7(3) ultimately puts only one explicit condition for the legitimacy of sanctions: it demands to the Council to 'take into account the possible consequences of such a suspension on the rights and obligations of natural and legal persons' when it imposes sanctions. This clause creates a proportionality-like test,[17] which strives in particular to protect the position of those individuals – both citizens and entities of the Member States concerned and of other Member States – that bear no responsibility for the breach to the Union values. The Court of Justice could be called to perform this proportionality check on the basis of Article 269 TFEU, which allows the Court to review whether the procedural stipulations of Article 7 have been respected.[18]

What is however clear from the text of Article 7 is that the system does not allow for the expulsion of a Member State from the Union, and this has been implicitly confirmed by the CJEU in the *Wigthman* case.[19] Article 7 does not even provide for the full suspension of membership rights: the Council may suspend only 'certain' of the rights. Furthermore, membership obligations 'shall in any case continue to be binding': forms of reciprocity from the offending Member State are prohibited.[20] Thus, although Arti-

---

may be suspending the State's participation and voting rights in the European Council, or the possibility to nominate candidates for posts in other EU institutions such as the Commission or the Court of Justice. On the other hand, it would arguably not be possible to remove Commissioners or Judges of the Court already in charge, considering that they are not representatives of a Member State.

[16] See M. Novak, 'Human Rights "Conditionality" in relation to Entry to, and full Participation in, the EU', in P. Alston (ed.) *The EU and Human Rights* (Oxford University Press, 1999); Besselink, *supra* note 5), 131.

[17] In this sense, Besselink, *supra* note 5, and Dumbrovsky, *supra* note 13. The latter distinguishes 'general' proportionality obligations – according to which sanctions should be 'suitable to change the objectionable policy of the target state'; they must be necessary, in the sense that 'the objectionable policy cannot be changed by a less intrusive measure'; and finally, they must not 'have an excessive effect on the target state's rights' – and the 'special' obligation of respecting individual positions.

[18] Yet, in view of the political nature of the Article 7 system, the Court most likely would grant the Council broad leeway in terms of the choice of sanctions.

[19] See CJEU, Case C-621/18 *Wightman* ECLI:EU:C:2018:999. Para. 72: a Member State 'cannot be forced to leave the European Union against its will'. There was however some discussion on the possibility to introduce an expulsion clause at the time of the Amsterdam Treaty; the idea was ultimately rejected because it would have called into question the idea of 'irreversibility' of EU membership: see Sadurski, *supra* note 8, also for a general overview of the drafting history of the provision.

[20] For example, even in the case in which budget transfers to a Member State were suspended, the Member State sanctioned under Article 7(3) would still be called to contribute to the EU budget.

cle 7 in many respects resembles procedures of other international organizations that have parallel aims, it provides for a typical and fairly unique sanctions regime. In most other international organizations, including the Council of Europe and the United Nations, expulsion of members is possible;[21] or in the alternative, the relevant statutes at least generally provide for the full suspension of membership. In the EU, on the other hand, neither option is available. The stricter limits to the sanctions' regime point to the constitutional nature of the EU project: as it happens in fully-fledged federations, it is simply out of the question to remove one of the members from the entity, even if it breaches the common values of the polity.[22] Expelling a Member State would also entail the unacceptable outcome of potentially stripping millions of individuals of EU citizenship and connected rights. Rather than 'kicking out' a Member State, it is crucial to offer a concrete solution to the breach, bringing it to an end: as the Commission pointed out in a 2019 communication on the rule of law instruments, the final and paramount objective of EU action 'must not be to impose a sanction but to find a solution that protects the rule of law, with cooperation and mutual support at the core'.[23]

It is worth emphasising two other consequences, though not sanctions strictly speaking, that the activation of Article 7 mechanisms may have. First, Protocol 24 on asylum for nationals of Member States contains a general presumption that Member States are 'safe countries of origins' and thus applications for asylum made by a Member State national in another Member State are generally not admissible. Yet, an exception provides that when the Council or the European Council have adopted a decision under Article 7(1) or (2), or even when the procedure of Article 7(1) has been merely activated, applications for asylum 'may be taken into consideration or declared admissible'. Second, the European Arrest Warrant Framework Decision contains in its preamble a recital (no 10) that allows the European Council, after a decision under Article 7(2) has been adopted, to suspend the EAW system in the Member State responsible for the breach of the common values. The CJEU clarified in the *LM* case (also known as *Celmer*)[24] that two steps are necessary: first, a decision of the European Council under Article 7(2) and then a second determination, still by the European Council. After the second decision, judicial authorities 'would be required to refuse automatically to execute any European arrest warrant' issued by the Member State concerned.[25] In the absence of such a determination, in order to suspend

[21] See Article 8 of the CoE Statute, Articles 5 and 6 of the UN Charter.

[22] I have developed this point at a grater length in M. Bonelli, 'A Federal Turn? The European Union's Response to Constitutional Crises in the Member States' (2018) *Perspectives on Federalism* 10, 41.

[23] European Commission, Communication 'Further strengthening the Rule of Law within the Union - *State of play and possible next steps*', Brussels, 3 April 2019, COM(2019) 163 final, 7.

[24] See CJEU, C-216/18 *Minister for Justice and Equality v. LM (Deficiencies in the system of justice)* ECLI:EU:C:2018:586.

[25] CJEU, C-216/18 *LM,* para. 72.

the execution of a European Arrest Warrant on fundamental rights and rule of law grounds, the executing judicial authorities need to conduct a systemic *and* an individual assessment of the situation, as explained by the Court in *LM* and earlier in *Aranyosi and Căldăraru*.[26]

4.2.4. Article 7: concluding thoughts

To summarize, Article 7 TEU offers to the EU institutions the possibility to adopt sanctions against a Member State that breaches in a 'serious and persistent' manner the basic values of the Union. Sanctions are however the last, and merely possible, step of a process that also allows for softer and more dialogical responses that have a preventive function. Still today, Article 7 TEU is the *only* provision in the Treaties that is specifically dedicated to the protection of EU values: the question on how to protect EU values has been kept separate from that of enforcing 'ordinary' Union law,[27] though, as shall be seen, traditional mechanisms can also contribute to the goal of ensuring respect for democracy, the rule of law, and human rights.

Article 7 TEU is a political mechanism. The key determinations are firmly in the hands of political actors: the EP and the Council, under Article 7(1), and the EP and the European Council, under 7(2); the Council is then exclusively competent on the adoption and removal of sanctions. On the other hand, the Court of Justice is not involved in the substantive decisions, but can only check respect for the procedural stipulations of Article 7.[28] The political nature of the mechanisms is a feature, as noted above, that is common to similar procedures of other international organizations.

4.3. From sanctions to prevention...

After this brief overview of the procedures of Article 7, the second section follows with a broader historical perspective on this instrument. As explained above, the system of Article 7 is a fairly recent construction: the provision was introduced only a little more than twenty years ago, with the Treaty of Amsterdam. The next paragraphs have the objective first to explain the rationale that guided the Member States to introduce a sanctions regime for domestic breaches of democracy, the rule of law, and human rights; and second, to show how and, after the introduction of Article 7, the focus of the debate shifted from the topic of sanctions to that of prevention, in order to anticipate the moment of possible EU intervention.

---

[26] CJEU, C-404/15 *Aranyosi and Căldăraru* ECLI:EU:C:2016:198.

[27] See also A. Jakab, D. Kochenov, 'Introduction', in Jakab and Kochenov, *supra* note 5.

[28] See Article 269 TFEU.

4.3.1. The origins of the procedure: a sanctions regime

Going back to the first decade of the European integration project, a first predecessor of what is now Article 7 TEU could be found in the proposed – but never entered into force – European Political Community (EPC) Treaty of 1953. The EPC was meant as a platform for political cooperation working alongside the European Coal and Steel Community (ECSC), on the one hand, and the European Defence Community (EDC), on the other. Article 104 of the EPC Treaty would have allowed the Community's institutions to intervene in order to '[maintain] constitutional order and democratic institutions' in the Member States 'territory'.[29] However, after the French Parliament failed to ratify the parallel EDC Treaty, the EPC project was abandoned as well. As is widely known, the Member States opted for a project that while extremely ambitious, had a more limited substantive scope: the European Economic Community (EEC). In this context, there was simply no need for a provision comparable to Article 104 EPC or current Article 7 TEU. The EEC was indeed meant to be an economic organization, one where political questions on the democratic conditions in the Member States were simply not meant to arise.

The situation gradually changed over the years as a result of the 'constitutionalisation process' of the Communities and then the Union. The well-known and much discussed[30] process has several dimensions. What matters for our purposes is that – to put it in fairly general terms – the European integration process as a whole has eventually become associated with the 'constitutional values' now listed in Article 2 TEU. Part and parcel of this transformation was that the common institutions of the Communities and then of the Union began to be interested in the democratic, rule of law, and human rights situation of the Member States.

The accession to the EEC of Greece, Portugal and Spain gave a first impulse to this development. In pre-accession documents, the Commission included for the first time some paragraphs dedicated to the political-constitutional situation of the three countries, which had just established still fragile democratic systems after decades of authoritarianism. Following these first timid steps, the EP advanced a proposal for a post-accession mechanisms in the 1984 Draft Treaty on European Union: it recommended giving to the Court of Justice the competence to determine the existence of 'a serious and persistent violation of democratic principles or fundamental

---

[29] For an overview, see G. de Búrca, 'The Road Not Taken: The EU as a Global Human Rights Actor' (2011) *American Journal of International Law* 105, 649. The concrete procedures for intervention were supposed to be specified by secondary law.

[30] See for example the groundbreaking works of E. Stein, 'Lawyers, Judges and the Making of a Transnational Constitution, (1981) *American Journal of International Law* 25, 1; G.F. Mancini, 'The Making of a Constitution for Europe', (1989) *Common Market Law Review* 26, 395; and J.H.H. Weiler, 'The Transformation of Europe' (1991) *The Yale Law Journal* 8, 100.

rights by a Member State'[31] and to the European Council the power to adopt sanctions after the Court's decision. These sanctions could have included the suspension of participating and voting rights in the Council and more generally the suspension of membership rights. The Member States declined however to introduce similar mechanisms on the occasion of the Single European Act or later the Maastricht Treaty.

A second and even more fundamental stimulus came then from the Eastern Enlargement process.[32] Having established in Copenhagen in 1993 that accession to the EU formally required respect for democracy, the rule of law and human rights, including minority rights (the so-called 'Copenhagen political criterion'), the Commission then put in place a strong system of political conditionality for candidate countries.[33] With accession of Central and Eastern European countries approaching, though, the institutions and the Member States finally realized that there was also a need for mechanisms that could ensure respect for the same values *post*-accession. In particular, it was evident that the EU lacked instruments to monitor issues that were crucial during the accession process, such as the independence of the judiciary, but also minority rights, but fell outside the scope of Union law. In the negotiations leading to the Amsterdam Treaty of 1997, the Member States finally agreed on the creation of what are now Article 7(2), (3), and (4) TEU. The introduction of the Article 7 system was not crucial for the enlargement process itself, because of the strong conditionality regime existing in the accession policy, but it was meant for the next 'ordinary' period'.[34]

The decision to introduce Article 7 was at the same time the result of the EU constitutionalisation process and a further contribution to it, and a true sign of the 'coming of age' of the EU human rights regime.[35] Yet, at the same time, the creation of Article 7 did not produce a fundamental shift in concrete Union policies. The desire of the Member States to retain strict control over the procedure[36] –

---

[31] See Article 4(4) of the Draft Treaty on European Union.

[32] On the link between the introduction of Article 7 and the Eastern enlargement process: Sadurski, supra note 8; B. De Witte, 'The Impact of Enlargement on the Constitution of the European Union', in M. Cremona (ed.), *The Enlargement of the European Union* (Oxford University Press, 2003), p 209.

[33] See Cremona, supra note 32; C. Pinelli, 'Conditionality and Enlargement in Light of the EU Constitutional Developments, (2004) *European Law Journal* 10, 354; W. Sadurski, *Constitutionalism and the Enlargement of Europe* (Oxford University Press, 2012) and, for a more critical assessment, D. Kochenov, *EU Enlargement and the Failure of Conditionality* (Kluwer Law International, 2008).

[34] Sadurski, *supra* note 8, 425, argued that the introduction of Article 7 had a 'marginal' role in Central European candidate states.

[35] G. de Búrca, 'Beyond the Charter: How Enlargement Has Enlarged the Human Rights Policy of the European Union', (2003) *Fordham International Law Journal* 27, 679.

[36] See also Sadurski, supra note 8, 393, while Austria and Italy proposed to introduce mecha-

shown for example by the extremely high thresholds required for the activation of Article 7(2), namely the unanimity of the Member States in the European Council – led to the creation of a system that was mostly intended to have a deterrent effect, rather than being actually used. These choices may also mirror the general reluctance of the Member States to confer to the EU strong sanctioning powers, described elsewhere in this volume.[37] In any event and at the very least, Article 7 was never meant to be used often.[38] It was included in the Treaties as a safeguard clause for extreme situations. Perhaps, at that stage, it could truly be considered a 'nuclear option', as it came to be known over the years. Although the label now creates confusion, especially when it is applied to the entire framework created by Article 7 and thus also to the preventive part, there is little doubt that deterrence was originally in the minds of the drafters of the provision.

In the Amsterdam setting, the strong sanctioning regime of Article 7 was not accompanied by other softer instruments that could also contribute to protect EU values. In particular, the Member States rejected the EP's calls for the setting up of a general monitoring system that could constantly verify respect for EU values at the national level. Thus, Article 7 granted at the time only one possibility: finding a serious and persistent breach of EU values and then, if considered necessary, imposing sanctions. The system did not allow for a more gradual approach.[39] Soon however, the EU and the Member States began to be confronted with the fact that, while a full-scale collapse of a state that could immediately warrant the activation of Article 7(2) and (3) was fairly unlikely, other serious but softer threats to the common values were much more realistic, even in the Western part of the continent. The attention began to shift from the topic of sanctions to that of prevention.

4.3.2. The Haider case: moving towards prevention

After the 1999 Austrian parliamentary elections, the decision of the center-right People's Party to form a coalition with the far-right Freedom Party, led by Jörg Haider, shocked the European leaders. The other fourteen EU Member States im-

---

nism with qualified majority voting, the other Member States 'were more reluctant regarding the creation of a broad sanctions mechanism, which could impinge on their sovereign rights'.

37 See also the Chapter by S. Montaldo, F. Costamagna and A. Miglio in this volume.

38 This was immediately clear after its introduction: see A. Verhoeven, 'How democratic need European Union members be? Some thoughts after Amsterdam' (1998) *European Law Review* 23, 217, p 224: the 'chances of a Member state ever being condemned or punished ... are limited, and 'it is the deterrent effect that counts'.

39 In the Amsterdam formulation, Article 7 did not even allow the Council or the European Council to adopt recommendations before the finding of a serious and persistent breach of the values.

mediately decided to react to the Austrian developments, but it was evident that Article 7 could not be used in that situation. The mere fact that the Freedom Party joined the ruling coalition could not be considered to fulfill the substantive threshold of a 'serious and persistent breach' of EU values, as the Austrian government had not yet adopted any concrete measure violating or even concretely threatening the values. Thus, the fourteen Member States opted for a series of diplomatic sanctions that were however adopted outside the EU legal framework.[40] These sanctions were in any case revoked fairly soon, after the so-called 'Wise Men committee' informally put in charge of monitoring the situation found that there was no clear violation of EU values.[41]

The Haider affair clearly proved the deficits of the Article 7 system as designed in Amsterdam: there was no procedure available at the EU level in order to react to cases that fell short of a 'serious and persistent breach' of the values, but that could still be considered problematic in a broader sense. Diplomatic sanctions outside the EU framework could not become long-term solutions. The Wise Men Report suggested a possible way forward: it argued for the introduction of 'preventive and monitoring procedures', which could allow the EU institutions to conduct a non-confrontational dialogue from an early stage. Meeting on the occasion of the next Inter-Governmental Conference in Nice, the Member States followed the report's recommendation and agreed on the creation of what is now Article 7(1) TEU.[42] The addition of the new provision, while signaling a shift towards prevention, did not water down the system; quite on the contrary, it actually strengthened and completed it, creating a new procedure for political dialogue within the Treaties' framework.[43] It was, in other words, a necessary addition to the sanctioning mechanism, which was moved to Article 7(2) and (3).

4.3.3. The Commission's Rule of Law Framework: doubling down on prevention

Despite the introduction of the preventing arm of Article 7(1), the provision remained dormant in the following decade. It did not play any role whatsoever even

---

[40] See B. De Witte, G.N. Toggenburg, 'Human Rights and Membership of the European Union', in S. Peers, A. Ward (eds), *The EU Charter of Fundamental Rights* (Hart Publishing, 2004). On the 'Haider affair', see also M. Merlingen, C. Mudde, U. Sedelmeier, 'The Right and the Righteous? European Norms, Domestic Politics and the Sanctions Against Austria', (2001) 39 *Journal of Common Market Studies* 59.

[41] M. Ahtisaari, J.A. Frowein, M. Oreja, 'Report on the Austrian Government's Commitment to the Common European Values, in particular concerning the Rights of Minorities, Refugees and Immigrants, and the Evolution of the Political Nature of the FPO' ('The Wise Men Report'), Paris, 8 September 2000.

[42] For an overview, see Section 4.2.1 of this Chapter.

[43] See also Sadurski, *supra* note 8, 397.

in controversial cases such the UK's invasion of Iraq, challenges to freedom of information and media pluralism under Berlusconi's government in Italy, or the CIA renditions affair. The point is not that Article 7 *should* have been used in those cases, rather that it was not even part on the European debate on these topics. In the 2000s, the entire Article 7 system began to be associated with the 'nuclear option' label, a definition that is both unhelpful and mistaken. In fact, there is nothing nuclear in the preventive procedure of Article 7(1), and even Article 7(2) ultimately allows for a gradual approach, since the Council is not obliged to adopt sanctions after the determination of a serious and persistent breach of EU values.

When a new, and more severe, challenge came into the picture – the Hungarian constitutional crisis [44] – there was unfortunately a general political unwillingness to use Article 7, to which the 'nuclear option' label certainly contributed. The Commission opted to react to the Hungarian developments with another mechanism, namely infringement procedures under Article 258 TFEU, following an 'indirect' approach. [45] However, those infringement procedures only tackled the few aspects of the constitutional reforms that fell within the scope of EU law, and transformed the democratic and rule of law challenges in more technical issues. [46] It is now evident that this approach did not produce adequate results. [47]

Implicitly acknowledging the difficulties in tackling the Hungarian developments with the traditional enforcement toolkit, the Commission began to work on a new instrument. It argued that it was necessary to 'fill the gap' between Article 7 and infringement actions based on Article 258 TFEU. The outcome of the process was the 'Rule of Law Framework', presented in spring 2014, which sought 'to resolve future threats to the rule of law in Member States before the conditions for activating the mechanisms foreseen in Article 7 TEU would be met'. [48] The Framework was therefore conceived as an instrument of prevention, a mechanism that allows the Commission to conduct a political dialogue with the national government concerned on the basis of 'Rule of Law Opinions' and 'Rule of Law Recommendations'. The substantive threshold for the activation of the Rule of Law Framework is that of 'systemic threats to the rule of law', and the Framework thus

---

[44] See von Bogdandy and Sonnevend, *supra* note 2. On the first moments of the crisis, see also K. Kovacs, G.A. Toth, 'Hungary's Constitutional Transformation', (2011) 7 *European Constitutional Law Review* 183.

[45] M. Dawson, E. Muir, 'Hungary and the Indirect Protection of EU Fundamental Rights and the Rule of Law' (2013) *German Law Journal* 14, 1959.

[46] For example, questions related to the independence of the judiciary became an age discrimination problem: see Case C-286/12 *Commission v. Hungary*, ECLI:EU:C:2012:687.

[47] See for a critical assessment L. Pech, K.L. Scheppele, 'Illiberalism Within: Rule of Law Backsliding in the EU' (2017) *Cambridge Yearbook of European Legal Studies* 19, 3.

[48] European Commission, Communication 'A New EU Framework to Strengthen the Rule of Law', Brussels, 19 March 2014, Doc. COM(2014) 158 final/2.

stops one step before the condition for the activation of Article 7(1), namely a 'clear risk of a serious breach' of the rule of law, is met. Regrettably, however, the Commission failed to clearly distinguish these two types of situations.

If adding the preventive arm of Article 7 truly strengthened the overall oversight system, it is more debatable whether the Rule of Law Framework was truly necessary.[49] On the one hand, the Framework can be seen as a much-needed step to bolster monitoring before and beyond Article 7, as well as an important attempt to clarify the substantive standards for assessing national rule of law system.[50] In this respect, it works alongside other monitoring mechanisms at the EU and the Council of Europe level, including the European Commission's 'Justice Scoreboard'. The latter was designed, approximately in the same period, in order to measure the functioning of the national judiciaries on the basis of a series of quantitative and qualitative criteria, and a further example of the shift from 'sanctions' to 'prevention'.

On the other hand, the very decision to adopt an instrument such as the Rule of Law Framework could be considered a side effect of the confusing nuclear option label attached to Article 7 even by top Commission officials such as Presidents Barroso and Juncker. Additionally, the choice might have derived from a reading of the Hungarian crisis that has in the meantime proved to be mistaken: while the Commission tried to bolster dialogical and preventive instruments, authorities in Budapest did not truly engage in a genuine dialogue with EU institutions. Instead, they used strategies of symbolic and creative compliance[51] in order to delay stronger EU reactions, until it became simply too late to restore the previous situation.[52] Thus, with the Rule of Law Framework, the Commission doubled down on a strategy of preventing threats to EU values. It maintained the view already expressed in 2003 that in a 'Union of values', 'it will not be necessary to apply penalties pursuant to Article 7 of the Union Treaty'.[53] Dialogue and constructive engagement with the Member State concerned were meant to be adequate responses to rule of law challenges, complemented, if need be, by the occasional infringement action, rather than by sanctions under Article 7.

4.3.4. The Council Rule of Law Dialogue: a 'culture' of prevention?

Shortly after the presentation of the Commission's Rule of Law Framework and af-

---

[49] Expressing doubts in this respect: D. Kochenov, L. Pech, 'Monitoring and Enforcement of the Rule of Law in the EU: Rhetoric and Reality', (2016) *European Constitutional Law Review* 11, 512.

[50] See in particular the Annex to the Rule of Law Framework.

[51] A. Batory, 'Defying the Commission: Creative Compliance and Respect for the Rule of Law in the EU', (2016) *Public Administration* 94, 685.

[52] See Pech and Scheppele, *supra* note 47.

[53] European Commission, *supra* note 7, p. 12.

ter a negative opinion of the Council's Legal Service on the compatibility of the Framework with the Treaties,[54] the Council designed yet another instrument that was meant to contribute to rule of law protection throughout the Union. The 'Rule of Law Dialogue' of the Council has even less bite than the Commission Framework, though. Let alone imposing sanctions, it is not even meant to tackle specific crises, but to 'promote a culture of respect' for the rule of law: it boils down to an annual meeting of the General Affairs Council, in which the competent ministers hold a debate on a theme selected by the temporary Presidency. [55] Arguably, it cannot be considered a true peer review exercise, as there are no horizontal analyses of possible problematic profiles in different Member States. The Dialogue is thus a much lighter instrument than Article 7 or the Rule of Law Framework. It strives to prevent threats or crises by fostering a culture of compliance, but is toothless if and when a crisis actually arises.

4.4. ... and now back to sanctions?

The inability to find effective answers to the Hungarian crisis, and later to the Polish one, ultimately showed to the institutions and the public the deficits of the EU oversight system and of the approach followed until then. First, the deterrent effect of the Article 7 system proved to be very weak: the mere fact that the provision existed did not actually dissuade Hungarian and Polish authorities to pursue their constitutional and institutional reforms. Second, as illustrated in particular by the Polish case,[56] where the Commission relied uniquely on the Rule of Law Framework for a quite long time, preventive and dialogical mechanisms alone cannot achieve the expected results. Third and finally, the Hungarian developments showed that traditional enforcement mechanisms such as the infringement procedure are not a sufficient response either, at least if not complemented by parallel political action.

As a consequence, the attention of both the institutional and the academic debate shifted again to the topic of sanctions, and more generally to EU enforcement tools. This has led to two developments, which could, at least at first sight, be viewed as partially contradictory. On the one hand, Article 7 has regained its centrality as the key instrument to protect EU values, although any actual imposition of sanctions still remains extremely unlikely at the moment, because it requires a previous unanimous

---

[54] Council of the European Union, Opinion of the Legal Service 'Commission's Communication on a new EU Framework to strengthen the Rule of Law: compatibility with the Treaties', Brussels, 27 May 2014, Doc. 10296/14

[55] Including: fight to terrorism and the rule of law (2016), or 'The Rule of Law in the Age of Digitalisation' (2015).

[56] For an analysis of the use of the Rule of Law Framework in the Polish case, see Pech and Scheppele, *supra* note 47.

decision within the European Council under Article 7(2). On the other hand, precisely in light of the difficulties in reaching a final decision under Article 7(2) and (3) TEU, EU institutions, and the Commission in particular, have attempted to find new ways to tackle breaches of the common values, proposing new sanctioning procedures or rethinking and readapting existing ones.[57]

4.4.1. The new centrality of Article 7

Almost twenty years after its introduction, Article 7 finally 'came of age' in December 2017, when the Commission activated it for the first time against Poland. The Commission took the decision after three unsuccessful Rule of Law Recommendations under the Rule of Law Framework, which did not stop the controversial reforms of the judiciary.[58] A few months later, the Parliament decided to follow the Commission's step and adopted a resolution calling for the activation of Article 7(1) against Hungary.[59] Both procedures are now pending before the Council, which will take the final decision on the existence of a 'clear risk of a serious breach' of the rule of law (in the Polish case) and of EU values (in Hungary). In the Polish case, the Council has already held three formal hearings in June, September and December 2018,[60] while the first formal hearing on Hungary took place in September 2019.[61]

The activation of Article 7 has not had the 'catastrophic' effects that some feared.[62] On the contrary, it has made evident that the procedure, or at the very least its first paragraph, is not a nuclear option. It is a tool that *can* and actually *should* be used when the Commission, the Parliament or some Member States consider that its substantive thresholds have been fulfilled. In this respect, it is crucial that the institutions are finally developing a concrete practice under Article 7, meaning that there are now precedents on how to conduct the formal hearings, how to exchange views with the national governmentw concerned, and other relevant elements of the procedure.[63] Institutional cooperation between the

---

[57] N Lazzerini's chapter in this volume also underlines how EU institutions are exploring alterantive routes.

[58] For an overview of the reforms, see Sadurski, supra note 2.

[59] European Parliament, Resolution on a proposal calling on the Council to determine, pursuant to Article 7(1) of the Treaty on European Union, the existence of a clear risk of a serious breach by Hungary of the values on which the Union is founded, Strasbourg, 12 September 2018, Doc. 2017/2131(INL).

[60] For a summary, see Council Conclusions, Brussels, 18 December 2018, Doc. 15396/18.

[61] Council Conclusions, Brussels, 16 September 2019, Doc. 12111/19. A second hearing took place in December 2019: see Council Conclusions, Brussels, 10 December 2019, Doc. 14959/19.

[62] See Williams, *supra* note 1, p. 27.

[63] In July 2019, the Council issued a note on 'standard modalities' for Article 7(1) hearings: see Council, Note 'Standard modalities for hearings referred to in Article 7(1) TEU', Brussels, 9 July 2019, Doc. 10641/2/19

Commission and the Council[64] has been fairly positive, with the former taking active part in the debates in the Council, though less positively the Council has refused to give a formal role to the Parliament in the Hungarian procedure. In substance, while it is evident that the activation of Article 7 has not brought the crises to an end, it has undoubtedly raised political pressure on the two governments, for example fostering the debate within the European People's Party on Fidesz's membership. All considered, for at least some time, it might have contributed to crystallizing the situation, in the sense that the Hungarian and Polish authorities seemed to be more reluctant to advance other controversial reforms.[65] All considered, Article 7 does not seem to be an empty gesture anymore, but a real tool in the hands of the institutions to tackle threats to the common values. In other words, EU institutions are developing a true 'Article 7 policy', though, as acknowledged by the Commission, further reflections on how to best conduct the procedure are still needed.[66]

4.4.2. New tools: rule of law conditionality

The decisions of the Commission and of the EP have therefore given new centrality to Article 7. At the same time, EU institutions, as well as the academic debate, have also attempted to find alternative solutions, implicitly acknowledging the difficulties that are inherent in reaching a final unanimous decision under Article 7(2) and (3). Poland and Hungary have in fact often pledged to help each other, vetoing any possible decision under Article 7(2) TEU.

The European Parliament presented a proposal that still focused by and large on prevention: in its 'Democracy, Rule of Law, and Fundamental Rights Pact', it called for the introduction of a detailed monitoring framework that would serve to verify Member States' respect for all Article 2 TEU values. On the contrary, the Commission has concentrated on possible new sanctions. Most importantly, in spring 2018, it issued a proposal for a Regulation on 'Rule of Law Conditionality'.

The proposed Regulation is based on Article 322(1)(a) TFEU, according to which the Parliament and the Council can adopt 'the financial rules which determine in particular the procedure to be adopted for establishing and implementing the budget and for presenting and auditing accounts', and it would allow the Commission to propose the suspension of EU funding in case of 'generalised defi-

[64] Another positive aspect of the activation of Article 7 is that it has forced the Council to finally take up its responsibility, which had escaped until that moment: see P. Oliver, J. Stefanelli, 'Strengthening the Rule of Law in the EU: The Council's Inaction' (2016) *Journal of Common Market Studies* 54, 1075.

[65] In the months after the submission of this book chapter, however, both the Hungarian and the Polish government pushed forward new controversial reforms. Any positive effect of the activation of Artifcle 7 seems thus to have vanished.

[66] See Commission Communication, *supra* note 23.

cencies'[67] in the rule of law system of a Member State. The measures suggested by the Commission include 'the suspension of payments when the budget is implemented through 'direct or indirect management' and the suspension or reduction of commitments and payments under 'shared management'. The proposal of the Commission would be then sent to the Council, which would be called to decide under the principle of reverse qualified majority, meaning that a qualified majority would be necessary to *reject* or amend the proposal.[68] The Commission also included in the system a clause protecting individual beneficiaries of EU funds,[69] in order to avoid that they are unfairly affected by a suspension of EU funding.

Even before the Commission's proposal, the suspension of EU funding for those Member States breaching the rule of law had been long discussed as a possible new tool for protecting EU values.[70] The Commission ultimately opted for a new procedure that would create a separate sanctions' regime. It is precisely in this respect that the proposed regulation raises some doubts relating to its compatibility with the Treaties. Is it possible to adopt sanctions for breaches of the rule of law *outside* the procedures of Article 7? The Legal Service of the Council, in an Opinion not yet public, has expressed doubts.[71] The EP, on the other hand, has endorsed the Commission's proposal.[72] Irrespectively, the Commission's initiative shows a clear change of perspective: since prevention has not sufficed to address the current crises, Brussels is attempting to design new sanctioning tools with a view to enhance the EU oversight scheme.

---

[67] According to Article 2 of the draft Regulation, there would a generalized deficiency when 'a widespread or recurrent practice or omission, or measure by public authorities ... affects the rule of law'.

[68] The reverse qualified majority system has been borrowed from Stability and Growth Pact system, see Regulation 1173/2001 on the effective enforcement of budgetary surveillance in the euro area. See F. Costamagna and A. Miglio's chapter in this volume.

[69] See Article 4(2) of the draft Regulation.

[70] For early proposals, see K.L. Scheppele, 'Enforcing the basic principles of EU law through systemic infringement actions', in Closa, and Kochenov, *supra* note 9; J.W. Müller, 'Should the EU Protect Democracy and the Rule of Law inside Member States?' (2015) *European Law Journal* 21, 141; and then G. Halmai, 'The Possibility and Desirability of Rule of Law Conditionality' (2019) *Hague Journal of the Rule of Law* 11, 171.

[71] For a discussion, K.L. Scheppele, L. Pech, and D.R. Kelemen, 'Never Missing an Opportunity to Miss an Opportunity: The Council Legal Service Opinion on the Commission's EU budget-related rule of law mechanism', Verfassungsblog, 12 November 2018, www.verfassungsblog.de/never-missing-an-opportunity-to-miss-an-opportunity-the-council-legal-service-opinion-on-the-commissions-eu-budget-related-rule-of-law-mechanism/.

[72] European Parliament, Legislative resolution on the proposal for a regulation of the European Parliament and of the Council on the protection of the Union's budget in case of generalised deficiencies as regards the rule of law in the Member States, 4 April 2019.

4.4.3. Reviving 'old' tools: the infringement procedure

Finally, the Commission, backed by the Court, is trying to give new boost and bite to a traditional instrument, i.e. the infringement procedure, and use it to contribute to protect the common values of the Union. Firstly, as illustrated more in detail in another chapter in this volume, the Court has allowed the imposition of penalty payments ex Article 260 TFEU in case of non-compliance with an interim order of the Court delivered on the basis of Article 279 TFEU.[73] This happened in a case concerning Poland, though not related to the constitutional backsliding phenomenon. In this manner, the Commission and the Court can make use of an already existing sanctioning tool in a new and creative manner.

Secondly, the Commission has recently read its mandate to launch infringement actions in a broader manner. In the 'Portuguese judges' decision,[74] the CJEU found, on the basis of the second paragraph of Article 19(1) TEU, that the Member States are obliged to ensure the judicial independence of all national courts potentially called to apply or interpret Union law.[75] Building on this judgment, the Commission has begun relying on Article 19 TEU in infringement actions. The first action launched on this basis tackled the reform of the Polish Supreme Court. The action was quickly brought before the Court of Justice and decided in June 2019. After two interim orders in which it had already asked Polish authorities to suspend the reform and restore the preexisting situation, the Court of Justice eventually acknowledged an infringement of Article 19 TEU.[76] The Court found another infringement in second action, concerning the reforms of the ordinary courts' system, decided in November 2019.[77] Generally, the broad interpretation of Article 19 TEU allows the Commission to take into consideration and possibly bring before the Court any judicial reform that has the effect of undermining the independence of national courts.

Lastly, after a period of reluctance,[78] the Commission is now starting infringement actions also on the basis of the Charter of Fundamental Rights. Most notably, this happened in a string of procedures against Hungary, concerning for example the 'Higher Education law' that has forced the Central European University to relo-

---

[73] See L. Prete's chapter in this volume.

[74] CJEU, C-64/16 *Associação Sindical dos Juízes Portugueses* ECLI:EU:C: 2018:117.

[75] For a more detailed analysis, see M. Bonelli, M. Claes, 'Judicial serendipity: how Portuguese judges came to the rescue of the Polish judiciary', (2018) *European Constitutional Law Review* 14, 622.

[76] CJEU, C-619/18 *Commission v. Poland* ECLI:EU:C:2019:531.

[77] CJEU, C-192/18 *Commission v. Poland* ECLI:EU:C:2019:924.

[78] A. Łazowski, 'Decoding a Legal Enigma: the Charter of Fundamental Rights of the European Union and infringement proceedings', ERA Forum (2013).

cate to Vienna, and on measures restricting NGOs funding opportunities.[79]

Compared to the earlier actions started after the adoption of the 2012 Hungarian constitutional reforms, the new procedures seem much more promising. Firstly, relying on Article 19 TEU or the Charter as an infringement ground makes more difficult for the Member State to engage in forms of symbolic or creative compliance: the national government must not only prove compliance with technical EU rules, but also remedy the structural breaches to judicial independence or fundamental rights. Secondly, breaches of Article 19 TEU or of the Charter could lead the Court to determine a higher coefficient in the case of an Article 260 TFEU proceeding.[80] Third and more generally, these grounds add some political pathos to what can otherwise be perceived as an ordinary and ultimately fairly technical procedure. All considered, these new developments may significantly bolster the EU capacity to enforce its basic values and sanction possible breaches also through an ordinary instrument such as the infringement procedure, read in a creative and expansive manner.

4.5. Concluding remarks and possible future developments

This chapter has mapped the evolution of the EU's mechanisms to respond to national breaches of the founding values of the European project, listed in Article 2 TEU: first, the introduction of a sanctioning scheme (Article 7 TEU), mostly meant to have a deterrent effect; then, a progressive shift towards prevention; and then, most recently, the institutional rediscovery of sanctions, both within and outside the Article 7 system, which by and large is yet to be followed by concrete steps to tackle the most evident breaches of EU values in Hungary and Poland.[81]

As noted in the third section of this chapter, the very decision to endow the EU with these sanctioning powers came more than four decades after the beginning of the integration project and is one of the key moments of the EU constitutionalisation process. The decision taken in Amsterdam and then confirmed in Nice and Lisbon was to create a separate, special instrument for protecting EU values, rather than extending the applicability of ordinary EU law enforcement tools. In origin, Article 7 was exclusively a sanction procedure. Yet, soon after the introduction of the new sanction scheme, and mostly as a result of the Haider affair, the attention of

[79] See *CJEU, Commission v. Hungary, C-66/18 (CEU) & C-78/18 (NGOs) (both pending).*

[80] See also M. Schmidt, P. Bogdanowicz, 'The Infringement Procedure in the Rule of Law Crisis: How to Make Effective Use of Article 258 TFEU' (2018) *Common Market Law Review* 55, 1061.

[81] See however the promising judicial steps taken by the Court of Justice, most notably in CJEU, C-619/18 *Commission v. Poland* ECLI:EU:C:2019:531 and C-192/18 *Commission v. Poland* ECLI:EU:C:2019:924.

EU institutions and the Member States shifted to theme of prevention, and this led to the introduction of the preventive arm with the Treaty of Nice. Despite this decision, Article 7 – mistakenly – began to be considered a nuclear option, which could not be used in practice but was only meant to have a deterrent effect. Even when confronted with the Hungarian and Polish constitutional crises, at least in the first phases, EU institutions preferred to react with softer means and both the Commission and the Council even opted to adopt new preventive tools. Only when it became clear that dialogical tools failed, did the focus of the institutions finally return to the theme of possible sanctions.

There are now two trends, which, as argued earlier, might seem to some extent paradoxical. On the one hand, after the activation of the first paragraph of the provision against both Poland and Hungary, the Article 7 system is regaining its centrality. EU institutions are finally developing a concrete practice under Article 7: the provision is not an 'empty gesture'[82] anymore, but sets out a concrete Union policy. Even the Council, so far reluctant to take on its responsibilities,[83] has finally agreed on a standard procedure for conducting the formal hearings under Article 7(1) TEU.[84] While the results are yet to be seen, from a systemic perspective this is finally a step in the right direction.

On the other hand, the institutions are also trying to find new ways to protect the common values outside the system of Article 7. Implicitly, they acknowledge that in the present situation, it is if not impossible, at least extremely unlikely to reach the unanimous decision under Article 7(2) TEU that is required in order to unleash sanctions against the Member State responsible for a breach of the common values. In this light, the Commission has proposed the creation of a rule of law conditionality clause for the EU funding system, and, together with the Court, is bolstering the use of infringement actions to tackle judicial independence and fundamental rights problems.

At closer sight, the two trends are not paradoxical, but actually complement each other. The fundamental challenge posed by the Hungarian and Polish crises can only be resolved if EU institutions make use of the entire toolkit that is available, composed by both political sanctions procedures, such as Article 7 TEU, and by judicial instruments such as the infringement procedure. Creating new tools is another option to be considered, especially for dealing with possible future crises. In this sense, the Commission proposal on rule of law conditionality positively fosters a discussion on how to best use the EU budget in order to guarantee the common values, but the perplexities raised by the Council Legal Service seem so far well

---

[82] See Williams, *supra* note 1.

[83] See Oliver and Stefanelli, *supra* note 63.

[84] See Council Conclusions, Brussels, 18 July 2019, Doc. 1137/19.

grounded. In particular, it does not seem possible at this stage, and in the absence of a broad reform of the Treaties, to 'escape' from Article 7 TEU and establish a sanctions' regime for breaches of the rule of law (or other EU values) completely independent from it.[85] One should not forget that Article 7 is the only provision[86] that is blind to any distinction between national and EU competences: its fundamental relevance is that it extends EU oversight to areas falling outside the scope of Union law. To put it simply, without Article 7, the EU would just not have a general competence to protect democracy, the rule of law and human rights in the Member States.

Yet, for Article 7 to regain not only symbolical, but also practical centrality, further institutional steps are necessary. Leaving aside any implausible – in the current political context – reform of the Treaties, it would be beneficial if institutions would take action to complete the system in two respects. First, in order to further strengthen prevention, they could agree on the creation of a common monitoring framework, covering all Member States and delivering yearly reports on respect for EU values at the national and EU level. All institutions have been working on a similar proposal: the EP proposed a 'European DRF Report' already in 2016;[87] the Commission announced that it will launch a 'Rule of Law Review Cycle';[88] and finally the Finnish Presidency of the Council worked on a revision of the 'Rule of Law' dialogue scheme, which would be transformed in a true peer review exercise.[89] In order to avoid duplication and improve institutional coordination, it would arguably be beneficial if the three institutions could agree on a single framework, not only limited to rule of law aspects, but also to democracy and human rights. Second, the concrete procedures under Article 7 should be further clarified. Here too, the Council took a positive step when it agreed on the modalities for a

[85] On the other hand, more specific conditionality clauses that would suspend EU funding when the identified rule of law deficiencies have a direct impact on the system of administration and control of EU funding could be more easily acceptable, and easier to reconcile with the proposed legal basis of Article 322 TFEU. See also the recommendations of Court of Auditors, 'Opinion No 1/2018 Concerning the Proposal of 2 May 2018 for a Regulation of the European Parliament and of the Council on the Protection of the Union's Budget in Case of Generalised Deficiencies as Regards the Rule of Law in the Member States'.

[86] The broad interpretation of Article 19 TEU recently given by the Court of Justice suggest that the latter also has a broader scope than other EU law provisions, though it still requires a degree of connection with EU law: it only covers (and protects) courts acting 'in the fields covered by Union law'.

[87] See European Parliament, Resolution on the establishment of an EU mechanism on democracy, the rule of law and fundamental rights, Strasbourg, 25 October 2016.

[88] European Commission, Communication 'Strengthening the rule of law within the Union – a blueprint for action', Brussels, 17 July 2019, COM(2019) 343 final.

[89] Council Conclusions, Brussels, 16 September 2019, Doc. 12111/19. The Croatian Presidency has however not picked up the work of the predecessor.

formal hearing under Article 7(1) TEU,[90] but once again a common effort of the institutions is necessary in order to develop a coherent framework to operationalize the mechanisms.[91] An inter-institutional agreement covering all Article 7-related aspects – monitoring, prevention, sanctions – would be a positive and necessary political complement to the developments on the judicial front, first and foremost the case law of the Court of Justice based on Article 19 TEU.

---

[90] Council Conclusions, Brussels, 18 July 2019, Doc. 1137/19.

[91] As also acknowledged by the Commission in its Communication - Communication 'Strengthening the rule of law within the Union – a blueprint for action', Brussels, 17 July 2019, COM(2019) 343 final, p. 14: 'the institutions should work together to intensify the collective nature of decision-making between them'.

Chapter 5

INFRINGEMENT PROCEDURES AND SANCTIONS UNDER ARTICLE 260 TFEU: EVOLUTION, LIMITS AND FUTURE PROSPECTS

Luca Prete *

ABSTRACT: *After illustrating the evolution of the sanctioning procedures provided for in the Treaties, in the context of infringement proceedings (Articles 258 to 260 TFEU) and proceedings for interim meausres (Article 279 TFEU), the present contribution will focus on the main limitations and future prospects of those procedures, in the light of the recent decisions of the Court in Commission v Belgium (High-speed electronic communications networks) and Commission v Poland (Białowieża Forest).*

KEYWORDS: *infringement proceedings – interim measures – lump sum – periodic penalty payments*

5.1. Introduction

The procedures for establishing infringements of European Union law by Member States, set out in Articles 258 to 260 TFEU, have, slowly but surely, evolved over time. This evolution is the result of actions undertaken by three main actors: the drafters of the Treaties (which have, on two occasions, amended the relevant provisions), the Court (which has, through its case-law, filled in certain gaps left by the bare Treaty provisions) and the Commission (which has progressively revised and streamlined its internal practice, and published reports and communications with a view to improving the transparency of the procedures). These developments, which

---

* Référendaire at the Court of Justice of the European Union and Guest Professor at the Vrije Universiteit Brussel. The views are expressed in a purely personal capacity. The author would like to thank Roland Klages, Jacques Radoux and the editors for useful discussions and comments. This article reflects the state of the law on 31 March 2020.

have spanned more than 50 years, turned rarely used, opaque and policy-driven procedures into common, fairly transparent and highly technical ones. [1]

These observations apply especially to the standard proceedings under Article 258 TFEU. [2] They are also, to a large extent, valid with regard to proceedings under Article 260(2) TFEU: the main provision on sanctions, introduced by the Treaty of Maastricht and subsequently amended by the Treaty of Lisbon. Starting from the first case, decided in 2000, [3] the Court has, by end of 2019, delivered some 50 judgments under Article 260(2) TFEU. The procedure under Article 260(2) TFEU has become commonplace: cases are often heard by chambers of five judges that rule without an Opinion of the Advocate General ('AG'). [4]

That said, recent months have seen the Court deliver two decisions of great importance with respect to sanctions in the context of infringement proceedings. These decisions do not, however, concern procedures brought pursuant to Article 260(2) TFEU, but procedures started under Article 260(3) TFEU and under Article 279 TFEU, respectively. The most recent of those decisions – the judgment of the Grand Chamber in *Commission v. Belgium (High-speed electronic communications networks)* [5] – is the very first in which the Court had the opportunity to interpret and apply Article 260(3) TFEU: the new provision introduced by the Treaty of Lisbon aimed at strengthening the effectiveness of the judicial procedures against Member States for failures to transpose directives. The other decision – the order delivered by the Grand Chamber in the interim procedure *Commission v. Poland (Białowieża Forest)* [6] – is even more innovative: it makes clear that the interim measures that may be adopted under Article 279 TFEU include periodic penalty payments.

After illustrating the evolution of the sanctioning procedures provided for in the Treaties, the present contribution will focus on the main limitations and future prospects of those procedures, in the light of the aforementioned decisions of the Court.

---

[1] L. Prete, B. Smulders, 'The Coming of Age of Infringement Proceedings' (2010) *Common Market Law Review* 9.

[2] Conversely, the Member State to Member State procedure under Article 259 TFEU has been used very rarely: see D. Kochenov, 'Biting Intergovernmentalism: The Case for the Reinvention of Article 259 TFEU to Make It a Viable Rule of Law Enforcement Tool' (2015) *Hague Journal on the Rule of Law* 153-174; and L. Prete, *Infringement Proceedings in EU Law* (Kluwer, 2017) 201-205. The last such cases adjudicated by the Court are C-591/17, *Austria v. Germany*, EU:C:2019:504, and C-457/18, *Slovenia v. Croatia*, EU:C:2020:65.

[3] Case C-387/97, *Commission v. Greece*, EU:C:2000:356.

[4] See e.g. Cases C-328/16, *Commission v. Greece*, EU:C:2018:98; C-584/14, *Commission v. Greece*, EU:C:2016:636; and C-576/11, *Commission v. Luxembourg*, EU:C:2013:773.

[5] Case C-543/17, EU:C:2019:573.

[6] Case C-441/17 R, EU:C:2017:877.

5.2. Evolution

The original EEC and Euratom Treaties, unlike the ECSC Treaty,[7] did not provide for any system of penalties in the framework of infringement proceedings. For that reason, from the 1970s onwards, the then Community institutions voiced concerns about the lack of mechanisms of enforcement, and suggested that the Treaties be amended in order to give the Court and/or the Commission more effective powers in that regard.[8]

The Member States eventually agreed to tackle this issue at the 1990-1991 Intergovernmental Conference. After intense discussions, it was decided that the Treaty of Maastricht would add a new second paragraph to then Article 171 EEC, allowing the Commission to initiate proceedings against a Member State which has not complied with a previous judgment, requesting the Court to impose financial penalties upon it.[9] The newly devised procedure was the same as the ordinary infringement procedure, with a pre-judicial phase (letter of formal notice followed by a reasoned opinion) and a judicial phase. Subsequent attempts, in the context of the Amsterdam and Nice Treaties, to amend the Treaty provisions in order to improve the efficiency of the infringement and sanctions procedures did not succeed.[10]

However, with the Treaty of Lisbon, two important changes were eventually introduced with a view to simplifying and accelerating the procedure for the imposition of financial penalties upon recalcitrant Member States. Those changes had already been envisaged in the (failed) Treaty establishing a Constitution for Europe, which in turn reflected certain proposals put forward in the Final Report issued by the Discussion Circle on the Court of Justice set up within the Convention on the Future of Europe.[11] First, the requirement to issue a reasoned opinion prior to

---

[7] Article 88 of the ECSC Treaty. The penalties provided therein, however, have never been applied: see G. Tesauro, 'La sanction des infractions au droit communautaire', FIDE Report, 1992, p. 152.

[8] See, in particular, Court of Justice, Suggestions of the Court of Justice on European Union (Bull. EC Supp. 9/75, p. 17); European Parliament, Resolution on the Responsibility of Member States for the Application of and Compliance with Community, Law of 9 February 1983(OJ 1983 C 68, p. 32) (the 'Sieglerschmidt Resolution'), and European Parliament, Draft Treaty Establishing the European Union (OJ 1984 C 77, p. 33) (the 'Spinelli Project').

[9] See, generally, I. Kilbey, 'Financial Penalties under Article 228(2)EC: Excessive complexity?' (2007) *Common Market Law Review* 744, and I. Kilbey, 'The Interpretation of Article 260 TFEU (ex 228 EC) (2010) *European Law Review* 371.

[10] See e.g. Report from the Working Party on the Future of the European Communities' Court System (the 'Due Report'), January 2000, Section II.B. See also J. Tallberg, *European Governance and Supranational Institutions: Making States Comply* (Routledge, 2003) 82-91.

[11] See especially Documents CONV 636/03 and CONV 734/03. More generally, see R. Passos,

bringing the case before the Court under Article 260(2) TFEU was eliminated. Second, pursuant to a new paragraph 3 of Article 260 TFEU, where an infringement concerns a failure to notify the Commission of measures transposing a directive adopted under ordinary legislative procedure, the Commission may request the imposition of financial penalties in the context of the original infringement proceedings, avoiding proceedings under Article 260(2) TFEU altogether.

A proper understanding of the functioning of the sanctioning procedures, and appreciation of their limitations and future prospects, requires a more in-depth examination of the case-law.

5.2.1. Article 260(2) TFEU: *nihil sub sole novum?*

As AG Jarabo Colomer noted in the first case brought pursuant to Article 260(2) TFEU, the concise nature of the provision, and the inherent complexity of the subject-matter, raised a large number of interpretative issues. [12] However, subsequent case-law has, by and large, progressively clarified those issues. In particular, the Court made clear that the procedure provided for in Article 260(2) TFEU is a special judicial procedure for the enforcement of judgments. [13] The sanctions provided for in Article 260(2) TFEU – lump sum and penalty payments – are both intended to induce a defaulting Member State to comply with an adverse ruling. However, those sanctions pursue this objective in a complementary manner: while the imposition of a penalty payment seeks to induce a Member State to put an end as soon as possible to a breach of obligations which, in the absence of such a penalty, would tend to persist, the imposition of a lump sum aims at preventing similar infringements in the future. For that reason, simultaneous recourse to both types of sanction is not precluded, in particular where the breach of obligations both has continued for a long period and is inclined to persist. [14]

According to settled case-law, the imposition of a penalty payment is, in principle, justified only in so far as the failure to comply with an earlier judgment continues up to the time of the Court's examination of the facts. [15] The imposition of a lump sum is not automatic, but depends on all the relevant factors pertaining to both the nature of the established infringement and the conduct of the Member State in question. [16] In exercising its discretion in this matter, the Court sets the

---

'Le système juridictionnel de l'Union', in G. Amato, E. Bribosia, B. de Witte (eds), *Genesis and Destiny of the European Constitution* (Bruylant, 2007) 565-598.

[12] Opinion in Case C-387/97, *Commission v. Greece*, EU:C:1999:455, para 1.

[13] See Case C-95/12, *Commission v. Germany*, EU:C:2013:676, para. 23 and the case-law cited.

[14] See Case C-304/02, *Commission v. France*, EU:C:2004:274, paras 80-86.

[15] See Case C-576/11, *Commission v. Luxembourg*, EU:C:2013:773, para. 43 and the case-law cited.

[16] See Case C-121/07, *Commission v. France*, EU:C:2008:695, paras 62-63.

sanctions in a way which is appropriate to the circumstances, and proportionate to the established infringement and the Member State's ability to pay.[17] The Commission's proposals in that respect cannot bind the Court, being merely a useful point of reference. For the purposes of determining the amount of the sanctions, the basic criteria taken into consideration by the Court are, in principle, the seriousness of the infringement, its duration and the Member State's ability to pay. In applying those criteria, the Court gives due regard, in particular, to the effects on public and private interests of the failure to comply, and the urgency of the matter.[18] The final amount is determined in the light of all the circumstances of each case and, in particular, of mitigating and aggravating factors.[19] The Court also enjoys discretion with regard to the periodicity of the penalty payment, and how, if at all, the Member State's progress towards full compliance may be taken into account in order to gradually decrease the amount of the penalty payment.[20]

Having clarified these key issues over the past years, the latest case-law of the Court has not given rise to any major innovation. Recent developments, in the Commission's practice or in the Court's case-law, concerned less significant aspects of the procedure, such as one of the criteria used to determine the amount of the penalties.[21]

5.2.2. Article 260(3) TFEU: (some) clarity at last

By virtue of Article 260(3) TFEU, the Commission may propose to the Court, in the context of an infringement action lodged pursuant to Article 258 TFEU, to impose a lump sum or penalty payment in the same judgment in which it finds that a Member State has failed to fulfil its obligation to notify measures transposing a directive adopted under a legislative procedure. The purpose of this new provision is, naturally, to give Member States a stronger incentive to transpose directives within the period prescribed.

The text of Article 260(3) TFEU, however, raises a number of novel issues. Interestingly, until very recently there was no authoritative interpretation of the provision: all previous cases brought by the Commission under Article 260(3) TFEU were sub-

---

[17] See, to that effect, Cases C-576/11, *Commission v. Luxembourg*, EU:C:2013:773, para. 46; and C-653/13, *Commission v. Italy*, EU:C:2015:478, para. 89.

[18] See e.g. case C-251/17, *Commission v. Italy*, EU:C:2018:358, paras 70-71.

[19] See, with further references, L. Prete, *supra* note 2, 262-265.

[20] See Cases C-278/01, *Commission v. Spain*, EU:C:2003:635, paras 47 seq.; C-496/09, *Commission v. Italy*, EU:C:2011:740, paras 48-52; and C-533/11, *Commission v. Belgium*, EU:C:2013:659, paras 70 seq.

[21] See Case C-93/17, *Commission v. Greece*, EU:C:2018:903, paras 132-142; and European Commission, Communication on modification of the calculation method for lump sum payments and daily penalty (OJ 2019 C 70, p. 1).

sequently withdrawn, given that the Member States concerned had achieved compliance with the earlier judgment in the course of the proceedings.[22] Nevertheless, in two of those cases the Opinion of the Advocate General was delivered before the withdrawal: that of AG Wathelet in *Commission v. Poland,*[23] and that of AG Tanchev in *Commission v. Spain.*[24] Moreover, AG Szpunar also delivered an Opinion in *Commission v. Belgium,*[25] the case in which, on 8 July 2019, the Court handed down its first judgment in this matter. Undoubtedly, that judgment goes to great lengths to clarify some of the main doubts which, for ten years, surrounded the interpretation of Article 260(3) TFEU. However, regrettably the Court either did not expressly address, or did not address at all, some other issues debated by the parties and discussed in the mentioned Opinions.

5.2.2.1. The nature and purpose of the provision

A first issue raised by Article 260(3) TFEU concerned the purpose of the provision. In a nutshell, the issue was whether the new mechanism is meant to penalise failures to notify transposition measures or failures to comply with judgments declaring Member States to be in breach of their obligation to notify the Commission of transposition measures. Put differently, is Article 260(3) TFEU to be understood as an 'enhanced' Article 258 TFEU, or as an exception to (or a variant of) Article 260(2) TFEU? The issue had an important practical consequence, as AG Szpunar pointed out in his Opinion.[26] In the former case, a failure to notify transposition measures within the period prescribed could, as such, give rise to the imposition of financial penalties. Conversely, in the latter case, a financial penalty imposed by the Court in the judgment would not take effect until a later date, because connected to the failure to comply with that judgment.

---

[22] In that connection, in its Communication - Application of Article 260(3) of the Treaty (OJ 2011 C 12, p. 1) of 2011, the Commission stated that, in the cases brought before the Court it would only seek the imposition of penalty payments. This meant that the Commission was to withdraw a case where the Member State managed to reach compliance during the proceedings (p. 5). However, in its Communication - EU Law: Better Results through Better Application (OJ 2017 C 18, p. 10) of December 2016, the Commission announced that it would change its policy on this point: in the future, it would systematically ask the Court to impose both a lump sum and a periodic penalty payment. The logical consequence of the new approach is, in the Commission's view, that in cases where a Member State rectifies the infringement by transposing the directive in the course of the proceedings, the action will not be withdrawn. According to the Commission, the Court would be still entitled to impose a lump sum penalising the duration of the infringement up to the time the situation was rectified (p. 3). No case brought after this change of policy has, by March 2020, been decided by the Court.

[23] Case C-320/13, EU:C:2014:2441.

[24] Case C-569/17, EU:C:2019:271.

[25] Case C-543/17, EU:C:2019:322.

[26] Paras 37-38 of the Opinion.

The former interpretation, suggested by the Commission in its Communication of 2011, was supported, implicitly or explicitly, by a number of authors in their writings.[27] Without openly addressing the issue, the Opinions of AG Wathelet in *Commission v. Poland* and of AG Tanchev in *Commission v. Spain*, also appear to be based on that premise. Conversely, other authors prefer the latter interpretation of Article 260(3) TFEU.[28] AG Szpunar is his Opinion in *Commission v. Belgium* also favoured this approach.[29] A number of arguments based on a textual, contextual, and historical interpretation of Article 260(3) TFEU had been invoked in this regard. Moreover, that reading of the provision would, arguably, be more in line with the principle of proportionality and better respect the Member States' rights of defence. In essence, the latter approach is based on the idea that the procedure under Article 260(3) TFEU is intended to avoid a second set of proceedings under Article 260(2) TFEU in cases where they would be manifestly unnecessary. Since determining whether a Member State has failed to communicate transposition measures is a rather straightforward exercise, the drafters of the Treaties decided to empower the Court to impose sanctions in the first set of proceedings, and to determine that those penalties should take automatic effect at a later date, unless the judgment is complied with.

In its judgment, the Court did not expressly deal with this issue. However, by ordering that the imposed penalty payments would start to run from the date the judgment was delivered,[30] it is clear that the Court endorsed the interpretation of Article 260(3) TFEU as an 'enhanced' Article 258 TFEU. The absence of a discussion on this point is disappointing nonetheless: one is left to wonder why the Court found the, arguably forceful, arguments put forward in support of the alternative approach to be unpersuasive. The only conceivable counterargument is a possible decrease of effectiveness of the provision: interpreting Article 260(3) TFEU as an exception to Article 260(2) TFEU might have reduced the incentive for the Member State to transpose directives within the prescribed period. Indeed, they would be able to escape any sanction until the end

---

[27] See, e.g. I. Kilbey (2010), *supra* note 9, 383-384; N. Wunderlich, in von der Groeben, Schwarze, Hatje (eds), *Europäisches Unionsrecht (Kommentar)* (7th ed., Nomos, 2015) Artikel 260 AEUV, para. 31; M. Pechstein, in Pechstein, Nowak, Häde (eds), *Frankfurter Kommentar zu EUV, GRC und AEUV*, Band IV (2017, Mohr Siebeck) Artikel 260 AEUV, para. 18; and P. Wennerås, 'Making effective use of Article 260 TFEU', in András, Kochenov (eds), *The enforcement of EU law and values* (OUP, 2017) 79.

[28] See A. Adinolfi, 'Le istituzioni giudiziarie nel progetto di Costituzione europea' (2003) *Rivista di Diritto Internazionale* 655; R. Alonso García, 'Lisbon and the Court of Justice of the European Union' (2010) WP IDEIR 1, 18; N. Wahl, L. Prete, 'Between Certainty, Severity and Proportionality: Some Reflections on the Nature and Functioning of Article 260(3) TFEU' (2014) *European Law Reporters* 171-174; T. Van Rijn, 'Les Sanctions Pécuniaires de l'Article 260 TFUE: 5 ans après le Traité de Lisbonne' (2016) *Cahiers de droit européen* 588; and M. Klamert, 'Die Durchsetzung finanzieller Sanktionen gegenüber den Mitgliedstaaten' (2018) *Europarecht* 162.

[29] See paras 35-57 of the Opinion.

[30] Paras 91-92 of the judgment.

of the 'grace period' that the Court had to grant them to comply with the judgment. Such an argument is not without force. However, in that respect, the principle of effectiveness in EU law cannot be understood as allowing the EU judiciary to *maximise* the effects of a provision of EU law, but rather should be interpreted as preventing the EU judiciary from *depriving* a provision of the drafters' intended effects.[31]

5.2.2.2. The scope of the provision

A second issue raised by the text of Article 260(3) TFEU concerns the meaning of the requirement which makes recourse to the new mechanism available: the Member State's failure to 'notify measures transposing a directive'.[32] The wording of the new provision was considered odd by many:[33] the mechanism does not seem to target a substantive failure (that of not transposing a directive), but a procedural failure (that of not communicating the transposition measures to the Commission). Nevertheless, it cannot be disputed that the more serious breach is the former, not the latter.

In that respect, four lines of interpretation were suggested. The most restrictive reading of the provision was proposed by some Member States who lodged their observations before the Court. They relied on a strictly literal interpretation of the new provision: put simply, a failure to communicate is a failure to *communicate*. No breach other than total inactivity of the Member States could, in their view, be subject to the procedure under Article 260(3) TFEU.[34] A broader interpretation was put forward by the Commission in its 2011 Communication. The Commission took the view that Article 260(3) TFEU cannot be limited to failures to comply with the procedural obligation of notification, but had to also cover certain failures to *transpose* the directives. In particular, instances of *incomplete* or *partial* transposition of directives could be caught by the new provision, whereas cases of *erroneous* transposition of directives had to be dealt with under the standard procedures.[35]

At the other end of the spectrum, one could find the even broader interpretation suggested by AG Wathelet and by AG Tanchev in the above-mentioned Opinions. In their view, the distinction made by the Commission between cases of incomplete or

---

[31] See P. Pescatore, 'Monisme, dualisme et «effet utile» dans la jurisprudence de la Cour de justice de la Communauté européenne', in Colneric and Others (eds), *Une communauté de droit : Festschrift für Gil Carlos Rodríguez Iglesias* (Nomos, 2003) 340; and N. Wahl, L. Prete, *supra* note 28, 179 and 185. See also Opinion of AG Szpunar in *Commission v. Belgium*, paras 7 and 74-75.

[32] A second requirement is that the directive has been 'adopted under a legislative procedure'. The interpretation of this condition, however, gives rise to less doubts and, in any event, was not raised in the proceedings in question. On this issue, see generally Opinion of AG Wathelet in Case C-320/13, *Commission v. Poland*, paras 95-103; and S. Peers, 'Sanctions for Infringement of EU Law after the Treaty of Lisbon' (2012) European Public Law 40-41.

[33] See e.g. A. Arnull, *The European Union and Its Court of Justice* (2nd ed., OUP, 2006) 51.

[34] See Case C-543/17, *Commission v. Belgium*, para. 39.

[35] Para 19 of the 2011 Communication, *supra* note 22.

partial transposition and cases of incorrect transposition was unworkable.[36] They thus proposed to interpret Article 260(3) TFEU as encompassing also cases of incorrect transposition of directives.[37] A number of academic writers too suggested that, despite the terminology employed, Article 260(3) TFEU could be used against some or all failures to transpose directives.[38] Finally, a fourth interpretation – that is middle ground between the position expressed by the Member States referred to above, and that defended by the Commission – had been suggested in legal scholarship,[39] and embraced by AG Szpunar.[40] According to this final approach, based mainly on a textual and historical interpretation of Article 260(3) TFEU, the new mechanism could only be used against Member States' failure to notify transposition measures. However, that failure would not be limited to instances of total inactivity of the Member State in question but include those cases where, despite some measures having been formally notified to the Commission, the information communicated fell short of the requirements of clarity, precision and completeness that are necessary for the Commission to fulfil its role as guardian of the Treaties.

In its judgment of 8 July 2019, the Court formally endorsed the latter approach. However, by interpreting the obligation of the Member States to communicate the transposition measures to the Commission in a very broad and consequential manner, the Court came, in substance, relatively close to the position expressed by the Commission. Schematically, the different interpretations proposed before the judgment of the Court, and the one eventually retained by the Court, can be illustrated as follows.

---

[36] The problem was identified also by AG Szpunar: see paras 71-73 of the Opinion in *Commission v. Belgium*. Similarly, P. Wennerås, 'Sanctions against Member States under Article 260 TFEU: Alive, but not kicking?' (2012) *Common Market Law Review* 167; and N. Wahl, L. Prete, *supra* note 28, 176.

[37] See, respectively, paras 114-145 of the Opinion of AG Wathelet in *Commission v. Poland* and paras 41-71 of the Opinion of AG Tanchev in *Commission v. Spain*.

[38] See, with different nuances, T. Joris, S. Van der Jeught, 'Tien jaar financiële sancties in de Europese inbreukprocedure ex artikel 260, lid 2 VWEU - Tijd voor een stand van zaken' (2010) *Tijdschrift voor Europees en economisch recht* 435; T. Materne, *La Procédure en Manquement d'État – Guide à la lumière de la Jurisprudence de la Cour de Justice de l'Union européenne* (Larcier, 2010), 42-43; S. Van der Jeught, 'L'action en manquement "renforcée": sanctions pécuniaires en cas de non-transposition des directives européennes' (2011) *Journal de droit européen* 68-70; S. Peers, *supra* note 32, 39; and D. Blanc, 'Les procédures du recours en manquement, le traité, le juge et le gardien: entre unité et diversité en vue d'un renforcement de l'Union de droit', in Mahieu (ed.), *Contentieux du droit de l'Union européenne* (Larcier, 2014) 446-447.

[39] Again, with different nuances, see N. Wahl, L. Prete, *supra* note 28, 174-179; and T. Van Rijn, *supra* note 28, 585. More generally, emphasizing the importance of the wording of the provision: U. Everling, 'Rechtsschutz in der Europäischen Union nach dem Vertrag von Lissabon' (2009) *Europarecht* 82; and D. Simon. 'Sanctions pécuniaires', *Revue Europe*, March 2011, 15.

[40] Paras of the 58-81 of the Opinion in *Commission v. Belgium*.

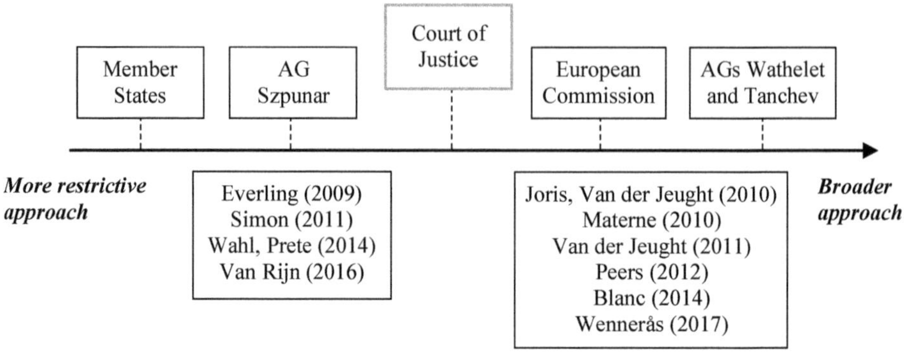

In its judgment, the Court on the one hand rejected the formalistic arguments expressed by some of the Member States: their restrictive reading would compromise the objective pursued by the new provision. On the other hand, the Court also dismissed the more extensive interpretation proposed by the Commission: the wording of the provision, its genesis and the broader context make it very clear that it was intended to be applied in cases of failures to *notify*, and not to *adopt*, transposition measures. The Court then explained that the proper interpretation of the provision must ensure its effectiveness, while protecting the right of defence of the Member States and enabling the Court to check the existence and gravity of the failures alleged by the Commission. Accordingly, the notification obligation referred to in Article 260(3) TFEU must be understood as requiring Member States to indicate, for each provision of a directive, the corresponding provisions of national law. When a Member State has satisfied this condition, where appropriate through the use of corresponding tables, it is for the Commission to prove that the measures notified are manifestly inexistent or do not cover the whole territory of the Member State.[41]

5.2.2.3. The *an* and *quantum* of the sanctions

Having clarified that, the Court went on to deal with other outstanding issues. With regard to the *an* and *quantum* of the sanctions, the Court indicated that principles developed under Article 260(2) TFEU are fully applicable in the context of the new mechanism. In particular, the Court stated that the imposition of penalty payment is justified when the infringement continues up until the Court's *examination of the facts*.[42] With regard to the determination of the amount of the sanction, the Court appeared to follow the same criteria used in the context of proceedings

[41] Paras 48-59 of the judgment.

[42] The precise meaning of this expression is, however, not entirely clear. It should probably be understood as referring to the start of the Court's deliberation. This normally corresponds to the end of the oral procedure (that is, the delivery of the AG Opinion if there is one, otherwise the end of the oral hearing). However, where the Court proceeds to judgment without an hearing and an Opinion, it corresponds to the end of the written procedure.

under Article 260(2) TFEU. In the case at hand, in the light of the gravity and duration of the infringement, the Court decided to impose penalty payments of EUR 5 000 per day.[43] That amount was not set by following a mathematical formula, such as that used by the Commission, but according to an *ex aequo et bono* approach.[44] The Court then rejected Belgium's request to set a degressive penalty payment which could take into account the progressive adoption and notification of the transposition measures. According to the Court, that measure would have limited the effectiveness of the sanction imposed. Finally, the Court decided that, if the failure persisted at the date of delivery of the judgment, the penalty payments were to take effect from that very moment, and not at a later date as Belgium had asked.[45]

5.2.3. Article 279 TFEU: penalty payments as *interim* measures

In July 2017, the Commission brought infringement proceedings against Poland for possible breaches of the Habitats and Birds Directives[46] due to the increase of active forest management operations in the Białowieska Forest, a Natura2000 site. On the same day, the Commission also lodged an application for interim measures. Essentially, the Commission asked the Court to order the Polish authorities to halt those operations, pending the judgment in the main action, except where there was a threat to public safety. The Vice-President of the Court, owing to the risk of serious and irreparable damage for the integrity of the site, provisionally granted the requested measures, *inaudita altera parte*, by order of 27 July 2017.

In the following weeks, however, the Commission took the view that the Polish authorities had deliberately ignored that order, as the contested operations continued unaffected. Thus, during an hearing that took place before the Vice-President of the Court on 11 September 2017, the question arose as to whether any means exists to enforce compliance with an order issued under Article 279 TFEU. In the light of that discussion, on 13 September 2017, the Commission supplemented its

---

[43] In the light of its low amount, the penalty payment might appear almost symbolic (compare it, for example, with that imposed in the *Białowieża Forest* case: infra section II.3). However, the daily amount set by the Court is not much lower than that requested by the Commission (EUR 6 071,04).

[44] Generally, regarding these two approaches, see A. Kornezov, 'Imposing the Right Amount of Sanctions Under Article 260(2) TFEU: Fairness v. Predictability, or How to "Bridge The Gaps"' (2014) *Columbia Journal of European Law* 307-331.

[45] Paras 60-68 and 78-93 of the judgment.

[46] Respectively, Council Directive 92/43/EEC of 21 May 1992 on the conservation of natural habitats and of wild fauna and flora (OJ 1992 L 206, p. 7) and Directive 2009/147/EC of the European Parliament and of the Council of 30 November 2009 on the conservation of wild birds (OJ 2010 L 20, p. 7).

application with a request for an additional order obliging Poland to pay a *periodic penalty payment* if it failed to comply with the orders made in those proceedings. The case was assigned to the Grand Chamber, before which, on 17 October 2017, the parties presented oral observations.

5.2.3.1. The Court's order of 20 November 2017

On 20 November 2017, the Court adopted the final order in the proceedings. In its order, the Court found that the requirements of *fumus boni iuris* and urgency were met. It thus decided that the measures provisionally granted by the Vice-President had to be maintained. With regard to the Commission's additional application, the Court first recalled that the purpose of the procedure for interim relief is to guarantee the full effectiveness of the final decision in the main action. To that end, Article 279 TFEU confers on the Court the power to prescribe any interim measures that it deems necessary. Although it is for the applicant to request such measures as it is considered appropriate, the Court must satisfy itself that the measures which it intends to order are sufficiently effective to achieve their aim. The Court enjoys broad discretion in that respect. If deemed appropriate, the Court may also adopt, where necessary *ex officio*, any ancillary measure intended to ensure that its order is complied with. Such a measure may include – the Court found – the imposition of periodic penalty payments. That measure must not be regarded as a punishment, but merely as a means to encourage the relevant Member State to comply with the order. The Court further stressed that that measure is not irreversible, as it in no way prejudices the future decision in the main action.[47]

In the case at hand, the Court found it unnecessary to establish whether the first order had not been complied with. There was enough evidence in the case-file for doubting that Poland had complied, or that it intended to comply with the new order. Thus, if the new order were to do no more than confirm the first order, there would be a risk that its effectiveness would be limited. In such circumstances, the Court considered it necessary to 'enhance the effectiveness' of the interim measures ordered by providing for a periodic penalty payment to be imposed if Poland failed to comply with them immediately and fully. Poland was thus requested to send to the Commission, within 15 days, details of all measures adopted in order to comply. If the Commission was of the view that Poland had failed to comply with the order, it could request that proceedings be resumed. The Court would then give a decision by way of a new order. If the Court found an infringement, it would order Poland to pay to the Commission 'a periodic penalty payment of at least EUR 100 000 per day', from the date of notification of the new order until compliance was achieved, or until the judgment in the main proceedings was delivered. Accordingly, the

[47] Paras 89-108 of the order.

Court reserved its final decision on the Commission's additional application.[48]

In essence, the Court's order of 20 November 2017 is based on two main principles. First, the wording of Article 279 TFEU, which refers to '*any* necessary interim measures'.[49] Second, the principle of effectiveness: since the purpose of the procedure under Article 279 TFEU is to ensure the effectiveness of the decision to be taken in the main proceedings, the Court must have the requisite powers to guarantee such effectiveness by adopting, where necessary, ancillary measures such as periodic penalty payments. These arguments are, objectively, not unpersuasive.

5.2.3.2. Did the Court see the full picture?

However, in the aftermath of the order, doubts were raised as to whether the Court had overlooked some other arguments that might have suggested a more restrictive approach to the issue.

Firstly, according to settled case-law, 'although the conditions for the Court's jurisdiction must be interpreted in the light of the principle of effective judicial protection, such an interpretation cannot have the effect of setting aside the conditions in question, expressly laid down in the Treaties, without going beyond the jurisdiction conferred by the Treaties on the EU Courts. While it is, admittedly, possible to envisage a system of judicial review different from that established by the founding Treaties, it is for the Member States, if necessary, in accordance with Article 48 TEU, to reform the system currently in force'.[50] Seen from this perspective, the sanctions provided for in Article 260(2) and (3) TFEU – introduced, as mentioned, with amendments of the Treaties – appear to constitute *leges speciales*. This explains why, to date, the lack of means of enforcement for interim measures has generally been considered as a *lacuna* in the EU Treaties.[51]

Secondly, the Court's power to impose sanctions under Article 279 TFEU might sit uneasily with the *purpose* of the procedure for interim measures. The aim of the sanctions seems more to be one of enforcement: to ensure compliance with a decision of the Court. The objective of maintaining the existing situation or restore the *status quo ante*,[52] pending a decision in the main action, is pursued rather indirectly. Notably, in the early 1980s the Commission lodged an application for interim measures in the context of two infringement actions brought against France during the so-called 'sheepmeat war'. The purpose of that application was, ostensibly, to enforce previous judgments of the Court which had remained dead letter. However,

---

[48] Paras 109-119 of the order.

[49] Emphasis added.

[50] See especially Case C-50/00 P, *Unión de Pequeños Agricultores*, EU:C:2002:462, paras 44-45.

[51] See inter alia C.W.A. Timmermans, 'La sanction des infractions au droit communautaire – Rapport communautaire', FIDE Report 1992, p. 26; and L. Prete, *supra* note 2, 396-397.

[52] See Case 352/88 R, *Commission v. Italy*, EU:C:1989:55, para. 23.

the Court dismissed the application, finding no grounds to order the interim measures requested. The Court emphasised that those measures consisted, in substance, in requiring France to comply with previous judgments. The Court took the view that such kind of measures fell outside the scope of the Treaty provision on interim measures.[53]

Thirdly, various lines of authority from the EU Courts concerning the nature, type and function of interim measures seem difficult to reconcile with the broad (and bold) approach taken in the order at issue. The EU Courts have stated that the interim measures sought may not 'exceed the jurisdiction of the Court in interlocutory matters',[54] and 'must not fall outside the scope of the final decision which the Court may reach on the main application'.[55] In addition, the EU Courts have also held that interim measures must have 'a sufficiently close link [with] the subject-matter of the main action',[56] and must not give rise to an irreversible situation.[57] In fact, the Court has traditionally shown a certain reluctance to order measures which go beyond the mere suspension of the act whose validity or compatibility is disputed by the parties.[58] Against that background, certain doubts may arise: may the imposition of penalty payments be considered to remain *within the scope* of the main action? Is there a *sufficiently close link* between the penalties and the subject-matter of the main action? In the event that the Member State concerned succeeds in the main action, would the monies paid by a Member State in default nonetheless remain in the EU budget and, if so, does that not give rise to an *irreversible situation*?

Fourthly and finally, the finding that the concept of 'any measure' within the meaning of Article 279 TFEU encompasses also any *ancillary* measure, even those adopted *ex officio*, is not going beyond Article 160(3) of the Rules of Procedure of the Court, according to which an application for interim measures must 'state the subject matter of the proceedings, the circumstances giving rise to urgency and the pleas of fact and law establishing a prima facie case for the interim measure applied for'? [59]

---

[53] Joined Cases 24 and 97/80 R, *Commission v. France*, EU:C:1980:107. On those procedures, see extensively T.C. Hartley, 'Interim Measures Against France in the 'Lamb War'' (1980) *European Law Review* 363.

[54] See e.g. Case C-191/88 R, *Co-Frutta*, EU:C:1988:418, para. 24.

[55] See e.g. Case T-18/01 R-I, *Goldstein*, EU:T:2001:110, para. 14 and the case-law cited.

[56] See Case T-78/04 R, *Sumitomo*, EU:T:2004:204, para. 43.

[57] Opinion of AG Capotorti in Joined Cases C-24 and 97/80 R, *Commission v. France*, EU:C:1980:95, pp. 1338-1339.

[58] See, to that effect, Case 25/62 R, *Plaumann*, EU:C:1962:32, p. 124; Case 50/69 R, *Germany v. Commission*, EU:C:1969:42, pp. 450-451, Case 88/76 R, *Exportation des Sucres*, EU:C:1976:140, p. 1587; and Case C-352/88 R, *Commission v. Italy*, EU:C:1989:55, para. 23.

[59] Cf. L. Coutron, 'La Cour de justice au secours de la forêt de Bialowieska - Coup de tonnerre dans le recours en manquement!' (2018) RTD Eur. 321.

5.2.3.3. A more thoughtful reflection

However, notwithstanding those doubts, thoughtful reflection on the subject appears to confirm the soundness of the Court's findings. As a preliminary observation, it must be stressed that the decision at issue is an order issued in the context of summary proceedings in which, evidently, time is of essence. The Court may not be expected, in those circumstances, to answer in detail each and every argument put forward by the parties, let alone explain why its findings are not called into question by provisions, principles or case-law which the parties have not even invoked.

More importantly, several factors justifying the Court's approach emerge when the order at issue is examined within its broader context. To begin with, Article 279 TFEU unquestionably applies in the context of proceedings brought under Article 258 TFEU: the first cases go as far back as to the mid-1970s. [60] Moreover, the Court has already clarified that 'the provisions on judicial protection in the field of interim measures cannot be interpreted narrowly, as otherwise there would be the risk of a lacuna in the Treaties'. [61] Thus, although the Court cannot interpret the Treaty provisions in a manner that extends its jurisdiction beyond the limits set out therein, it does not mean that those provisions should be given a *narrow* interpretation, particularly where that might deprive them of effectiveness. Such logic applies especially to the procedure provided for in Article 279 TFEU, considering its broad formulation and its specific role within the system of judicial remedies set out in the Treaties.

In the light of the provision's very wording, it is clear that the range of possible measures under Article 279 TFEU is not predetermined: arguably, any measure … must mean *any* measure. As AG Reischl stated, that provision 'is expressed in very general terms and lays down no exceptions for certain types of procedures or measures'. [62] More recently, Lasok wrote: 'there is in principle no limit (other than practicalities) to the type of measure that the Court may order'. [63] It is, for example, undisputed that, on the basis of Article 279 TFEU, the judge hearing the application for interim relief may issue, on a provisional basis, injunctions or 'appropriate directions' to the parties. [64] Accordingly, at this interlocutory stage, the Court may require a

---

[60] See, e.g. Cases 61/77 R and 61/77 R-II, *Commission v. Ireland*, EU:C:1977:122 and EU:C:1977:126; Joined Cases 31/77 R, *Commission v. United Kingdom*, and 53/77 R, *United Kingdom v. Commission*, EU:C:1977:86.

[61] See e.g. Case C-399/95 R, *Germany v. Commission*, EU:C:1996:193, para. 46 and the case-law cited.

[62] Opinion in Case C-61/77 R, *Commission v. Ireland*, EU:C:1977:122, pp. 953-954.

[63] K.P.E Lasok, *Lasok's European Court Practice and Procedure* (3rd ed., Bloomsbury, 2016) 640.

[64] See, to that effect, Cases 118/83 R, *Muratori*, EU:C:1983:225, para. 53; C-76/08 R, *Commission v. Malta*, EU:C:2008:252, para. 19; and T-203/95 R, *Connelly*, EU:T:1995:208, paras. 24-25.

Member State to do something, whereas that is not possible in the main action, since a judgment given under Article 258 TFEU is merely declaratory.[65]

With regard, then, to the effects of the measures that may be ordered, the Court has pointed out that recourse to measures which give rise to *irreversible effects* are not excluded as matter of principle. The Court has accepted that such measures may be granted 'where the *prima facie* case appears particularly strong and the urgency of the measures sought undeniable'.[66] Those requirements were obviously met in the *Białowieska Forest* case. Furthermore, the imposition of penalty payments would have by no means prejudiced the substance of the case in the main action, meaning the future final decision of the Court. Finally, it is true that the EU Courts typically refuse to grant interim measures where alternative avenues to avert the damage exist under EU and/or national law.[67] In the case at hand, however, there seemed to be no alternative avenue to protect the integrity of the natural site (not to mention alternative measures to protect the authority of the Court). It is also worth recalling, in this context, that damage to the environment is generally considered irreparable.[68]

5.3. Limits and future prospects

Infringement proceedings are generally regarded as being rather effective:[69] the Commission processes, on a yearly basis, over 3 000 complaints which concern suspected infringements of EU law by Member States' authorities. In the last five years, the Commission opened, on average, almost 800 new procedures per year, the vast majority of which could be closed during the pre-litigation phase. Only some 30 cases were eventually referred to the Court each year, with around half of those being withdrawn before the judgment, given that the Member States concerned had, in the meantime, taken the necessary measures to comply with EU law. Where the cases proceeded to judgment, the Commission was predominantly successful.[70]

However, that does not mean that the procedure under Article 258 TFEU is necessarily free from flaws. In particular, the significant duration of the procedure has

---

[65] See e.g. K. Lenaerts, I. Maselis, K. Gutman, *EU Procedural Law* (OUP, 2014) 571.

[66] Case C-393/96 P(R), *Antonissen*, EU:C:1997:42, para. 41.

[67] See e.g. Cases C-310/85 R, *Deufil*, EU:C:1986:58, para. 22; and T-417/05 R, *Endesa,* EU:T:2006:41, para. 50.

[68] Case C-320/03 R, *Commission v. Austria*, EU:C:2004:231, para. 92.

[69] See, inter alia, B. Schima, 'Comment to Article 258 TFEU', in Kellerbauer, Klamert, Tomkin (eds), *The EU Treaties and the Charter of Fundamental Rights: A Commentary* (OUP, 2019) 1775.

[70] See European Commission, Monitoring the Application of Union Law - 2018 Annual Report – Part I: general statistical overview, especially pp. 10-22.

been a perennial problem.[71] Indeed, the administrative stage of the procedure may easily last for 2 years or more,[72] and another 17-20 months must be added for the judicial stage.[73] Furthermore, the imposition of sanctions may normally come only after the completion of a second set of proceedings. Thus, it is inevitable that the alleged infringements may continue for several years before the recalcitrant Member States may be hit by any sanction.[74] To address this issue, a number of proposals *de lege ferenda* have been explored but, so far, with little or no success. The only measure that could significantly impact the overall duration of the proceedings would probably be to empower the Commission (in all cases, or only in some) to declare an infringement by way of decision, which the Member State in question could, where appropriate, challenge before the EU Courts. This would 'cut in half' the procedure by making the judicial phase only optional. However, such a change would require a Treaty amendment and thus the agreement of all the Governments of the Member States.[75]

Against that background, the recent decisions of the Court in *Commission v. Belgium* and *Commission v. Poland* are of the greatest interest.

In the first place, given its relatively broad scope of application, the procedure set out in Article 260(3) TFEU should substantially reduce the duration of the proceedings necessary to compel Member States to transpose more quickly (and in full) directives adopted under the ordinary legislative procedure. In those cases, the threat of sanctions kicks in from the very first proceedings brought by the Commission before the Court, and the Member States will not be able to escape them by simply sending the Commission incomplete or unclear notifications. To that end, the Court's ruling had to leverage the Member States' obligation to notify transposition measures to the Commission, an obligation which is not *expressis verbis* in the Treaties but that the Court derives from Article 4(3) TEU.

The consequences of this obligation, as the Court sees it, are very far reaching: in practice, the judgment makes the submission of correlation tables by Member States almost mandatory. However, it must be borne in mind that there has been a long-standing disagreement between the Commission and Parliament on the one

---

[71] See e.g. European Parliament, Report on the twenty-seventh annual report on monitoring the application of European Union law (2009) point 33; and EU Court of Auditors, Special Report 7/2007, paras 96-100 and 123. In legal scholarship, see e.g. D. Chalmers, G. Davies, G. Monti, *European Union Law – Text and Materials* (3rd ed., CUP, 2014), 357; and R. Muñoz, 'The Monitoring of the Application of Community Law: The Need to Improve the Current Tools and an Obligation to Innovate', Jean Monnet Working Paper 04/06, 33.

[72] See European Commission, 2018 Annual Report, *supra* note 70, p. 11.

[73] Court of Justice of the European Union, Annual Report 2018, Judicial Activity, 134.

[74] See e.g. Cases C-610/10, *Commission v. Spain*, EU:C:2012:781, paras 121-122; and C-374/11, *Commission v. Ireland*, EU:C:2012:827, para. 38.

[75] For an ample discussion, with further references, see L. Prete, *supra* note 2, 369-378.

side, and the Council and the Member States on the other, on whether correlation tables could be systematically required. A common position on this matter was eventually found in 2011, when two Joint Political Declarations ('JPD') were issued.[76] In essence, according to the JPD, the Commission could request, on a case-by-case basis and with proper justification, the transmission of 'explanatory documents' by the Member States which, if the Member States consider it useful, could also take the form of correlation tables. The explanatory documents were meant to illustrate the relationship between national transposing rules and the specific provisions of a given directive.[77] One may wonder whether the JPD on this point have not been superseded by the judgment of the Court.

It is true that the new mechanism concerns only one specific type of infringement cases (so-called 'non-communication cases'). However, one must not overlook the fact that they have consistently represented a significant percentage of the overall number of infringement cases started by the Commission. That said, there are naturally a number of interpretative issues which the Court will need to address in the future which might have an impact on the functioning of the new mechanism. Some cases are currently pending before the Court. In two such cases a hearing before the Grand Chamber took place on 10 December 2019, and AG Tanchev delivered his Opinions on 5 March 2020.[78]

To begin with, the Court has, wisely, avoided falling into the trap of having to distinguish between partial transposition and erroneous transposition. Yet, the *prima facie* test devised by the Court to check whether a notification of transposition measures is sufficiently clear and complete does not seem very different from that proposed by the Commission. It remains to be seen how the Court's examination on this matter will work in practice, especially in those cases where — unlike Belgium in the case at hand[79] — the defendant Member State does not expressly acknowledge the shortcomings of its communication.

In addition, should the Commission explain why it has chosen to make use of the mechanism set out in Article 260(3) TFEU in a specific case[80] and, if so, elaborate on its choice made with regard to the requested sanctions? On the one hand, an argument could be made that the expression 'when it deems appropriate' included in Article 260(3) TFEU (and not in Article 260(2) TFEU) means that that

---

[76] Joint Political Declarations on explanatory documents dated 28 September 2011 (OJ 2011 C 369, p. 14) and 27 October 2011 (OJ 2011 C 369, p. 15).

[77] See, amply, C. Harlow, R. Rawlings, *Process and Procedure in EU Administration* (Hart, 2014) 177, and L. Prete *supra* note 2, 315-316.

[78] See Opinions in Cases C-549/18, *Commission v. Romania*, EU:C:2020:173, and C-550/18, *Commission v. Ireland*, EU:C:2020:175.

[79] See especially paras 20-22, 25 and 64-67 of the judgment.

[80] In its 2011 Communication the Commission announced its intention to make use of this mechanism in all cases (p. 5).

institution is to duly outline the motivations for its choices. On the other hand, however, the Commission has so far enjoyed almost unfettered discretion in deciding whether, when, on which grounds and against which Member States to institute infringement proceedings,[81] any different approach under Article 260(3) TFEU appears unlikely. It would also be hard to imagine how the Court could actually review the Commission's (largely policy-based) choices, even under a manifest error of assessment standard. In any event, would such an exercise be reasonable? After all, if the Court comes to the conclusion that the sanctions requested are not proportionate to the infringement committed, it could always reduce the amounts or impose no sanction at all. AG Tanchev, in his Opinions of 5 March 2020, also proposed to dismiss the arguments of the defendants on this point.[82]

In this context, it must be stressed that the boundaries of the Court's discretion with regard to the choice of types and amounts of sanctions under Article 260(3) TFEU are not entirely clear. According to that provision the Court may impose a lump sum or penalty payment 'not exceeding the amount specified by the Commission'. Consequently, unlike in proceedings under Article 260(2) TFEU, the amount of the penalties proposed by the Commission constitutes a ceiling which the Court cannot go beyond. Two issues in that regard remain, however, not settled.

First, is the Commission entitled to use the same *methods of calculation* of the sanctions it proposes under Article 260(2) and (3) TFEU? Some Member States have argued that the Commission should use, under Article 260(3) TFEU, a 'lighter touch' than under Article 260(2) TFEU. The reason would be that the former provision penalises a simple infringement (non-communication of transposition measures), whereas the latter provision concerns a 'compound' infringement[83] (original infringement *and* subsequent failure to comply with the judgment of the Court given under Article 258 TFEU). The judgment in *Commission v Belgium* does not provide detailed guidance in that regard. AG Wathelet, AG Tanchev and AG Szpunar, however, saw no problem in adopting a coherent approach under both provisions.[84]

Second, the text of Article 260(3) TFEU does not explicitly state whether the

---

[81] See e.g. Cases C-200/88, *Commission v. Greece*, EU:C:1990:422, para. 9; C-523/04, *Commission v. Netherlands*, EU:C:2007:244, paras 27-29; and C-323/13, *Commission v. Italy*, EU:C:2014:2290, para. 43.

[82] See Opinion in *Commission v. Romania*, paras 43-49 and Opinion in *Commission v. Ireland*, paras 45-50.

[83] For the first use of this expression: Opinion of AG Fennelly in Case C-197/98, *Commission v. Greece*, EU:C:1999:59, para. 19.

[84] See Opinion of AG Wathelet in *Commission v. Poland*, paras 146-160, Opinion of AG Szpunar in *Commission v. Belgium*, para. 96, and Opinions of AG Tanchev in *Commission v. Spain*, para. 73, in *Commission v. Romania*, paras 50-53, and in *Commission v. Ireland*, paras 51-54.

Court may depart from the Commission's request as to the *type* of sanction(s) to be imposed. Therefore, whether Article 260(3) TFEU restricts the Court's discretion in that regard is unclear. On the one hand, AG Tanchev suggested that the Court should be able to alter the type of sanctions, as long as it remains within the amount proposed by the Commission.[85] On the other hand, AG Wathelet and AG Szpunar,[86] took the opposite view: the Commission's choice of sanctions would be binding on the Court. The latter position seems based on a combined reading of the first subparagraph of Article 260(3) TFEU ('the Commission … may … specify the amount of the lump sum or penalty payment to be paid') with the second subparagraph of that provision ('the Court … may impose a lump sum or penalty payment … not exceeding the amount specified by the Commission'). More importantly, given the intrinsic difference between lump sums (one-off payments) and periodic penalty payments (recurring payments for a period that cannot be determined a priori), how could their amounts be combined (or converted) in order to ensure that the overall amount does not exceed that specified by the Commission? That accounting operation seems very hard, if not impossible, to carry out.

A related question is whether the Court may impose both a lump and a penalty payment *at the same time* (regardless of whether that is possible only at the Commission's request or also *ex officio*). Arguably, the Court's reasons for answering positively to the question in respect of Article 260(2) TFEU[87] should apply equally with regard to Article 260(3) TFEU, given the identical wording on this point.[88] However, one may wonder whether the fact that, as mentioned, the new provision concerns a simple infringement whereas the old provision concerns a 'compound' infringement might be relevant in this context. Finally, it may be noted that, in paragraph 90 of the judgment, the Court stated that, in a case such as that at issue, the imposition of degressive penalty payments would be likely to compromise the effectiveness of that penalty. Does that mean that such adjustments to the penalty payments are generally excluded under Article 260(2) TFEU?

In the second place, as far as Article 279 TFEU is concerned, there is little doubt that the Court order in the Białowieża Forest case is nothing less than revolutionary. The Court decision opens new scenarios for the enforcement of EU law against Member States in default. In particularly serious and urgent cases, the Commission now has at its disposal a very effective and rapid tool that may coerce recalcitrant

---

[85] See Opinions in *Commission v. Spain*, paras 75-78, in *Commission v. Romania*, paras 54-59, and in *Commission v. Ireland*, paras 55-57.

[86] See Opinion of AG Wathelet in *Commission v. Poland*, paras 153-155, and Opinion of AG Szpunar in *Commission v. Belgium*, paras 97-100.

[87] See Case C-304/02, *Commission v. France*, paras 80-86 (*supra* note 14).

[88] Cf. Opinions of AG Tanchev in in *Commission v. Spain*, paras 76-78, in *Commission v. Romania*, paras 54-59, and in *Commission v. Ireland*, paras 55-57.

Member States to comply without delay with any measure provisionally issued by the Court pursuant to Article 279 TFEU.[89]

That said, it must be recognised that this decision too leaves a number of issues open. To begin with, what will the procedure look like, when a Member State does not comply with an order from the Court and the penalty payments become due? The order does clarify the respective roles of the Commission and defendant Member State in the resumed procedure However, one cannot fail to note that, in that context, the Court would have to carry out a substantive and final assessment of whether the Member State in question has failed to comply with the previous order. Such an assessment is typical of a main action brought under Article 260(2) TFEU. It is, conversely, a novelty in the context of a summary procedure where any determination by the Court is meant to be provisional and the analysis is limited to the establishment of a *prima facie* case.

The Court's accounting principles are also unclear: how did it arrive at the amount of the daily penalty payment of '*at least*' EUR 100 000? More importantly, had Poland not complied, what criteria could the Court have made use of to fix the specific amount of the penalty payments?[90] Interestingly (and regrettably), there was nothing on this point in the Commission's additional application. Furthermore, it is not a given that the principles laid down in the Commission's communications regarding Article 260(2) and (3) TFEU could, *mutatis mutandis*, be applied in this rather different context. Indeed, the logic followed by those communications, and the criteria and parameters used therein may, or may not, be easily transposable to a procedure under Article 279 TFEU. From a more practical angle, what if penalty payments are finally imposed, but the Commission's main action is subsequently dismissed: are the monies paid by the Member State concerned to be paid back (arguably, plus interest)? Logically, the answer should be negative: those monies were meant to induce compliance with an order that was, as a matter of fact, not complied with. Accordingly, their fate should not depend on the result of the main action. However, may that consequence be reconciled with the Court's statement according to which penalty payments should not 'be seen as a punishment'?

Finally, and crucially, it remains to be determined whether penalties under Article 279 TFEU will be granted only in circumstances as exceptional as those of the *Białowieża Forest* case.[91] Few would disagree that, quite apart from the particularly serious threat of environmental damage, the explicit refusal by Poland to

[89] For a more detailed analysis, see L. Prete, 'Can't see the Forest for the Trees? Penalties Under Article 279 TFEU', in Sarmiento et al (eds), *Yearbook on Procedural Law of the Court of Justice of the European Union: First Edition – 2019*, MPILux Research Paper 2020, 157-170.

[90] Cf. A. Łazowski, 'Editorial - Winter Is Coming. The Polish Woodworm Games' (2017) *European Papers* 801.

[91] Cf. P. Wennerås, 'Saving a forest and the rule of law: Commission v. Poland' (2019) *Common Market Law Review* 548-550 and 557.

abide by a previous order of the Court called for some drastic measure. Yet, now that the principle is acquired, could penalty payments also be ordered in more mundane situations?

In conclusion, the two recent decisions of the Court in *Commission v. Belgium* and *Commission v. Poland* should be warmly welcomed, notwithstanding the many issues that remain open under both Article 260(3) and Article 279 TFEU. These decisions enlarge and strengthen the arsenal at the disposal of the Commission to act before the Court against infringements of EU law committed by Member States' authorities. They also enable the Court, in some specific situations, to impose sanctions upon Member States in default more rapidly than under the standard infringement procedures. However, it is hardly necessary to point out that the simplification and acceleration of the sanctioning procedures is not an end in itself. The purpose is not to create a draconian system of enforcement to the benefit of the Union budget. As for any other regime of penalties, the underlying idea is, obviously, that the mere *threat* of sanctions should, ideally, induce recalcitrant Member States to act more quickly beforehand, in order to avoid proceedings altogether.

Chapter 6

FUNDAMENTAL RIGHTS AS CONSTRAINTS ON THE POWER OF THE EUROPEAN UNION TO IMPOSE SANCTIONS

Nicole Lazzerini *

ABSTRACT: *The chapter argues that, in the post-Lisbon era, the protection of fundamental rights is a major driving force for the evolution of the Union's power to impose sanctions. The dual role of fundamental rights as* constraints *on, and as* justification *for, the activity of the Union implies that their relationship with the power to adopt sanctions is* ordinarily antagonistic *and* occasionally synergic. *Whilst any sanctions imposed by the Union must comply with the fundamental rights granted by the EU Charter, the latter's enforcement can sometimes be assisted by sanctions.*

With a view to complement the analysis developed elsewhere in this Book, the chapter focuses on the role of fundamental rights as constraints on the Union's power to sanction. The analysis is divided into two main parts. First, having regard to the general provisions of the EU Charter, the scope of the Union's duty to respect fundamental rights will be outlined and the main structural implications on the power to sanction will be identified. Second, the specific substantive and procedural constraints that the EU Charter poses on the exercise of that power will be explored.

Rather than focus on specific fields or categories of sanctions, the chapter engages in a general mapping exercise of the fundamental rights that can act as general limits to the sanctioning power of the Union. Notably, the analysis considers three different expressions of the Union power to sanction, which are logically and chronologically connected: the shaping of sanctions, their actual imposition and, ultimately, the judicial review on them. Attention is paid to the protected scope of the relevant fundamental rights, including the possibility to impose restrictions on their enjoyment. The interactions with the system of protection established by the ECHR and the case-law of the Strasbourg Court are also considered.

A conclusive section summarizes the main findings and considerations stemming from the analysis developed.

KEYWORDS: *EU Charter of Fundamental Rights – ECHR – ECJ – constraints – sanctioning cycle – judicial review*

SUMMARY: 6.1. Introduction: the twofold relationship between fundamental rights and the power of the Union to impose sanctions. – 6.2. The duty of the Union to respect funda-

---

* Assistant Professor of EU Law, University of Florence.

mental rights and its implications on the power to sanction. – 6.3. Substantive and procedural fundamental rights constraints in the sanctioning cycle: a mapping exercise. – 6.3.1 "Shaping" sanctions. – 6.3.2 Proceedings that may lead to the imposition of sanctions and related investigatory activities. – 6.3.3 Judicial review of sanctions. – 6.4. Concluding remarks.

6.1. Introduction: the twofold relationship between fundamental rights and the power of the Union to impose sanctions

Fundamental rights have acquired a prominent role in the post-Lisbon EU legal order. The evolution of the direct power of the Union to sanction is not immune from this constitutional development.[1] A twofold relationship exists whereby the protection of fundamental rights acts *ordinarily* as a *constraint* on that power, and *occasionally* as a *justification* for its exercise. This reflects the dual role that fundamental rights play *vis-à-vis* the institutions and other bodies of the Union.[2]

As is well established, fundamental rights made their appearance in the legal order of the (then) European Economic Community ('EEC') with a 'negative' function, notably as *constraints* on the actions of the EEC institutions. Back in the 1970s, in the absence of explicit references in the Treaties, the European Court of Justice (or 'ECJ') affirmed that it had jurisdiction to ensure the observance of the fundamental rights 'enshrined in the general principles of Community law', which constituted both parameters for the interpretation of Community law provisions and grounds for the review of the acts adopted by the EEC institutions. The Lisbon Treaty has given new impetus to the negative function of fundamental rights. In addition to confirming the duty of the Union to respect fundamental rights guaranteed as general principles of EU law,[3] it has provided the written 'Bill of rights' of the Union, the EU Charter of Fundamental Rights (hereinafter 'Charter' or 'CFR'), with the same primary law status as the EU Treaties.[4] Describing the nature of the post-Lisbon Union, the ECJ has stated that 'at the heart of [the] legal structure [of the European Union] are the fundamental rights recognised by the Charter, respect for

---

[1] This chapter is concerned only with the *direct* power of the Union to impose sanctions; the adjective 'direct' will therefore be omitted in what follows.

[2] EU fundamental rights are binding also on the Member States 'only when they are implementing Union law': see Article 51(1) of the EU Charter of Fundamental Rights and the interpretation provided by the ECJ in Case C-617/10 (Grand Chamber), *Åklagaren* v. *Hans Åkerberg Fransson*, EU:C:2013:105, paras 21-22 (on which see, notably, D. Sarmiento, 'Who's afraid of the Charter? The Court of Justice, national courts and the new framework of fundamental rights protection in Europe' (2013) *Common Market Law Review* 50, 1267). The Charter therefore acts as a limit to the Member States when they adopt sanctions that are required by EU primary or secondary law. However, this topic goes outside the scope of this chapter.

[3] See Article 6(3) TEU. On this provision, see also infra, under section II.

[4] See Article 6(1) TEU.

those rights being a condition of the lawfulness of EU acts, so that measures incompatible with those rights are not acceptable in the EU'.[5]

The 'positive' function of fundamental rights, i.e. as a *justification* for the activity of the Union, is much less developed, given that the Treaties do not entrust the EU institutions with a general competence on protecting and promoting fundamental rights, i.e. a competence transcending the specific fields of action foreseen by the Treaties. This does not mean, however, that that function is absent. Within the powers conferred on them by the Treaties, the EU institutions must promote the respect of the fundamental rights granted by the Charter.[6] Moreover, over the years, specific objectives and powers related to the protection of fundamental rights – within the EU and in the relations with third States – have been gradually conferred on the Union.[7] In addition, since the Amsterdam Treaty, Article 7 TEU provides the political institutions of the Union (notably, the European Council and the Council) with certain mechanisms to react to situations in which a Member State is seriously endangering the Union's founding values, stated in Article 2 TEU to be: 'respect for human dignity, freedom, democracy, equality, the rule of law and respect for human rights, including the rights of persons belonging to minorities'. In this context, the Council can potentially adopt sanctions consisting of the suspension of certain membership rights.[8]

The positive and the negative functions of fundamental rights contribute to shaping (also) the scope, the objectives and the limits of the power of the Union to sanction. On the one hand, the EU institutions must always ensure that, when they adopt sanctions, the fundamental rights guaranteed by the Charter are respected. On the other hand, the lack of a general fundamental rights competence does not preclude that, in some instances, the relationship between the power of the Union to sanction and fundamental rights can be synergic, with the EU institutions relying on the former to assist the enforcement of the latter.

This second dynamic is well-consolidated in the external action of the Union,[9] which since the 1990s has adopted 'restrictive measures' – such as arms embargoes,

---

[5] Opinion 2/13 (Full Court), *Draft Accession Agreement of the EU to the ECHR*, EU:C:2014:2454, para. 169.

[6] See Article 51(1) of the Charter.

[7] See Article 3 TEU and G. De Burca. 'Fundamental Rights and Citizenship', in B. De Witte (ed.), *Ten Reflections on the Constitutional Treaty for Europe* (European University Institute, RSCAS/AEL, 2003). The Author maps the connections between the provisions of the Charter and the legal bases of the Constitutional Treaty, most of which can also be found in the TFEU.

[8] See Article 7(3) TEU and, within this Book, the chapter by M. Bonelli.

[9] One can note, in this respect, that the external fundamental rights competence of the Union appears to be broader than its internal counterpart: Article 3(5) TEU, on the objectives of EU external action, includes the contribution to 'the protection of human rights, in particular the rights of the child'; moreover, Article 21(2) TEU states that the Union 'shall work for a high degree of cooperation in all fields of international relations, in order to: (…) b) consolidate and support democracy, the rule of law, human rights and the principles of international law'.

restrictions on sales, asset freezing orders and visa or travel bans – targeting (formally) Third States and (in substance) non-state entities and individuals responsible for, inter alia, human rights violations, or which represent a threat thereof. [10] However, the rule of law backsliding trends that have emerged in recent years in some Member States have drawn attention to the intra-EU dimension of the 'positive' relationship between fundamental rights and sanctions. For the first time, the Commission and the European Parliament have formally proposed the activation of the 'preventive mechanism' delineated in paragraph 1 of Article 7 TEU, respectively against Poland in December 2017 and against Hungary in September 2018. [11] At the same time, the EU institutions, are exploring alternative routes to enforce Article 2 TEU, such as promoting an infringement procedure in relation to the violation of Treaty provisions that give expression to the Union's values, [12] or suspending certain payments – notably, in the context of structural funds – to Member States affected by generalized deficiencies as regards the rule of law. [13] The preliminary ruling has also emerged as an important instrument to challenge domestic legislation affecting the independence of judges. [14]

Importantly, however, the attention devoted to the potential of the infringement procedure as a means to uphold the founding values of the Union should not overshadow the role that this procedure – which may eventually lead to the imposition of penalties – [15] can play as regards 'ordinary' violations of the fundamental rights granted in the EU. Whilst the alleged violation of the Charter is not enough to trigger an infringement procedure, [16] the latter can be initiated against the Member

[10] See, within this Book, the chapter by C. Beaucillon.

[11] Disappointingly enough, at the time of writing this chapter, these procedures have not progressed further.

[12] At present, the Commission and the Court of Justice have focused on the combination between Articles 2 and 19(1) TEU: see, notably, Case C-192/18 (Grand Chamber), *Commission v. Poland (Indépendance des juridictions de droit commun)*, EU:C:2019:924, para. 98, and Case C-619/18 (Grand Chamber) *Commission v. Poland (Indépendance de la Cour supreme)*, EU:C:2018:910, para. 47. The combination between Articles 2 and 19(1) TEU was inaugurated in the preliminary ruling in Case C-64/16 (Grand Chamber) *Associação Sindical dos Juízes Portugueses*, EU:C:2018:117, para. 32 (on which see, notably, M. Bonelli, M. Claes, 'Judicial serendipity: How Portuguese judges came to the rescue of the Polish judiciary' (2018) *European Constitutional Law Review* 14, 622.

[13] See the proposal for a Regulation of the European Parliament and of the Council on the protection of the Union's budget in case of generalised deficiencies as regards the rule of law in the Member States, COM (2018) 324 final. The European Parliament adopted its position at first reading on 4 April 2019. The following procedural steps can be monitored at https://eur-lex.europa.eu/legal-content/EN/HIS/?uri=CELEX:52018PC0324.

[14] See, notably, Case C-585/18 (Grand Chamber), *A.K. (Indépendance de la chambre disciplinaire de la Cour suprême)*, EU:C:2019:982.

[15] See Article 260 TFEU and, within this Book, the chapter by L. Prete.

[16] This is a corollary of the fact that the Charter cannot extend the competences conferred on the Union by the Treaties: see Article 6(1) TEU and Article 51(2) CFR. That would be the case if

States' failure to (correctly) implement or apply Union measures that give specific expression to the fundamental rights protected by the Charter. [17]

Given that the mechanisms and procedures through which the Union's power to impose sanctions can assist the enforcement of fundamental rights are dealt with elsewhere in this Book, the focus of this chapter will be exclusively on the role of fundamental rights as constraints on that power. The analysis is divided into two main parts. First, moving from the system of fundamental rights protection that has resulted from the Lisbon Reform, the scope of the Union's duty to respect those rights will be outlined, having regard to its implications on the power to sanction (section II). Second, the specific substantive and procedural constraints that the Charter poses on the exercise of that power will be identified and discussed (section III). The key findings of the analysis will then be summarized (section IV).

6.2. The duty of the Union to respect fundamental rights and its implications on the power to sanction

The role of fundamental rights as constraints on the power of the Union to sanction is a corollary of the general duty to respect the fundamental rights guaranteed in the EU law order, by the Charter and as general principles, which binds any components of the institutional architecture of the Union, cutting across all the competences and powers foreseen in the Treaties. [18].

The Lisbon Treaty clarified the general scope of the Union's duty to respect general principles concerning fundamental rights. Article 6(2) of the pre-Lisbon TEU referred to the duty of the Union to respect fundamental rights 'as general principles of *Community law*'. [19] This provision could be read, alternatively, as a *limit* to the relevance of the fundamental rights identified by the Court of Justice only to Community law (the first-pillar of the post-Maastricht Union), [20] or, on the

---

the provisions of the Charter were invoked to challenge national provisions in situations that are not governed by other EU law provisions: see, for instance, Case C-466/11, *Currà and others*, EU:C:2012:465, para. 25.

[17] For some proposals to improve the potential of the infringement procedure in this respect, see O. De Schutter, *Infringement Proceedings as a Tool for the Enforcement of Fundamental Rights in the European Union*, study commissioned by the Open Society Foundation, October 2017, available online.

[18] In fact, that duty also binds the institutions (or other bodies) of the Union when they perform functions 'outside the framework of the European Union legal order': see infra, in this section.

[19] Emphasis added.

[20] See G. Gaja, 'The Protection of Human Rights Under the Maastricht Treaty', in D. Curtin and T. Heukels (eds), *Institutional Dynamics of European Integration: Essays in Honour of Henry G. Schermers* (Martinus Nijhoff, 1994), 559.

contrary, as the *confirmation* that the duty of the Union to respect those general principles also extends to the fields of the Common Foreign and Security Policy (CFSP) and Justice and Home Affairs (i.e. the second and third pillars of the post-Maastricht Union).[21] At the end of the 1990s, the issue became highly sensitive from the perspective of the power of the Union to impose sanctions, in light of the growing reliance on restrictive measures against natural or legal persons or other non-State entities, which are decided through CFSP acts. Shortly before the entry into force of the Lisbon Treaty, in the context of some preliminary rulings concerning the validity of such restrictive measures, the ECJ had the occasion to clarify that the Union was also bound by the general principles of Community law in its activities within the second and third pillars.[22] The Lisbon Treaty then formally abolished the pillar-structure and introduced a reference to fundamental rights as 'general principles of the *Union's law*'[23] in Article 6(3) of the current TEU.

However, the most important novelty introduced by the Lisbon Treaty has been the Charter being granted with 'the same legal value as the Treaties'. The catalogue of the fundamental rights guaranteed by the Charter draws significantly on the previous case law of the ECJ on the general principles, on the European Convention on Human Rights ('ECHR') and the related case law of the European Court of Human Rights ('ECtHR'), and on other international human rights treaties. This does not mean, however, that the Charter is a mere consolidation of the fundamental rights *acquis* previously developed by the ECJ through the general principles. A more accurate assessment is that the content of the Charter 'goes beyond the fundamental rights recognized so far by the Court of Justice, but falls short of what on the basis of the current criteria for fundamental rights protection in the EU potentially belongs to the *acquis communautaire*'.[24]

For sure, a more innovative part of the Charter is represented by its Title VII, headed 'General provisions governing the interpretation and application of the Charter'. This set of rules, which concern all the fundamental rights granted in Titles I to VI, does not constitute a mere codification of the previous case law of the ECJ.[25] The very idea of 'constraining', at least to some extent, the role of the ECJ as

---

[21] See the Opinion of AG Poiares Maduro in case C-160/03, *Spain v. Eurojust*, EU:C:2004:817, para. 32.

[22] See case C-354/04 P (Grand Chamber), *Gestoras Pro Amnistía and Others* v. *Council*, EU:C:2007:115, para. 51, and case C-355/04 P (Grand Chamber), *Segi and Others v. Council*, EU:C:2007:116, para. 51.

[23] Emphasis added.

[24] E. de Smijter, K. Lenaerts, 'A "Bill of Rights" for the European Union' (2001) *Common Market Law Review* 28, 280.

[25] The general provisions address questions such as the scope of application of the Charter (51 CFR), the regime of limitations (52(1) CFR), and their relationship with other sources of fundamental rights protection, notably the ECHR (52(3) CFR), the constitutional traditions common to

regards the interpretation of EU fundamental rights is unedited and unfolds from the Member States' fear that the Charter could become a powerful tool for the expansion of the Union's competences.[26] In this respect, it must be recalled that some important guidance on the interpretation of the Charter is also provided by a separate document, the so called 'Explanations'.[27] Whilst they have not been granted legally binding status, the Explanations must be given 'due regard' in the interpretation of the Charter.[28]

In addition to the significant overlap between the Charter and the general principles in terms of the fundamental rights granted, the Treaties do not establish any hierarchical relationship between the two sources, nor has the ECJ elaborated upon this issue. On several occasions, the ECJ has rather opted for a combined reference, ensuring the continuity between its pre-Lisbon case law on fundamental rights and the Charter. Nonetheless, it is important to stress that the Charter and the general principles, whilst much intertwined in substance, remain two formally distinct sets of rules, with some degree of autonomy between them. In this respect, at least two implications deserve attention for the purpose of this chapter.

Firstly, the Court may offer protection to a fundamental right which is not granted by the Charter through the general principles.[29] Secondly, so far the ECJ has not offered a clear answer as to whether (Member) States or their emanations[30] can invoke the protection of the Charter.[31] In an infringement procedure

---

the Member States (52(4) CFR), and national constitutions and international human rights treaties other than the ECHR (Article 53 CFR).

[26] Both Article 6(1) TEU and Article 51(2) CFR point out that the Charter cannot expand the competences or powers of the Union.

[27] Explanations relating to the Charter of Fundamental Rights, OJ (2007), C 303/17.

[28] See Article 6(1) TEU and Article 52(7) CFR.

[29] It must be observed that, in line with its predecessors, Article 6(3) TEU refers only to the general principles deriving from the European Convention on Human Rights ('ECHR') and from the constitutional traditions common to the Member States. By contrast, since its 1974 judgment in *Nold*, the ECJ has made a more general reference to 'the international treaties for the protection of human rights on which the Member States have collaborated or of which they are signatories'. In spite of the narrow formulation endorsed by the Treaty drafters, the ECJ has not stepped back from its initial position. Whilst the Charter contains *some* fundamental rights drawn from *some* human rights treaties other than the ECHR, there may still be space for an autonomous relevance of those (or future) treaties as sources of inspiration for new general principles. For a recent analysis of the use of human rights treaties other than the ECHR by the ECJ see A. Adinolfi, 'Qualche riflessione sulla rilevanza nell'ordinamento dell'Unione europea dei trattati sui diritti umani diversi dalla CEDU', in AA.VV., *Temi e questioni di diritto dell'Unione e europea. Scritti offerti a Claudia Morviducci* (Cacucci, 2019) 133.

[30] The ECJ has relied on the notion 'emanation of the State' in its case law on the effects of unimplemented, or badly implemented, EU directives (thus, with respect to Member States); reference is made to 'organisations or bodies which are subject to the authority or control of the State or which possess special powers beyond those which result from the normal rules applicable to

where Spain sought to rely on Article 41 CFR *vis-à-vis* the Commission, the Court observed that 'that right reflects a general principle of EU law' and, on this basis, expressly refrained from 'adopting a position as to whether a Member State may be regarded as or equated with a 'person' within the meaning of [Article 41 CFR], and can on that basis rely on the right that it lays down'.[32] It then added, referring to its previous case law, that 'the EU institutions are required to observe that general principles of law in the context of administrative procedures that are initiated against Member States and are liable to result in decisions adversely affecting them'.[33] What remains dubious, also with respect to the general principles, is whether States or their emanations can rely on fundamental rights other than those enshrining procedural safeguards, within the limits of the compatibility of those rights with their nature as legal entities.

The negative function of the Charter as a constraint on the Union's activities is clearly stated in Article 51(1) CFR. According to this provision, the Charter '[is] addressed to the institutions, bodies, offices and agencies of the Union (…) and to the Member States only when they are implementing Union law'. A clear difference is thus established between the scope of the Member States' duty to respect the Charter, which is limited to the situations in which they 'implement' Union law,[34] and the scope of the Union's duty, which is unqualified. Accordingly, the latter must be understood as extending to any articulation of the EU institutional framework, regardless of the formal label, and to any of the Union's actions, internal or external. In other words, that duty is inherent in the very fact of being an entity of the Union. An implicit confirmation of this has come from the *Ledra* judgment, where the ECJ stated that 'the Charter is addressed to the EU institutions, including (…) when they act outside the EU legal framework' in the performance of tasks at-

---

relations between individuals' (see Case C-413/15 *Elaine Farrell v. Alan Whitty and Others*, EU:C:2017:745, para. 33). According to the General Court, an emanation of a Third State is 'an entity which participated in the exercise of governmental powers or which ran a public service under governmental control' (see Case T-496/10, *Bank Mellat v. Council*, EU:T:2013:39, para. 42).

[31] By contrast, *private* legal entities can invoke the protection of the Charter (inasmuch as the fundamental right at issue is compatible with their nature). Some provisions make an express reference to legal entities; when the provision is silent, the issue of the personal scope is a matter of interpretation: see Case C-279/09 *DEB*, EU:C:2010:811, and, for a comment, P. Oliver, 'Case C-279/09, DEB v. Germany, Judgment of the Court of Justice (Second Chamber) of 22 December 2010' (2011) *Common Market Law Review* 48, 2023.

[32] Case C-521/15 (Grand Chamber), *Spain v. Council*, EU:C:2017:982, paras 88-89.

[33] *Ibidem*, para. 90. The Court referred to its judgments in Case C-501/10, *Spain v. Commission*, EU:C:2004:438, para. 52, and in the Joined Cases C-549/12 P and C-54/13 P, *Germany v. Commission*, para. 89. For a comment also touching on the issue addressed here, see M. Chamon, 'Fining Member States under the SGP, or how enforcement is different from implementation under Article 291 TFEU: *Spain* v. *Council*' (2018) *Common Market Law Review* 55, 1495.

[34] On the meaning of this notion see fn. 6 *supra*.

tributed on them by the Member States.[35] No doubts can therefore exist about the relevance of the Charter *vis-à-vis* the Union in the exercise of the powers conferred by the Treaties.

This conclusion is not challenged by the fact that some EU acts fall outside (at least *prima facie*) the jurisdiction of the ECJ. This is the case of CFSP provisions and measures, which are altogether excluded from the jurisdiction of the ECJ, with very limited exceptions.[36] This situation may be problematic from the point of view of the judicial protection of natural and legal persons. For sure, it can hardly be reconciled with the founding value of the rule of law, which, as the ECJ has been repeating since its 1986 judgment in *Les Verts*, requires that the acts of the EU institutions can be the subject of a review of their conformity with 'the basic constitutional charter, the Treaty'.[37] Nonetheless, the duty of the Union to respect the Charter when acting within the CFSP remains unaltered, and the question arises as to whether, and possibly to what extent, the Charter – notably, Article 47 on the right to an effective judicial remedy – can help in filling some of the existing gaps in judicial protection.[38] A similar situation exists, as we shall see,[39] with respect to the measures – which could possibly include sanctions – that the European Council and the Council may adopt, pursuant to Article 7 TEU, *vis-à-vis* a Member State that is (potentially) acting in violation of the Union's founding values.

Finally, it is worth recalling that, even if the Union, unlike its Member States, is not (yet) formally bound by the ECHR,[40] the Lisbon Treaty has elevated the protection granted by the ECHR to a minimum standard in the context of the Charter. Article 52(3) CFR prescribes that 'the meaning and scope' of the provisions of the Charter that affirm fundamental rights already guaranteed by the ECHR '*shall* be

---

[35] Case C-8/15 (Grand Chamber), *Ledra Advertising v. Commission and ECB*, EU:C:2016:701, para. 67. From the case law of the Court, it follows that 'the Member States are entitled, in areas which do not fall under the exclusive competence of the Union, to entrust tasks to the institutions, outside the framework of the Union, (…) provided that those tasks do not alter the essential character of the powers conferred on those institutions by the EU and FEU Treaties': see Case C-370/12 (Full Court), *Thomas Pringle v. Government of Ireland and Others*, EU:C:2012:756, para. 158.

[36] See Article 24(1) TEU and Article 275(2) TFEU. One exception concerns the 'review of the legality' of decisions providing for restrictive measures against natural or legal persons adopted by the Council within the CFSP, which was introduced by the Lisbon Treaty: on this, see infra, under section III, c).

[37] Case C-294/83, *Les Verts v. Parliament*, EU:C:1986:166, para. 23.

[38] See section III below, under point iii).

[39] *Ibidem.*

[40] As is well known, the Lisbon Treaty has introduced an *ad hoc* legal basis (in Article 6(2) TEU) for the accession of the EU to the ECHR. However, the accession process is frozen in limbo since the ECJ delivered its negative opinion on the Draft Accession Agreement of 2013 (see *supra* fn. 5).

the same as those laid down by the said Convention', without excluding the possibility that a 'more extensive protection' is provided by Union law. According to the Explanations, the case law of the ECtHR shall be considered when reconstructing the meaning, the scope and the regime of limitations of the abovementioned Charter provisions. As will be seen, the 'bridge' between the Charter and the ECHR built by Article 52(3) CFR has some important implications on the limits that fundamental rights pose on the power of the Union to impose sanctions.

6.3. Substantive and procedural fundamental rights constraints in the sanctioning cycle: a mapping exercise

At present, the role of fundamental rights as constraints on the Union's power to sanction mostly emerges, unsurprisingly, from the case law of the ECJ concerning sanctions for breaches of competition law, or restrictive measures adopted within the CFSP. However, rather than focus on specific fields or categories of sanctions, this chapter engages in a general mapping exercise of the fundamental rights that can act as general limits to the sanctioning power of the Union. In doing so, the Charter will be regarded as the main reference framework.[41] Moreover, the analysis considers three different expressions of the Union power to sanction, which are, however, logically and chronologically connected: the "shaping" of sanctions, their actual imposition and, ultimately, the judicial review on them. Attention is paid to the protected scope of the relevant fundamental rights, including the possibility to impose restrictions on their enjoyment.

6.3.1. "Shaping" sanctions

The Charter acts as a constraint at the time when the EU institutions pre-determine the main features of a sanction, such as the addresses, the conditions of application, the content or amount, and the limits thereto.

In this respect, some important requirements flow from the principles of legality and proportionality of criminal offences and penalties, which constitute general principles of Union law and are now affirmed in Article 49 CFR.[42] Whilst the powers of the Union in the field of criminal law are still rather limited, the abovementioned principles also apply to administrative sanctions that can be regarded as 'criminal' on the basis of substantive criteria, such as, for instance, some restrictive measures addressed to natural or legal persons in the fight against terrorism.

[41] For a similar analysis, mostly from the point of view of limits to EU law-related *national* sanctions, see P. De Hert, 'EU criminal law and fundamental rights', in V. Mitsilegas, M. Bergström, and T. Konstadinides (eds), *Research Handbook on EU Criminal Law* (Edwar Elgar Publishing, 2016) 105.

[42] On proportionality, see the chapter by S. Montaldo within this Book.

Article 49 CFR has codified the long-established rules of the non-retroactivity of criminal offences and criminal penalties (*nullum crimen sine lege*, *nulla poena sine lege*); in this respect, the provision corresponds with Article 7 ECHR, so that the rule of parallel interpretation established in Article 52(3) CFR applies. Drawing on the case law of the ECtHR, the ECJ has stated that Article 49 CFR encompasses the principle of *nulla poena sine lege certa*, which is 'a specific expression of the general principle of legal certainty [implying] inter alia, that legislation must clearly define the offences and the penalties which they attract'; this requirement is met 'where the individual concerned is in a position, on the basis of the wording of the relevant provision and, if necessary, with the help of the interpretation made by the courts, to know which acts or omissions will make him criminally liable'.[43] However, the principle of *nulla poena sine lege certa* does not preclude 'the gradual clarification of rules of criminal liability by means of interpretations in the case-law', provided that the following clarifications are 'reasonably foreseeable'.[44]

In line with the previous case law of the ECJ on the general principles of EU law, Article 49 CFR also enshrines the rule of the retroactivity of a more lenient criminal law, which is not expressly stated in Article 7 ECHR.[45] In this respect, the protection provided by Union law is already more extensive than that granted by the (text of the) ECHR, which cannot be used to develop a parallel interpretation. Interestingly, the reverse process has occurred: the Strasbourg Court has interpreted Article 7 ECHR as encompassing also the guarantee of the retrospective application of a law providing for a more lenient penalty, supporting its reasoning also through an explicit reference to the formulation of Article 49 CFR.[46]

Furthermore, different fundamental rights enshrined in the Charter may be relevant depending on the measure at issue. For instance, freezing orders or travel bans are likely to impinge on, *inter alia*, the right to respect for private and family life, the freedom to conduct a business, and the right to property, which are guaranteed, respectively, by Articles 7, 16, and 17 CFR. Whilst these fundamental rights are not un-

---

[43] Case C-72/15 (Grand Chamber), *Rosneft*, EU:C:2017:236, para. 162. The Court referred to the leading case concerning the general principle of the legality of criminal offences and penalties (*nullum crimen, nulla poena sine lege*), notably Case C-303/05 (Grand Chamber), *Advocaten voor de Wereld*, EU:C:2007:261, paras 49-50.

[44] *Rosneft*, para. 167.

[45] See the explanation of Article 49 CFR and the Court's judgment in Joined Cases C-387/02, C-391/02 and C-403/02 (Grand Chamber), *Berlusconi and Others*, EU:C:2005:270, para. 68.

[46] See the ECtHR's judgment in *Scoppola v. Italy* (No 2), application no. 10249/03, para. 105. The Strasbourg Court found that the contrary position initially endorsed by the ECHR Commission should be overcome in light of important developments occurring under international and EU law, observing, inter alia, that 'the wording of Article 49 of the Charter differs – and this can only be deliberate – from Article 7 [ECHR]'.

fettered prerogatives,[47] restrictions to their exercise must comply with the requirements laid down by Article 52(1) CFR: they must have a legal basis and prove necessary to pursue objectives of general interest recognised by the Union, or to protect competing rights or freedoms, without impinging on the essence of the right(s) at issue or constituting a disproportionate interference with it (or them).

According to the General Court, freezing orders and travel bans, given their temporary and precautionary nature, do not deprive their addressees of the rights to property or respect for private and family life, whereas objectives such as the fight against the threats to international peace and security posed by acts of terrorism and protection of civilian populations are 'fundamental to the international community'.[48] Moreover, in the Court's view, a system of prior authorisation or the obligation to justify *ex post* how the funds were used would not be equally effective to achieve the goals pursued.[49]

However, the abovementioned considerations concern (only) the *abstract* compatibility of the measures at issue with the requirements stated in Article 52(1) CFR. It is essential that the EU act allows sufficient space to ensure that the actual imposition of sanctions does not result into a disproportionate interference with fundamental rights. For instance, the ECJ has stressed the importance of including derogations from the freezing of assets for medical and humanitarian purposes or for access to legal services.[50] When they process a request for a derogation, national authorities responsible for the execution of EU restrictive measures do not enjoy an absolute discretion; rather, they must act in compliance with the fundamental rights granted in the Charter. The Court found that those national authorities cannot rely on the potential for legal aid to be available as a valid reason for rejecting a request for the release of some frozen funds, which the person concerned wished to use to pay for a lawyer of their choosing when seeking to bring an annulment action against the freezing order before the General Court. This would be contrary to Article 47(2) CFR, which states that '[e]veryone shall have the possibility of being advised, defended and represented'; access to legal aid is a different entitlement, dealt with in Article 47(3) CFR, which concerns 'those who lack sufficient resources'.

Furthermore, the principle of equality, now also affirmed by Article 20 of the Charter, acts as a limit to the exercise of the Union exercising its power to sanction. It requires that comparable situations must not be treated differently, and, in turn, different situations must not be treated in the same way unless there is an objective justification. An application can be found in competition cases, where the ECJ has

---

[47] See, for instance, Joined Cases C-402/05 P and C-415/05 P *Kadi and Al Barakaat International Foundation v. Council and Commission*, paras 359-366; Case C-348/12 P, *Council v. Manufacturing Support & Procurement Kala Naft*, EU:C:2013:776, para. 121.

[48] Case T-383/11, *Makhlouf*, EU:T:2013:431, paras 99-100.

[49] *Ibidem*, para. 101.

[50] Case C-314/2014, *Peftiev and Others*, EU:C:2014:1645, paras 24 to 26 and 29.

often stated that the amount of fines must take into account the differences between the undertakings that have participated in an agreement or concerted practice contrary to Article 101(1) TFEU.[51] However, the principle of equality is a general limit, which applies regardless of the field concerned.

6.3.2. Proceedings that may lead to the imposition of sanctions and related investigatory activities

Several fundamental rights granted in the Charter act as constraints in the context of proceedings instituted by the Union, which may lead to the imposition of sanctions. Notably, this is the case of some guarantees relating to the 'right to good administration' under Article 41 CFR, which every person is entitled to in their relationship with the Union.

According to Article 41(1), 'every person has the right to have his or her affairs handled impartially, fairly and within a reasonable time by the institutions and bodies of the European Union'. Even though the term 'right' is used in the singular, the requirements of impartiality, fairness and reasonable time-limit for taking decisions have some degree of autonomy from one other, so that they can provide distinct parameters by which to assess the lawfulness of the Union's action which is at issue.[52] Moreover, Article 41(2) outlines three additional subjective guarantees which the right stated in the previous paragraph 'includes', namely: the right of every person to be heard before any individual measure which would affect him or her adversely is taken; the right of every person to have access to his or her file; and the obligation on the part of the administration to give reasons for its decisions. The expression 'includes' clearly indicates that Articles 41(2) reflects only some components of the right under Article 41(1), which remain open to interpretation by the ECJ.[53] The EU legislature can also contribute to shaping the content of the right in specific areas. However, the rights stated in Article 41, or grounded on it by the Court, must be observed regardless of whether the relevant legislation makes express provision for them.[54]

Of course, the rights encompassed by Article 41 do not constitute unfettered

---

[51] See, for instance, Case C-604/13 P, *Aloys F. Dornbracht v. Commission*, EU:C:2017:45, paras 78-79.

[52] Cf. Articles 11 and 17 of the European Ombudsman's European Code of Good Administrative Behaviour. As regards impartiality, the ECJ has made clear that it has two distinct dimensions, subjective and objective: see, for instance, Case C-680/16, *August Wolff and Remedia v. Commission*, EU:C:2019:257, paras 24-28.

[53] The European Ombudsman's European Code of Good Administrative Behaviour could provide inspiration for an expansive interpretation: see P. Craig, 'Article 41', in S. Peers, T. Hervey, J, Kenner, A. Ward (eds), *The EU Charter of Fundamental Rights: A Commentary* (Hart, 2014), 1072.

[54] See, for instance, Case C-383/13 PPU, *G. and R.*, EU:C:2013:533, para 32.

prerogatives. Echoing the case law of the Court in competition cases,[55] Article 41(2) expressly refers to 'the respect for the legitimate interests of confidentiality and of professional and business secrecy' as a limit to the right of access to the file. Beyond this specific provision, the general rule laid down by Article 52(1) CFR applies.[56] For instance, the ECJ has acknowledged that the effectiveness of restrictive measures such as the freezing of funds would be jeopardised if the addressee had to be informed in advance, so that, as an exception to Article 41(2) CFR 'it is as a rule enough if the institution notifies the person or entity concerned of the grounds and affords it the right to be heard at the same time as, or immediately after, the decision is adopted'.[57] Moreover, concerns related to 'overriding considerations connected with State security' may justify the decision not to disclose, in the context of an administrative (or judicial) proceedings, some information to the person concerned.[58] However, for this limitation to be legitimate, Member States must ensure effective judicial review over the secrecy claim and put in place mechanisms enabling the court in charge of the decision to strike a balance between security needs and due process guarantees.[59] One can infer that the addressee of a sanction should always know at least the essence of the case against him or her.

Based on the wording of Article 41, the right to good administration is granted only *vis-à-vis* the EU institutions, bodies, offices and agencies. This is an exception to the general provision in Article 51(1) CFR, whereby the Charter is binding also on the Member States 'when they are implementing Union law' (i.e., when they act within the scope of EU law).[60] It follows that national administrative proceedings concerning the application of EU law fall outside the scope of Article 41, and the same applies to the national element in composite administrative procedures where both Union institutions (or other bodies) and Member States' authorities are involved. However, according to the ECJ, Article 41 'reflects a general principle of EU law', which, as such, is also binding in the context of national administrative procedures located within the scope of Union law.[61] One can note that this double-track solution works if the protected scope of the general principle concerning the

[55] See Joined Cases C-204/00 P, C-205/00 P, C-211/00 P, C-213/00 P, C-217/00 and C-219/00 P, *Aalborg Portland and Others* v. *Commission*, EU:C:2004:6, para. 64.

[56] Similarly, with respect to the right to good administration as a general principle, *see* Case C-383/13 PPU, para. 33.

[57] See, for instance, Case C-27/09 P, *France v. People's Mojahedin Organization of Iran*, EU:C:2011:853, paras 61 and 72.

[58] See Case C-300/11, *ZZ*, EU:C:2013:363, para. 54. In the context of judicial proceedings (this was the case in ZZ), the reference provision in the Charter is Article 47 on the right to an effective remedy and a fair trial, on which see section III.3 *infra*.

[59] *Ibidem*, para. 58.

[60] See *supra* note 2.

[61] See, *ex multis*, Case C-230/18, *PI*, EU:C:2019:383, paras 56-57.

right to good administration is the same as Article 41. At the same time, the status of the right as a general principle implies that 'the EU institutions are required to observe [it] in the context of administrative procedures that are initiated against Member States and are liable to result in decisions adversely affecting them',[62] such as an infringement procedure or a procedure under Article 7 TEU.

Some additional constraints derive from Article 48(2) CFR on the rights of defence. The ECJ has indeed clarified that '[in] all proceedings in which sanctions, especially fines or penalty payments, may be imposed observance of the rights of the defence is a fundamental principle of European Union law'.[63]

A provision that deserves attention is Article 50 CFR on the *ne bis in idem* principle, which prohibits the duplication of 'criminal' proceedings 'within the Union'. The latter expression implies that – speaking in the abstract – the scope of the prohibition encompasses different scenarios, which include the duplication of 'criminal' proceedings instituted by one or more Union institutions, or by an EU institution and a Member State or a third State.[64] As regards the 'criminal' character of the proceedings, according to a well-settled interpretative approach of the ECJ, which draws on the Strasbourg case law, the scope of the *ne bis in idem* rule extends to proceedings that, though being classified as administrative, are 'criminal' by virtue of their nature and the degree of severity of the penalty that the person is liable to incur.[65] This interpretation triggers the relevance of the *ne bis in idem* in relation to Union sanctions, for instance in the field of competition law.[66]

It is worth noting that the abovementioned cumulation does not necessarily infringe Article 50 CFR, which tolerates limitations that are justified on the basis of Article 52(1) CFR.[67] Interestingly, the ECJ has not adhered to the case law of the Strasbourg Court whereby a duplication of administrative and criminal proceedings and penalties does not infringe the *ne bis in idem* principle where proceedings at issue 'have a sufficiently close connection in substance and time'.[68] Proportionality is the main thread of the ECJ's reasoning. First, it has observed that 'a duplication of criminal proceedings and penalties may be justified where those proceedings and penalties pursue (…) complementary aims relating (…) to different aspects of the

---

[62] *Commission* v. *Spain*, cit., paras 89-90.

[63] Case C-550/07 P, *Akzo Nobel Chemicals Ltd and Akcros Chemicals Ltd v. European Commission*, EU:C:2010:512, para. 92. This corresponds with the court's long-established case law: see Case C-85/76, *Hoffmann-La Roche v. Commission*, EU:C:1979:36, para. 9.

[64] See J. Tomkin, 'Article 51', in *The EU Charter of Fundamental Rights: A Commentary*, 1374.

[65] See ECtHR, *Engel and Others v. the Netherlands,* application no. 5100/71; 5101/71; 5102/71; 5354/72; 5370/72, paras 80 to 82, and Case C-489/10, *Bonda*, EU:C:2012:319, para. 37.

[66] On the qualification of sanctions in competition cases, see, within this Book, the chapter by L. Calzolari.

[67] Case C-129/14 PPU (Grand Chamber), *Spasic*, EU:C:2014:586, paras 55 and 56

[68] ECtHR, 15 November 2016, *A and B* v. *Norway*, para. 132.

same unlawful conduct'.[69] That said, however, the Court has relied not only on the proportionality test required by Article 52(1) CFR, but also to the *ad hoc* principle of proportionality of penalties, now affirmed by Article 49(3) CFR, in order to circumscribe the possibility of duplication. The legislation which allows it 'must provide for the obligation for the competent authorities, in the event of the imposition of a second penalty, to ensure that the severity of all of the penalties imposed correspond with the seriousness of the offence concerned'.[70]

Finally, Article 7 CFR on the respect for private and family life circumscribes the power of Union institutions (or bodies) to carry out investigatory activities aimed at ascertaining, for instance, breaches of EU competition rules or conducts incompatible with the financial interest of the Union, which may be preliminary to the imposition of sanctions. Activities such as searches of a person's premises, interceptions of communications or the seizure of documents or e-mails constitute restrictions on the fundamental right guaranteed in Article 7 CFR, which encompasses the protection of the private and family life, home and communications.[71] The lawfulness of these activities depends on whether the requirements in Article 52(1) CFR have been satisfied. Given that Article 7 CFR corresponds to Article 8 ECHR, the rule of parallel interpretation provided by Article 52(3) CFR must be observed (unless a more extensive protection is granted under Union law). Adhering to that rule, the Court of Justice has recognised that the protection afforded by Article 8 ECHR may encompass certain professional and commercial premises and activities, but the interference by a public authority could be more intrusive than in other cases.[72] For instance, the ECJ has stated that a post-inspection judicial review covering both questions of fact and questions of law, such as that which Regulation 1/2003 entrusts on Union courts, may counterbalance the absence of prior judicial authorisation. In another competition case, the Court pointed out that the undertaking concerned could not rely on Article 7 CFR 'to complain of a loss of reputation which is the foreseeable consequence of his own actions'; the violation alleged stemmed from the disclosure of information directly relevant to the infringement contested and to the undertaking's participation in it.[73]

6.3.3 Judicial review of sanctions

As stated by the ECJ, the EU 'is a union based on the rule of law in which the acts of its institutions are subject to review of their compatibility with (…) the Treaties, the

---

[69] Case C-524/15, *Menci*, EU:C:2018:197, para. 44.

[70] *Ibidem*, para. 55. As regards the role of proportionality in *Menci*, see, within this Book, the chapter by S. Montaldo.

[71] Case C-419/14, *WebMindLicenses*, EU:C:2015:832.

[72] Case C-583/13 P, *Deutsche Bahn and Others* v. *Commission*, EU:C:2015:404, para. 20.

[73] Curia C-162/15 P, *Evonik Degussa* v. *Commission*, EU:C:2017:205, paras 117-118.

general principles of law and fundamental rights'.[74] At the same time, Article 47 CFR grants to 'everyone whose rights and freedoms guaranteed by the law of the Union are violated' the fundamental right to an effective judicial remedy and to a fair trial. This brings up the question of the role of Article 47 CFR in the EU judicial system. Focusing on EU acts that impose sanctions, Article 47 CFR sets the minimum standard for the effective judicial review of those acts; in addition, it can be relied upon to test some limits to the jurisdiction of the EU Courts as foreseen by the Treaties.

As regards the first function, three aspects of Article 47 CFR are worthy of attention. First, as with Article 41 CFR, this provision enshrines a set of guarantees, concerning: the right to an effective remedy before a court, fair trial rights, and access to legal aid for those who lack sufficient resources. Second, as the Explanations point out,[75] Article 47 CFR reflects, at least in part, the content of Articles 6(1) and 13 ECHR (or the Strasbourg case law on legal aid). Article 52(3) CFR therefore applies. Thus, Article 47 CFR substantially incorporates into the EU legal order the protection offered by those ECHR provisions, which constitutes a *minimum* standard. However (and third), Article 47 CFR is framed in broader terms than Articles 6(1) and 13 ECHR, at least in two main respects: the remedy must be granted before a 'court' (whereas Article 13 ECHR refers to 'a national authority'), and the protection guaranteed is not limited to civil and criminal proceedings (in contrast to Article 6(1) ECHR). The scope of Article 47 CFR rather covers all situations in which someone's 'rights and freedoms guaranteed by the law of the Union are violated'. Interestingly, the case law of the ECJ suggests that this condition is automatically met when a dispute concerns a matter regulated by EU law.[76] It is submitted that a proper reading of the two interpretative rules provided by Article 52(3) CFR requires that the ECHR standard must be regarded as setting a minimum level of protection also in relation to the parts of Article 47 CFR that do not merely reflect Article 6(1) or Article 13 ECHR.

The ECJ has confirmed the compatibility with Article 47 CFR of the control that EU Courts can perform on the decisions of the Commission imposing fines for competition infringements (which consists of a combination of the review of legality of the

---

[74] Case C-538/11 P (Grand Chamber), *Inuit Tapiriit Kanatami and Others v. Parliament and Council*, EU:C:2013:625, para 91.

[75] See the explanations relating to Articles 47 and 52(3) CFR.

[76] D. Shelton, 'Article 47', in *The EU Charter of Fundamental Rights: A Commentary*, cit., 1211. The Author argues that 'Article 47 has the same scope as Article 51 of the Charter'. This interpretation is coherent with Article 19(1) TEU, which requires the Member States to 'provide remedies sufficient to ensure effective legal protection in the fields covered by Union law'. It must be noted, however, that in the most recent case law of the ECJ a process of decoupling is emerging between the scope of application of the Charter and the (broader)scope of the Member State's duty under Article 19(1) TEU: see Case C-619/18 (Grand Chamber), *Commission v. Poland (Indépendance de la Cour suprême)*, EU:C:2019:531, para. 50, and Case C-64/16 (Grand Chamber), *Associação Sindical dos Juízes Portugueses*, EU:C:2018:117, para. 29.

decision under Article 263 TFEU and the unlimited jurisdiction to review the fine imposed).[77] In doing this, the Court has taken the opportunity to substantiate that control, stressing that 'whilst, in areas giving rise to complex economic assessments, the Commission has a margin of discretion (...), that does not mean that the [EU Courts] must refrain from reviewing the Commission's interpretation of information of an economic nature. Not only must those Courts establish, among other things, whether the evidence relied on is factually accurate, reliable and consistent but also whether that evidence contains all the information which must be taken into account in order to assess a complex situation and whether it is capable of substantiating the conclusions drawn from it'.[78]

In the field of the CFSP, the ECJ has relied on Article 47 CFR to shape the standard of judicial review that, after the Lisbon Treaty, EU Courts can exercise over decisions of the Council providing for restrictive measures against natural or legal persons, in accordance with Articles 24(1) TEU and 275(2) TFEU.

It derives from the Court's case law that a person or entity included in a black list has *locus standi* to challenge its inclusion in that list, which is tantamount to an act of direct and individual concern to that person within the meaning of Article 263(4) TFEU.[79] The applicant must be able to know the reasons on which the decision is based, possibly by requesting their disclosure.[80] However, it is the task of the EU institution concerned to demonstrate that the decision challenged was grounded on a sufficiently solid factual basis.[81] Whilst there is no duty to produce all the information relating to the reasons allegedly substantiating the decision, the EU Courts must disregard any reasons which are not supported by sufficient evidence and must establish the probative value of the information provided, taking into ac-

---

[77] See Council Regulation (EC) No 1/2003 of 16 December 2002 on the implementation of the rules on competition laid down in Articles 81 and 82 of the Treaty, OJ 2003, L 1/1. Article 31 entrusts the Court of Justice 'with unlimited jurisdiction to review decisions whereby the Commission has fixed a fine or periodic penalty payment. It may cancel, reduce or increase the fine or periodic penalty payment imposed'. See also Article 261 TFEU.

[78] See, inter alia, Case C-272/09 P, *KME Germany and Others v. Commission*, EU:C:2011:810, para. 94. Questioning the impact on the standard of judicial review applied in previous cases, see R. Nazzini, 'Judicial Review after *KME*: An Even Stronger Case for the Reform That Will Never Be' (2015) *European Law Review* 490. See also C-199/11 (Grand Chamber), *Otis and Others*, EU:C:2012:684, in which the Court found that the possibility for the Commission to act as a plaintiff in an action for damages for the loss caused to the European Union by a cartel is not incompatible per se with the principle of equality of arms. For a comment, see A. Andreangeli, 'Private but can it do so? Comments on *Otis*' (2014) *European Law Review* 717.

[79] See, *inter alia*, Case C-348/12 P, *Council* v. *Manufacturing Support & Procurement Kala Naft*, EU:C:2013:776, para. 50.

[80] Case C-584/10 P (Grand Chamber), *Commission and Others v. Kadi* (*Kadi II*), EU:C:2013:518, para. 100.

[81] *Ibidem*, para. 119.

count the observations submitted by the person concerned.[82] Furthermore, the ECJ has found that, after the removal of their name from the list, the person retains a legal interest in seeking the annulment of the Council decision under Article 263 TFEU, as a finding of the illegality of the act may constitute 'a form of reparation for the non-material harm which [she] has suffered by reason of that illegality'.[83]

The second function of Article 47 CFR concerns, as anticipated, its capacity to test the limits on the jurisdiction of the EU Courts as foreseen by the Treaties. According to the ECJ's mantra, the Treaties provide for 'a complete system of legal remedies and procedures designed to ensure judicial review of the legality of European Union acts'.[84] Now, whilst it is undisputed that the Lisbon Treaty introduced some important novelties as regards the judicial protection of natural and legal entities *vis-à-vis* EU acts, there are still some gaps, also with respect to the judicial review of EU sanctions. The case law of the Court is clear in the sense that Article 47 CFR cannot be used 'to change the system of judicial review laid down by the Treaties', and particularly to neutralize the *locus standi* conditions of direct actions under Article 263 TFEU,[85] or to confer jurisdiction on the EU Courts where the Treaties exclude it.[86] At the same time, Article 47 CFR – more precisely, the underlying principle of 'effective judicial review [which] is of the essence of the rule of law', a founding value of the Union – implies that any limits to the jurisdiction of the EU Courts must be interpreted strictly.[87]

So far this function of Article 47 is most evident in the field of the CFSP, where the jurisdiction of EU Courts is excluded entirely, with only some limited exceptions. One of these concerns, as anticipated, the 'review of legality' by Union courts of Council decisions providing for restrictive measures against natural or legal persons. Given that Article 275(2) TFEU refers to 'proceedings (…) brought in accordance with the conditions laid down in [Article 263(4) TFEU]', one could have argued that the only way to challenge the abovementioned measures is through an annulment action. Remarkably, the ECJ has also affirmed its jurisdiction to perform the 'review of legality' in the context of a preliminary ruling concerning the validity of the decisions at issue. In reaching this conclusion, the Court observed, inter alia, that 'it would be contrary to (…) the principle of effective judicial protection to adopt a strict interpretation of the jurisdiction conferred on the Court by [Article 275(2) TFEU], to which reference is made by Article 24(1) TEU'.[88]

---

[82] *Ibidem*, paras 120 to 124.

[83] Case C-239/12 P (Grand Chamber), *Abdulrahim v. Council and Commission*, EU:C:2013:331, para. 72.

[84] The ECJ has reiterated this expression on numerous occasions since its seminal judgment in Case 294/83, *Les Verts v. Parliament*, EU:C:1986:166, para. 23.

[85] *Inuit Tapiriit Kanatami*, cit., paras 97-98.

[86] *Rosneft*, cit., para. 74.

[87] *Ibidem*, paras 73-74.

[88] *Ibidem*, para. 75. For a comment, see S. Poli, 'The Common Foreign Security Policy after

The Court may follow a similar approach to affirm its jurisdiction to review, in the context of proceedings instituted by natural or legal persons, the sanctions that the Council is empowered to adopt under Article 7(3) TEU.

According to this provision, following a unanimous 'determination' by the European Council about the existence of a serious and persistent breach by a Member State of the EU values stated in Article 2 TEU, the Council, acting by a qualified majority, 'may decide to suspend certain of the rights deriving from the application of the Treaties to the Member State in question'. Reference is made to the suspension of the voting rights of the representative of the government of the Member State concerned in the Council. However, this is only an example. The formulation of Article 7(3) TEU suggests that *any* rights deriving from the State's membership of the Union may be suspended, though not *all* those rights. Moreover, it is stated that 'the Council shall take into account the possible consequences of such a suspension on the rights and obligations of natural and legal persons'. In other words, Article 7(3) TEU acknowledges that the sanctions at issue, though being addressed to a Member State, may have an adverse impact on the legal sphere of natural and legal persons, including, possibly, their fundamental rights granted by the Charter.

Now, Article 269 TFEU states that 'the Court of Justice shall have jurisdiction to decide on the legality of an act adopted by the European Council or by the Council pursuant to Article 7 [TEU] solely at the request of the Member State concerned by a determination of the European Council or of the Council and in respect solely of the procedural stipulations contained in that Article'. There seems to be space to argue that this limit concerns only the acts qualified as 'determinations' under Article 7 TEU, which do not encompass the decisions of the Council to suspend some membership rights. The latter would fall outside the scope of Article 269 TFEU so that the 'ordinary' jurisdiction of EU courts would extend to them.[89] A reasoning similar to that developed in the context of the CFSP would assist this conclusion. One would be tempted to say 'time will tell', yet in this case it seems better to hope that the issue remains a matter for academic speculation.

Rosneft: Still imperfect but gradually subject to the rule of law' (2017) *Common Market Law Review* 54, 1799. The same approach was endorsed by the Court in relation to other aspects of its limited jurisdiction in the field of the CFSP: see, notably, Case C-658/11 (Grand Chamber), *Parliament v. Council*, EU:C:2014:2025, para. 70, Case C-439/13 P, *Elitaliana v. Eulex Kosovo*, EU:C:2015:753, para. 42, and Case C-455/14 P (Grand Chamber), *H v. Council and Commission*, EU:C:2016:569, para. 40. For a comprehensive appraisal, see M. Cremona, '«Effective judicial review is of the essence of the rule of law»: Challenging Common Foreign and Security Policy measures before the Court of Justice' (2017) 2 *European Papers* 671.

[89] See B. Nascimbene, 'La violation grave des obligations découlant du Traité UE. Les limites de l'application de l'art. 7', in *Liber Amicorum Antonio Tizzano. De la Cour CECA à la Cour de l'Union: le long parcours de la justice européenne* (Giappichelli, 2018), 679.

6.4. Concluding remarks

The analysis developed in the previous sections has shown that, in the post-Lisbon era, the protection of fundamental rights is a major driving force for the evolution of the Union's power to impose sanction. This relationship is both antagonistic and synergic, because the exercise of the Union's power to sanction, which is always constrained by fundamental rights, can sometimes assist the enforcement of the latter.

As regards the role of fundamental rights as constraints, which was the main focus of the chapter, it is worth stressing the following main findings. First of all, the duty to respect fundamental rights is a limit inherent to any expressions of the Union's power to impose sanction, in the relations with both the Member States and third States, regardless of the EU institution or body involved, or the field concerned. The fundamental rights acting as constraints are those granted in the Charter and those recognized as general principles of EU law, which overlap to a large extent with the former, but remain a formally distinct set of rules. This has some interesting implications. For instance, whilst the question of whether States or their emanations can invoke the Charter *vis-à-vis* the Union is still open, the Court of Justice has given a positive answer with respect to the general principles, notably those concerning procedural safeguards. The Charter, for its part, has created a 'bridge' with the ECHR and the relevant case-law of the Strasbourg Court, which therefore contribute – indirectly – to shaping the scope and limits of the constraints deriving from the Charter itself on the Union's power to sanction. Moreover, the Charter can improve the possibility for individuals or legal entities to obtain effective judicial protection *vis-à-vis* the Union, either by shaping the standard for the review of EU sanctions or supporting a narrow interpretation of the Treaty provisions that excludes the jurisdiction of the Court of Justice on certain sanctions.

Even though this other dynamic was referred to only in passing in this chapter, it seems important to stress that the role of sanctions as a tool for the enforcement of fundamental rights should not be limited to situations where the Union's values are severely endangered. The infringement procedure is an important instrument to pressure Member States to comply – fully, properly and in due time – with their obligations flowing from EU measures that give specific expression to fundamental rights granted in the Charter. In this respect, an attitude of 'zero tolerance' by the Commission, in line with the commitment expressed by this institution in the aftermath of the entry into force of the Lisbon Treaty, [90] would be beneficial in the 'daily practice' of fundamental rights' compliance, whilst adding to the legitimacy of a reaction of the Union against attacks to its founding values.

---

[90] Commission communication (COM(2010) 573 final) – Strategy for the effective implementation of the EU's Charter of Fundamental Rights, 10.

Chapter 7

EU SANCTIONING POWER AND THE PRINCIPLE OF PROPORTIONALITY

Stefano Montaldo [*]

ABSTRACT: *The chapter discusses the role that the principle of proportionality plays in shaping the EU power to impose sanctions. It addresses two main aspects, namely the direct imposition of sanctions by the EU institutions and bodies and the national authorities' obligation to resort to sanctions as a means to enforce EU law. The analysis underscores that proportionality covers all phases of the sanctioning cycle, from the abstract pre-determination of a measure to its actual imposition, thereby requiring appropriate monitoring and remedies at the normative and judicial layers. Due to its inherent elusiveness and to the many facets of EU sanctioning power, proportionality and its monitoring follow very different trajectories, depending on the domain at issue and the tasks of the European and national institutions involved. However, the analysis identifies some recurring features, which provide an illustration of the current magnitude of and constraints on EU sanctioning power.*

KEYWORDS: *sanction – proportionality – decision-making process – judicial review – implementation*

7.1. Introduction: proportionality and sanctions in EU law

In the legal context, proportionality reflects the idea underpinning liberal democracies that the individual should be protected from the excessive or unnecessary use of public powers.[1] As such, it calls for *ex ante* institutional and normative constraints, particularly through the accurate pre-determination of the boundaries of

---

[*] Associate Professor of EU Law, University of Turin.

[1] A. Barak, *Proportionality. Constitutional Rights and Their Limitations* (CUP, 2012).

public authority. From a complementary perspective, proportionality also represents a ground for *ex post* judicial review of the outcome of any discretionary administrative or political decision-making process.

The underlying articulation of the proportionality test varies in structure and intensity from jurisdiction to jurisdiction, and also depends on the domain and the public and private interests at issue. In any case, the more intense a public power and its effects on individuals are, the more demanding this principle becomes. This is why proportionality is particularly significant in the domain of sanctions, where the magnitude of public coercive powers reaches its peak.

In this area, proportionality primarily questions the nature, level and effects of the exercise of *ius puniendi*. The immediately ensuing obligation is to "determine what justice requires", meaning that any punishment should pursue a legitimate objective and be reasonably commensurate to the blameworthiness of an action, both *in abstracto* and *in concreto.*[2] Again, the twofold dimension of proportionality, including both the normative layer and the subsequent judicial scrutiny, covers all phases of the sanctioning cycle, from the abstract pre-determination of a measure to its actual imposition.

EU law is not immune from these considerations. In the 1970s, the Court of Justice qualified proportionality as a general principle stemming from the rule of law,[3] requiring that individual freedom (of action) cannot be limited beyond what is necessary in the public interest.[4] Since then, proportionality has gradually developed from a supranational emanation of some domestic legal traditions – especially that of Germany – to a fully-fledged general principle of EU law encompassing any aspect of the Union's action.[5] Such an evolution has progressed in parallel with the attribution and subsequent strengthening of the then European Community's direct sanctioning power. In the wake of the debate on the scope of the European repressive system, where EC *ius puniendi* was confined to a limited set of secondary law provisions,[6] the Court took the clear stance that any such provision had to respect general principles governing the power to impose sanctions, with the principle of proportionality playing an overarching role.[7]

On this basis, the chapter aims to analyse how the principle of proportionality influences the EU's direct sanctioning power. To do so, it builds on the broad definition of the notion of sanction provided in the introduction.

---

[2] M. Thoburn, 'Proportionate sentencing and the rule of law', in L. Zedner and J. Roberts (eds.), *Principles and Values in Criminal Law and Criminal Justice* (Oxford, 2012) 26.

[3] 4/73, *Nold*, ECLI:EU:C:1974:51.

[4] 11/70, *Internationale Handelsgesellschaft*, ECLI:EU:C:1970:114.

[5] Opinion of AG Jacobs, C-120/94, *Commission v. Greece*, ECLI:EU:C:1995:109.

[6] See *supra,* p. XXX.

[7] 122/78, *Buitoni*, ECLI:EU:C:1979:43, para. 20.

In particular, the analysis focuses on how this general principle influences two complementary aspects of the sanctioning chain: the abstract imposition of a sanction and of its features at a normative and regulatory layer (Section 2), and the CJEU's *ex post* judicial review of sanctioning measures on grounds of proportionality (Section 3).

In both cases, the analysis reflects the multi-layered structure of the EU legal order and the general rule according to which implementation and enforcement of EU law are traditionally – but not exhaustively and exclusively – entrusted to the domestic authorities. Decentralisation makes monitoring compliance with the principle of proportionality particularly pressing and multi-faceted. Centrally-steered EU patterns might raise proportionality concerns in themselves, but could also turn out to be problematic in light of their implementation and application by domestic authorities. Therefore, the chapter touches upon Union and domestic levels, and the related different trajectories of the principle of proportionality. The analysis of the normative dimension addresses some of the (soft) rules governing purely EU sanctions (Section 2.1.) and the duty incumbent upon national authorities to sanction violations of EU law by means of "effective, proportionate and dissuasive" measures (Section 2.2.). In a similar way, Section 3 focuses on the CJEU's judicial review of national measures (Sections 3.1. and 3.2.) and of EU ones (Section 3.3.). Lastly, Section 4 provides some closing remarks on the main implications of the principle of proportionality in the EU sanctioning cycle.

As a final note, it is worth pointing out that the exercise of EU sanctioning powers is fragmented into the pieces of an extremely diversified puzzle. This chapter does not aim to provide a comprehensive analysis. Instead, it considers selected areas so as to highlight the core aspects of the role played by the principle of proportionality in shaping the Union's *ius puniendi*.

7.2. EU sanctions and proportionality: the normative layer

7.2.1. EU direct sanctions

The Court has consistently held that it is the task of the EU legislature alone to determine the most appropriate solutions for achieving the objectives established by primary and secondary law and that these include the imposition of sanctions for breaches of Union law.[8] Of course, the possibility of relying on this power is not *carte blanche* in the hands of the Union. All relevant provisions of EU law must be interpreted – *inter alia* – through the lens of proportionality, which sheds light on the methods and extent of the EU's *ius puniendi*.[9] In fact, this principle requires

---

[8] C-240/90, *Germany v. Commission*, ECLI:EU:C:1992:408.

[9] The proportionality of sanctions does not feature in EU primary law; as such, Article 49(3) of the Charter enshrines this principle only in relation to criminal offences and penalties.

such a power to be exercised only insofar as it is necessary to achieve the pursued policy objectives and through the means strictly necessary. In addition, the intensity of the reaction to an infringement of EU law should, accordingly, be measured carefully. Depending on the situation at issue, the intensity of the reaction may involve aspects such as the duration in time, the extent, and the objective and subjective scope of application of a sanction.

The EU *acquis* and the practice of EU institutions show some attempts to align the aforementioned methods and extent of EU sanctioning powers to requirements of appropriateness, necessity and proportionality at normative or regulatory level, as the outcome of a proportionality-oriented decision-making process.

From a general perspective, the diversified forms of EU direct sanctioning power often share a common denominator, namely the fact that the respective measures represent a photographic negative of the infringement or misconduct that justifies their imposition.[10] Sanctions, such as recovery or reduction of unduly obtained benefits, pecuniary sanctions in an amount equivalent to a given unlawful economic advantage or quantified in light of the severity of the conduct and its material effects, withdrawal of administrative decisions, and temporary exclusion from the right to apply for specific funding opportunities, are recurring examples, cross-sectional to many EU policies. The obligation to return unlawfully granted State aid and the recovery of structural and investment funds in the event of fraud or mismanagement are illustrative examples. Similarly, EU nation sanctions against third countries aiming to prevent conflicts and the proliferation of weapons, to promote democracy and human rights, and to combat terrorism include, depending on the circumstances, arms embargoes, trade restrictions, import or export prohibitions, and travel and visa bans or restrictions.

Tailoring the form of a sanction to the conduct it addresses and to the aim(s) it pursues is not conclusive in terms of compliance with the principle of proportionality. However, ensuring coherence in the causal link between a breach and the ensuing penalty is an effective way of securing the sound exercise of public coercive powers, since – at least in principle – it avoids plainly unreasonable normative choices. Thereafter, the compelling question is the extent to which an *in abstracto* tailor-made sanction can be, regardless of its qualification, *in concreto* problematic from a proportionality viewpoint, due to its severity and its effects.

The EU legal framework and the practice of EU institutions are matters of debate in this respect. In fact, all key areas lack binding EU legislation establishing clear and pre-determined limits to the Union's direct sanctions. The enforcement of Articles 101 and 102 TFEU and the sanctions that the Court of Justice has the power to impose on a Member State pursuant to Article 260(2) TFEU are particularly telling examples.

---

[10] As we will see, this approach applies regardless of whether the measure is imposed directly by EU institutions or is formally issued at domestic level based on a national legislation implementing common Union standards.

Firstly, as Calzolari discusses in detail later in this book,[11] the enforcement of EU competition rules still relies heavily on pecuniary sanctions issued by the Commission and by the national competition authorities. Since the early 1980s, the Commission has prioritised the deterrent effect of penalties for breaches of Articles 101 and 102 TFEU, thereby provoking a sharp increase in the severity of sanctions, up to their recent remarkable peaks.[12] Nonetheless, this trend has not been accompanied by *ad hoc* legislative constraints and the Commission has always been endowed with extensive discretion in determining the fines and calculation methods. Widespread criticism of the lack of transparency and predictability eventually forced the Commission to adopt the Fining Guidelines,[13] a self-imposed (and unilaterally devised) soft law instrument detailing the exercise of its sanctioning prerogatives. Although this document is a useful reference point, the absence of formal legislation still raises claims of the unconstrained – or, at least, not duly constrained – sanctioning power of the Commission, with remarkable effects on the companies concerned and on the market as a whole.[14]

The Fining Guidelines do not refer explicitly to proportionality, but this principle underlies the calculation method, which is split into three steps. Following the determination of the basic amount of the fine, the second phase aims to tailor that sum to all relevant (aggravating and mitigating) circumstances. In addition, the third and final assessment establishes the so-called turnover cap, according to which a fine may not exceed 10% of the undertaking's total global turnover in the previous year. This criterion primarily aims to avoid disproportionately harsh penalties.

The Commission made a similar effort to secure the transparency and predictability of the lump sum and the penalty payment that may be imposed on a Member State pursuant to Article 260(2) TFEU, following a failure to take the necessary measures to comply with a judgment of the Court of Justice in the framework of infringement proceedings. Since 1996, the Commission has issued several Communications providing guidance on the calculation methods of these sanctions,[15] paying great attention to penalty payments. In fact, due to their reiteration over time and

[11] See *infra*, Chapter 12.

[12] See, for instance, Commission Decision of 18 July 2018, AT.40099 – Google Android, where a fine of four billion Euros was imposed on a single undertaking.

[13] Guidelines on the method of setting fines imposed pursuant to Article 15(2) of Regulation no. 17 and Article 65(5) of the ECSC Treaty, OJ 1998, C 9/3 and Guidelines on the method of setting fines imposed pursuant to Article 23(2)(a) of Regulation no. 1/2003, OJ 2006, C 210/2.

[14] R. Nazzini, 'Administrative Enforcement, Judicial Review and Fundamental Rights in EU Competition Law: A Comparative Contextual-Functionalist Perspective' (2012) 49 *CMLRev*. 971. This loophole is filled *ex post* by the scope of the judicial scrutiny entrusted to the General Court over the fines. See *infra*, Section 3.3.

[15] The list and the texts of the Communications are available at https://ec.europa.eu/atwork/applying-eu-law/infringements-proceedings/financial sanctions/index_en.htm.

the ensuing budgetary pressure on the Member States, they were deemed to hold significant deterrent potential, with a real risk of disproportionate financial burdens. This concern was incorporated into the mechanism for determining the penalty amount: the objective assessment of the gravity of the infringement and its duration was to be filtered by an *n* factor, reflecting the budgetary magnitude of each Member State, established on the basis of its Gross Domestic Product in the year preceding the imposition of the sanction. [16] The development of the *n* factor is an interesting aspect for our purposes.

The 2004 enlargement to ten new Member States – most of which were characterised by weaker economies than those of the EU-16 – and the *Commission v. France* case of 2005, [17] in which the Court of Justice decided, for the first time, to cumulate both a lump sum and a penalty payment, prompted new adjustments to this mechanism. To reflect more accurately the differences between the Member States in the enlarged EU, the Commission included the voting weight of a Member State in the Council in the method of determining the *n* multiplier. Moreover, it undertook to update its approach on a regular basis, to reflect both contingent factors – such as inflation – and the Court's evolving case law.

More recently, the economic crisis provided an opportunity for further reviews, as the Court took the stance that the criteria pre-determined by the Commission – in particular, the reference to the previous year's GDP – did not accurately reflect the abrupt and sharp decrease of some Member States' ability to pay. Consequently, from 2011, the Commission decided to issue yearly updates to its approach, to reflect more attentively the continent's rapidly evolving economic situation.

The final step of this development occurred in 2019, [18] after the expiry of the transition period regarding the fully-fledged application of the new double majority voting system within the Council. Even though the Commission was willing to continue to use the weighting of votes for the purpose of calculating the *n* factor, at least for pending cases, [19] the Court began to determine penalty payments by referring only to the GDP. [20] Consequently, the Commission once again had to reconsider the calculation of penalty payments. In fact, referring to the GDP alone would have led to a disproportionate increase of the differential of the *n* factor between Member States,

---

[16] The *n* factor was later extended to the determination of the lump sum, with some differences.

[17] C-304/02, *Commission v. France*, ECLI:EU:C:2005:444.

[18] Modification of the calculation method for lump sum payments and daily penalty payments proposed by the Commission in infringement proceedings before the Court of Justice of the European Union, 2019/C 70/01, OJ C70/1.

[19] C-93/17, *Commission v. Greece*, ECLI:EU:C:2018:903, para. 100.

[20] C-328/16, *Commission v. Greece*, ECLI:EU:C:2018:98; C-251/17, *Commission v. Italy*, ECLI:EU:C:2018:358.

based on their ability to pay,[21] with detrimental consequences on the fairness of the system and on the deterrent effect of the sanctions. Therefore, the Commission decided to use another objective institutional criterion, namely the number of representatives in the European Parliament.

Overall, the Commission's Guidelines aim to ensure the consistency, transparency and proportionality of the system and of the proposals of determination of a sanction, although the Court is not bound by the proposed amount and has the final say on the determination of a specific lump sum and/or penalty payment.[22] However, the Commission's role once again becomes dominant in the enforcement phase, after the Court has passed its second judgment. At that time, the actual effects of the imposition of a sanction on the Member State concerned materialise, as the Guardian of the Treaties is entitled to request the payment. To do so, the Commission has the power to decide whether or not the infringement persists and whether or not the Member State concerned has made any improvement. Depending on the outcome of this crucial assessment, also following submissions and requests from the national authorities, the Commission may collect the entire penalty, grant reductions or instead decide that there is no longer any need to enforce the judgment. Surprisingly, this phase is blanketed with silence. The Treaties do not rule on how it should be managed, and the Commission has never issued any soft law instrument to self-orient its activity and make it more transparent, as occurs in the pre-judgment phase. Even though the Member States should be entitled to challenge any final decision taken by the Commission in this context pursuant to Article 263 TFEU.[23] the misalignment between the institutional efforts to tailor the lump sum and the penalty to the specific circumstances of a case and the lack of indications on the Commission's approach to the material enforcement of such sanctions is striking. Moreover, the stance taken by the Commission raises serious issues of proportionality, particularly in relation to the duration of the obligation to pay the penalty and to any reductions of its amount in light of the Member State's improved conduct.

7.2.2. EU indirect sanctions: the adoption of common standards concerning the duty incumbent upon the Member States to sanction breaches of Union law

As an inherent feature of the EU composite legal order, the Member States are the traditional enforcers of EU law, by virtue of the duty of loyal cooperation enshrined in Article 4(3) TEU. In most policy areas, the broad obligation incumbent upon the

[21] As pointed out by the Commission, "The difference between the lowest and the highest *n*-factor today is 55 – this would increase to 312 with the exclusive use of GDP".

[22] C-93/17, *Commission v. Greece*, cit., para. 119. Its proposals cannot bind the Court and are "merely a useful point of reference".

[23] In this regard, see *infra*, Section 3.3.

Member States to take all measures necessary to implement and apply EU law effectively encompasses the adoption of sanctions. From a domestic perspective, this multi-level dynamic of compliance could be seen as a much needed self-restraint of the Union, on the deeply held assumption that all aspects of the sanctioning cycle – from the abstract normative choices on the type and severity of the relevant measures to their enforcement – touch upon the *noyau dur* of national sovereignty.

In line with this, until the early 1980s, the Union offered leeway to national authorities on their choice of measures for enforcing EU law, refraining from imposing specific harmonised sanctioning standards. Accordingly, in *Amsterdam Bulb*, the Court took the stance that loyal cooperation "allows the Member States to choose the measures which they consider appropriate", without further specific constraints.[24] Yet, in 1989, the *Greek Maize* case marked the rise of a second season of the EU legislature's practice. While setting the scene for a stricter assessment of the compatibility of national sanctions with the general principles of EU law,[25] the Court clarified that the relevant domestic sanctions must comply with three cumulative criteria, namely effectiveness, proportionality and dissuasiveness. In the aftermath of this judgment, the European legislature began to include the "effective, proportionate and dissuasive" refrain as a matter of routine in any provisions requiring the Member States to sanction an infringement of EU law,[26] although it can be considered to merely codify pre-existing general obligations already deriving from Article 4(3) TEU.

Building on the advances made by *Greek Maize*, the European institutions decided to develop further the normative approach to the indirect exercise of their sanctioning powers. In an increasing set of policy domains, the EU legislature – and sometimes the Commission, in its capacity as a delegated authority – began to provide more specific indications on the type and level of sanctions to be implemented in the national legal orders. This third normative season is now well-established, to the extent that the persisting reference to effective, proportionate and dissuasive sanctions very often takes the shape of specific legal contours within which the domestic authorities must contextualise their (now more limited) discretion. Even though the panorama is extremely diversified, some recurring features can be identified. EU legislation usually provides for abstract types of measures – or at least some of them[27] – to be made available to the competent national authorities and

[24] 50/76, *Amsterdam Bulb*, ECLI:EU:C:1977:13, para. 32. In the same paragraph, the Court also clarified that such measures "may even be criminal in nature".

[25] 68/88, *Commission v. Greece*, ECLI:EU:C:1989:339, paras 24 and 25.

[26] The same refrain appears in Article 325 TFEU.

[27] The panorama of sanctions that EU law requires Member States to implement is increasingly wide. For instance, Article 16(2) of the so-called Emission Trading Scheme Directive 2003/87/EC states that, among the relevant measures, the national authorities must ensure the publication of the names of the operators that are held responsible for certain conduct.

sometimes clarifies the type and severity of conduct to which these pre-determined measures should apply. Moreover, these instruments often include quantitative thresholds, such as the minimum and/or maximum scale of nominal sanction common to all Member States,[28] or at least provide a series of factors to be taken into consideration when determining the amount of a penalty.[29] Finally, as already outlined above for direct EU *ius puniendi*, on many occasions, the forms of sanctions prescribed by EU acts lead to domestic measures that reflect the infringement concerned and are tailor-made to it.

The development outlined above entails a partial paradigm shift from the traditional way of conceiving EU law enforcement, although the formal allocation of this task is still centred on the necessary intervention of the Member States. From a functional perspective, it also represents an example of how the EU legislature attempts to maximise the scope of the legal bases enshrined in the Treaties, with a view to securing the full effectiveness of EU law. These normative constraints to national legislatures can be seen as an instrument for avoiding undue departures from EU law. Their main rationale is to establish an EU-wide level playing field in which sanctions can effectively punish and deter violations of EU law, while avoiding the detrimental implications of the two opposite poles of the sanctioning range: the creation of safe havens where significantly less severe measures can encourage non-compliance and, conversely, the choice of types and levels of sanctions which are – *per se* or in specific cases – disproportionate to the infringement they are intended to address.

In this respect, the identification of the essential elements of the sanctions to be transposed into national law pre-determines the forms and severity of sanctions that are likely to be considered as "effective, proportionate and dissuasive". While it contributes to securing the implementation of EU policies, this approach also contributes to preventing these measures from being cancelled following a judicial review at national and European levels, unless the EU normative choices are *per se* disproportionate or a Member State departs from the EU-pattern when transposing them.[30] Of course, the trend outlined above does not automatically secure the compatibility of domestic enforcement activity with the general principles of EU law. Leaving aside situations of erroneous implementation, the actual sanctioning scales may be influenced by other branches or aspects of national legislation falling outside the scope of EU competences, thereby leading to the imposition of excessively harsh measures.

---

[28] See, for instance, Arts 63 and 64 of Regulation 1306/2013 of the European Parliament and of the Council of 17 December 2013 on the financing, management and monitoring of the common agricultural policy, OJ 2012, L 347/549.

[29] See, for instance, Article 19 of Regulation (EU) no. 995/2010 of the European Parliament and of the Council of 20 October 2010 laying down the obligations of operators who place timber and timber products on the market, OJ 2010, L 295/23.

[30] See *infra*, Section 3.3.

Interestingly, this third wave of EU sanctions regarding the Member States has gradually expanded to the Union's competence to impose duties of criminalisation. This domain is of particular significance from the viewpoint of proportionality, as confirmed by Article 49(3) of the Charter, which enshrines the principle of proportionality of criminal offences and penalties.

Article 83 TFEU has equipped the EU with the competence to adopt minimum rules common to the Member States regarding the definition of certain offences and the determination of the type and level of the related sanctions. While the Third Pillar legal bases only provided for the competence to harmonise "minimum maximum penalties", namely the minimum threshold of the maximum penalty available for sentencing at national level, Article 83 TFEU has, in principle, amplified the Union's role, extending its harmonisation powers to the lowest degree of the nominal penalty scale. Although, thus far, the EU has not exercised the latter competence, the codification of the EU's competence to harmonise national criminal legislation has further boosted the Union legislature's practice to established detailed rules on penalty scales,[31] aggravating and mitigating circumstances, and other factors influencing the severity of nominal sanctions that should be made available to law enforcement and judicial authorities. Overall, the Union appears to be increasingly eager to articulate a minimum common basis for a shared understanding of interests requiring protection and of the intensity of the reaction of domestic penal systems to a given criminal conduct. For our purposes, the question is then whether or not the principle of proportionality of criminal sanctions plays any role in the EU decision-making process in this area.

The 2011 Commission Communication on European criminal policy provides useful guidance in this respect.[32] On that occasion, the Commission stressed the importance of adopting common rules on penalties, as a means of guaranteeing deterrence and avoiding "safe havens "with attractively lenient sanctioning systems, fostering security across Europe.[33] The Commission usually reiterates these arguments as a mantra for substantiating its proposals for new legislative acts harmonising substantive criminal law and the related minimum or penalties. Crucially, the relevant EU legislation translates these underlying objectives into the aforementioned refrain that sanctions must be "effective, proportionate and dissuasive". In

[31] See, for instance, Directive (EU) 2017/541 of the European Parliament and of the Council of 15 March 2017 on combating terrorism, OJ 2017, L 88/6 which prescribes different penalty scales for a series of criminal behaviours included in the category of terrorist offences.

[32] Communication from the Commission COM(2011)573 of 20 September 2011, Towards an EU Criminal Policy: Ensuring the effective implementation of EU policies throughout criminal law.

[33] The Commission also contends that common standards on punishment can foster judicial collaboration, as they contribute to ensuring that reactions to a crime will not differ greatly from one State to another.

line with an overarching deterrence narrative, many expected to see an increase in penalty scales at national level, due to the harsher EU minimum common rules. It has been highlighted that harsher punishment is an easy way of (apparently) strengthening dissuasiveness while coping with the fragmentation of national legal orders with regard to the type and level of penalties. However, studies conducted thus far lead to the rejection of the idea of a generalised EU-driven aggravation of penalty scales in the national scenarios.[34]. Moreover, and *a fortiori* when dealing with minimum harmonisation instruments, nominal penalties rarely correspond to actual levels of (and trends in) punishment. A wide range of exogenous factors pertaining, *inter alia*, to national criminal law and criminal law enforcement contribute to amplifying the fragmentation of domestic legal regimes and the solutions to which they could lead. This means that, provided that the minimum common rules on penalties adopted at EU level are not plainly unreasonable or disproportionate, the proportionality match is mainly played at the level of national penal systems, which are expected to ensure that, either systemically or in each individual case, this general principle is respected.

7.3. The judicial review of EU direct and indirect sanctions: the role of the Court of Justice

7.3.1. The judicial review of national measures: derogations from EU law

The proportionality test developed by the Court of Justice requires a measure to be appropriate to the aim pursued, necessary to achieve it – meaning that no more desirable or less restrictive alternatives are reasonably available – and proportionate in a strict sense.[35] From a general perspective, it has been argued that proportionality provides a sound basis for a judicial review of sanctioning measures, as it allows the Court to carry out, where appropriate, a detailed scrutiny.[36] In fact, the review of national measures through the lens of proportionality does not only cover the formal legality of a sanction, but also the merits of its adoption, substance and effects, both on the individual concerned and on the objectives pursued by EU law. This assessment covers all steps of the sanctioning cycle, as the "Member States are required to comply with the principle of proportionality not only as regards the determination of factors constituting an infringement and the determination of the rules concerning the

---

[34] T. Elholm, 'Does EU Cooperation Necessarily Mean Increased Repression in the Nordic Countries?' (2009) 17 *European Journal of Crime, Criminal Law and Criminal Justice*, 204.

[35] In the past, the Court sometimes used a bipartite test, assessing if the means employed corresponded to the importance of the aim and were necessary for its achievement. See C-66/82, *Fromançais v. FORMA*, ECLI:EU:C:1983:42.

[36] G. de Búrca, 'The principle of proportionality and its application in EC law', (1993) 13 *YEL* 105.

severity of fines, but also as regards the assessment of the factors which may be taken into account in the fixing of a fine".[37]

Against this background, the review of national measures differs, depending on whether the Member State concerned is implementing EU law or departing from it. In the latter case, the Court's primary concern is to avoid evasions of EU law, especially when a fundamental freedom is at stake. Two complementary situations must briefly be considered: reliance on a derogation codified in the Treaties or in secondary law and the exercise of national exclusive competences indirectly affecting EU law.[38]

In the former situation, judicial scrutiny is mainly centred on the need to interpret formal derogations restrictively and to ensure that the domestic measure genuinely pursues an objective of public interest and is, in any event, compatible with the general principles of EU law, such as non-discrimination on grounds of nationality and, of course, proportionality. This approach sometimes leads the Court to cancel national provisions on criminalisation as they are incompatible with EU law, affecting fundamental freedoms.[39] In other cases, the Court focuses directly on the compatibility of a national penalty. In particular, case law consistently holds that any penalty must represent a balanced reaction to a given wrongful conduct, also in terms of avoiding unnecessary restrictions to the rights and freedoms stemming from the EU legal order.[40] In addition, sanctions must not be automatic and absolute in nature; instead, they must be imposed and determined in light of the specific circumstances of a case.[41] Moreover, "the national authorities should not impose penalties for disregard of a provision which is incompatible with [EU] law".[42]

In the second situation, namely when the Member State does not rely on a derogation enshrined in primary or secondary legislation and instead invokes the legitimate exercise of its residual competences, a domestic measure could affect EU law.[43] Even in such cases, however, longstanding case law clarifies that the Member

---

[37] C-210/10, *Marton Urban*, para. 54. This is the only judgment in which the Court uses this description. Usually, case law refers to a more nuanced formula, which basically identifies the key components of the proportionality review of a sanction and leaves the door open for possible further assessment criteria: "In order to assess whether a penalty is consistent with the principle of proportionality, account must be taken of, *inter alia*, the nature and the degree of seriousness of the infringement which that penalty seeks to sanction, and of the means of establishing the amount of that penalty". See C-712/17, *EN.SA.*, ECLI:EU:C:2019:374, para. 40.

[38] M. Dougan, 'From the Velvet Glove to the Iron Fist: Criminal Sanctions for the Enforcement of Union Law', in M. Cremona (ed.), *Compliance and Enforcement in EU Law* (OUP, 2012) 74.

[39] See, *ex multis,* C-360/04, *Placanica*, ECLI:EU:C:2006:71.

[40] C-47/15, *Affum*, ECLI:EU:C:2016:408.

[41] C-348/96, *Calfa*, ECLI:EU:C:1999:6, paras 26-28.

[42] 8/77, *Sagulo*, ECLI:EU:C:1977:131, para. 6.

[43] A. Hinarejos, 'Law and Order and Internal Security Provisions in the Area of Freedom, Security and Justice: Before and After Lisbon', in C. Eckes, T. Konstadinides and T. Yorke (eds.), *Crime Within the Area of Freedom, Security and Justice. A European Public Order* (CUP 2011) 249.

States must exercise their reserved powers in a manner that does not affect the general principles of the EU legal order. A particularly illustrative case in this respect is *Wijsenbeek*,[44] which involved a national provision requiring a person, whether or not an EU citizen, under threat of criminal penalties, to establish his nationality upon entering the territory of that Member State via an internal border of the Union. As Mr. Wijsenbeek's refusal to comply with such a national law dated back to 1993, when the Community lacked common rules on controls at external borders and an immigration, visa and asylum policy, the Court held that, "as Community law stood at the time of the events",[45] the Treaty did not preclude the Member States from criminalising such conduct. At the same time, it is worth pointing out that the Court reiterated that the discretion entrusted to national authorities was dependent on the condition that "the penalties applicable [...] are not disproportionate, thus creating an obstacle to the free movement of persons".[46]

Domestic sanctions must not go beyond what is strictly necessary and must not be so disproportionate to the gravity of an infringement of national legislation as to become an obstacle to the exercise of a fundamental freedom.[47] More generally, the (disproportionate) exercise of national *ius puniendi* cannot amount to hampering the full effectiveness of EU law and excessively restrict the individual rights stemming from the European legal order. This twofold systemic and individual dimension is well-depicted by the *El Dridi* case.[48] Italy had failed to transpose Directive 2008/115/EC[49] and the Court was asked if its Arts 15 and 16 precluded an Italian provision imposing a custodial sentence on illegally staying third country nationals, solely because of a failure to comply with an order to leave the national territory within a given period. On the premises that the national criminalising provision was *per se* lawful, the Court contended that the sentence of imprisonment was disproportionate to the aim pursued by the Italian authorities and that it was detrimental both to achieving the objective of an effective system of rapid returns and to the need to minimise the restriction of liberty of illegally-staying third country nationals.[50]

Crucially, the less direct the link with EU law, the more delicate the case can be,

---

[44] C-378/97, *Wijsenbeek*, ECLI:EU:C:1999:439.

[45] *Ibidem*, para. 45.

[46] *Ibidem*, para. 44.

[47] 203/80, *Casati*, ECLI:EU:C:1981:261, para. 27.

[48] C-61/11 PPU, *El Dridi*, ECLI:EU:C:2011:268.

[49] *Ibidem*, para. 45.

[50] *Ibidem*, paras 42-43 and 57-58. The Court primarily refers to the need to secure the effectiveness of the system of returns set up by the Directive. The individual dimension is a corollary to it, although the Court reiterates that the imposition of coercive measures on illegally staying third country nationals for the purposes of removal must not exceed the length of time strictly required for that purpose.

not only because of the dilemma between achieving EU goals and the risk of an undue intrusion into the legitimate exercise of domestic sovereign competences, but primarily in terms of the fairness of the legal system as a whole and of the just application of a coercive measure to a person in an individual case. In fact, in both situations outlined above, the Court usually allows the individual to benefit from more lenient treatment, by tempering the severity of the sanctions at issue or even suggesting that the national authorities exclude them. This outcome could lead to reverse discrimination, depending on whether or not a given factual circumstance falls within – or has effects on – the scope of the branch of EU law under consideration, for instance, where a national sanction hampers the free movement of persons but also applies to third country nationals. It would then be for the national authorities to decide how to deal with this situation.

From the opposite perspective, it might be the case that a breach of EU law requires harsher sanctions than those applied to violations of national laws in a similar domain, on grounds of the requirement of effectiveness. The Court has already accepted that such a differentiated situation is compatible with EU law and, in particular, with the principle of equivalence, provided that the measure imposed by Union law is proportionate.[51]

7.3.2. The judicial review of national measures: implementation of EU law

When a Member State implements EU law, the proportionality scrutiny maintains its inherent structure, but includes the step of a more complex check covering the *Greek Maize* criteria.[52] Proportionality plays a major role here, as the Member State is caught between two potentially competing obligations. The duty of loyal cooperation requires it to sanction infringements of EU law and to do so effectively, whereas the general principles place limits on the national authorities' discretion to sanction those breaches. In addition, the national implementing provisions usually embody further national policy goals, which might not be fully in line with the EU objectives.

Against this background, the proportionality scrutiny can be seen, in essence, as a balancing exercise of various interests underpinning a national sanctioning measure. The intensity of this check varies, depending on the (EU and/or national) objectives in the public interest under consideration, as well as – according to some commentators – how far the Court is prepared to defer to the decisions of the authorities con-

---

[51] C-432/05, *Unibet*, ECLI:EU:C:2007:163.

[52] For the purposes of this Chapter, we focus only on the judicial review performed by the EU Courts. However, the national courts are often charged with determining whether or not a domestic sanction is proportionate, and the Court of Justice provides them with the criteria for developing such an assessment. See, for instance, C-487/14, *Total Waste Recycling*, ECLI:EU:C:2015:780, para. 55.

cerned.[53] All in all, therefore, proportionality entails a variable and open-structured assessment, the stringency of which alters in light of the circumstances of each individual case, the underlying public interests, and the individual rights at stake. It is therefore difficult to identify a specific trend or standard of review, since it very much depends on the context, the type of measure at issue, its severity and material effects, the nature of the evidence, and the arguments raised to the Court. Despite this, some common features can be identified.

Usually, the Court seems to be sympathetic to the broad discretion of the Member States with regard to the choice of the means of enforcing EU law, where no common provisions have been adopted at European level. Case law shows respect for national-centred cultural, social and economic factors leading to a diversified perception of the degree of wrongfulness of an action, and to ensuing varied options in terms of the type and severity of sanctions. In *Louloudakis*,[54] for instance, the Court accepted that a harsh penalty of a criminal nature for evading car registration fees in Greece was, in principle, proportionate, due to the high incidence of such frauds in that Member State.[55] The Court also argued that, *in abstracto*, the national legislature is free to discount the person's good faith as a codified alleviating circumstance, on the grounds of the principle that everyone is presumed to know the law, enshrined in national legislation. However, the relevant judicial authority must be able to assess this aspect when determining the actual amount of the sanction. At the same time, the Court has consistently held that when a choice between several appropriate measures can be made, the least onerous one should be selected, so as to contribute to preventing disadvantages which are too cumbersome and therefore disproportionate to the aims underpinning a sanction.[56] The Court similarly rules out national provisions imposing the same penalty for a set of actions on an ascending scale of seriousness. Thus, it is very strict in assessing those penalties that are not *in abstracto* and *in concreto* tailor-made to the breach they are intended to sanction. In *Marton Urban*,[57] for instance, the Court struck down a Bulgarian penalty addressing the breaches of a national regulation concerning the transport by road of goods and persons and listing the information that drivers

---

[53] T. Tridimas, *The General Principles of EU Law* (OUP 2006) 139.

[54] C-262/99, *Louloudakis*, ECLI:EU:C:2001:407.

[55] See, also, C-156/04, *Commission v. Greece*, ECLI:EU:C:2007:316.

[56] See, *inter alia,* C-562/08, *Müller Fleisch*, ECLI:EU:C:2010:93, para. 43, on the implementation of EU rules governing the system for monitoring bovine spongiform encephalopathy, or the joined cases C-379/08 and C-380/08, *ERG and Others*, ECLI:EU:C:2010:127, in the field of environmental law and the polluter pays principle. In other cases, the Court has acknowledged the compatibility of a severe sanction also thanks to the provision in the national legal order of even harsher penalties for similar but more serious actions: see, for instance, 354/95, *National Farmers' Union*, ECLI:EU:C:1997:379.

[57] C-210/10, *Marton Urban*, cit.

must fill-in to demonstrate that they are complying with relevant legislation on road safety and drivers' working conditions. The domestic measure took the shape of a flat-rate fine for any infringements of that regulation, no matter how serious, reiterated or continued in time.[58]

Finally, most recent case law reveals an increasingly close link between proportionality and the risk of a breach of the sanctioned person's rights. Two main categories of cases can be identified. On one hand, the Court is keen to make general references to the principle of proportionality *per se* as a means of shedding light on unbalanced restrictions of the rights of the person concerned. An illustration of this stream of cases is the preliminary ruling issued in *Haqbin.*[59] The Court was confronted with the Belgian law implementing Directive 2013/33/EU, which prescribed the reduction or the withdrawal of the material reception conditions granted to any asylum seeker who was held responsible for violent behaviour and serious breaches of the rules governing accommodation centres. The Grand Chamber ruled out the proportionality of a withdrawal – even of temporary nature – of the full set of material reception conditions relating to housing, food or clothing, since such a measure affects the individual's dignified standard of living and precludes him or her from being allowed to meet his or her most basic needs.[60] Instead, with regard to the reduction of material reception conditions, the Court stressed that "it is for the competent authorities to ensure under all circumstances that such a sanction, having regard to the particular situation of the applicant as well as all of the circumstances of that case, complies with the principle of proportionality and does not undermine the dignity of the applicant".[61]

The Court has also made effective use of Article 49(3) of the Charter. In particular, from the *Menci* case of 2018 onwards,[62] it began to refer to this provision in combination with Article 52(1) of the Charter, to assess if various national normative schemes involving the imposition of an administrative sanction and a criminal penalty against the same person for the same facts constituted a justified restriction to the *ne bis in idem* principle.[63] In *Menci* as well as in *Garlsson Real Estate*,[64] the Court developed a three-step argument. Firstly, the principle of proportionality does not auto-

---

[58] It is worth clarifying that the Court has acknowledged that national systems penalising breaches of EU law on the basis of strict liability are not, in themselves, incompatible with the principle of proportionality.

[59] C-233/18, *Haqbin*, ECLI:EU:C:2019:956.

[60] *Ibidem*, paras 47 and 48.

[61] *Ibidem*, para. 51.

[62] C-524/15, *Menci*, ECLI:EU:C:2018:197.

[63] Article 50 of the Charter.

[64] C-537/16, *Garlsson Real Estate*, ECLI:EU:C:2018:193. See also C-596/16 and C-597/16, *Di Puma*, ECLI:EU:C:2018:192.

matically preclude this kind of sanctioning approach, otherwise the Member States' freedom to choose the applicable measures for securing the EU's (financial) interests through the collection of VAT revenue would be unduly restricted.[65] However – and this is the second step – the Member States must set up an appropriate normative scheme, ensuring *in abstracto* that the disadvantages resulting from the duplication of sanctions are limited to what is strictly necessary to achieve the objectives pursued by such measures. Thus, those rules must include the obligation for the competent authorities to align the severity of the imposed penalties with the seriousness of the offence. Thirdly, although national legislation complying with the previous requirement could appear, in principle, capable of balancing the different interests at issue, it should also lead *in concreto* to a proportionate outcome. Therefore, the scrutiny of formal legal provisions must be followed by a further review of how these rules have actually been applied by the national authorities and courts.

7.3.3. The judicial review of EU sanctions

Before considering the main features of the judicial scrutiny of EU direct sanctions, it is worth making some general comments on the proportionality review of the acts of the Union's institutions and bodies.

In this regard, the Court traditionally acknowledges that EU institutions and bodies enjoy broad discretion in matters regarding the exercise of the political responsibilities given to them by the Treaties. Therefore, if the evaluation of a complex situation is at issue and the Union has a broad measure of discretion, the check on the legality of its activity "must confine itself to examining whether that exercise discloses manifest error or constitutes a misuse of powers or a clear disregard of the limits of its discretion".[66] The "manifestly inappropriate test"[67] means that, in principle, only macroscopic violations of the limits inherent to the use of political discretionary powers are ruled out on grounds of proportionality.[68] This light proportionality review is cross-sectional to many fields of EU competence, and applies to a varied set of legal schemes and measures adopted by Union institutions and bodies, ranging from the general governance of a CAP market organisation to the adoption of protective measures in trade with third States.[69]

At first sight, such an approach appears to be a mild version of the (potentially)

---

[65] C-524/15, *Menci*, cit., para. 47.

[66] *Inter alia*, C-122/00, *Omega Air*, ECLI:EU:C:2002:161, para. 64.

[67] C-331/88, *Fedesa*, ECLI:EU:C:1990:391, para. 14. In other cases, the Court refers for instance to a patently disproportionate (138/78, *Stölting*, ECLI:EU:C:1979:46, para. 7) or manifestly unsuitable (59/83, *Biovilac*, ECLI:EU:C:1984:380, para. 17) measure.

[68] It is worth emphasising that this light test applies to each of the components of the proportionality check, namely suitability, necessity and proportionality in the strict sense.

[69] C-205/94, *Binder*, ECLI:EU:C:1996:234, para. 17.

intense proportionality scrutiny over domestic measures derogating from EU law or implementing it. As we have seen, the open-textured nature of the proportionality review allows the EU (and the national) courts to develop an in-depth analysis of the form and substance of domestic measures, even when the latter represents the outcome of important political choices. On the contrary, a more cautious approach seems to apply to EU law, in comparable situations.

This differentiated test has two main explanations, both stemming from the nature and rationale of the judicial reviews under consideration. Firstly, the scrutiny over EU provisions involving discretionary choices reflects the balance of powers between EU institutions and the necessary restraint that a judicial body must self-impose when dealing with primarily political decisions. It is not for the Court to second guess the merits of such choices, at least in terms of suitability for the objectives they pursue, necessity and proportionality in the strict sense. Secondly, the empowerment of the Court when reviewing national laws or practices is mainly justified on grounds of effectiveness and uniformity of EU law across the Union. Even though the structure of the test is the same, the multi-level context in which it is performed models its intensity and requires the Court of Justice to act as a guardian of its correct interpretation and application throughout the EU.[70]

The key question is then whether or not these considerations justify a diversified attitude also in relation to the validity of EU direct sanctions and to those provisions which orient the actions of the Member States when they are faced with the *Greek Maize* duty to adopt effective, proportionate and dissuasive sanctions.

Since the 1970s, the Court has held that European institutions are endowed with sanctioning powers and that the exercise of this competence is not immune from the general principles governing *ius puniendi.*[71] Therefore, both EU rules orienting national sanctions and 'purely' European ones can be challenged before the EU judiciary to check if they comply with the principle of proportionality.[72] The Court accordingly and consistently states that, as a general rule, the acts of EU institutions and bodies undergo a comprehensive judicial review, including a fully-fledged proportionality test over direct Union sanctions.[73]

At the same time, the Court often adopts a tolerant stance when carrying out its proportionality assessment, paying due regard to the broad discretion of EU institutions when implementing EU policies.[74] This happens, in particular, in *Greek Maize*

[70] A similar imparity can be detected in federal systems, between the review developed by central courts on state laws and on federal ones. F. Jacobs, 'Recent Developments in the Principle of Proportionality in European Community Law', in E. Ellis (ed.) *The Principle of Proportionality in the Laws of Europe* (Edward Elgar, 1999) 3.

[71] 11/70, *Internationale Handelsgesellschaft* and 122/78, *Buitoni*, cit.

[72] 56/86, *Société pour l'exportation du sucre*, ECLI:EU:C:1987:146.

[73] C-7/95, *Deere*, ECLI:EU:C:1998:256, para. 34.

[74] C-331/88, *Fedesa*, cit., and C-180/96, *Schrader*, ECLI:EU:C:1998:192.

situations, namely when the Court is called upon to review EU provisions establishing common rules on the extent and amount of sanctions to be applied at domestic level.[75] The exercise of EU indirect *ius puniendi* is basically confined to the adoption of minimum shared standards and leaves a broad margin of manoeuvre to the Member States. Moreover, the penalty scales imposed at Union level do not prevent national legislatures from imposing stricter measures and can, in any event, be modified *de facto* pursuant to further domestic procedural or substantive provisions influencing the determination of the amount of a sanction. At the same time, as already discussed above, the more recent normative trend of the Union testifies to an attempt to boost the EU's indirect sanctioning powers, by means of increasingly specific rules, such as carefully diversified types and scales of penalties for different actions or behaviours with a different degree of seriousness. This developing approach could trigger stricter judicial scrutiny in future.

When it comes to the EU's direct sanctioning powers, the recurring "manifestly inappropriate" formula conceals a more varied scenario. Although the Court very often formally builds on this premise, a closer look at its legal arguments demonstrates that it does not exclude the possibility of performing a robust proportionality assessment. In particular, the Court, on some occasions, declassifies the due respect for EU policy choices from a justification for a lighter review to a criterion of assessment, along with other considerations. This means that the breadth of the EU institutions and bodies' discretion influences the intensity of the proportionality review, just as other elements do. From this point of view, case law unveils three main lines of reasoning that often intertwine.

Firstly, the Court often focuses on the aims pursued by the sanction in question. Even though the practice is fragmented, judicial scrutiny through the teleological lens is usually tenuous and allows the sanction at stake to pass the necessity test. More specifically, the Court mainly considers whether or not a measure, in principle, guarantees the achievement of the objectives of the legal framework to which it is related and is usually sympathetic to the decisions made by the Union institutions and bodies, particularly with regard to the extent of the sanctions. For instance, case law on EU restrictive measures relies on the objectives that the freezing of funds, properties and assets pursues, such as international peace and security, the promotion of democracy and the fight against terrorism, to point out that only clearly inappropriate measures would be deemed illegitimate. Moreover, these objectives allow the Council to enjoy broad discretion in determining the categories of recipients of restrictive measures and the main features of these sanctions.[76]

Secondly, the Court attaches particular importance to the rule whose breach de-

---

[75] See *supra*, Section 2.2.

[76] See, *inter alia,* C-348/12 P, *Kala Naft*, ECLI:EU:C:2013:776, para 120; C-630/13, *Issam Anbouba v. Council*, ECLI:EU:C:2015:247, para 42.

termines the imposition of a sanction. More specifically, it makes a distinction between primary and secondary obligations. In relation to the former category, the Court has usually been cautious in ruling out even harsh sanctions covering obligations deemed to be essential for the functioning of a given policy or mechanism.[77] Conversely, in the event of violations of rules of lesser importance, the intensity of judicial scrutiny increases.

Thirdly, the Court does not dismiss the individual dimension and states that the exercise of EU institutions and bodies' discretion cannot lead to excessive disadvantages for the recipients of a sanction. The requirement of necessity plays a prominent role here,[78] as it means that if a choice between various measures can be made, the least restrictive sanction available should be imposed.[79] In addition, just as it does for national sanctions, the Court has used the necessity criterion to invalidate EU direct sanctions, whose quality and amount were not tailored to the wrongfulness of an action, as they applied indistinctly to a range of breaches of clearly different severity, thereby imposing disproportionate burdens.[80]

Finally, the EU Courts take a path of their own in some areas of EU law in terms of sanctions. The analysis briefly considers competition fines pursuant to Arts 101 and 102 TFEU and the penalties and lump sums that the Court may impose by virtue of Article 260 TFEU, both discussed above from a normative perspective.[81]

As already argued, the Commission is endowed with a significant margin of manoeuvre when determining antitrust sanctions, to such an extent that it can even derogate from the Fining Guidelines to secure the deterrent effect of the relevant measures.[82] The main institutional consequence of this power is that Regulation 1/2003 grants unlimited jurisdiction to the General Court over competition fines. The General Court can conduct an in-depth assessment of the merits of the case and of the Commission's evaluation concerning the seriousness of the violation that occurred

---

[77] C-345/95, *National farmers' Union*, cit.; C-8/89, *Zardi*, ECLI:EU:C:1990:260.

[78] Tridimas holds that "necessity is more important because, in applying the principle of proportionality, the Court does not act as an appellate body exercising review of the merits but is concerned primarily with the restrictive effects of the measure on the freedom of the individual". T. Tridimas, *The General Principles*, cit., 143.

[79] 181/84, *Man Sugar*, ECLI:EU:C:1985:359; 15/83, *Denkavit*, ECLI:EU:C:1984:183. At the same time, even harsh sanctions have been accepted, considering that - even though they were not the most lenient available - more severe ones could have been chosen: C-354/95, *National Farmers' Union*, cit.

[80] See, for instance, C-356/97, *Molkereigenossenschaft Wiedergeltingen*, ECLI:EU:C:2000:364, on a penalty imposed for delayed statement of quantities of milk, regardless of any consideration concerning the length of the delay and its impact on the system of milk quotas.

[81] See *supra*, Section 2.1.

[82] Guidelines on the method of setting fines, cit., para. 37.

and the quantification of the sanction.[83] It can even replace the Commission's assessment with its own.[84] On the other hand, the Court of Justice's power of review is limited to the broad check on whether or not the General Court considered all the main factors in assessing the seriousness of the infringement and issuing an appropriate fine, which could then be re-calculated to guarantee its fairness.

Moving on to infringement proceedings, it should be noted that, under Article 260 TFEU, the Court of Justice does not conduct a formal judicial review of an action of another EU institution or body; rather, it is itself tasked with the power directly to impose a penalty and/or a lump sum on a Member State. Despite the Commission's proposal, it is only for the Court to determine the nature and amount of the sanction. Case law has clarified the basic criteria which must be considered for this purpose, namely "the seriousness of the infringement, its duration and the ability to pay of the Member State in question".[85] Both the penalty payment and the lump sum must be tailored to the circumstances of a case and should avoid excessive burdens to the Member State involved.[86] The Court is particularly attentive in assessing the Member State's ability to pay, especially in the event of budgetary difficulties, which have been taken into account to re-calculate the *n* factor.[87] or, more generally, as a mitigating element.[88] Alleviating circumstances constitute a recurring concern and cover a wide range of situations, such as the lack of a previous similar infringement or – conversely – the existence of several negative precedents against the same Member State,[89] the cooperation in good faith and the efforts made by the national authorities,[90] partial compliance and how difficult and lengthy it would be to achieve full compliance. In particu-

---

[83] This judicial scrutiny entails "an in-depth review both of the legality of the contested decision and of whether the amount of the fine set out in that decision was appropriate". C-411/15 P, *Timab*, ECLI:EU:C:2017:11, para. 109. Case law clarifies that the General Court's full jurisdiction also aims to ensure the overall fairness of the sanction imposed: T-486/11, *Orange Polska*, ECLI:EU:T:2015:1002, para. 68.

[84] The General Court can therefore "cancel, reduce or increase the fine or periodic penalty payment imposed": C-617/13 P, *Repsol*, ECLI:EU:C:2016:416, para. 84.

[85] *Ex multis*, C-251/17, *Commission v. Italy*, ECLI:EU:C:2018:358, para. 71. The Court further adds that "regard must be had, in particular, to the effects on public and private interests of the failure to comply and to how urgent it is for the Member State concerned to be induced to fulfil its obligations".

[86] The tailor-made nature of the penalty payment is also reflected by the frequency for calculating the amount to be paid, which the Court can establish on a case-by-case basis. See, for instance, *inter alia*, C-533/11, *Commission v. Belgium*, ECLI:EU:C:2013:659, for a six-month frequency.

[87] C-70/06, *Commission v. Portugal*, ECLI:EU:C:2008:3.

[88] C-407/09, *Commission v. Greece*, ECLI:EU:C:2011:196; C-279/11, *Commission v. Ireland*, ECLI:EU:C:2012:834.

[89] C-653/13, *Commission v. Italy*, ECLI:EU:C:2015:478, para. 92.

[90] C-576/11, *Commission v. Luxembourg*, ECLI:EU:C:2013:773, para. 62.

lar, case law consistently holds that a penalty payment might not be proportionate if it does not take into due account the progress made by the Member State, such that, for instance, gradually decreasing sums could better fit the situation,[91] In addition, the Court has sometimes imposed a lump sum significantly more lenient than the amounts indicated in the Commission's Guidelines.[92]

Overall, case law demonstrates that the Court takes proportionality concerns seriously when determining the lump sum and/or penalty payment imposed on a Member State. Interestingly, the recent reform of the Statute of the Court strengthened its control over respect of the proportionality requirement. As outlined in Section 2.1, it is the Commission's task to enforce the sanctions at issue and this institution has leeway to verify the (degree of) persistence of the infringement. The Member State involved could then have an interest in challenging the Commission's decisions in the enforcement phase. In the past, the jurisdiction for dealing with these actions for annulment was granted to the General Court,[93] which was – so to speak – "quite uncomfortable" about carrying out this review.[94] The amended wording of Article 51 of the Statute includes a new letter *c*), expressly giving to the Court of Justice the competence to adjudicate on this matter.

7.4. Conclusions

Over the decades, sanctions have become an increasingly important instrument in the Union's toolbox. The gradual strengthening of the EU *ius puniendi* is telling evidence of the progress made by the integration process, not only in relation to the acquisition of new competences, but primarily in terms of the establishment of institutional settings and of legal remedies securing the appropriate use of such powers.

The analysis developed in this Chapter highlights the efforts made by the Union to shape the whole sanctioning cycle – from the normative determination of the features of a sanction to its imposition and the judicial scrutiny of its effects on the recipient – after the requirements of suitability, necessity and proportionality, in the strict sense, which make up the proportionality test.

Crucially, due to its inherent elusiveness and to the many facets of EU sanctioning power, proportionality and its monitoring follow very different trajectories, depend-

---

[91] C-496/09, *Commission v. Italy*, ECLI:EU:C:2011:740. paras 48-52. At the same time, the Court dismisses the good faith cooperation and progress arguments when the action taken by the Member State has not brought about an actual improvement of the situation (and, therefore, to a lesser degree of seriousness of the infringement): C-557/14, *Commission v. Portugal*, ECLI:EU:C:2016:471, paras 79-80.

[92] C-241/11, *Commission v. Czech Republic*, ECLI:EU:C:2013:773.

[93] T-139/06, *France v. Commission*, ECLI:EU:T:2011:605; T-70/06, *Portugal v. Commission*, ECLI:EU:T:2008:266.

[94] L. Prete, *Infringement Proceedings in EU Law* (Wolters Kluwer, 2017) 395.

ing on the domain at issue and the tasks of the European and national institutions involved. However, some recurring features can be identified, which provide an illustration of the current magnitude of and constraints on EU sanctioning powers.

Firstly, the substantive and flexible approach to the notion of sanction maximises the scope of the principle of proportionality. The Court of Justice consistently holds that it is the EU legislature alone which must determine the most appropriate measures to secure compliance with EU law and the achievement of the objectives pursued by Union policies. Thus, the enforcement of EU law is equipped with a remarkably wide set of instruments facilitating the imposition of a – pecuniary, operational, organisational, personal – burden on an individual or an entity. Regardless of their formal qualification, the Court has always conditioned the legality of these measures on a proportionality test, so that the Union's coercive powers are subject to due constraints, regardless of the form they take.

Secondly, this approach also strengthens the judicial scrutiny of a measure, adding substance to the review that the Court may conduct. Proportionality requires a sanction to be *in abstracto* tailor-made to the conduct it addresses and to be appropriately pre-determined in all its main features. At the same time, this principle entails an individualised assessment of the criteria available to the competent authority in order to determine and impose a sanction, as well as the effects of a measure, in order to avoid unnecessary burdens. Although a normative measure of general nature cannot take into account any possible individual situation, the relevant legal framework and its actual application must not lead to a disproportionate use of coercive powers.

Of course, the more a sanction reflects wide policy choices, the fewer the possibilities there are to challenge it successfully, due to the light proportionality test to which the Court traditionally resorts when confronted with an act of the EU. However, case law demonstrates that this lenient review is not a blanket rule and leaves room for a detailed assessment of EU sanctions. Beyond general policy objectives underpinning a sanction, its imposition involves the assessment of factual elements and the use of factors and calculation methods that are generally suitable for a strict judicial review. In this respect, in the complementary area of indirect sanctioning powers, the current trend towards the adoption of increasingly specific rules concerning the type and level of sanctions that the Member States must implement in their legal orders to deal with breaches of EU law pave the way for further future advances of the Court of Justice case law, both in terms of the review of EU acts and of stricter guidance to national courts regarding the constraints on domestic *ius puniendi* stemming from the principle of proportionality.

Chapter 8
SANCTIONS IN THE EMU ECONOMIC PILLAR

Francesco Costamagna, Alberto Miglio[*-**]

ABSTRACT: *In the context of the economic pillar of the EMU, "soft" coordination mechanisms are backed by "hard" sanctions under the Stability and Growth Pact and the Macroeconomic Imbalances Procedure. Crisis-induced reforms have expanded the scope of EU sanctioning power and devised new procedural rules to facilitate their exercise. However, actual recourse to sanctions in EU economic governance has thus far been negligible. This apparent paradox can be explained on two counts. On the one hand, the EMU enforcement machinery provides a considerable degree of flexibility. On the other hand, alternative or complementary means of enforcement – based either on the power of financial markets or on conditionality – have emerged, reducing the need to resort to formal sanctions. The Chapter critically analyses these trends and indicates the main legal problems they raise.*

KEYWORDS: *EMU – sanctions – enforcement – Stability and Growth Pact – conditionality*

8.1. Introduction

The economic pillar of the Economic and Monetary Union (EMU) is one of the policy areas in which EU sanctioning powers have been debated most widely and intensely. In order to secure compliance with fiscal constraints by euro area Member

---

[*] Respectively, Associate Professor of EU Law and Postdoctoral Research Fellow in EU Law, University of Turin.

[**] The chapter is the outcome of a joint scientific effort by the authors. Paragraphs 8.1, 8.3, 8.4.1 and 8.4.3 were written by Francesco Costamagna, while Alberto Miglio is the author of paragraphs 8.2, 8,4.2, 8.5 and 8.6. The authors wish to thank Susanna Cafaro, Menelaos Markakis and Annamaria Viterbo for their insightful comments on the earlier drafts. As for any remaining errors and omissions, the usual disclaimer applies.

States, the Treaty drafters and the EU legislature devised special enforcement mechanisms that rely heavily on sanctions. Article 126 TFEU and the Stability and Growth Pact (SGP) grant EU institutions the power to monitor Member States' budgetary decisions and to impose fines if they deviate from the established benchmarks. In the wake of the financial and debt crisis of the 2010s, the 2011 Six-Pack considerably strengthened the sanctioning component of the SGP and, by introducing a Macroeconomic Imbalances Procedure (MIP), extended the sanctions beyond fiscal discipline to ensure compliance with macroeconomic performance parameters. There is also a significant degree of overlapping between EU rules and commitments to fiscal discipline undertaken by the Member States outside the EU framework, under the Treaty on Stability, Coordination and Governance in the Economic and Monetary Union (TSCG).[1]

At first sight, economic policy may thus appear to be the area in which the EU would most effectively exercise sanctioning powers over the Member States. Yet, despite the prominence of enforcement tools in the EMU architecture and the emphasis on fiscal discipline, the actual recourse to sanctions has been negligible.

This Chapter seeks to shed light on this apparent paradox. At the outset, we briefly illustrate the origin of the "hard" enforcement machinery in the economic pillar of the EMU, tracing its roots back to the original design of the Maastricht Treaty (section 2). In the following section, we outline the role played by sanctions for the enforcement of EU budgetary and macroeconomic rules (section 3). Against this background, we seek to explain the limited application of sanctions in practice by highlighting two possible reasons. On the one hand, in spite of the popular belief in their strictness, the rules on fiscal discipline actually provide a considerable degree of flexibility and discretion. On the other hand, sanctions are neither the only nor the most effective tool for ensuring that Member States comply with budgetary constraints. They share this function with different mechanisms, based either on the power of the market or on various forms of conditionality (section 4). The final part of the Chapter focuses on the procedural rules introduced since the Six-Pack with a view to improving the effectiveness of enforcement by injecting greater automaticity into the application of sanctions and into the operation of conditionality (section 5). The conclusion summarises the main findings and indicates the challenges raised by alternative enforcement tools and by adaptations to decision-making rules (section 6).

8.2. The structure of the EMU and the rationale for sanctions

As is well known, the legal architecture of the EMU is based on a fundamental di-

---

[1] On this overlapping, see P. Craig, 'The Stability, Coordination and Governance Treaty: Principle, Politics and Pragmatism' (2012) 37 *European Law Review* 231, 247.

vide between monetary policy and economic policy.[2] Although it may be somewhat inaccurate in terms of economic theory – as monetary policy is part of general economic policy[3] – this distinction forms the basis for the allocation of competence between the EU and the Member States. Monetary policy is an exclusive EU competence for euro area Member States[4] and it relies on a heavily centralised institutional setup, with the European Central Bank (ECB) at its core. By contrast, competence on economic policy rests primarily with the Member States,[5] with EU intervention mostly being limited to coordinating and supporting the Member States' policies.[6]

One reason for the limited scope of EU economic policy competence was the reluctance of Member States to relinquish their autonomy in this key policy area and to endow the Union with a substantial budget comparable to that of federal states.[7] Another reason was the belief in the stabilising effects of the financial markets, reflecting the influence monetarism, as a school of thought, had on the drafting of the Maastricht Treaty.[8] According to the monetarist view, fully integrated financial

---

[2] See, amongst others, F. Snyder, 'EMU Revisited: Are We Making a Constitution? What Constitution Are We Making?' EUI Working Paper LAW No. 98/6; S. Cafaro, *Unione monetaria e coordinamento delle politiche economiche. Il difficile equilibrio tra modelli antagonisti di integrazione europea* (Giuffrè, 2001); R.M. Lastra, J.-V. Louis, 'European Economic and Monetary Union: History, Trends, and Prospects' (2013) 32 *Yearbook of European Law* 57, 60-62.

[3] See A. Verdun, 'An Asymmetrical Economic and Monetary Union in the EU: Perceptions of Monetary Authorities and Social Partners' (1996) 20 *Journal of European Integration* 59; B. Laurens, E.G. de la Piedra, 'Coordination of Monetary and Fiscal Policies', IMF Working Papers No. WP/25/98, March 1998.

[4] Article 3(1)(c) TFEU.

[5] Whereas "*[t]he Union* shall establish an economic and monetary union" (Article 3(4) TEU), it is for "*Member States*" to "coordinate *their* economic policies with a view to contributing to the achievement of the objectives of the Union" (Article 120 TFEU). Emphasis added.

[6] The central Treaty provisions in this regard are Article 5 TFEU ("The Member States shall coordinate their economic policies within the Union. To this end, the Council shall adopt measures, in particular broad guidelines for these policies") and Article 2(3) TFEU ("The Member States shall coordinate their economic and employment policies within arrangements as determined by this Treaty, which the Union shall have competence to provide"). The extent to which this *sui generis* allocation of competences grants the EU power to intervene in economic affairs is debated: see R. Bieber, 'The Allocation of Economic Policy Competences in the European Union', in L. Azoulai (ed.), *The Question of Competence in the European Union* (Oxford University Press, 2014), 86-87. In addition, there are legal bases authorising the EU to intervene in specific fields, such as the Treaty provisions on economic, social and territorial cohesion – an area of shared competence according to Article 4(2)(c) TFEU – or Article 136 TFEU concerning the adoption of measures applicable to euro area Member States.

[7] Snyder, *supra* note 2, 6; J. Snell, 'The Trilemma of European Economic and Monetary Integration, and Its Consequences' (2016) 22 *European Law Journal* 157, 160.

[8] See P. De Grauwe, 'What Have we Learnt about Monetary Integration since the Maastricht Treaty?' (2006) 44 *Journal of Common Market Studies* 714, 726; J.-P. Fitoussi, F. Saraceno, 'Euro-

markets are sufficient to absorb asymmetric shocks, thereby safeguarding the stability of the common currency.

A corollary of this approach, which emphasises the role of markets in ensuring stability and the importance of structural reforms for the sustainability of a monetary union, is a set of legal rules restraining discretionary fiscal policy.[9] Despite retaining competence on matters of economic policy, the Member States are thus not free from EU law constraints in its exercise. In fact, the Member States do not enjoy absolute freedom in any policy area, as the principle of primacy implies that national law and practices must be compatible with EU law, irrespective of the allocation of competence.[10] However, the EMU is a special case in this regard. Member States are not merely under a general obligation to comply with EU law when they exercise their own competences, but they have assumed a specific set of commitments that directly impinge on their economic and fiscal policies. Indeed, in a normative and institutional setting based on the primacy of price and financial stability and lacking a common macroeconomic policy, a federal fiscal capacity and a strong EU budget, the Member States' commitment to budgetary discipline appeared necessary to guarantee the viability of the monetary union.[11] In order to prevent uncoordinated, discretionary fiscal policies at national level that could undermine the EMU, the drafters of the Maastricht Treaty devised two institutional mechanisms. On the one hand, the Treaty introduced a multilateral surveillance procedure aimed at coordinating the economic policies of the Member States (now Article 121 TFEU).[12] On the other hand, it established the excessive deficit procedure (EDP) to tackle Member States' failures to contain deficit and debt below agreed targets (now Article 126 TFEU). Both procedures were supplemented a few years later by the SGP, consisting of two Council regulations and a European Council resolution.[13] The preventive arm of the SGP strengthened the supervision over national budgets by requiring euro area Member States to submit a stability programme and

---

pean Economic Governance: The Berlin–Washington Consensus' (2013) 37 *Cambridge Journal of Economics* 479; M.K. Brunnermaier, H. James, J.-P. Landau, *The Euro and the Battle of Ideas* (Princeton University Press 2016).

[9] See C. Kaupa, *The Pluralist Character of the European Economic Constitution* (Hart, 2016), 285.

[10] See L. Azoulai, 'The "Retained Powers" Formula in the Case Law of the Court of Justice: EU Law as Total Law?' (2011) 4 *European Journal of Legal Studies* 192.

[11] M. Herdegen, 'Price Stability and Budgetary Restraints in the Economic and Monetary Union: The Law as Guardian of Economic Wisdom' (1998) 35 *Common Market Law Review* 9, 15-18.

[12] J-P. Keppenne, 'Economic Policy Co-Ordination: Foundations, Structures, and Objectives', in F. Amtenbrink, C. Herrmann (eds), *EU Law of Economic and Monetary Policy* (OUP 2020), 787.

[13] J-P. Keppenne, 'EU Fiscal Governance on the Member States: The Stability and Growth Pact and Beyond', in Amtenbrink and Herrmann (eds), *supra* note 12, 813.

entrusting the Council with monitoring its implementation.[14] Its corrective arm was intended to govern the EDP and to enhance its effectiveness.[15]

According to the logic underlying the Treaty provisions on economic policy and the SGP, sanctions and the threat thereof are an important instrument of compliance.[16] Their main function is deterrence:[17] the mere possibility of sanctions is intended to entrench the Member States' commitment to sound financial management and to the sustainability of public debt, which are, in turn, viewed as major factors contributing to the stability of the common currency.[18] However, the enforcement of constraints on Member States' economic policy departs significantly from the ordinary enforcement machinery generally available under EU law. The most important difference is the institutional setting that characterises each enforcement mechanism and, more specifically, who has the last say when it comes to deciding if the State concerned violated EU law. As is well known, in infringement proceedings the power to ascertain a breach of EU law by a Member State lays with the Court of Justice, which may also impose penalties in certain cases.[19] By contrast, the enforcement of fiscal constraints under the EDP and the SGP is entrusted to political institutions pursuant to special procedures. Indeed, the EDP and the infringement procedure are mutually exclusive, in so far as the Treaty precludes the possibility of bringing infringement actions pursuant to Articles 258 and 259 TFEU within the framework of an EDP.[20]

In the aftermath of the crisis that struck the Eurozone in 2009-2010, the SGP, including its sanctioning component, was considerably strengthened. In order to prevent euro area Member States' public finances from spiralling out of control again, the Six-Pack, a set of measures adopted in 2011,[21] sharpened sanctions and expanded their scope. In the

---

[14] Regulation 1466/97.

[15] Regulation 1467/97.

[16] F. Amtenbrink, R. Repasi, 'Compliance and Enforcement in Economic Policy Coordination in EMU' in A. Jakab, D. Kochenov (eds), *The Enforcement of EU Law and Values. Ensuring Member States' Compliance* (OUP 2017), 145.

[17] See J.-V. Louis, 'The Economic and Monetary Union: Law and Institutions' (2004) 41 *Common Market Law Review* 575, 577-578.

[18] Herdegen, *supra* note 11, 18.

[19] On sanctioning in the context of infringement proceedings, see the chapter by L. Prete in this book.

[20] See Article 126(10) TFEU.

[21] Regulation (EU) no. 1173/2011 of the European Parliament and of the Council on the effective enforcement of budgetary surveillance in the euro area OJ L306, 23.11.2011, 1-7; Regulation (EU) no. 1174/2011 of the European Parliament and of the Council on enforcement measures to correct excessive macroeconomic imbalances in the euro area OJ L 306, 23.11.2011, 8-11; Regulation (EU) no. 1175/2011 of the European Parliament and of the Council amending Council Regulation (EC) no. 1466/97 on the strengthening of the surveillance of budgetary positions and the surveillance and coordination of economic policies OJ L 306, 23.11.2011, 12-24; Regulation (EU)

next paragraph, we provide an overview of the existing sanctioning mechanisms in the economic pillar of the EMU.

8.3. "Hard" sanctioning powers in the EMU economic pillar

8.3.1. Sanctions under the Stability and Growth Pact

The above-mentioned SGP is a set of rules enforcing the so-called 'basic budgetary rule',[22] as envisaged by Article 126(1) TFEU and the Protocol on EDP.[23] According to this rule, Member States must avoid excessive deficits, which occur when the deficit-to-GDP ratio exceeds the 3% threshold, and excessive debt, i.e. a debt-GDP ratio higher than 60%.

The SGP has two components: a preventive arm, focusing on the surveillance of budgetary positions and the coordination of economic policies, and a corrective one, aiming "to deter excessive government deficits and, if they occur, to further prompt their correction".[24] Quite understandably, the exercise of sanctioning powers by EU institutions in the context of the SGP has traditionally been associated with the corrective arm of the SGP. However, post-crisis reforms and, in particular, the Six-Pack introduced the possibility of exercising such prerogatives as early as in the preventive arm. The choice is fully in line with the idea that pervaded the crisis-induced reform, according to which strengthening the SGP's sanctioning machinery was the main step to be taken to restore its credibility and its ability to deter the Member States from adopting unsound budgetary policies.

In particular, under Article 4 of Regulation 1173/2011, the Council, acting on a recommendation by the Commission, can request a Member State to lodge an interest-bearing deposit amounting to 0.2% of its GDP when it has significantly deviated from its Medium-Term Objective (MTO) or the adjustment path toward it. Before adopting such a measure, the Commission, when it observes a significant deviation, must address a warning to the Member State concerned "to prevent the occurrence of an excessive deficit".[25] Within one month of the warning, the Council may

no. 1176/2011 of the European Parliament and of the Council on the prevention and correction of macroeconomic imbalances OJ L 306, 23.11.2011, 25-32; Council Regulation (EU) no. 1177/2011 amending Regulation (EC) no. 1467/97 on speeding up and clarifying the implementation of the excessive deficit procedure OJ L 306, 23.11.2011, 33–40; and Council Directive 2011/85/EU on requirements for budgetary frameworks of the Member States OJ L 306, 23.11.2011, 41-47.

[22] F. Amtenbrink, 'The Metamorphosis of European Economic and Monetary Union', in A. Arnull, D. Chalmers (eds), *The Oxford Handbook of European Union Law* (Oxford University Press, 2015), 723.

[23] Protocol (No 12) on the excessive deficit procedure.

[24] Article 1 Regulation 1467/97.

[25] Article 6(2) Regulation 1466/97.

recommend the State to adopt specific policy measures to address the situation by a certain deadline. If the State fails to adopt those measures, the Council may adopt a decision establishing that no effective action has been taken. That decision is a pre-requisite for requiring the Member State concerned to lodge a deposit. The introduction of this possibility was intended to fill what many commentators considered a lacuna of the preventive component of the SGP, i.e. "the absence of any legally binding means to sanction Member States for non-compliance". [26]

The core of the EU institutions' sanctioning power in the context of the SGP lies with the EDP. This procedure, set out in Article 126 TFEU and regulated in detail by Regulation 1467/97, allows EU institutions to sanction Member States for failing to comply with the basic budgetary rule. The overall structure of the EDP has remained largely unaltered since its introduction in 1997, but the Six-Pack and the TSCG have broadened its scope of application and considerably increased the stringency of the mechanism.

The EDP begins with a decision by the Council on the existence of an excessive deficit, i.e. exceeding 3% of the GDP, based upon a recommendation by the Commission. The crisis-induced reforms of the SGP clarified that the deficit criterion is not the only relevant one and that an EDP may also be launched where public debt exceeds 60% of the GDP and the State has failed to reduce it at an average rate of $1/20^{th}$ per year. [27] When it decides that an excessive deficit or debt exists, the Council may address recommendations to the Member State concerned, demanding the adoption of specific measures to correct the situation. Since the entry into force of the Six-Pack, these recommendations have now been incorporated into the Country Specific Recommendations adopted in the context of the European Semester. [28]

---

[26] Amtenbrink, *supra* note 22, 726.

[27] Article 2 Regulation 1467/1997.

[28] The European Semester is a framework that, after being launched as a code of conduct for the implementation of the SGP, was fully codified by the Six-Pack and, in particular, by Regulation (EU) No. 1175/2011. It brings under the same umbrella different strains of EU policy coordination and surveillance which touch upon both economic and social policies. The Semester rests upon three main pillars, namely the Europe 2020 Integrated Guidelines, the Stability and Growth Pact, and the Macroeconomic Imbalances Procedure (MIP). It starts in November, when the Commission adopts the Annual Growth Survey (AGS), whose content, after being endorsed by the European Council, should feed into Member States' National Reform Programmes (NRPs) and Stability or Convergence Programmes (SCPs). In May, the Commission evaluates national reform and fiscal plans and issues Country-Specific Recommendations (CSRs) which indicate the actions to be taken by the State concerned. In July, the CSRs are finally approved by the ECOFIN Council. The approval of the 'Two-Pack' added a further step to the Semester, at least with regard to Euro States. Indeed, since 2013, the latter have been required to submit to the Commission by 15 October a draft budgetary plan for the following year. This allows the Commission to look into the measures proposed by national Governments at a time when these measures, and their modes of implementation, are being discussed by the national parliaments. If the Commission identifies serious non-compliance with SGP obligations, it can request the State concerned to submit a revised plan within three weeks.

The TSCG and Regulation 473/2013 imposed a further obligation upon a Member State under the EDP. Indeed, the State must present to the Commission and the Council an economic partnership programme, detailing "the policy measures and structural reforms that are needed to ensure an effective and lasting correction of the excessive deficit".[29] Moreover, the State is subjected to enhanced reporting requirements, if so requested by the Commission.[30]

Lastly, the decision on the existence of an excessive deficit or debt can also trigger a non-interest bearing deposit requirement. Pursuant to Article 5 of Regulation 1173/2011, this can occur either when the State had already been requested to lodge a deposit within the preventive arm of the SGP or when the Commission has identified "particularly serious non-compliance with the budgetary policy obligations".

When the Council – again acting upon a recommendation from the Commission – finds that the State has taken no effective action, it can decide to make its recommendations public.[31] Following the logic according to which reasserting the centrality of the sanctioning component was the only way to restore the SGP's lost credibility, the Six-Pack sought to add teeth to this decision, introducing the possibility for the Council to impose a fine on the State that has failed to take effective action.[32]

Prior to the adoption of the Six-Pack, the final phase of the EDP was the only one in which EU institutions could adopt sanctions against the State that persisted in not adopting the requested corrective measures. According to Article 126(11) TFEU, in determining the most appropriate 'sanction', the Council may choose from different options: requiring the State to publish additional information, inviting the European Investment Bank to reconsider its lending policy towards the State, requiring the State to lodge a non-interest bearing deposit, or imposing a fine. The original version of Article 11 of Regulation 1467/97 sought to articulate more clearly the relationship between the last two options, clarifying that the Council first had to impose a deposit. Only then could it issue a fine. The 2011 reform of this provision subverted the order, by specifying that "[w]henever the Council decides under Article 126(11) TFEU to impose sanctions on a participating Member State, a fine shall, as a rule, be required".

8.3.2. The Macroeconomic Imbalances Procedure

A further element of novelty introduced by the Six-Pack was the creation of the

---

[29] Article 9 Regulation 473/2013.

[30] Article 10 Regulation 473/2013.

[31] Article 126(8) TFEU.

[32] Article 6 Regulation 1173/2011.

Macroeconomic Imbalances Procedure (MIP). Structurally, the MIP is largely modelled on the SGP, having a preventive arm and a corrective one.[33] Substantively, it aims to overcome the SGP's exclusive focus on fiscal policy, by taking into account macro-financial and macro-structural aspects that, as the crisis dramatically showed, contributed to the accrual of internal and external imbalances triggering balance of payment crises and debt crises.

The starting point of the MIP is the Alert Mechanism Report (AMR), [34] which contains the Commission's assessment of the Member States' economic developments based upon a scoreboard of indicators looking at external imbalances and competitiveness, internal imbalances and employment trends. In the AMR, the Commission also identifies those States at risk of being affected by imbalances and thus worthy of further scrutiny. For each of these countries, the Commission carries out an in-depth review, to assess the existence and the gravity of economic imbalances.[35] On this basis, the Council, acting upon a recommendation from the Commission, may take preventive action, recommending that the Member State involved adopt corrective measures.

If the Commission is convinced that the State is facing excessive imbalances, it can recommend that the Council certify the existence of this situation and can recommend the State to adopt corrective measures. This is the opening step of the Excessive Imbalance Procedure (EIP), which is the corrective phase of the MIP. At that point, the Member State concerned must present a corrective action plan, which is then monitored and assessed by the Council and the Commission. If the Council, based upon a report by the Commission, considers that the measures adopted are not in line with those planned, it can adopt a decision establishing non-compliance, together with a recommendation setting a new deadline for the adoption of the corrective measures.[36] For euro area Member States, the non-compliance decision can trigger a sanctioning mechanism pursuant to Regulation 1174/2011.[37] The sanctions are similar to those that can be adopted in the context of the SGP, since the Council can impose an interest-bearing deposit or a fine. More specifically, the Council, after having issued the non-compliance decision, can first impose a deposit, when it concludes that the Member State concerned has failed to adopt the

---

[33] See, respectively, Regulation 1176/2011 and Regulation 1174/2011. See generally L. Flynn, 'Non-Fiscal Surveillance of the Member States', in Amtenbrink and Herrmann (eds), *supra* note 12, 850.

[34] Article 3 Regulation 1176/2011.

[35] Article 5 Regulation 1176/2011.

[36] Article 10(4) Regulation 1176/2011.

[37] The Regulation is based on Article 121 TFEU in combination with Article 136 TFEU and only applies to Member States whose currency is the euro.

recommended corrective action.[38] Conversely, the State may be requested to pay a fine if, in the same imbalance procedure, the Council adopts either two successive recommendations finding that the corrective plan is insufficient or two successive non-compliance decisions.[39]

8.4. The limited application of sanctions: reasons and alternatives

8.4.1. Elements of flexibility in the sanctioning machinery

Despite recent reforms of EU economic governance focusing on strengthening the sanctioning machinery, the actual recourse to sanctions against Member States in this context has been negligible. Although every Member State, except Estonia and Sweden, has been subject to an EDP,[40] none of them have been sanctioned so far. In 2016, Spain and Portugal narrowly escaped fines when the Commission proposed that sanctions be imposed on those Member States due to the failure to tackle their excessive deficit, which it later recommended be cancelled.[41] The Council followed the Commission's recommendation and cancelled the fines.[42] The only instance where a sanction was adopted against a Member State in the context of the SGP occurred in 2015, when Spain was fined for presenting incorrect budgetary statistics.[43]

The mismatch between the perceived centrality of sanctions as enforcement tools in the EMU and their lack of application in practice can be explained on two counts: the intrinsic flexibility embedded in the SGP and in the MIP, and the existence of alternative, possibly more effective, enforcement mechanisms which, despite not being sanctions in the proper sense, play a comparable role.

Traditionally, the SGP has been considered as being rather mechanical and rigid in its functioning. In reality, both its preventive and its corrective arm contain several elements of flexibility that make the process of adopting a sanction far from straightforward. Flexibility is certainly essential in a context where eminently politi-

---

[38] Article 3(1) Regulation 1174/2011.

[39] Article 3(2) Regulation 1174/2011.

[40] See https://ec.europa.eu/info/business-economy-euro/economic-and-fiscal-policy-coordination/eu-economic-governance-monitoring-prevention-correction/stability-and-growth-pact/corrective-arm-excessive-deficit-procedure/excessive-deficit-procedures-overview_en.

[41] See Stability and Growth Pact: fiscal proposals for Spain and Portugal, press release, 27 July 2016, https://ec.europa.eu/commission/presscorner/detail/en/IP_16_2625.

[42] Council Decision (EU) 2017/984 of 8 August 2016 giving notice to Spain to take measures for the deficit reduction judged necessary in order to remedy the situation of excessive deficit, OJ 2017 L 148/38; Council Decision (EU) 2017/985 of 8 August 2016 giving notice to Portugal to take measures for the deficit reduction judged necessary in order to remedy the situation of excessive deficit, OJ 2017 L 148/42.

[43] Council Decision (EU) 2015/1289 of 13 July 2015 imposing a fine on Spain for the manipulation of deficit data in the Autonomous Community of Valencia.

cal choices on the allocation of scarce resources are at stake. This, in turn, entrusts supranational institutions – and the Commission, in particular – with a broad margin of discretion.

An initial element of flexibility lies with the inherent vagueness of the terms used to define some of the benchmarks against which the State's fiscal or macroeconomic position is to be assessed. This is the case, for instance, with the notion of "excessive deficit", to be determined by taking into account whether it is due to "an unusual event outside the control of the Member State concerned" or "a severe economic downturn",[44] or with the definition of "excessive imbalance" in the context of the MIP.[45]

Secondly, in the aftermath of the financial crisis, the Commission, giving in to the pressure of several Member States, sought to inject greater flexibility into the SGP, without formally changing the rules.[46] To this end, it identified certain investments that were not to be taken into account when determining the fiscal adjustment under the preventive or the corrective arm of the SGP and it announced that it would interpret extensively the so-called "structural reforms clause" contained in Article 5 of Regulation (EC) 1466/97.

A further element of flexibility is the so-called 'general escape clause' enshrined in Articles 3(5) and 5(2) of Regulation 1467/2011. Pursuant to this mechanism, in the case of a severe economic downturn in the euro area or in the Union as a whole, the Council may decide, on a recommendation from the Commission, to adopt a revised fiscal trajectory.[47] Recently, this 'general escape clause' was activated in the face of the expected severe economic downturn caused by the COVID-19 pandemic.[48] Finally – and most importantly – quantitative benchmarks are not decisive *per se* in determining whether or not a State should be sanctioned for its failure to implement a sustainable budgetary policy or to correct excessive macroeconomic imbalances. As is already clarified by Article 126 TFEU with regard to the EDP, a sanction can be triggered by the failure of the Member State concerned to adopt the corrective measures recommended by the Council. The same applies to the MIP, as

---

[44] Article 2 Regulation 1467/2011.

[45] Article 2 Regulation 1176/2011 is of little help in this regard, simply stating that "'excessive imbalances' means severe imbalances, including imbalances that jeopardise or risk jeopardising the proper functioning of the economic and monetary union".

[46] Commission Communication, Making the Best Use of Flexibility within the Existing Rules of the Stability and Growth Pact, COM(2015) 12 final.

[47] Regulation 1467/2011, respectively Articles 5(1) and 9(1) for the preventive arm, and Articles 3(5) and 5(2) for the corrective arm of the SGP.

[48] The Commission recommended activating the 'general escape clause' on 20 March 2020 (Commission Communication on the activation of the general escape clause of the Stability and Growth Pact, COM(2020) 123 final). On 23 March 2020, the Council endorsed the Commission's recommendation.

Article 10(4) of Regulation 1176/2011 provides that the Council may adopt a decision of non-compliance – which is the precondition for applying pecuniary sanctions – only "[w]here it considers that the Member State has not taken the recommended corrective action".

Over the years, the control exercised by supranational institutions has progressively shifted its focus from quantitative benchmarks to adopted policy measures. [49] The Six-Pack pushed this evolution further, by combining hard sanctioning mechanisms and soft coordination processes under the European Semester. In this context, the possibility of adopting coercive measures is now seen primarily as an instrument to pressure Member States into adopting the structural reforms recommended by EU institutions.

This trend is exemplified by those cases in which the Commission decided to close an EDP after the State concerned adopted the recommended policy measures, despite its fiscal position not improving. The adoption of the so-called *Loi Khomri* (or *Loi Travail*) in France is a case in point. [50] In the wake of the crisis, France struggled to meet the SGP debt and deficit benchmarks and was placed under an EDP in April 2009. [51] In 2013, the Commission and the Council began to place greater emphasis on the link between the "correction of the fiscal imbalances" and "a credible implementation of ambitious structural reforms to increase the adjustment capacity and boost growth and employment". [52] In particular, France was recommended to reduce the cost of labour and to "ensure that developments in the minimum wage are supportive of competitiveness and job creation". [53] The same happened, with only minor terminological variations, in 2014 [54]

[49] D. Chalmers, 'The European Redistributive State and a European Law of Struggle' (2012) 18 *European Law Journal* 667, 679-681. Further, on this point, D. Chalmers, 'Crisis Reconfiguration of the European State', in D. Chalmers, M. Jachtenfuchs and C. Joerges (eds.) *The End of the Eurocrats Dream* (Cambridge University Press, 2016), 266. See also F. Costamagna, 'National Social Spaces as Adjustment Variables in the EMU: A Critical Legal Appraisal' (2018) *European Law Journal* 163, 175.

[50] R. Erne, 'A Supranational Regime that Nationalizes Social Conflict: Explaining European Trade Unions' Difficulties in Politicizing European Economic Governance', (2015) 56 *Labor History* 345, 348.

[51] Council Decision No. 2009/414/EC of 27 April 2009 on the existence of an excessive deficit in France, OJ L 135 of 30.05.2009, 19-20.

[52] Council Recommendation of 9 July 2013 on the National Reform Programme 2013 of France and delivering a Council opinion on the Stability Programme of France, 2012-2017, OJ C 217 of 30.07.2013, 31.

[53] *Ibidem*.

[54] Council Recommendation of 8 July 2014 on the National Reform Programme 2014 of France and delivering a Council opinion on the Stability Programme of France, 2014, OJ C 247 of 29.07.2014, 47-48.

and 2015.[55] In February 2015, the French Government bowed to the pressure, passing a law that aimed to make the labour market more business-friendly. The decision paid off, as the Commission refrained from sanctioning France despite its failure to bring the deficit under the 3% threshold.[56]

8.4.2. Enforcement by the market

Flexibility alone cannot account for the extremely limited recourse to the EMU sanctioning apparatus. A second factor that contributes to explaining this phenomenon is the existence of other enforcement tools which may not fall as evidently within the traditional understanding of 'sanctions' in legal terms, but nevertheless perform a similar function.

The most important enforcement tool in EU economic policy is arguably market discipline.[57] It is often assumed that surveillance over fiscal discipline and macroeconomic performance by Member States is essentially a task for public institutions, since private enforcers would be "hardly available".[58] In fact, private entities play a central role in ensuring the effectiveness of EU budgetary constraints. Rather than the threat of sanctions, it is pressure from financial markets that provides incentives for fiscal probity. Crucially, reliance on the disciplinary effect of financial markets was an intentional choice and has been a structural feature of the EMU design since the Maastricht Treaty.[59] The TFEU contains a set of prohibitions aimed at subjecting Member States to the disciplining power of the market. Article 123 TFEU prohibits the monetary financing of public authorities by central banks, ensuring that the financing of Member States' public debt occurs at market conditions. Article 124 supplements that prohibition by ruling out privileged access to financial institutions by public authorities, whereas Article 125 TFEU (so-called 'no-bailout clause') stipulates that neither the Union nor the other Member States may be liable for or assume the commitments of a Member State. In essence, these prohibitions aim to ensure that Member States resort to capital markets to finance their debt. In order

---

[55] Council Recommendation of 14 July 2015 on the 2015 National Reform Programme of France and delivering a Council opinion on the 2015 Stability Programme of France, OJ C 272 of 18.08.2015, 55.

[56] Commission recommendation for a Council Recommendation with a view to bringing an end to the excessive government deficit in France, 27 February 2015, COM(2015) 115 def. The French case is discussed in European Court of Auditors, *Special Report No 10/2016: Further Improvements Needed to Ensure Effective Implementation of the Excessive Deficit Procedure* (Publications Office of the European Union 2016).

[57] See Amtenbrink and Repasi, *supra* note 16, 169.

[58] R. Bieber, F. Maiani, 'Enhancing Centralized Enforcement of EU Law: Pandora's Toolbox?' (2014) 51 *Common Market Law Review* 1057, 1058.

[59] M. Ioannidis, 'Europe's New Transformations: How the EU Economic Constitution Changed during the Eurozone Crisis' (2016) 53 *Common Market Law Review* 1237, 1249-1259.

to be able to raise capital, they must inspire confidence in their solvency. Accordingly, pressure from capital markets should provide a crucial incentive for Member States to pursue a 'sound' and sustainable fiscal policy.[60] In addition to those prohibitions, other rules are intended to amplify the disciplining effects of market pressure: in both the macroeconomic surveillance procedure and the EDP, the possibility of making recommendations public[61] serves this purpose, making markets aware of the conduct expected of the Member State concerned.[62] From a strictly legal perspective, pressure from financial markets may not easily fit within the notion of sanction.[63] However, it performs a comparable function in economic terms, since it aims to prevent moral hazard and to incentivise fiscal probity.

After the financial crisis dramatically exposed the weakness of this design and the risk that the default of a euro area Member State would pose to the common currency, a somewhat permissive interpretation of the no-bailout clause and of the prohibition on monetary financing prevailed. The Court of Justice held in *Pringle* that the establishment of the European Stability Mechanism (ESM) for the purpose of granting financial assistance to euro area Member States was compatible with the Treaties[64] and upheld the legality of ECB non-conventional monetary policy measures in *Gauweiler*[65] and *Weiss*[66]. The Court's assessment of crisis-induced measures may be viewed as ushering in a transformation of the EU economic constitution,[67] yet it certainly did not discard the assumption that market pressure would be needed to preserve the stability of the common currency.[68] In *Pringle*, the statement that Article 125 TFEU did not prohibit outright financial assistance between euro area Member States was accompanied by the proviso that assistance would be permissible only if it did not remove the incentive to maintain budgetary discipline

[60] See M. Ruffert, 'The European Debt Crisis and European Union Law' (2011) 48 *Common Market Law Review* 1777, 1786.

[61] Article 121(4) TFEU; Article 126(8) TFEU.

[62] A. von Bogdandy, F. Arndt, J. Bast, 'Legal Instruments in European Union Law and their Reform: A Systematic Approach on an Empirical Basis' (2004) 23 *Yearbook of European Law* 91, 113.

[63] According to the Black's Law Dictionary, "a 'sanction' is a penalty or punishment provided as a means of enforcing obedience to a law".

[64] C-370/12 *Pringle*, ECLI:EU:C:2012:756.

[65] C-62/14 *Gauweiler and Others*, ECLI:EU:C:2015:400.

[66] C-493/17 *Weiss and Others*, ECLI:EU:C:2018:1000. However, the German Federal Constitutional Court declared this judgment, as well as the underlying decisions adopted by the ECB, as being *ultra vires*. See BVerfG, Judgment of the Second Senate of 05 May 2020 - 2 BvR 859/15 -, ECLI:DE:BVerfG:2020:rs20200505.2bvr085915.

[67] See Ioannidis, *supra* note 59.

[68] H. Schepel, 'The Bank, the Bond, and the Bail-out: On the Legal Construction of Market Discipline in the Eurozone' (2017) 44 *Journal of Law and Society* 79.

provided by the "logic of the market".[69] The Court reached a similar conclusion with respect to Article 123 TFEU in *Gauweiler*, where it held that purchases of sovereign bonds on the secondary market may not be used to circumvent the objective underpinning the prohibition on monetary financing.[70]

Since the outbreak of the financial crisis, market incentives have proven complementary to legal constraints in forcing Member States to pursue fiscal austerity policies. It was ultimately market pressure and the threat of being forced by lack of liquidity to exit the Eurozone that convinced the Greek government to agree to a deal over the bailout package in summer 2015 despite the outcome of a domestic referendum.[71] Italy is another case in point. The need to contain the rise of interest rates on public debt was a source of restraint on expansive fiscal policy by the Italian authorities, making the recourse to formal sanctions by EU institutions unnecessary.

8.4.3. Conditionality

Market discipline is not the only enforcement mechanism that performs a function comparable to sanctions in the proper sense. Aside from the pressure from the financial markets, since the outbreak of the Eurozone crisis, conditionality has emerged as the most effective tool for enforcing fiscal constraints. Conditionality has been employed primarily in the context of financial assistance.[72] Drawing from the experience of pre-accession negotiations and from IMF practice, loan disbursements under assistance programmes were made conditional upon the adoption by the Member State concerned of fiscal consolidation measures and structural reforms.[73] Despite the variety of legal instruments employed to collect and transfer

---

[69] *Pringle*, para. 135-136.

[70] *Gauweiler*, para. 101.

[71] See V. Dendrinou, E. Varvitsioti, *The Last Bluff* (Papadopoulos Publishing 2019).

[72] See M. Ioannidis, 'EU Financial Assistance Conditionality after "Two Pack"' (2014) 74 *Zeitschrift für ausländisches öffentliches Recht und Völkerrecht* 61; A. Viterbo, R. Cisotta, 'La crisi del debito sovrano e gli interventi dell'U.E.: dai primi strumenti finanziari al *Fiscal Compact*' (2012) 17 *Il Diritto dell'Unione Europea* 323, 342-348. Prior to the crisis-induced reforms, a similar mechanism only existed for non-euro area Member States under Regulation 332/2002 on the provision of medium-term financial assistance for Member States' balances of payment. According to Article 3(2)(b) of the Regulation, which does not apply to Member States whose currency is the euro, upon granting financial assistance to a Member State the Council shall determine "the economic policy conditions attaching to the medium-term financial assistance with a view to re-establishing or ensuring a sustainable balance of payments situation".

[73] In some cases, EU institutions and, in particular, the ECB resorted to informal tools, such as secret letters, to put pressure on some Member States to force them to enter into a structural adjustment programme or to adopt budgetary consolidation measures. On this form of implicit conditionality, see S. Sacchi, 'Conditionality by Other Means: EU Involvement in Italy's Structural Reforms in the Sovereign Debt Crisis' (2015) 13 *Comparative European Politics* 77; A. Viterbo, 'Legal and Accountability Issues Arising from the ECB's Conditionality' (2016) 1 *European Papers* 501.

financial resources to the requesting Member State, either integrated into or external – but connected – to the EU legal order,[74] the recourse to conditionality in the form of memoranda of understanding was a key feature in all financial assistance programmes. In this context, conditionality can be seen as a continuation of the enforcement mechanisms described above by other, and far more stringent, means. Operating in a situation of emergency, EU institutions, especially those forming part of the so-called 'Troika',[75] enjoyed an unprecedented capacity of policy formulation, supervision and guidance on key economic and social issues. However, under this form of control, the Member State concerned is relieved of its reporting obligations under the SGP and the MIP, as envisaged by Article 7 of Regulation 472/2013.

More recently, EMU-related conditionality was also embraced in the operation of the European Structural and Investment Funds ('ESI Funds'). This new type of 'spending conditionality'[76] is one of the major innovations in the 2013 reform of structural funds ahead of the launch of the 2014-2020 programme period. Regulation 1303/2013[77] transformed ESI Funds into compliance tools backing EMU governance mechanisms.[78] Pursuant to Article 23 of the Regulation, ESI Funds' commitments and payments may be suspended where a Member State has failed to comply with its obligations under an EDP, in the case of particularly serious macroeconomic imbalances or if a Member State receiving financial assistance has breached its commitments under a macroeconomic adjustment programme.[79] As to

---

[74] See A. Hinarejos, 'The Legality of Responses to the Crisis', in Amtenbrink and Herrmann (eds), *supra* note 12, 1376-1380; C. Kilpatrick, 'Are the Bailouts Immune to EU Social Challenge Because They Are not EU Law?' (2014) 10 *European Constitutional Law Review* 363; Ioannidis, *supra* note 72.

[75] See A. Sapir, G.B. Wolff, C. de Sousa, A. Terzi, *The Troika and financial assistance in the euro area. Successes and failures* – Study for the Directorate-General for Internal Policies of the Union (European Parliament) (EU Publications 2014).

[76] V. Viţă, 'Revisiting the Dominant Discourse on Conditionality in the EU: The Case of EU Spending Conditionality' (2017) 19 *Cambridge Yearbook of European Legal Studies* 116.

[77] Regulation (EU) No 1303/2013 of the European Parliament and of the Council of 17 December 2013 laying down common provisions on the European Regional Development Fund, the European Social Fund, the Cohesion Fund, the European Agricultural Fund for Rural Development and the European Maritime and Fisheries Fund and laying down general provisions on the European Regional Development Fund, the European Social Fund, the Cohesion Fund and the European Maritime and Fisheries Fund and repealing Council Regulation (EC) no. 1083/2006.

[78] See, generally, Amtenbrink and Repasi, *supra* note 16, 157.

[79] The Commission proposed to include the same clause also in the Recovery and Resilience Facility, the mechanism offering financial support for investments and reforms in response to the economic and social crisis generated by the COVID-19 pandemic and in relation to the green and digital transitions. See Article 9 of the Proposal for a Regulation of the European Parliament and the Council *estabilishing a Recovery and Resilience Facility*, 28.05.2020, COM(2020) 408 final.

the first case, the Commission may propose to suspend ESI disbursements when the Council has decided that the Member State concerned has failed to address its excessive deficit.[80] In the context of an MIP, the Commission may propose to put ESI Funds on hold where the Council has adopted either two successive recommendations finding that the corrective action plan proposed by the Member State concerned is insufficient[81] or two successive decisions establishing non-compliance by a Member State that failed to take the recommended corrective action.[82] Finally, funding can be suspended if a Member State receiving financial assistance has not implemented the adjustment programme referred to in Regulation 407/2010 or has failed to honour its commitments under a macro-economic adjustment programme referred to in Article 7 of Regulation 472/2013.

Both conditionality under financial assistance programmes and 'spending conditionality' under Regulation 1303/2013 are relative novelties compared to pre-existing, more established forms of conditionality in the EU legal order. Traditionally, conditionality has been employed in relations with third countries, either as a tool in pre-accession negotiations[83] or as a means to advance EU values in trade and aid policies.[84] By making a given benefit (for instance, the provision of development aid or privileged access to the EU market) conditional upon compliance with certain commitments, the EU is able to project its own values, particularly on human rights, the rule of law, and democracy, onto the international scene.[85] By contrast, 'internal' conditionality enshrined in post-crisis reforms serves a different function. It does not aim to export EU values to third countries, but to stimulate compliance with fiscal rules and to boost the effectiveness of the EMU enforcement machinery. In a long-term perspective, 'spending conditionality' appears to be more innovative than financial assistance conditionality. Whereas the latter is seen as exceptional and temporary, the former is an ordinary component of the EU enforcement machinery.[86] As such, it

---

[80] In accordance with Article 126(8) and (11) TFEU.

[81] Article 8(3) Regulation 1176/2011.

[82] Article 10(4) Regulation 1176/2011.

[83] See D. Kochenov, *EU Enlargement and the Failure of Conditionality: Pre-accession Conditionality in the Fields of Democracy and the Rule of Law* (Kluwer, 2008); E. Gateva, *European Union Enlargement Conditionality* (Palgrave Macmillan, 2015).

[84] See L. Bartels, *Human Rights Conditionality in the EU's International Agreements* (Oxford University Press, 2005).

[85] On values in EU external policy, see M. Cremona, 'Values in EU Foreign Policy', in M. Evans, P. Koutrakos (eds), *Beyond the Established Orders: Policy Interconnections between the EU and the Rest of the World* (Hart, 2011), p. 275.

[86] EMU governance has proven to be an important laboratory for the design of institutional mechanisms that may be replicated in other policy areas. The Commission's proposal for a regulation on the protection of the EU budget in case of generalised deficiencies of the rule of law in the Member States suggests that conditionality could become an instrument for the enforcement of EU values on recalcitrant Member States, well beyond the boundaries of economic policy. Under

is likely to trigger a more in-depth transformation in the relationship between the EU and the Member States.[87] Governance by conditionality departs from the traditional toolbox available for guaranteeing compliance with EU law and calls into question the very need to resort to sanctions, as it offers an easy alternative to the enforcement procedures laid down in the Treaties. In particular, the 'spending conditionality' embedded in the operation of ESI Funds allows EU institutions to fully exploit the asymmetry of power that underpins the relationship between a party controlling financial resources and a party hoping to reap a benefit from their provision.

8.5. Towards quasi-automatic enforcement? Reverse qualified majority voting

Sanctions under the SGP and conditionality mechanisms were either introduced or considerably strengthened in response to the Eurozone crisis. However, in addition to substantive rules, the pro-sanction logic that permeated post-crisis reforms also affected procedural rules. The Six-Pack and the TSCG intervened on what was considered a major flaw of the original EMU setup, i.e. the decision to leave the final say on the adoption of sanctions to the Council. This was identified as a major factor explaining the inability of the SGP to prevent Member States from adopting unsustainable budgetary policies.[88] The usual example cited in this regard is the 2003 Council's decision to brush aside a Commission recommendation requiring France and Germany to bring their deficits below the 3% threshold by the following year.[89] Against this background, the Six-Pack sought to inject greater automa-

---

the scheme envisaged by the Commission, disbursements of EU funds could be suspended in case of rule of law deficiencies in a Member State liable to impair sound financial management and threaten the financial interests of the Union (Proposal for a Regulation of the European Parliament and the Council on the protection of the Union's budget in case of generalised deficiencies as regards the rule of law in the Member States, COM(2018) 324). See the chapter by M. Bonelli in this book.

[87] Viţă, *supra* note 76, 119.

[88] D. Adamski, 'National Power Games and Structural Failures in the European Economic Governance' (2012) 49 *Common Market Law Review* 1319, 1322-1323; R. Palmstorfer, 'The Reverse Majority Voting under the "Six Pack": A Bad Turn for the Union?' (2014) 20 *European Law Journal* 191. See, for a different perspective, Snell, *supra* note 7, 160-164, who observes that this was one of the elements concurring to preserve policy space for national authorities.

[89] Decision 2003/89/EC on the existence of an excessive deficit in Germany—Application of Article 104(6) of the Treaty establishing the European Community, OJ L34 of 11.02.2003; Decision 2003/487/EC on the existence of an excessive deficit in France—Application of Article 104(6) of the Treaty establishing the European Community, OJ L165 of 03.07.2003. On 25 November 2003, the Council voted on the recommendations, failing to reach the required majority. The Commission brought an action of annulment against the non-decision of the Council, but the Court dismissed it (see Judgment of 13 July 2004, *Commission v. Council*, C-27/04, paras. 25-36).

ticity in the system by introducing reverse qualified majority voting (RQMV) in all cases where the Council decides on the adoption of sanctions or the imposition of a deposit.[90] This means that a Commission recommendation to impose a sanction is adopted unless the Council votes against it by qualified majority. The TSCG further extended the applicability of RQMV, stating that "Contracting Parties whose currency is the euro commit to supporting the proposals or recommendations submitted by the European Commission where it considers that a Member State of the European Union whose currency is the euro is in breach of the deficit criterion in the framework of an excessive deficit procedure".[91] The same voting procedure also applies in the context of the MIP: Article 3(3) of Regulation 1176/2011 clarifies that this is the way in which a decision imposing a deposit or a fine is to be adopted.

Later legislative instruments further extended the scope of RQMV beyond the SGP and the MIP to various conditionality mechanisms. Firstly, Regulation 472/2013 introducing specific rules on conditionality for Member States receiving financial assistance makes the adoption of corrective measures for Member States under post-programme surveillance subject to RQMV.[92] The adoption of recommendations under post-programme surveillance also occurs according to the same voting procedure.[93] Moreover, all decisions on the suspension of ESI Funds pursuant to Regulation 1303/2013 are taken by way of RQMV.[94]

Arguably, the extension of RQMV beyond the SGP and the rules on economic policy coordination to the operation of conditionality represents a significant development in the EU enforcement machinery. Indeed, while the introduction of RQMV in the Six-Pack may be viewed as an exceptional, emergency-driven measure enacted to cope with pressure from the capital markets in the direst phase of the Eurozone crisis,[95] its replication in other pieces of legislation is evidence of its value as a general governance mechanism. It reveals a willingness to give teeth to the enforcement of fiscal constraints by replacing political discretion with semi-automatic decision-making on a permanent basis.

Undoubtedly, the introduction of RQMV strengthens the Commission's position at the expense of the intergovernmental logic prevailing in the Council. From the per-

---

[90] The category is to be seen in a broad sense, including, for instance, also the case where the Council requires a State to lodge a non-interest bearing deposit in the context of the preventive arm of the SGP (see Article 5 Regulation 1173/2011).

[91] Article 7 TSCG.

[92] Article 14(1) Regulation 472/2013.

[93] Article 14(4) Regulation 472/2013.

[94] Article 23(10) Regulation 1303/2013. An identical mechanism is also envisaged, beyond the EMU, by the Commission proposal for a regulation on the protection of the EU budget in case of generalised deficiencies of the rule of law in the Member States. See Article 5(7) of the proposal.

[95] See Editorial Comments, 'Some thoughts concerning the Draft Treaty on a Reinforced Economic Union' (2012) 49 *Common Market Law Review* 1-2.

spective of the effectiveness of EU law, it could be hailed as a remarkably positive development, as it allows the Commission to play its role as Guardian of the Treaties more fully and boosts the strength of the EU enforcement machinery. However, this very effect also raises doubts on the compatibility of RQMV with EU primary law, particularly with the rules governing Council decision-making and with the principle of institutional balance.[96] Apparently, the categorisation of sanctioning measures under the Six-Pack[97] and decisions on conditionality as implementing measures[98] offers some support for the legality of RQMV. Indeed, it has long been accepted that the legislature may introduce new procedures, other than those laid down in the Treaties, for the purpose of regulating the adoption of implementing acts.[99] However, it is questionable whether the legislature, in laying down provisions for the adoption of implementing measures, may derogate from Article 16(3) TEU, which states that the Council "shall act by a qualified majority except where the Treaties provide otherwise". Moreover, the new voting mechanism is also problematic in light of the principle of institutional balance.[100] By reversing the requirements of 'ordinary' majority voting and enhancing the Commission's position to the detriment of the Council, it upsets the balance of power between institutions designed by the Treaty in the context of EU economic governance.

8.6. Conclusion

Crisis-induced reforms significantly increased the centrality of sanctions in the EMU enforcement machinery. In addition to the expansion and the hardening of sanctions, post-crisis legislation brought about a major procedural innovation by introducing RQMV for the adoption of sanctions. Despite this, the application of sanctions in the EMU economic pillar is virtually non-existent. Various elements of flexibility embedded in EU economic governance mechanisms and the emergence of other enforcement tools account for this apparent paradox. In particular, means such as market pressure and conditionality have contributed to the fulfilment of EMU objectives, acting either as a

---

[96] See Ruffert, *supra* note 60, 1800; J. Bast, F. Rödl, 'Jenseits der Koordinierung? Zu den Grenzen der EU Verträge für eine Europäische Wirtschaftsregierung' (2012) 39 *Europäische Grundrechte Zeitschrift* 269; H. Rathke, '"Umgekehrte Abstimmung" in der Fiskalunion: neue Stabilitätskultur oder halbautomatischer Vertragsbruch' (2012) *Die Öffentliche Verwaltung* 751; Palmstorfer, *supra* note 87, 191-202; A. Miglio, 'Reverse Qualified Majority Vote in Post-crisis EU Economic Governance: A Circumvention of Institutional Balance?', Working Paper REScEU no. 23, 2019, https://www.resceu.eu/publications/working-papers/wp-1-2019-reverse-qualified-majority-vote-in-post-crisi-eu-economic-governance-a-circumvention-of-institutional-balance.html.

[97] See C-521/15, *Spain v. Council*, ECLI:EU:C:2017:982.

[98] See, in particular, Article 23(6) and (10) Regulation 1303/2013.

[99] See 230/78, *Eridania*, ECLI:EU:C:1979:216, para. 7.

[100] Palmstorfer, *supra* note 87, 200-201; Miglio, *supra* note 95, 13-15.

complement to or, more often, as a substitute for formal sanctions. Both the hardening of sanctions proper and the emergence of new enforcement techniques strengthen the Commission's role in the EMU.[101] On a procedural level, RQMV reinforces the Commission's position to the detriment of the Council when it comes to deciding on sanctions. On a substantive level, conditionality likewise enhances its power by relying on financial incentives.

The evolutionary patterns outlined above give rise to a number of legal questions. The flexibility embedded in the EMU enforcement machinery makes sanctions dependent on vague criteria and emphasises political discretion.[102] Against this background, the traditional lack of parliamentary and judicial accountability in the context of the EMU is problematic.[103] Recourse to decision-making procedures based on reverse majority voting for the purpose of facilitating enforcement further amplifies those shortcomings. Not only is the application of sanctions left to the decision of political bodies, the Council's discretion, which is a basic feature of the enforcement system set out in the Treaties,[104] is also curtailed to the benefit of the Commission. The implications of this shift on the EU's constitutional balance[105] should not be underestimated.

The emergence of enforcement mechanisms other than formal sanctions raises additional concerns. Firstly, these mechanisms tend to prioritise financial stability, as the primary EMU objective,[106] over concurrent policy objectives, upsetting the balance between the economic and the social dimension in European integration.[107] The primacy of EMU requirements over different EU objectives has been extensively discussed with regard to financial assistance conditionality.[108] A similar evolution

---

[101] R. Smits, 'From Subordinated to Prominent. The Role of the European Commission in EMU. Reflections on Euro Area Democracy', in L. Daniele, P. Simone, R. Cisotta (eds), *Democracy in the EMU in the Aftermath of the Crisis* (Springer and Giappichelli 2017), p. 51.

[102] See Bieber and Maiani, *supra* note 58, 1071.

[103] See, generally, C. Fasone, 'European Economic Governance and Parliamentary Representation. What Place for the European Parliament?' (2014) 20 *European Law Journal* 164; R. Repasi, 'European Parliament and National Parliaments', in Amtenbrink and Herrmann (eds), *supra* note 12, 455-504; M. Markakis, *Accountability in the Economic and Monetary Union: Foundations, Policy, and Governance* (OUP 2020).

[104] See AG Tizzano, C-27/04, *Commission v. Council*, ECLI:EU:C:2004:313, para. 45.

[105] See M. Dawson, F. de Witte, 'Constitutional Balance in the EU after the Euro-Crisis' (2013) 76 *Modern Law Review* 817.

[106] For a general overview, see G. Lo Schiavo, *The Role of Financial Stability in EU Law and Policy* (Kluwer 2016); L. Lionello, *The Pursuit of Stability of the Euro Area as a Whole. The Reform of the European Economic Union and Perspectives of Fiscal Integration* (Springer 2020).

[107] See Costamagna, *supra* note 49; K. Tuori, K. Tuori, *The Eurozone Crisis: A Constitutional Analysis* (CUP 2014).

[108] For a forceful critique, see C. Kilpatrick, 'The Displacement of Social Europe: A Productive Lens of Inquiry' (2018) 14 *European Constitutional Law Review* 62.

can be seen with regard to 'spending conditionality'. The contribution of ESI Funds to EMU stability is given precedence over the pursuit of specific objectives of social, economic and territorial cohesion. Indeed, the possible suspension of payments operates only where a Member State does not comply with recommendations issued in the context of the European Semester or with other requirements established within the economic governance framework. Conversely, the mechanism pays little attention to the negative implications that the suspension of payments and commitments can have on their specific objectives. Secondly, alternative enforcement mechanisms largely evade the application of the general set of limits that, as shown elsewhere in this book,[109] apply to the exercise of sanctioning powers. Particularly when enforcement is left to the 'logic of the market', legal constraints imposed by respect for fundamental rights and by the principle of proportionality may prove to be largely illusory.

[109] See, in particular, the chapter by N. Lazzerini in this book.

Chapter 9
THE SANCTIONING POWER OF THE ECB: FROM ONE TO SEVERAL LEGAL REGIMES

Frédéric Allemand [*]

ABSTRACT: *The European Central Bank is the only non-judicial institution of the Union with a power to impose sanctions based directly on the EU treaties. Linked to the implementation of the ECB regulations and decisions, this sanctioning power has so far remained little exercised. In 2013 the Regulation establishing the single supervisory mechanism conferred on the ECB a new specific sanctioning power to enforce European directly applicable prudential rules. Two complementary but separate legal regimes regulate the use of sanctioning power by the ECB in monetary and in supervisory matters respectively. The duality of the applicable legal bases, their cross-referencing and the decentralisation of the implementation of the ECB's powers make the legal framework as a whole highly complex and non-transparent. The increasing use by the ECB of its sanctioning especially in the prudential supervision area requires clarification of the specific features of each legal regime from a substantive and procedural perspective.*

KEYWORDS: *european central bank – monetary policy – prudential policy – sanctions*

9.1. Introduction

The sanction is "one of the best and simplest means of ensuring effective compliance with obligations". [1] It is a legal norm whose function is to guarantee the effective application of another so-called 'primary norm', according to Hart's typology. [2] This finding does not preclude the primary norm from being complied with regardless of

---

[*] Associate Researcher, Robert Schuman Initiative, University of Luxembourg; Lecturer in EU Law, SciencesPo, ENA.

[1] M. Virally, *La pensée juridique* (LGDJ 1960), 68.

[2] H. Hart, *Le concept de droit* (LGDJ 2006), 105.

the existence of a sanction. Other legal and non-legal means exist to ensure that the behaviour of the addressees complies with legal requirements,[3] e.g. the establishment of a system of liability for fault or the nullity of contrary acts, political procedures relating to the legitimacy of the authority issuing the legal norm, or economic procedures based on a cost-benefit analysis of compliance with the rule of law.

Economic and Monetary Union (EMU) law is an area where the effectiveness of legal obligations depends partly on sanctions. The discipline of the Member States' budgetary policies is based on a mixed system where market surveillance is supported by a coordination procedure of administrative and political nature, which provides for the adoption of fines by the Council.[4] No sanctions have ever been applied to a Member State for budgetary or macroeconomic indiscipline.[5] In the monetary pillar, the ECB may "impose fines and periodic penalty payments on undertakings for failure to comply with its regulations and decisions"[6], especially in the case of non-compliance by credit institutions with the obligation to hold minimum reserves.[7] The limits and conditions of this sanctioning powers are laid down in Council Regulations.[8] In the context of the establishement of the European Banking Union ('BU'), the ECB is vested with specific sanctioning powers to carry out new supervisory tasks conferred on by a Council Regulation adopted in 2013.[9] Unlike the Council in the Economic Union, the ECB makes full use of its

[3] J. Rivero, 'Sur l'effet dissuasif de la sanction juridique' in, Mélanges offerts à Pierre Raynaud (Dalloz-Sirey 1985), 675.

[4] Article 126(11) TFEU. For an analysis of the sanctioning regime applicable in the Economic Union area, see F. Allemand, F. Martucci, 'La nouvelle gouvernance économique européenne' (2012) 48 *Cahiers de Droit européen* 17, and the chapter by F. Costamagna and A. Miglio in this book.

[5] See Article 8 of Regulation (EU) No 1173/2011 of the European Parliament and of the Council of 16 November 2011 on the effective enforcement of budgetary surveillance in the euro area, OJ L 306/1, 23.11.2011. However, Spain was has been fined by the Council for its "serious negligence" following an undeclared expenditure amounted to EUR 4.5 billion in its 2011 budget deficit. In its judgment of 20 December 2017 (case C-521/15, *Spain v Council*, ECLI:EU:C:2017:982), the Court of justice dismissed the action for annulment brought by Spain against the Council decision.

[6] Article 132(3) TFEU, and Article 34(3) of the Statute of the ESCB and of the ECB.

[7] Article 19 of the Statute.

[8] Article 132 TFEU, Articles 5(4) and 19(2) of the Statute. See Council Regulation (EC) No 2532/98 of 23 November 1998 concerning the powers of the European Central Bank to impose sanctions, OJ L 318/4, 27.11.1998, amended by Council Regulation (EU) 2015/159 of 27 January 2015, OJ L 27/1, 3.2.2015; Council Regulation (EC) No 2531/98 of 23 November 1998 concerning the application of minimum reserves by the ECB, OJ L 318/1, 27.11.1998, amended by Council Regulation (EC) No 134/2002 of 22 January 2002, OJ L 24/1, 26.1.2002; and Council Regulation (EC) No 2533/98 of 23 November 1998 concerning the collection of statistical information by the ECB, OJ L 318/8, 27.11.1998, last amended by Council Regulation (EU) 2015/373 of 5 March 2015, OJ L 64/6, 7.3.2015.

[9] Council Regulation (EU) No 1024/2013 of 15 October 2013 entrusting the ECB with specif-

sanctioning power, although a distinct practice can be observed depending on the monetary or prudential area where this power is exercised. Between 1999 and 2013, few pecuniary sanctions were imposed by the ECB; the total amount of the fines reached EUR 7 millions. In the majority of the breaches noted, the fines were less than EUR 500. [10] In the supervisory field, the ECB sanctioned ten credit institutions over the July 2017-October 2019 period; the total amount of administrative pecuniary penalties is EUR 21 millions, with a record total sanction of EUR 11.2 millions against the Italian bank Banco di Popolare di Vicenza in September 2017, [11] while the minimum amount of sanctions imposed to date is EUR 200,000. In addition, seven other credit institutions were sanctioned by national supervisors, following an infringement procedure initiated at the request of the ECB. [12]

The discrepancies between the number and amount of sanctions imposed by the ECB in the monetary field and in the prudential field may seem surprising at first. They reflect the profound differences in law enforcement approaches implemented in each area and, incidentally, their clear distinct 'philosophies' (Section 2). This dual legal situation deeply affects the definition of the legal regime of ECB's sanctioning power. The ECB shall exercise its sanctioning powers not in accordance with one single legal regime, but two (Section 3). The differences between these regimes do not preclude a high degree of convergence with regard to procedural aspects (Section 4).

9.2. The distinct philosophy of the ECB's monetary and prudential tasks

9.2.1. Monetary policy: favouring the market approach

The Union shall have exclusive competence in monetary and exchange-rate matters for those Member States whose currency is the euro. [13] The ECB, together with the national central banks (NCBs) of these Member States constitute the Eurosystem. [14] The Eurosystem is governed by the decision-making bodies of the ECB (i.e. the

---

ic tasks concerning policies relating to the prudential supervision of credit institutions, OJ L 287/63, 29.10.2013.

[10] Author's estimates based on ECB Annual Reports.

[11] ECB, 24 August 2017, Imposition of administrative penalties on Banco Popolare di Vincenza S.p.A. in liquidazione coatta amministrativa. Available at: https:// www.bankingsupervision.europa.eu/banking/sanctions/shared/pdf/ssm.170911_publication_template.en.pdf, accessed on 02.12.2019.

[12] ECB, Supervisory sanctions. Available at: https://www.bankingsupervision.europa.eu/banking/sanctions/html/index.en.html, accessed on 02.12.2019.

[13] Article 3(1) c) TFEU.

[14] Article 282(2), 2nd sentence, TFEU, repeated in Article 1., 2nd sentence, of the Statute.

Governing Council and the Executive Board) and is responsible for carrying out a number of "basic tasks" of a monetary nature, including the definition and implementation of monetary policy. [15] The Eurosystem and the ECB are entrusted with additional tasks. [16] The Eurosystem carries out its tasks in accordance with the dual operating principle of centralised decision-making at ECB level and decentralised execution at the level of the NCBs. [17]

The implementation of those tasks by the Eurosystem is objective-oriented: the primary objective of the Eurosystem shall be to maintain price stability and, without prejudice to this objective, to support the general economic policies in the Union. [18] These objectives are to be pursued in accordance with the principle of an "open market economy with free competition". [19] When carrying out the tasks conferred on it by the Treaties or the Statute, the ECB shall, for example, determine the Eurosystem's monetary policy strategy, quantify the level of price stability to be achieved, and choose among the instruments at its disposal to achieve its objectives. In this regard, the ECB has to choose between two approaches: (i) regulatory control of the money supply in circulation in order to influence prices directly; [20] or (ii) indirect control of prices in the medium term through the exercise of its monetary power. This second option is favoured by the Treaties and corresponds to the practice of modern central banks. This is the choice made by the ECB since the very beginning.

It is essential to understand that monetary power is of a fundamentally different nature from regulatory power. The monetary power represents the ECB's ability to create money, either by issuing euro banknotes [21] or by granting credit in 'central bank money' to counterparties (e.g. credit institutions) which have an account in NCBs of the Eurosystem. [22] Whenever the ECB lends 'central bank money' to a credit institution, this loan is recorded in the balance sheet of that institu-

---

[15] See Article 127(2) TFEU.

[16] Article 127(4) TFEU on advisory tasks and Article 127(6) on specific tasks relating to prudential supervision carried out by the ECB; Article 127(5) TFEU on the contribution of the ESCB to the smooth conduct of prudential policy and the stability of the financial system.

[17] See R.M. Lastra, 'The Division of Responsibilities between the European Central Bank and the National Central Banks within the European System of Central Banks', in J.-V. Louis, H. Bronkhorst (eds), *The Euro and European Integration / L'euro et l'intégration européenne* (Euro Institute / P.I.E. Peter Lang 1999), 199-216.

[18] Article 127(1) TFEU, and Article 2 of the Statute.

[19] Articles 119(2) and 127(1) TFEU, and Article 2 of the Statute.

[20] Control may consist in setting ceilings on credit openings by credit institutions, setting minimum limits on Treasury bill subscriptions by credit institutions, etc. Abandoned in practice by the monetary authorities since the 1970s, the use of instruments of monetary control is still considered in the Treaties.

[21] Article 128 TFEU, and Article 16 of the Statute.

[22] Article 17 of the Statute.

tion as a liability. At the same time, the liquidity obtained from the ECB constitutes a resource available to the credit institutions to meet their refinancing needs. Although the ECB unilaterally defines the conditions under which credit institutions may participate in monetary policy operations,[23] credit institutions have no legal obligation to participate. Under normal circumstances, credit institutions cover their financial needs by turning to the interbank market. The exercise of monetary power does not preclude the use of regulatory power. On the contrary, they are complementary. The ECB requires credit institutions established in the euro area to hold minimum reserves with the NCBs of the Eurosystem. The increase or decrease in the level of minimum reserves affects the structural liquidity needs of credit institutions. Although regulatory power contributes to the effectiveness of monetary power, the influence of monetary power on the alignment of credit institutions' behaviour derives from elsewhere. The ECB has a *unlimited* monetary capacity and acts as a "bank for the commercial banks".[24] This unique feature is *the* reason why credit institutions are concerned to maintain access to the ECB's liquidity and comply as much as possible with the operational rules of monetary policy, the legal requirements for the transmission of statistical information and the holding of minimum reserves. Non-compliance with legal requirements is thus far from being common.

9.2.2. Prudential policy: improving the regulatory approach

The purpose of prudential policy is to provide a framework for measuring, managing and pricing the risks (credit, operational, counterparty, market, liquidity, etc.) that credit institutions may face in the course of their business.[25] Focused on "the safety and soundness of banks and the banking system"[26], this policy is known as micro-prudential. It differs from macro-prudential policy, which aims to understand and manage the systemic risks that may arise in the financial system.[27]

---

[23] Namely the open market operations, the standing facilities (marginal lending facilities and deposit facility). See Article 18 of the Statute.

[24] ECB, *What is money?* Available at: https://www.ecb.europa.eu/explainers/tell-me-more/html/what_is_money.en.html, accessed on 02.12.2019.

[25] J.-P. Pollin, 'La nouvelle régulation bancaire microprudentielle: principes, incidences et limites' (2011) 103 *Revue d'économie financière*, 155.

[26] Basel Committee for Banking Supervision, *Core Principles for Effective Banking Supervision*, Basel, 2012.

[27] ECB, *Financial stability and macroprudential policy*. Available at: https://www.ecb.europa.eu/ecb/tasks/stability/html/index.en.html, accessed on 02.12.2019. For a detailed discussion of the differences between the macro and microprudential policies, see J. Osiński, K. Seal, L. Hoogduin, 'Macroprudential and Microprudential Policies: Toward Cohabitation', *IMF Staff Discussion Note*, SDN 13/05, June 2013.

Prudential policy is traditionally based on two pillars: a set of substantive rules and a supervisory framework. The two go hand in hand. In a highly liberalised, competitive and open financial environment, credit institutions may be tempted to shirk from complying with their prudential obligations.[28] Faced with this risk of regulatory and supervisory arbitrage, it is essential that the rules be as uniform as possible and applied in a coherent and efficient way by supervisors. Because prudential policy is essentially regulatory in nature, "effective, proportionate and dissuasive sanctioning regimes are key to ensure compliance with EU banking rules, protect users of banking services and ensure safety, stability and integrity of banking markets".[29] The subprime credit crisis of 2008-2009 and then the sovereign debt crisis of 2010-2015 testified to the incompleteness of EU law on these two aspects. In response, the legislative framework has been thoroughly modernised and harmonised in the form of a 'single rule book' consisting of four texts adopted between 2013 and 2014: the capital requirements Directive IV[30] ('CRD IV'), the capital requirements Regulation[31] ('CRR'), the amended Directive on deposit guarantee schemes[32] ('DGS') and the bank recovery and resolution Directive[33] ('BRRD'). The CRR and the CRD IV are the two core components of this pilar. The CRD IV lays down rules concerning the access to the banking activity of credit institutions and

---

[28] See OECD, *Economic Reforms. Going for Growth* (OECD 2012), especially Chapter 6 'Prudential regulation and competition in the banking sector: finding the right mix', 209-219.

[29] Explanatory Memorandum, point 1.1.1 ('Sanctions'), of the Proposal for a Directive of the European Parliament and of the Council of 20 July 2011, on the access to the activity of credit institutions and the prudential supervision of credit institutions and investment firms and amending Directive 2002/87/EC of the European Parliament and of the Council on the supplementary supervision of credit institutions, insurance undertakings and investment firms in a financial conglomerate, COM(2011) 453 final.

[30] Directive 2013/36/EU of the European Parliament and of the Council of 26 June 2013 on access to the activity of credit institutions and the prudential supervision of credit institutions and investment firms, amending Directive 2002/87/EC and repealing Directives 2006/48/EC and 2006/49/EC, OJ L 176/338, 27.6.2013, as last amended by Directive (EU) 2018/843 of the European Parliament and of the Council of 30 May 2018, OJ L 156/43, 19.6.2018.

[31] Regulation (EU) No 575/2013 of the European Parliament and of the Council of 26 June 2013 on prudential requirements for credit institutions and investment firms and amending Regulation (EU) No 648/2012, OJ L 176/1, 27.6.2013, as last amended by Regulation (EU) 2019/876 of the European Parliament and of the Council of 20 May 2019, OJ L 150/1, 7.6.2019.

[32] Directive 2014/49/EU of the European Parliament and of the Council of 16 April 2014 on deposit guarantee schemes, OJ L 173/149, 12.6.2014.

[33] Directive 2014/59/EU of the European Parliament and of the Council of 15 May 2014 establishing a framework for the recovery and resolution of credit institutions and investment firms and amending Council Directive 82/891/EEC, and Directives 2001/24/EC, 2002/47/EC, 2004/25/EC, 2005/56/EC, 2007/36/EC, 2011/35/EU, 2012/30/EU and 2013/36/EU, and Regulations (EU) No 1093/2010 and (EU) No 648/2012, of the European Parliament and of the Council, OJ L 173/190, 12.6.2014.

investment firms as well as supervisory powers and tools for the prudential supervision of credit institutions by competent authorities. The CRR lays down uniform rules concerning general prudential requirements that credit institutions shall comply with. This set of secondary legislation is supplemented by binding technical standards drawn up by the European Banking Authority (EBA) and formally adopted by the European Commission in the form of delegated regulations or decisions. In addition to Union law, national measures transpose directives[34] or exercise the options left open in EU regulations.[35]

These developments in substantive law are accompanied by a 'revolution' with regard to the responsibility for prudential supervision in the Union. In its communication of 2010 on *Reinforcing sanctioning regimes in the financial services sector*, the Commission states that "ensuring proper application of EU rules is first and foremost the task of national authorities, who have the responsibility to prevent financial institutions from violating EU rules, and to sanction violations within their jurisdiction".[36] Three years later, Council Regulation No 1024/2013 ('SSM Regulation' or 'SSMR') conferred exclusive competence on the ECB to carry out specific supervisory tasks with regard to credit institutions established in the Euro Area Member States.[37] The SSM Regulation does not introduce amendments to the single rule book. When the ECB carries out its supervisory tasks, it is "*considered*, as appropriate, the competent authority or the designated authority in the participating Member States as established by the relevant Union law".[38] Any reference made in the CRD IV to a NCA shall thus be read as a reference to the ECB whenever the ECB is competent. To give but a few examples[39], the ECB shall be competent to authorise credit institutions and withdraw authorisations of credit institutions, and to ensure compliance with the EU legislative acts which impose prudential requirements or governance requirements on credit institutions.[40] All tasks not

[34] As of December 2019, the transposition of CRD IV resulted in the adoption of 515 national transposition measures, all Member States combined.

[35] The list of options and national discretions provided for by CRR and opted in by France is available on the website of the French supervisory authority: https://acpr.banque-france.fr/en/europe-international/banks/supervisory-disclosure/options-and-national-discretions, accessed on 02.12.2019.

[36] Communication from the Commission of 8 December 2010, COM(2010) 716 final, para. 1. See also Court of Justice, case C-222/02, *Peter Paul and Others v. Bundesrespublik Deutschland*, ECLI:EU:C:2004:606, stating that EU banking directives "impose on the national authorities a number of supervisory obligations vis-à-vis credit institutions" (para. 39).

[37] The task of the ECB shall concern the Member States of the Union whose currency is not the euro provided that a Memorandum of Understanding to this effect has been concluded between the ECB and the national supervisors of those States in accordance with Article 7 SSMR.

[38] Article 9 and Recital 45 SSMR.

[39] See Article 4(1) SSMR for the exahaustive list of tasks conferred on to the ECB.

[40] The competences for the resolution of failing credit institutions are conferred upon on a new European Agency, e.g. the Single Resolution Board. See Regulation (EU) No 806/2014 of

spelt out in the SSM regulation remain the competence of national supervisors.[41]

Conferring exclusive prudential tasks and supervisory powers to the ECB does not exclude cooperation with the NCAs. On the contrary, the latter remain closely involved in the conduct of most day-to-day verifications and other supervisory activities necessary to prepare and implement ECB's acts.[42] The SSM Regulation requires the ECB to carry out its supervisory tasks and to cooperate with national supervisors "within a single supervisory mechanism" (SSM).[43] Article 6 of the SSM Regulation sets out the general principles governing the SSM and the criteria to be applied in relation to the respective microprudential supervisory responsibilities of the ECB and the NCAs. The criteria are based on the size and the nature of credit institutions. While 'significant' credit institutions are supervised directly by the ECB, 'less significant' credit institutions are placed under the direct supervision of the NCAs. A few crucial supervisory tasks are not concerned by this responsibility sharing and remain under the exclusive responsibility of the ECB.[44] The practical arrangements of the cooperation within the SSM is detailed in ECB Regulation (EU) No 468/2014 of 16 April 2014,[45] aka 'ECB Framework Regulation' ('SSMFR'). This legal framework is complemented with the *SSM Supervisory Manual*, a not legally binding document established by the ECB.[46] The general framework lays down how the operational cooperation takes place within the SSM. The ECB may issue regulations, guidelines or general instructions to NCAs regarding less significant credit institutions to provide guidance and/or to ensure coherence and consistency of the performance of microprudential supervisory tasks by the NCAs.[47] The ECB may also, at any time, on its own initiative (and after consulting with NCA) or upon request by a national supervisor, decide to supervise directly one or more 'less significant' banks.[48]

---

the European Parliament and of the Council of 15 July 2014, establishing uniform rules and a uniform procedure for the resolution of credit institutions and certain investment firms in the framework of a Single Resolution Mechanism and a Single Resolution Fund and amending Regulation (EU) No 1093/2010, OJ L 225/1, 30.7.2014.

[41] See Article 1 and Recital 28 SSMR; Article 1(2) SSMFR.

[42] The NCAs have developed a strong knowledge of their national, regional and local banking markets. They benefit from significant dedicated human resources and are vested with a comprehensive range of investigatory powers. Incidentally, the number of credit institutions in the euro area was about 6 000 in late 2013.

[43] See Articles 6(1) and 7(1) of the SSM Regulation.

[44] For example the approval/withdrawal of a banking licence. See Articles 6(4) and 6(6) SSMR.

[45] OJ L 141/1, 14.5.2014.

[46] ECB, SSM Supervisory Manual, March 2018. Available at: https://www.bankingsupervision.europa.eu/ecb/pub/pdf/ssm.supervisorymanual201803.en.pdf, accessed on 02.12.2019.

[47] Article 6(5)(a) SSM Regulation.

[48] Article 6(5)(b) SSM Regulation.

The powers that the EU Treaties and the ESCB Statute confer on the ECB were designed in such a way as to enable the central bank to carry out its basic tasks, in particular its monetary tasks. The CRD IV and CRR require the Member States to ensure that "the competent authorities have the expertise, resources, operational capacity, powers and independence necessary to carry out the functions relating to prudential supervision, investigations and penalties set out in this Directive and in [CRR]." [49] Some of these powers are very specific to the supervisory field, such as investigatory powers or the power to remove a member of a credit institution's management body. As monetary authority, the ECB was originally not vested with all these powers. Thus, in order to enable the Bank to carry out its supervisory powers, the SSM Regulation gives the ECB the supervisory powers that the NCAs have under EU prudential legislation. [50] This being said, national supervisors may be vested with additional powers under national law. In that case, the ECB may require, by way of instructions, NCAs to make use of those powers in order to ensure the performance of full and effective supervision within the SSM. [51] The very complex solution adopted by Union law with regard to the ECB's sanctioning power is indeed illustrative of some discrepancies between the monetary and supervisory fields.

9.3. The duality and complexity of legal regimes

In 2009, within a context of high fragmention of the sanctioning regimes in the supervisory field, the report of the High Level Group on supervision chaired by Jacques de Larosière concluded that "[i]t is essential that within the EU and elsewhere, all supervisors are able to deploy sanctioning regimes that are sufficiently convergent, strict, resulting in deterrence". [52] The establishment of the Banking Union reflects this concern about the diversity of sanctioning regimes. The granting of exclusive competence to the ECB to supervise credit institutions in the Member States participating in the BU appears at first sight as the appropriate approach to provide a definitive solution to this problem. Article 18 of the SSM Regulation confers a sanctioning power on the ECB for the performance of its prudential tasks. However, the decentralisation of the exercise of supervision of the less significant credit institutions implies the sharing of supervisory sanctioning powers between the ECB and national supervisors, [53] which leads to an inappropriate complexity.

---

[49] Article 4(4) CRD IV.

[50] See Point 4.3.1 ('Supervisory and investigatory powers') of Communication COM(2012) 511 final.

[51] Article 9(1) of the SSM Regulation; and Articles 22 and 90 of the ECB Framework Regulation.

[52] De Larosière Group, *Final report of the High-Level Group on supervision*, 2009, para. 201.

[53] Point 4.2.2. of the explanatory memorandum of the Proposal for a Council Regulation of 12

9.3.1. General power to sanction

In accordance with Article 132(3) TFEU and Article 34 of the Statute, the ECB has a general power to impose pecuniary penalties on undertakings which have failed to comply with its regulations or decisions. In addition to this general power, the Statute provides for the application of specific sanction regimes in the field of statistics (Article 5(4)) and of minimum reserves (Article 19(1)).

The granting of an autonomous power of sanction to a specialised institution on the basis of the Treaties is exceptional in the institutional framework of the Union.[54] This notorious exception is justified by the concern of the authors of the Treaties to guarantee the functional autonomy of the ECB in the performance of its tasks. Nevertheless, with regard to political legitimacy issues, the European legislator, in this case the Council alone, is responsible for laying down the conditions and limits within which the ECB is entitled to exercise its powers.[55] Three Council Regulations form the general framework of the ECB's power to impose sanctions when carrying out its basic tasks. These are Regulations (EC) No 2532/98 on the powers of the ECB to impose sanctions, No 2531/98 on the maintenance of minimum reserves and No 2533/98 on the statistical powers of the ECB.[56] On the basis of its autonomous regulatory power, the ECB may also adopt other types of sanctions, such as disciplinary sanctions against staff members who have infringed the General Conditions of Employment.[57]

Council Regulation (EC) No 2532/98 aims to ensure consistency in the different areas of competence of the ECB and lays down the principles and procedures to be followed by the ECB in the exercise of its power to impose pecuniary penalties. It is an umbrella act for all legislation on the ECB's sanctioning power that can nevertheless be derogated from by Council regulations in specific areas.[58]

The ECB's power to adopt directly applicable acts (regulations, decisions) and

September 2012, conferring specific tasks on the European Central Bank concerning policies relating to the prudential supervision of credit institutions, COM(2012) 511 final.

[54] J.M. Fernandez Martin, P.G. Texieira, 'The imposition of regulatory sanctions by the European Central Bank' (2000) 25 *European Law Review* 392.

[55] Article 132(1) TFEU, in conjunction with Article 129(4) TFEU; and Article 34(1) of the Statute, in conjunction with Article 41 of the Statute.

[56] See *supra* note 8 for the references.

[57] See point 44 ff of the Conditions of Employement for Staff of the European Central Bank, adopted on 9 June 1998, latest amendments entered into force in 26 July 2019.

[58] Article 6(1) Council Regulation (EC) No 2532/98; Recitals 4 and 16, and Article 11(1) Regulation (EC) No 2157/1999 of the ECB of 23 September 1999 on the powers of the ECB to impose sanctions, OJ L 264/21, 12.10.1999, as amended by Regulation (EC) No 985/2001 of the European Central Bank of 10 May 2001, OJ L 137/24, 19.5.2001; Regulation (EU) No 469/2014 of the European Central Bank of 16 April 2014, OJ L 141/51, 14.5.2014; and Regulation (EU) 2017/2095 of the European Central Bank of 3 November 2017, OJ L 299/22, 16.11.2017.

its power to impose sanctions are closely linked. In accordance with Article 132(3) TFEU and Article 34(3) of the ESCB Statute, the ECB shall be entitled to impose sanctions to undertakings which fail to comply with the obligations under *its regulations and decisions*. Non-compliance with a legal act adopted by another European institution or body, a national measure transposing or implementing a Union act or any other national measure are thus excluded from the scope of this ECB's sanctioning power. Without prejudice to their legal qualification by the Court of Justice, guidelines and instructions issued by the ECB, although they may produce some external legal effects, constitute administrative acts[59] and do not fall within the scope of Article 132(3) TFEU either.

The areas in which the ECB has regulatory powers are set out exhaustively in the ESCB Statute: definition and implementation of monetary policy (Article 3(1), 1st indent), minimum reserves (Article 19(1)), payment systems (Article 22), specific tasks in the field of prudential supervision (Article 25(2)). In a range of other specified areas, the Council may entitle the ECB to exercise its regulatory power within the limits of the relevant Council Regulation.[60] The more the ECB's regulatory and decision-making power is exercised, the more its power to impose sanctions materially expands. Actually, the ECB has made very moderate use of its regulatory power in the monetary area. Since its establishment in June 1998, the ECB has adopted 59 regulations, most of which relate to statistical collection (33) or reserve requirements (11). Only one regulation was adopted for the definition and implementation of monetary policy tasks, and it was of temporary application.[61] This limited use of its regulatory power should be seen as an expression of the monetary authority's preference for less intrusive acts that favour the involvement of NCBs and preserve the specificity of the different national banking markets.[62] The situation is somewhat different when it comes to the adoption of decisions. By the end of 2019, the ECB has adopted 285 decisions.

Under Article 1(3) of Regulation (EC) No 2532/98 the ECB's sanctioning power apply to 'undertakings', ie. "those natural or legal persons, private or public, with the exception of public persons in the exercise of their public powers, in a participating Member State, which are the subject of obligations arising from ECB regula-

[59] R. Smits, *The European Central Bank* (Kluwer 1997), 103.

[60] See Article 134(1), 2nd indent, TFEU and Article 34(1), 2nd indent, of the ESCB Statute. This concerns the exercise of the ECB's advisory, statistical collection, minimum reserve requirements, the adoption of instruments of monetary control, as well as the financial provisions of the ECB.

[61] Regulation (EC) No 1053/2008 of the European Central Bank of 23 October 2008 on temporary changes to the rules relating to eligibility of collateral (ECB/2008/11), OJ L 282, 25.10.2008.

[62] J.-V. Louis, *L'Union européenne et sa monnaie, Commentaire Mégret* (Éditions de l'Université de Bruxelles 2009), 204; F. Martucci, *L'ordre économique et monétaire* (Bruylant 2015), 353.

tions and decisions." This broad definition is further clarified in Regulation (EC) No 2531/98 on reserve requirements and in Regulation (EC) No 2533/98 in statistical reporting.

In accordance with EU primary law, the ECB may adopt a wide range of sanctions[63] beyond the 'fines' and the 'periodic penalty payments' refered to in Article 132(3) TFEU: "penalty interest" and "other sanctions with comparable effect" (Article 19(1) of the Statute), or "the appropriate provisions for enforcement" (Article 3(4) of the Statute). Since the amendment of Regulation (EC) No 2532/98 in 2015 to enhance the consistency of the general sanctioning regime with the SSM Regulation,[64] 'fines' meant "a single amount of money which an undertaking is obliged to pay as a sanction", and 'periodic penalty payments' meant "amounts of money which, in the case of a continued infringement, an undertaking is obliged to pay either as a punishment, *or with a view to forcing the persons concerned to comply with the ECB supervisory regulations and decisions*".[65]

With regard to the upper limits and the calculation methods of the fines and the pecuniary penalty payments, the Council leaves the ECB little room for maneuver on this issue. As a matter of principle, the maximum fine is EUR 500 000 per infringement. The amount of daily penalty payments shall be limited to EUR 10 000 per infringement; periodic penalty payments may be imposed in respect of a maximum period of six months following the notification of the undertaking of the decision to initiate an infringement procedure. In order to strengthen the deterrent effect of the penalty and to deprive the infringing undertaking of any benefit, Regulation (EC) No 2531/98 and the SSM Regulation derogate from the maximum ceiling for fines provided for in Regulation (EC) No 2532/98. Conversely, Regulation (EC) No 2533/98 on statistical obligations limits the total cumulative amount of daily penalty payments to EUR 100 000 and the amount of fines to EUR 200 000.[66]

---

[63] K. Magliveras (2018), 'The sanctioning system of the European Central Bank: origins, analysis, comments and some suggestions', Paper prepared for the 2018 Conference of the Journal of Law, Finance, and Accounting, available at: https://papers.ssrn.com/sol3/papers.cfm?abstract_id=3132940, 5-6.

[64] Section 'General considerations' in the explanatory memorandum of the Recommendation for a Council Regulation amending Regulation (EC) No 2532/98 concerning the powers of the European Central Bank to impose sanctions (ECB/2014/19), OJ C 144/2, 14.5.2014; also Commission opinion of 18 December 2014 on the ECB's recommendation for a Council Regulation amending Regulation (EC) No 2532/98, OJ C 461/1, 20.12.2014.

[65] Article 1(1) of Council Regulation (EU) 2015/159 of 27 January 2015 amending Regulation (EC) No 2532/98 concerning the powers of the European Central Bank to impose sanctions, OJ L 27/1, 3.2.2015. The words in italics reproduces in almost identical terms the wording of Article 129 SSMFR.

[66] Article 7(4) Regulation (EC) No 533/98.

9.3.2. The specific sanctioning power of the ECB in the prudential supervision area

Article 132 TFEU makes no distinction according to the area where the ECB exercises its regulatory powers and its general sanctioning power. The ECB may thus impose fines or periodic penalty payments on undertakings which do not comply with its regulations or decisions adopted in the prudential supervision area.[67] As in the monetary area – albeit for different reasons – the ECB exercises little regulatory power in the area of prudential supervision. Under SSM Regulation, the ECB shall mainly apply the single rule book,[68] thereby limiting the use of its regulatory power: 1) to the exercice of the options open in the CRR;[69] 2) and to the functioning of the SSM,[70] especially the definition of the procedural rules to be followed by national supervisors when they supervise less significant credit institutions.[71] It is worth mentioning that the ECB may also take individual decisions in supervisory procedures and infringement proceedings. In 2019, the Supervisory Board (see *infra*) of the ECB took 1,924 decisions, most of which were on fit and proper assessments (1,006), internal models (160) and own funds (153).[72]

Article 64(1) CRD IV requires that "the competent authorities shall be given all supervisory powers to intervene in the activity of institutions that are necessary for the exercise of their function". According to paragraph 2, "Competent authorities shall exercise their supervisory powers and their powers to impose penalties in accordance with this Directive and with national law". The Member States shall thus lay down rules on administrative penalties and other administrative measures in respect of breaches of national provisions transposing the CRD IV and of the CRR.[73] According to Article 65(2) CRD IV, the administrative sanctions regime must be applicable to financial conglomerates, holding companies and, for these entities,

---

[67] See in that respect Article 18(7) SSMR.

[68] Recital (34) SSMR.

[69] Article 4(3) SSMR; also Recital 10 CRD IV. See for example Regulation (EU) No 2018/1845 of the ECB of 21 November 2018 on the exercise of the discretion under Article 178(2)(d) of Regulation (EU) No 575/2013 in relation to the threshold for assessing the materiality of credit obligations past due, OJ L 299/55, 26.11.2018.

[70] See the ECB SSM Framework Regulation, *supra*.

[71] See for example the reporting of supervisory financial information: Regulation (EU) No 2015/534 of the ECB of 17 March 2015, OJ L 86/13, 31.3.2015; Decision of the ECB of 2 July 2014 on the provision to the European Central Bank of supervisory data reported to the national competent authorities by the supervised entities pursuant to Commission Implementing Regulation (EU) No 680/2014, OJ L 214/34, 19.7.2014.

[72] ECB, Annual Report on supervisory activities 2018 spec. Section 5.3.1 (Figure 3). Available at: https://www.bankingsupervision.europa.eu/press/publications/annual-report/html/ssm.ar2018~927cb99de4.en.html, accessed on 02.12.2019.

[73] Article 65(1) CRD IV.

provide for sanctions against their management bodies or other natural persons who are responsible for the infringement. Finally, the Directive details a set of administrative sanctions and other administrative measures for breaches of a series of key provisions of CRD IV (Article 66) and CRR (Article 67). All these requirements enshrined in the CRD IV are primarily addressed to the Member States.[74] As the ECB has been regarded primarily as a monetary authority, it lacks the powers of prudential supervision of the NCAs. Ensuring the highest prudential standards in the participating Member States implies that the ECB's sanctioning power is at least similar to those of national supervisors. This is the purpose of the second paragraph of Article 9(1) of the SSM Regulation, the key provision for the conferral of powers on the ECB in the prudential field:

"For the same exclusive purpose, the ECB shall have all the powers and obligations set out in this Regulation. It shall also have all the powers and obligations, which competent and designated authorities shall have under the relevant Union law, unless otherwise provided for by this Regulation. In particular, the ECB shall have the powers listed in Sections 1 and 2 of this Chapter."

This general provision is completed with Article 18 SSM to deal specifically with the sanctioning power in the field of prudential supervision:

"For the purpose of carrying out the tasks conferred on it by this Regulation, where credit institutions, financial holding companies, or mixed financial holding companies, intentionally or negligently, breach a requirement under relevant directly applicable acts of Union law in relation to which administrative pecuniary penalties shall be made available to competent authorities under the relevant Union law, the ECB may impose administrative pecuniary penalties [...]"

Like Article 132(3) TFEU, Article 18 SSMR limits the scope of the ECB's sanctioning power that it vests on the ECB in several ways. This "specific supervisory power" applies only to breaches of requirements under "directly applicable acts of Union law" – an expression which is commonly interpreted as a reference to the Capital Requirements Regulation.[75] Beyond the CRR, the expression also includes all the delegated and implementing acts adopted by the Commission,[76] the ECB regulations on the exercise of discretion under the relevant provisions of the CRR[77] and, last but

---

[74] Article 162 CRD IV.

[75] See G. Lassagni, *Banking Supervision and Criminal Investigation: Comparing the EU and US Experiences* (Springer 2019), 131.

[76] The list of directly applicable EU acts adopted on the basis of the CRR is available at: https://eur-lex.europa.eu/legal-content/EN/ALL/?uri=CELEX:32013R0575&qid=1578874966006, accessed on 02.12.2019.

[77] See for example Regulation (EU) 2018/1845 of the European Central Bank of 21 November 2018 on the exercise of the discretion under Article 178(2)(d) Regulation (EU) No 575/2013 in relation to the threshold for assessing the materiality of credit obligations past due, OJ L 299/55, 26.11.2018.

not least, the ECB supervisory decisions. Conversely, the infringements of national rules transposing or implementing Union are excluded from the scope of Article 18 SSMR. Although the ECB is responsible for ensuring compliance with these national rules,[78] the sanctioning of non-compliance remain the sole competence of national supervisors.[79] As noted by the Commission in its 2017 report on the application of the SSM Regulation, this obvious asymmetry may have "the potential of impinging on the level playing field and would need to be closely monitored in terms of implications for the effectiveness of ECB's performance of supervisory tasks".[80] Article 18(5) SSMR modestly addresses this mismatch by providing that the ECB may request the NCAs to open proceedings in the cases out of the scope of its sanctioning power (see *infra*). Article 134(1) SSMFR lists the cases where such an assistance from the NCAs is required, but, as noted by an author, misses the potential case of breaches of national legislation exercising options in the CRR.[81]

The personal scope of Article 18 SSMR is quite limited, too, as compared to the scope of the ECB's general sanctioning power. The prudential policy aims to ensure the stability of the banking and financial sectors. Since the 1990s, the phenomenon of concentration of financial institutions through mergers and take-overs, the formation of financial conglomerates and the despecialisation/diversification of activities exercised by the banking industry and insurance companies have made prudential supervision ever more complex, as it must cover actors whose business extend across several fields.[82] From this perspective, Article 127(6) TFEU looks outdated and anachronistic, as it allows the Council to confer specific tasks upon the ECB "concerning policies relating to the prudential supervision of credit institutions and other financial institutions *with the exception of insurance undertakings*". This exclusion is to be regretted,[83] but will not disappear anytime soon, since it will require a Treaty revision under Article 48(2) TEU. The Treaties and the Statute do not define "credit institutions", nor does the SSM Regulation. Being closely related to the prudential regulation, the SSM Regulation contains few definitions on its own, refering mostly to the definitions provided for in the CRR (or Directive 2002/87/EC on financial conglomerates, as relevant), as it is the case for "credit institutions"[84]

---

[78] See Article 4(3) SSMR.

[79] Article 18(5) SSMR.

[80] Report from the Commission of 11 October 2017 on the Single Supervisory Mechanism established pursuant to Regulation (EU) No 1024/2013, COM(2017) 591 final, 14.

[81] G. Bassani, *The Legal Framework Applicable to the Single Supervisory Mechanism: Tapestry or Patchwork?* (Kluwer Law International 2019), 192.

[82] J. Le Cacheux, 'Réglementation et contrôle prudentiels dans l'espace bancaire et financier européen' (1993) *Revue ECU/EURO* 25.

[83] This exclusion is in response to a request made by France during the Maastricht negotiations.

[84] According to Article 4(1), point 1, 'credit institution' means "an undertaking the business of

and the “financial holding companies, or mixed financial holding companies” that Article 18 SSM Regulation includes within the category of “other financial institutions”.[85] By refering only to legal persons, Article 127(6) implicitly excludes natural persons from its scope.[86]

In addition, the ECB exercises its responsibilities within the SSM in cooperation with the NCAs (see *supra* Section 2.2). The latter shall carry out the direct supervision of less significant credit institutions and are thus responsible for adopting “all relevant supervisory decisions with regard to the credit institutions”.[87] In principle, only NCAs may impose appropriate sanctions on the credit institutions under their direct supervision. The exercise of the ECB’s sanctioning powers under Article 18 SSM Regulation is not applicable to the credit institutions supervised by NCAs,[88] without prejudice of the applicability of the general sanctioning power of the ECB under Regulation (EC) No 2532/98 (see *supra* Section 3.1).[89] Such an approach is consistent with the principle that responsibility for sanction follows responsibility for supervision.

Finally, the SSM Regulation applies only in respect of credit institutions that are established in participating Member States, i.e. euro area Member States and non-euro area Members States whose NCA has established a close cooperation with the ECB in accordance with Article 7 SSMR and Decision 2014/434/EU of the ECB.[90]

Depending on the nature of the rule of Union law which a credit institution has failed to comply with, the ECB may impose fines or periodic penalty payments under Regulation (EC) No 2532/98 (see Section 3.1 above) or “administrative pecuniary penalties” under Article 18 of the SSM Regulation. Taking over from CRD IV,[91] the qualification of the penalties as “administrative” aims to meet the criteria establised by the case law of the European Court of Human Rights[92]

---

which is to take deposits or other repayable funds from the public and to grant credits for its own account”.

[85] See Article 2, points 3 to 5, SSM Regulation.

[86] The personal scope of Article 18 SSM Regulation shall be understood in restrictive terms according to Recital 53. See also C. Gortsos, ‘The power of the ECB to impose administrative penalties as a supervisory authority: an analysis of Article 18 of the SSM Regulation’, *Working Paper Series*, European Center of Economic and Financial Law, No 2015/11, March 2015, 18.

[87] Article 6(6) SSMR.

[88] Article 124 SSMFR.

[89] Article 122, letter (b), SSMFR.

[90] Decision of the ECB of 31 January 2014 on the close cooperation with the national competent authorities of participating Member States whose currency is not the euro, OJ L 198/7, 5.7.2014.

[91] See Recitals 35 and 36, Articles 66(1), 66(2), letter (c), 67(2), letter (e) CRD IV.

[92] ECtHR, *Engel and Others v. the Netherlands*, App. No 5100/71, 5101/71, 5102/71, 5354/72, 5370/72, 8 June 1976, §§ 80 to 82, Series A no. 22.

and of the Court of Justice[93] concerning the criminal or administrative nature of sanctions imposed to economic operators.[94] As insisted on in the SSM Regulation, the penalties imposed by the ECB or the NCAs when required by the ECB to open proceedings (see *infra*), shall be 'dissuasive'.[95] These penalties shall amount "up to twice the amount of the profits gained or losses avoided because of the breach where those can be determined, or up to 10% of the total annual turnover, as defined in relevant Union law, of a legal person in the preceding business year or such other pecuniary penalties as may be provided for in relevant Union law".[96] Although the SSM Regulation does not explictly mention the possibility of imposing periodic penalty payments, such penalties remain available to the ECB in the prudential field in application of Article 132(3) TFEU.[97] The implementation of its supervisory powers listed in Articles 14 to 18 SSMR shall give rise to the adoption of decisions by the ECB,[98] non-compliance with which falls within the sanction regime established by Regulation (EC) No 2532/98.[99] The maximum ceiling for periodic penalty payments is set at 5% of the average daily turnover per day of infringement. The duration of the periodic penalty payment is limited to six months, as in the general case. Finally, the SSM Regulation does not provide for the ECB to impose non-pecuniary sanctions.

As a result of the multiple restrictions on its sanctioning power in the field of supervision, the ECB is less well-equipped than national supervisors to ensure the enforcement of prudential rules and to sanction their breach. Article 18(5) of the SSM Regulation, supplemented by Article 134 SSM Framework Regulation, sets out an exhaustive list of cases where the ECB "may require NCAs to open proceedings with a view to taking action in order to ensure that appropriate penalties are imposed".[100] Such cases may include, for example, the application of any pecuniary or non-pecuniary penalties in the event of a breach by legal or natural persons of any national law transposing relevant Union directives. By acting in the name and on behalf of the ECB in such cases, the NCAs must comply with EU fundamental

[93] Case C-489/10, *Bonda*, ECLI:EU:C:2012:319, para. 37; case C-617/10, *Åkerberg Fransson*, ECLI:EU:C:2013:105, para. 35; case C-537/16, *Garlsson Real Estate and Others*, ECLI:EU:C:2018:193, para. 37.

[94] Article 18(3) SSMR; Article 1, point 6, Regulation (EC) No 2532/98; ECB (2018), SSM Supervisory Manual, cit., para. 4.11.3, 103. For a discussion, see R. D'Ambrosio, 'Due process and safeguards of the persons subjects to SSM supervisory and sanctioning proceedings' (2013) 74 *Quaderni di Ricerca Giuridica*, Banca d'Italia, 17-18.

[95] Recital 36, Article 18(3), and Article 18(5) SSMR.

[96] Compare Article 66(2), letters (c) and (e), and Article 67(2), letters (g) and (e), CRD IV.

[97] Article 129(1) SSMFR.

[98] Article 22 SSMR; Article 25 SSMFR.

[99] Article 18(7) SSMR; Article 129 SSMFR.

[100] See also Recital 35 SSMR.

rights standards.[101] The ECB shall be notified of the completion of a penalty procedure initiated at its request and informed of the penalties imposed, if any.[102]

9.4. The convergence of sanctioning procedures

The adoption of a pecuniary sanction by the ECB is not subject to a single procedure but to two separate procedures depending on the area where the infringement or the breach is committed. The general procedural rules applicable to the sanctions which the ECB may impose in respect of the performance of its basic tasks are laid down in Regulation (EC) No 2532/98, as supplemented by ECB Regulation (EC) No 2157/1999. The procedure applicable to administrative pecuniary penalties is governed by the SSM Regulation and detailed in the SSM Framework Regulation (Articles 123 to 127). The Rules of Procedure of the ECB provide further details on the organisation of meetings and voting modalities of the Governing Council, the Executive Board and the Supervisory Board, ie. an internal ECB body responsible for the planning and execution of prudential supervision tasks. The 1998 and 1999 Regulations were amended following the assignment of new specific tasks to the ECB in the field of prudential supervision, as to align them on the latest developments in case law of the ECJ, as regards the protection of the rights of the defence, especially the separation of the investigation and decision-making phases. The procedural rules they laid down needed also to be complemented as to take into account fines and periodic penalty payments imposed by the ECB when carrying out its supervisory tasks. To avoid procedural differences with administrative pecuniary penalties, the substance of the relevant provisions of the SSM Framework Regulation is embedded in Regulation (EC) 2532/98, as much as possible. Two specific cases to be mentionned: infringements of minimum reserve requirements are subject to procedural rules derogating from the general rules in Regulation 2157/99,[103] and a simplified procedure is foreseen for minor infringements in the case of sanctions imposed by the ECB in the performance of its monetary tasks.[104]

9.4.1. Initiation and investigation phase

The decentralised execution of the Eurosystem's basic tasks by the ECB places the NCBs concerned at the forefront of detecting evidence that an infringement is be-

[101] R. D'Ambrosio, *supra* note 94, 11. For a general overview of fundamental right issues in relation to the exercise of EU sanctioning powers, see the chapter by N. Lazzerini in this book.

[102] Article 135(3) SSMFR.

[103] Article 11 Regulation (EC) 2157/1999.

[104] The amount of the penalty must be less than EUR 25 000. See Article 10 Regulation (EC) 2157/1999. The simplified procedure shall not apply to sanctions imposed for infringements of ECB regulations and decisions in the field of oversight of systemically important payment systems.

ing committed or has been committed. The initiation of the infringement procedure is therefore shared between the ECB and the NCB of the Member State where the alleged infringement has been committed. No more than one infringement procedure may be initiated against the same undertaking for the same facts.[105] The ECB and the NCBs shall keep each other informed of the procedures they initiate. Both the ECB and the relevant NCB may act either on their own initiative or following a motion to that effect by the other central bank.[106] If an infringement relates exclusively to a tasks entrusted to the Eurosystem or the ECB by EU primary law, the infringement procedure may be governed only by Regulation (EC) No 2532/98, as supplemented by Regulation (EC) No 2157/1999, irrespective of whether the procedure is initiated by the ECB or an NCB.[107] Only the infringement procedure initiated by the ECB is described below.

The ECB's responsibility to initiate an infringement procedure in the exercise of its prudential tasks is linked to the scope of its power to impose sanctions in this field. In accordance with Article 18(1), the ECB shall have exclusive competence to initiate a procedure where it considers that there is reason to suspect that one or more breaches under relevant directly applicable Union law or of an ECB regulation or decision are being or have been committed by a significant supervised institution.[108] This task is without prejudice to the competence of the NCAs to initiate infringement procedures in cases not covered by Article 18(1) SSMR. The procedure is initiated by the ECB on its own initiative, e.g. on the occasion of direct day-to-day supervision of significant institutions, of on-site inspections, after a positive evalution of a report of breaches submitted by a natural person directly to the ECB or through an NCA.[109] In accordance with the principle of sincere cooperation, the NCAs must also inform the ECB whenever they are aware of alleged infringement of ECB regulations and decisions by the credit institutions under their direct supervision. It should be noted that in the event of a change in the division of competence between the ECB and a national supervisor, the authority whose competence ends shall undertake efforts to complete any pending supervisory procedure which requires a decision prior to the date on which the change in the supervisory competence is to occur. If the supervisory procedure cannot be completed prior to this date, the authority whose competence ends shall remain competent to complete such pending supervisory procedure.[110]

---

[105] Article 2(1) Regulation (EC) No 2157/1999.

[106] Article 3(1) Regulation (EC) No 2532/98.

[107] Article 3(10) Regulation (EC) 2532/98.

[108] Article 124(1) SSMFR.

[109] Article 23 SSMR, and Articles 36-38 SSMFR.

[110] Article 48 SSMFR.

Without prejudice to the simplified procedure for minors breaches, the investigation of infringements shall be referred to an independent internal investigation unit. Introduced first in supervisory matters by the SSM Regulation,[111] this arrangement has been replicated in comparable terms for infringement procedures initiated in monetary matters.[112] The creation of an independent unit guarantees a separate exercise of investigative and decision-making powers.[113] The unit is composed of investigators appointed by the ECB from among its own staff,[114] duly mandated external experts, or staff of an NCB in the specific case of a breach of the prudential requirements for systemically important payment systems. In addition to the general regime of independence which they enjoy as staff of the ECB, investigators are independent in the performance of their duties vis-à-vis the bodies responsible for adopting decisions.[115] For the purpose of their investigations, the investigating units may exercise the powers granted to the ECB under relevant Union law. The investigating officers may request the undertakings to submit documents, examine/take copies of the books and records of the undertaking, obtain written or oral explanations.[116] They also have access to all documents and information gathered by the ECB and, where appropriate, by the relevant NCAs in the course of their supervisory activities.

Judicial rights and procedural safeguards are protected in a very similar way in the different infringement procedures even though some differences remain. Access rights to the ECB's files are guaranteed, except for confidential information.[117] In prudential supervisory matters, the undertakings concerned have the right to submit written observations in response to the notification of the initiation of an infringement procedure. The investigating unit may also invite the supervised entity concerned to attend an oral hearing. On completion of an investigation and before a proposal for a complete draft decision is prepared and submitted to the Supervisory Board, the investigating unit shall notify the supervised entity concerned in writing of the findings

---

[111] Article 123 SSMFR.

[112] See Article 1b(1) Regulation 2157/1999.

[113] Recital 5 SSMFR. See ECtHR, *Dubus v. France*, App. No 5242/04, 11 June 2009; *Menarini v Italy*, App. No 43509/08, 27 September 2011; *Grande Stevens*, App. No 18640/10, 4 March 2014.

[114] See Article 1b(1a) Regulation 2157/1999.

[115] Article 123(3) SSMR, Article 1b(1) Regulation 2157/1999.

[116] Article 3 Regulation (EC) No 2532/98; Article 11 SSMR. In that case, the EU regulations are everything but clear about the right of the persons heard to remain silent.

[117] Article 4b(3) Regulation (EC) No 2532/98; Article 32 SSMFR. See Decision (2004/257/EC) of the ECB of 19 February 2004 adopting the Rules of Procedure of the European Central Bank ('ECB RoP'), OJ L 80/33, 18.3.2004, as last amended by Decision (EU) 2016/1717 of the ECB of 21 September 2016, OJ L 258/17, 24.9.2016. In prudential supervisory matters, confidential information include internal documents of the ECB and of the NCAs, and correspondence between the ECB and an NCAs or between NCAs. See Article 32(5) SSMFR.

under the investigation carried out and of any objections raised thereto. In monetary matters, the investigating unit shall notify the undertaking concerned in writing of the factual results of any inquiry carried out and of the objections raised against the undertaking concerned before any decision is taken on the imposition of a sanction. The undertaking may object within 30 working days.[118] In addition, the untertaking concerned has the right to be heard by the ECB to present its defence. In the case of proceedings for infringement of minimum reserve requirements, the objective nature of the infringement (i.e. resulting from the difference between the amount of reserves to be held by the credit institution and the amount measured by the NCB with which the reserves are held) does not require investigative measures.[119]

Where, on completion of the investigation, the investigating unit (or, where appropriate, the competent NCB) considers that a sanction should be imposed on the undertaking, it shall submit a proposal for a decision to the Executive Board[120] or, in prudential supervisory matters, a proposal for a complete draft decision to the Supervisory Board.[121] The proposal shall be based only on facts and objections on which the undertaking concerned has had the opportunity to comment during the investigating phase. The proposal determines the infringement(s) or breach(es) committed and specifies the pecuniary penalties to be imposed.

The ECB initiated 27 sanctioning proceedings in the supervisory field in 2018 and handled a total of 51 sanctioning proceedings – 24 proceedings were still ongoing at the end of 2017. Of the 51 sanctioning proceedings handled in 2018, 22 were related to suspected breaches of directly applicable EU law (ECB decisions and regulations included) committed by 13 significant institutions. They led to 16 ECB decisions.[122]

9.4.2. The decision on sanction and its administrative review

The Governing Council and the Executive Board are the decision-making bodies of the ECB. Only the Governing Council and, by delegation, the Executive Board shall have the power to formally adopt legal acts with external effects, including decisions on sanction, irrespective of the field of competence where the infraction has been committed. In accordance with the principle of separation of the prudential supervisory function from the monetary policy function, the preparation and the adoption of a decision on a sanction follow different paths for prudential or mone-

[118] Article 5(1) Regulation 2157/1999.

[119] Article 11 Regulation 2157/1999.

[120] Article 3(4) Regulation (EC) No 2532/98, and Article 7a Regulation (EC) 2157/1999.

[121] Article 127(1) SSMFR.

[122] ECB, Annual Report on supervisory activities 2018, spec. Section 3.2. Available at: https://www.bankingsupervision.europa.eu/press/publications/annual-report/html/ssm.ar2018~927cb99de4.en.html, accessed on 02.12.2019.

tary tasks. The same applies to the administrative review procedure.

The decision-making bodies of the ECB are not bound by the proposal submitted by the investigating unit and can exercise their own assessment about the completeness of the file, the commission of an infraction and the appropriateness of the sanction proposed. To consider first the procedure in monetary matters, Regulation (EC) No 2157/1999 lists the options open to the Executive Board, which may accordingly: [123]

- return the file to the investigating unit (or the competent NCB, as relevant) together with a reasoned request for additional information. Guarantees relating to the rights of the defence must be respected when the investigation phase is reopened;
- agree with the proposal submitted and adopt it;
- consider that the facts do not constitute sufficient evidence of an infringement and close the case;
- agree that an infringement occurred, but disagree with the sanction: it adopts a decision specifying the sanction that it considers appropriate;
- disagree with the analysis of the investigating unit and considers that a different infringement has been committed by the institution.

The procedure followed in supervisory matters differs inasmuch the file prepared by the investigating unit is examined by the supervisory board before being submitted for adoption to the Governing Council of the ECB. The options open to the Supervisory Board are the same than those open to the Executive Board in monetary matters. The draft decision shall be deemed adopted unless the Governing Council objects within ten working days or 48 hours in emergency situations. [124] In the event of objections, the Supervisory Board is invited to submit an amended proposal for a decision. The NCAs shall be informed of the Governing Council's objections. In the event of disagreement between them regarding the ECB's objections, the case shall be referred to an internal ECB mediation committee. [125] It shall deliver a written opinion which shall be forwarded to the Supervisory Board and the Governing Council. The Supervisory Board may take it into account when drawing up its proposal for a decision. [126]

The undertaking concerned by a sanction has the right to request a review of the decision of the ECB within 30 days of its notification. [127] In monetary matters, the de-

---

[123] Article 7a Regulation (EC) 2157/1999.

[124] Article 13e ECB RoP.

[125] Article 27(8) and Article 25(5) SSMR

[126] Article 10 Regulation (EU) No 673/2014 of the ECB of 2 June 2014 concerning the establishment of a Mediation Panel and its Rules of Procedure, OJ L 179/72, 19.6.2014.

[127] Article 3(6) Regulation (EC) 2532/98; Article 24(5) SSMR.

cision of the Executive Board is to be reviewed by the Governing Council. The request for a review shall include all supporting informations and allegations. The Governing Council may request the undertaking, as well as the other relevant stakeholders (i.e. the Executive Board and/or the competent NCB) to provide additional information in order to review the decision of the Executive Board. In carrying out the review, the Governing Council may (i) confirm the decision of the Executive Board, (ii) amend the decision by modifying the amount of the sanction to be imposed and/or the grounds giving rise to an infringement; (iii) set aside the decision. In addition, if no decision has been taken by the Governing Council within two months of the request submitted by the undertaking concerned by the sanction, the decision of the Executive Board becomes final. [128]

In supervisory matters, the review process takes multiple steps. The request for administrative review of the Governing Council's initial decision is examined by a dedicated internal ECB body established by the SSM Regulation, the Administrative Board of Review ('ABoR'), prior to being forwarded to the Supervisory Board then to the Governing Council. [129] The ABoR is in charge of assessing the admissibility of the request for review, examining the grounds relied on by the applicant and adopting an opinion on the initial decision of the Governing Council. [130] The scope of ABoR's review is limited to the relevant procedural and substantive conformity with the SSM Regulation. The opinion adopted by the ABoR shall propose whether the decision should be either abrogated, replaced with a decision of identical content or replaced with an amended one. [131]. On the basis of the ABoR's opinion, the Supervisory Board shall prepare a new draft decision to the Council. Neither the ABoR's opinion, neither the grounds invoked by the applicant are binding on the Supervisory Board. The new draft decision is submitted to the Governing Council and shall be deemed adopted unless the latter objects within a maximum of ten working days. [132] At this stage, an objection by the Governing Council does not allow a new mediation. [133]

The final decision of the ECB shall be notified to the undertaking concerned, to the relevant supervisory authority and to the national central bank of the Member

---

[128] Article 3(8) Regulation (EC) No 2532/98.

[129] For a detailed analysis, see C. Brescia, R. Smits, A. Magliari, 'The Administrative Board of Review of the European Central Bank: Experience After 2 Years' (2017) 18 *European Business Organization Law Review* 567.

[130] Article 24 SSMR; Decision (2014/360/EU) of the ECB of 14 April 2014 concerning the establishment of an Administrative Board of Review and its Operating Rules, OJ L 175/47, 14.6.2014, as amended by Decision (EU) 2019/1378 of the ECB of 9 August 2019, OJ L 224/9, 28.8.2019.

[131] Article 16 Decision 2014/360/EU.

[132] Article 24(7) SSMR. For a detailed presentation, see ECB, SSM Supervisory Manual, *supra* note 46, 28.

[133] Article 11(3) Regulation (EU) No 673/2014.

State where the infringement occurred. It shall inform the undertaking of its right of judicial review. [134] According to Article 299 TFEU, decisions of the ECB which impose pecuniary penalties are enforceable. The enforcement of the sanction against the undertaking concerned is suspended during the review of the initial decision. [135] In supervisory matters, the suspension of the initial decision may be decided by the Governing Council, upon a proposal by the ABoR.

9.5. Concluding remarks

Any administrative penalty adopted by the ECB which imposes a pecuniary obligation on persons (other than States) takes the form of a decision and, under Article 299 TFEU, shall be enforceable in the territory of the Member state where the addressee of the decision is established. [136] The ECB decision shall be open to judicial review before the Court of justice, as well as national enforcement measures before national jurisdictions. It is worth mentioning that the ECB decision to impose a sanction is the final step of a complex procedure which usually involves national authorities in the preliminary or preparatory stages, such as the provision of information, the conduct of investigating measures or the submission of a proposal to the ECB. [137] As the Advocate-General noted in his opinion in Case T-212/15 *Berlusconi and Fininvest v Banca d'Italia*, such procedures are not uncommon in EU law, but the use made of them within the BU is, by far, much more intensive and more frequent than in other EU policy fields. [138] Whatever the field concerned, monetary or prudential, the ECB exercises, alone, the final decision-making power without being bound by the preparatory acts or the proposals of the national authorities. When deciding on the proposal submitted by a national authority in the monetary field or by the supervisory council in the supervisory field, the Governing Council and the Executive Board both have a large discretion. The judicial review of the ECB decision and the preparatory acts adopted by the national authorities shall be conducted only by the EU courts. [139] Conversely, the sanctions imposed by a national authority on the request of the ECB are to be appealed against in the national courts. [140] Since the entry into force of the SSM Regulation, only a few deci-

---

[134] Article 3(7) Regulation (EC) No 2532/98; Article 24(11) SSMR.

[135] Article 3(8) Regulation (EC) No 2532/98; and in the supervisory field: Article 25(8) SSMR, Article 34 SSMFR, and Article 9 Decision 2014/360/EU.

[136] Article 299 TFEU.

[137] Article 7a Regulation (EC) No 2157/1999.

[138] Opinion of AG Campos Sánchez-Bordona, case C-219/17, *Berlusconi and Fininvest v Banca d'Italia*, ECLI:EU:C:2018:502.

[139] Case C-219/17, *Berlusconi and Fininvest v. Banca d'Italia*, ECLI:EU:C:2018:1023, paras 49-51.

[140] Court of justice, judgment of 3 December 1992, *Borelli*, C-97/91, ECLI:EU:C:1992:491.

sions of the ECB to impose sanction have been brought before the European Courts and three cases are still pending as of December 2019.[141] These actions are without any doubt the first of many to come, given the very high complexity of the legal regimes governing the ECB's sanctioning power, and new developments are to be expected especially with regards to the respect of the EU Charter of fundamental rights.[142]

---

[141] Actions brought on 23 March 2018, case T-203/18, *VQ v ECB*; 18 July 2018, case T-451/18, *Triantafyllopoulos e.a. v ECB*; 25 September 2018, case T-576/18, *Crédit agricole v ECB*.

[142] See Lazzerini in this volume.

Chapter 10

RESTRICTIVE MEASURES AS TOOLS OF EU FOREIGN AND SECURITY POLICY: PROMOTING EU VALUES, FROM ANTITERRORISM TO COUNTRY SANCTIONS

Charlotte Beaucillon *

ABSTRACT: *This chapter questions the extent to which restrictive measures of the European Union contribute to the European Union's sanctioning powers. This is not so obvious if one considers that restrictive measures are part of the practice of international sanctions: they consist either of measures to enforce collective measures decided by the Security Council of the United Nations, or of unilateral measures adopted by the European Union proprio motu in reaction to behavior that it considers contrary to international law. However, could it not also be considered that the Union, while pursuing the objective of respecting international law, would also be pursuing the objective of respecting its own law, values and interest? In this chapter, I begin by demonstrating how the connection between sanctioning international law and sanctioning EU values is made in the practice of restrictive measures. I then highlight three legal mechanisms by which the European Union exports its values and its interpretation of law on the international scene: the coordination of Member States in third international organisations, the insertion of specific clauses in its international treaties, and the reaction to serious violations of customary international human rights law. Ultimately, it appears that while the practice of restrictive measures may be considered in some respects as a means of expressing the European Union's sanctioning powers, it is necessary to consider the consequences of the exercise of such a power - especially when it is unilateral - on third parties, who might ultimately challenge its legitimacy.*

KEYWORDS: *international sanctions – EU Restrictive measures – EU values – treaty breach – human rights violations*

* Professor of International and EU Law, University of Lille.

10.1. Introduction

To what extent does respect for human rights in Syria, the Iranian nuclear crisis or the international fight against terrorism fall within the scope of the enforcement of European Union law? Wondering whether EU restrictive measures contribute to EU law enforcement may seem surprising. However, EU restrictive measures differ very strongly from the other facets of EU law enforcement that have been developed in the other contributions to this collective volume. Their specificity deserves a twofold preliminary clarification. [1]

First, restrictive measures react to an alleged violation of international law by a third State or entity. For instance, the EU has adopted restrictive measures in reaction to the disrespect by Iran of its international obligations under the 1968 Non-Proliferation Treaty and the diverse resolutions adopted by the United Nations Security Council (UNSC) since 2006. It has also adopted restrictive measures to condemn the violation of Ukraine's territorial integrity when Russia annexed Crimea in 2014. Another example is the adoption of restrictive measures in reaction to the massive violations of human rights by the Syrian regime against its own population. The first question arising from the inclusion of EU restrictive measures in the study of the EU sanctioning powers is twofold: can the EU "sanction" the violation of international law by third States/entities? And, when doing so, is the EU also sanctioning a breach of EU law?

Second, EU restrictive measures contribute to the international practice of international sanctions. [2] When analyzed closely, the single EU law category of EU restrictive measures unfolds into two different international law instruments. On the one hand, EU restrictive measures can be aimed at implementing the resolutions that the UNSC has adopted under Chapter VII of the UN Charter to maintain international peace and security, which are binding on all EU Member States and which they implement collectively through the EU. On the other hand, the EU on its own initiative can impose EU restrictive measures. In this case, they range in the category of autonomous

---

[1] This chapter draws on some of the results of previous comprehensive research on European Union restrictive measures: Ch. Beaucillon, *Les mesures restrictives de l'Union européenne* (Bruylant 2014).

[2] The definition of international sanctions is dealt with in details in the following section: see below 2.2. *EU restrictive measures as sanctions*, esp. note 32.

unilateral sanctions together with the United-States' unilateral sanctions for instance. In both cases though, the political aim of UN-based or unilateral sanctions is the same: constraining their targets to change behavior in order to conform to their international obligations. The second question arising from the study of EU restrictive measures as a part of EU law enforcement is to what extent the EU is exporting its own values and its own interpretation of international law on the international stage, when it seeks to influence third parties' behavior in the name of respect for international law.

The European Union's export of its values to third parties, States or international organizations raises a preliminary issue: the very existence of values that would be specific to the European Union.

First of all, the notion of *EU* values refers to a set of values that would be characteristic of the European Union's identity on the international scene. A historical reading of this question reminds us that the genesis of the European project is inextricably linked to the end of the Second World War: the Union is being structured in response to its own devastation. Devastation on the one hand, due to the inability of European forces to maintain a sufficient balance between them, in order to avoid armed conflicts between European states. Devastation on the other hand, by the inability to stand up against nazi and fascist totalitarianism, their crimes against humanity and the Shoah, leading to the birth of a new international crime, genocide. The Union is thus structured around two pairs. The first, combining *peace* and *reconciliation*, responds to the need to bring lasting peace to the continent. The second, combining *freedom* and *solidarity*, puts the individual and his or her rights back at the heart of the European project.

All these values, which are enshrined in Articles 3(5) and 21 of the TEU, are undeniably liberal in nature and were consecrated at the universal level after the Second World War, as illustrated by the 1948 Universal Declaration of Human Rights (UDHR)[3] or the 1966 International Covenant on Civil and Political Rights (ICCPR).[4] To what extent, then, should the proper European character of such values be defined? From a political point of view, it will suffice here to recall that the universality of international human rights law has been the subject of various challenges, because of its European origin, in particular through the concept of the cultural relativity of human rights. From a legal point of view, the diversity of techniques for implementing legal principles as general as freedom or human dignity should be highlighted, as their universal nature does not prevent the development of regional protection mechanisms expressing all their specificity. The issue here will therefore

[3] A/RES/217(III), *International Bill of Human Rights*, 10 December 1948.

[4] Adopted and opened for signature, ratification and accession by A/RES/2200A (XXI), 16 December 1966, entered into force 23 March 1976, United Nations, *Treaty Series*, vol. 999, p. 171.

be to examine how the European Union reinterprets these liberal values in the light of its own legal order before re-exporting them to third parties, and not to seek a strictly European origin – as it were – for certain values.

In light of the above, I will first explain the extent to which EU restrictive measures can be considered international sanctions, and how they serve the exportation of EU values to third parties (2). Second, I will outline the different legal mechanisms at work to achieve this export of values, depending on whether the restrictive measures are linked to a UNSC measure, a treaty breach or a breach of customary international law (3). I will then conclude with a broader perspective on the possible consequences of such a power of the Union (4).

10.2. Normative synergies: promoting EU values through international sanctions

10.2.1. The two faces of Janus: a double qualification in EU and international law

The most immediate approach to EU restrictive measures is to examine the positive law provisions applicable to restrictive measures in the EU treaties. Title IV of the Treaty on the Functioning of the European Union (TFEU), "Restrictive measures", is the first recognition of the expression in the Union's primary law. Its single article states:

1. Where a decision, adopted in accordance with Chapter 2 of Title V of the Treaty on European Union, provides for the interruption or reduction, in part or completely, of economic and financial relations with one or more third countries, the Council, acting by a qualified majority on a joint proposal from the High Representative of the Union for Foreign Affairs and Security Policy and the Commission, shall adopt the necessary measures. It shall inform the European Parliament thereof.
2. Where a decision adopted in accordance with Chapter 2 of Title V of the Treaty on European Union so provides, the Council may adopt restrictive measures under the procedure referred to in paragraph 1 against natural or legal persons and groups or non-State entities.
3. The acts referred to in this Article shall include necessary provisions on legal safeguards.

This article, which entered into force on 1 December 2009 with the Lisbon Treaty, is the most recent codification of the European Union's practice in this field and is also the most elaborate version. The provisions of Article 215 of the TFEU reveal two elements for the definition of EU restrictive measures. Formally, restrictive measures are adopted through a decision taken within the framework of the EU

Common Foreign and Security Policy (CFSP),[5] as indicated by the reference in paragraphs 1 and 2 to the adoption of a decision "in accordance with Chapter 2 of Title V of the Treaty on European Union". They are then implemented within the framework of the Union according to its competences, following the procedure described at the end of paragraph 1. In material terms, restrictive measures cover cases where it has been decided to terminate or reduce the Union's economic relations with a third country,[6] or to impose certain constraints on individuals.[7] Restrictive measures are therefore instruments that the European Union uses exclusively in the context of its external relations.

The initial impression that the category of restrictive measures covers a wide range of elements is reinforced by a detailed examination of the content of these measures. Examining restrictive measures *ratione materiae*, no less than fifteen types of measures can be identified. These different tools of coercion include, for example, traditional measures such as an arms embargo, a ban on the import or export of certain goods or a ban on the provision of certain services. Other measures are more specific to a given target and aim, for example, at preventing illegal trafficking in nuclear, chemical or biological weapons,[8] or include restrictions on the payment of oil and gas.[9] A third type of measures pierces the veil of the State and directly affects certain individuals or entities. This applies to measures to freeze funds and financial assets, or to prohibit admission to the territory of the EU Member States. The persons involved vary. In addition to persons associated with international terrorism,[10] they include state leaders and their associates,[11] members of militias,[12] or

---

[5] Article 29 TEU.

[6] Article 215(1) TFEU.

[7] Article 215(2) TFEU.

[8] This is the case for the restrictive measures imposed on North Korea by the Common Position 2006/795/CFSP of 20 November 2006 concerning the adoption of restrictive measures against the Democratic People's Republic of Korea, OJ L 322/32, 22.11.2006.

[9] As provided for in the restrictive measures against Iraq: Council Common Position 2003/495/CFSP of 7 July 2003 on Iraq and repealing Common Positions 96/741/CFSP and 2002/599/CFSP, OJ L 169/ 72, 8.7.2003.

[10] Council Common Position 2001/931/CFSP of 27 December 2001 on the application of specific measures to combat terrorism, OJ L 344/93, 28.12.2001, and Council Common Position 2002/402/CFSP of 27 May 2002 on the application of specific measures against Osama bin Laden, members of the organization Al Qaeda and the Taliban and other associated persons, groups, undertakings and entities, and repealing Common Positions 96/746/CFSP, 1999/727/CFSP, 2001/154/ CFSP and2001/771/CFSP, OJ L 139/4, 29.5.2002.

[11] Council Common Position 2004/487/CFSP of 29 April 2004 concerning further restrictive measures against Liberia, OJ L 162/116, 30.4.2004; Council Common Position 2006/318/CFSP of 27 April 2006 renewing restrictive measures against Burma/Myanmar, OJ L 116/77, 29.4.2006.

[12] Council Common Position 2008/369/CFSP of 14 May 2008 concerning restrictive measures against the Democratic Republic of Congo and repealing the Common Position 2005/440/CFSP, OJ L 127/ 84, 15.5.2008.

persons indicted in some international courts.[13] These measures of freezing funds and banning entry into the territory in turn call for some comments from the point of view of their targets. Indeed, in parallel with the formal State targets of restrictive measures, their real targets appear to be either individuals or non-governmental entities. This now common practice, known as "targeted sanctions", raises some questions. Since this practice no longer limits itself to affecting trade or diplomatic relations with a State and directly targets certain persons because of their own activities, it creates a clear distortion between the formal target and the actual target of the measures adopted.[14]

The apparently homogeneous category of restrictive measures in European Union law covers two very different types of legal acts in international law. They correspond to different legal issues, depending on whether one focuses on the implementation by the EU of centralized measures adopted by the UNSC, or on the adoption by the EU of decentralized unilateral measures.

The European Union's restrictive measures are directly affected by the UN collective security system in which the primary responsibility for the maintenance of international peace and security is conferred on the UNSC, which acts on behalf of the organization's Member States.[15] The UNSC adopts measures not involving the use of armed force[16] when it "determines the existence of a threat to the peace, a breach of the peace or an act of aggression",[17] in order to "maintain or restore international peace and security".[18] The UN Charter thus enshrines the central role of the organization, through the UNSC, in adopting measures to protect international peace and security. The notion of *centralized* measures is justified here by the responsibility entrusted to the UNSC to maintain international peace and security. However, this centralization does not preclude decentralized implementation, as illustrated by the national (or regional at the EU level[19]) composition of the lists of persons covered by the counter-terrorism

[13] Council Common Position 2004/293/CFSP of 30 March 2004 renewing measures in support of the effective implementation of the mandate of the International Criminal Tribunal for the former Yugoslavia (ICTY), OJ L 94/65, 31.3.2004.

[14] This in turn raises the question of the appropriate legal regime for restrictive measures, depending on whether they affect a State or a private person. This question has already been analyzed in detail: See Beaucillon, *Les mesures restrictives de l'Union européenne*, *supra note* 1, 343-606; and Ch. Beaucillon, 'Opening up the horizon: The ECJ's new take on country sanctions' (2018) 55 *Common Market Law Review* 387. See also *infra*, section 4.

[15] Article 24(1) UN Charter.

[16] Article 41 UN Charter.

[17] Article 39 UN Charter.

[18] *Ibidem*.

[19] Council Regulation (EC) No 2580/2001 of 27 December 2001 on specific restrictive measures directed against certain persons and entities with a view to combating terrorism, OJ L 344/70, 28.12.2001.

measures decided by the UNSC under resolution 1373(2001).[20]

In the absence of an institutional mechanism for centralizing responses to violations of international law, subjects of public international law must ensure respect for their legal interests by means of private justice tools: "a subject pursues by his own means, without the intervention of an external authority, the protection or execution of what he considers to be his or her rights".[21] In this sense, these reactions to wrongfulness are *decentralized*, because it is the State or organization that considers that its legal interests have been ignored, which will qualify the illicit activity.[22] This process is therefore essentially inter-subjective.

Decentralized responses to wrongfulness can be divided into two categories, depending on whether the measures adopted are inherently lawful or, conversely, contrary to public international law. Unlike countermeasures, retaliatory measures are not, in themselves, measures contrary to international law. They consist of "unfriendly" conduct, which is not incompatible with an international obligation of the State, even if it intends to respond to an internationally wrongful act.[23] From the perspective of the European Union's restrictive measures, it is not the Member States but the Union as such that intends to react to certain international situations that it considers to be violations of the law. This intention is reflected in the adoption of a CFSP decision on the basis of Article 29 TEU.

10.2.2. EU restrictive measures as international sanctions

Are what are commonly referred to as "international sanctions", of which the Union's restrictive measures are a part, sanctions in the legal sense of the term? Whether it is the UNSC acting under the San Francisco Charter, or the EU adopting unilateral measures on its own initiative, it must be noted that the wrongful

---

[20] S/RES/1373(2001), *Threats to international peace and security caused by terrorist acts*, 28 September 2001.

[21] D. Alland, *Justice privée et ordre juridique international* (Pedone 1994), 1.

[22] We use the term "reaction to wrongfulness" in its general sense in public international law, and the term "decentralized reactions" with reference to L.-A. Sicilianos, *Les réactions décentralisées à l'illicite* (LGDJ 1990), 2.

[23] A/56/10, Supplement No 10, Report of the International Law Commission, Fifty-third Session, 23 April-1 June and 2 July-10 August 2001, 350. It should be noted that this definition of reprisals is proposed by the ILC as part of its work on State responsibility. It was therefore important to distinguish between the behaviors violating international law and those who are intrinsically lawful. We take note of the fact that the question of whether retaliation measures are acts taken in response to lawful or unlawful measures was less consensual than we present it here. This question was indeed discussed by some authors for whom the measures of retaliation would only be acts adopted in response to measures intrinsically legal but unfriendly. See A. Rivier, *Principes du droit des gens* (Arthur Rousseau 1899) vol. 2, quoted by L. Boisson de Chazournes, *Les contre-mesures dans les relations internationales économiques* (Pedone 1992), 24.

conduct of the target of the measures is not characterized by a judge.[24]

The institutionalization of international law is traditionally understood in opposition to the vision of an international community composed first and foremost of sovereign and legally equal States, and therefore essentially anarchic.[25] In this perspective, there is no organizing principle similar to what the State would be for the national legal order. Nor is there any total and *ex ante* centralization of *juris dictio*. It has thus been argued that the institutionalization of international law, illustrated by the multiplication of international organizations, contributes to its structuring.[26]

However, the enthusiasm that generally surrounds the identification of institutional sanctions must be met with caution when it comes to transposing it *mutatis mutandis* to any violation of the law, apart from the statutory sanctions imposed by organizations on their members.[27] Indeed, such a generalization would be based on the fiction that the organization would play a similar role in the international order to that of the domestic judge, who rules the law in complete independence.[28]

As Louis Cavaré expresses it:

> Let us add that in order to offer all the guarantees of justice, coercion must be decided and implemented by competent social bodies, among which it is desirable that a court be included. On the contrary, any coercion carried out by one subject of law against another, even for an illegal or harmful activity of the latter, cannot be qualified as a Sanction, but amounts to direct action, justice or private revenge.[29]

The theoretical or implicit attribution of a quasi-judicial function to political bodies as the UNSC or the Council of the EU leads to a clear distortion between

---

[24] For a comprehensive analysis of recent EU jurisprudence on restrictive measures targeting third countries: Ch. Beaucillon, 'Opening up the horizon: The ECJ's new take on country sanctions', *supra note* 14.

[25] 'Anarchy' in the strict sense of the term does not imply that the international system is not a legal order: "Therefore, the international order can be described as anarchic on the condition that it is understood that it is still a legal order, but one in which the law is precisely, to use Grotius' own expression, a 'voluntary right'", according to R.-J. Dupuy, 'Communauté internationale et disparités de développement', *Collected Courses of the Hague Academy of international law,* 1979, vol. 165, 52.

[26] W. Friedmann, *The Changing Structure of International Law* (Stevens 1964), 88-95.

[27] Of which Article 7 TEU is a topical example.

[28] Some international institutions as the European Union provide for elaborate mechanisms, since they establish a European judge in charge of the *juris dictio*. Who can do more can do the less, and it is therefore logical to consider that "[t]he real and primary source of 'sanction' in the Community, if it is permitted to use this word, resides in the authority recognized by the Court of Justice", L. Azoulai, 'Les formes de la sanction juridictionnelle', in I. Pingel (ed.), *Les sanctions contre les États en droit communautaire* (Pedone 2006), 18.

[29] L. Cavaré, 'Les sanctions dans le cadre de l'ONU', *Collected courses of The Hague Academy of international law*, 1952, vol. 80-I, 197.

what is expected from the practice of these bodies and what they are actually able to provide, thus exposing their legitimacy to significant criticism.

These considerations imply for this Chapter that the term sanctions should be understood *lato sensu*, or even in the broadest possible sense. Insofar as they are all intended to respond to the conduct of a third party deemed to be contrary to international law, EU restrictive measures fall into the category of legal sanction mechanisms, according to Georges Scelle's broad[30] and functional definition: "In a broad sense, we can call 'sanctions' all legal or material procedures designed to ensure the effectiveness of the law or the rule of law. Invalidity, damages, enforcement proceedings are sanctions".[31] It is in this sense that the term *international sanctions* will be used to refer to both *centralized* measures adopted by the UNSC and *decentralized* measures adopted by the European Union.

10.2.3. The double purpose of EU restrictive measures: respect for international law and EU values

The purpose of EU restrictive measures is twofold: to react to the violation of an international norm by a third party to the Union, and to pursue EU objectives in the field of the Common Foreign and Security Policy.

It is important to note that the objective of CFSP is to promote the values and interests of the Union, which, since the entry into force of the Lisbon Treaty, are formulated as follows:

> The Union is founded on the values of respect for human dignity, freedom, democracy, equality, the rule of law and respect for human rights, including the rights of persons belonging to minorities. These values are common to Member States in a society characterized by pluralism, non-discrimination, tolerance, justice, solidarity, solidarity and equality between women and men.[32]

The objectives of the CFSP must be read in conjunction with the Union's values, since the achievement of the former must serve the promotion of the latter, according to Article 21(1) TEU:

> The Union's action on the international scene is based on the principles that have governed its creation, development and enlargement, and which it seeks to

---

[30] For Ch. Leben, the following definition is "the broadest possible" of the sanction: 'Inter-State countermeasures and reactions to the illicit in international society', (1982) *French Yearbook of International Law* 17.

[31] G. Scelle, 'Le rôle et le risque des sanctions', in A. Mestre, L. Le Fur, G. Scelle (eds), *Les sanctions internationales, trois opinions de juristes* (Pedone 1936), 41. In the same vein, with regard to the "sanctions" (*sic*) of the European Community, J. Verhoeven, 'European Communities and International Sanctions', (1984-85) *Belgian Review of International Law* 79.

[32] Article 2 TEU.

advance in the wider world: democracy, the rule of law, the universality and indivisibility of human rights and fundamental freedoms, respect for human dignity, the principles of equality and solidarity, and respect for the principles of the United Nations Charter and international law.

The values of the European Union as formulated in the TEU refer to universal principles and standards.[33] However, their crystallization is the result of a historical process[34] and the aggregation of their interpretations by the Member States of the Union. In this sense, it has been possible for some political scientists to identify a European approach to these standards which results both from their historical significance for EU Members before the latter's instigation and from their interpretation and crystallization within the Community order itself and then within the Union. Peace is *sustainable*, freedom is *social* and democracy is *consensual*; human rights are *associative* in nature, the rule of law is ensured at *supranational* level, and equality is an *inclusive* concept; solidarity is *social* in nature, development is *sustainable* and governance is *good*.[35] Universal exogenous standards are thus integrated into the European Union's order and rethought into endogenous standards with a specific interpretation.

These EU values are then applied in turn to foreign policy. When the EU implements the measures adopted by the UNSC, it reacts to the violation of the UN Charter, as established by the UNSC, while pursuing its objective of "preserving peace, preventing conflicts and strengthening international security, in accordance with the purposes and principles of the United Nations Charter".[36] Again, when adopting decentralized autonomous measures, the EU reacts, for example, to the violation of human rights by a third country, while relying on its objective "to consolidate and support democracy, the rule of law, human rights and the principles of international law".[37]

As regards the aim pursued by the European Union in the conduct of its external action, the EU Treaty is unambiguous: "in its relations with the wider world, the Union shall uphold and promote its values and interests".[38] The European Union

---

[33] In the context of the fragmentation of international law, the consecration of certain norms by various legal regimes has been studied in the context of "equivalent standards from multiple sources". See among others T. Broude, Y. Shany, *Multi-Sourced Equivalent Norms in International Law* (Hart 2011).

[34] I. Manners, 'Normative Power Europe: A Contradiction in Terms?' (2002) 40 *Journal of Common Market Studies* 243-244.

[35] I. Manners, 'The Constitutive Nature of Values, Images and Principles in the European Union', in S. Lucarelli, I. Manners (eds), *Values and Principles in European Union Foreign Policy* (Routledge 2006), 32-38.

[36] Article 21(2)(c) TEU.

[37] Article 21(2)(b) TEU.

[38] Article 3(5) TEU.

must therefore not only promote these values, but also try to have them adopted by its third party partners, States or international organizations. As for the institutional practice corresponding to this mission given to the EU by its constituent treaties, it has been characterized since the 1990s by an essentially unilateralist approach to exports, in which the EU imposes its values on its partners as a condition for their relations. It is the relative success of this approach that has made it possible to qualify the EU as a normative power, an entity capable of exporting its own standards to the rest of the world.

The above results in an apparent contradiction between the liberal content of the values promoted by the EU on the one hand, and the unilateral export technique used by the EU on the other. In this respect, a realist reading of the European Union's external action as a normative power could lead to the conclusion that in promoting its values, the European Union is in reality seeking only the protection of its own interests. On the contrary, it is possible to examine how to translate the European Union's mission of "promoting" its values into concrete methods for international action. While the unilateralist promotion method is essentially oriented towards the export of values to third parties, there may well also be a concerted promotion method, oriented towards the proposal and discussion of values on the international scene. As it stands in practice, however, EU restrictive measures are a central tool of the unilateral export method of EU values.

10.3. The mechanics of normative exportation: linking EU values to international law

10.3.1. EU restrictive measures implementing UNSC counter-terrorism resolutions: exporting human rights to the international collective security system through the EU member States

i. *Member states obligations under EU and UN law: a combined reading*

Article 25 of the UN Charter states that: "The Members of the United Nations agree to accept and apply the decisions of the Security Council in accordance with the present Charter". This binding character is therefore attached to the resolutions adopted by the UNSC under Article 41 of the UN Charter, which are "decisions" of the Council under the letter of Article 41. This is confirmed *a contrario* by the reasoning of the International Court of Justice in its advisory opinion on Namibia, where it considers that the scope of Article 25 goes beyond Chapter VII of the Charter.[39] Article 48(2) of the Charter states that the Members of the United Na-

---

[39] *Legal Consequences for States of the Continued Presence of South Africa in Namibia (South West Africa) notwithstanding Security Council Resolution 276* (1970), Advisory Opinion, ICJ Reports 1971, para. 113.

tions shall carry out the measures decided by the UNSC "directly and through their action in the appropriate international bodies of which they are members". The reading of this article shows that the responsibility for implementing UNSC decisions adopted under Chapter VII rests with the Member States of the Organization, which, if necessary, use the organizations to which they belong. In this perspective, since all Member States of the European Union are Members of the UN, they are responsible for the obligation to implement Security UNSC decisions on the basis of Article 41 of the UN Charter, and are free to choose to carry out such implementation through the adoption of a decision to impose restrictive measures within the framework of the CFSP. In the perspective of Article 48(2) of the UN Charter, the European Union is a simple tool at the disposal of its Member States.

The well-known *Kadi* case is a topical example of the mechanism by which the EU has exported its values as part of its practice of restrictive measures implementing international sanctions against Osama Bin Laden and Al Qaeda. Following the rejection by the General Court of his request for annulment of the regulation implementing the UN sanctions against Al Qaeda,[40] Mr Kadi appealed against this decision to the Court of Justice. As we know, the Court concluded that the Community legal system should be autonomous from that of the United Nations and enshrined the principle of full judicial review of the regulations implementing a CFSP decision to impose restrictive measures.[41]

Following this logic, the Council's CFSP decision to implement measures decided by the UNSC in the form of Union restrictive measures plays a fundamental role. It is this decision based on Article 29 of the TEU which allows Member States to incorporate their obligations under the UN Charter into the Union's order. Consequently, the implementation of the UNSC measures is ensured by the execution of an obligation under Union law, based on Article 215 TFEU. The implementation of the measures decided by the UNSC is therefore a matter of incorporating the obligations of Members into Union law.[42]

Still in the *Kadi* case, the Advocate General drew some conclusions from the applicability of Article 351 TFEU to the EU-UN relationship. Article 351 TFEU reads as follows:

> The rights and obligations arising from agreements concluded before 1 January 1958 or, for acceding States, before the date of their accession, between one

[40] Case T-315/01, *Yassin Abdullah Kadi v Council of the European Union and Commission of the European Communities*, ECLI:EU:T:2005:332.

[41] Joined cases C-402/05 P and C-415/05 P, *Kadi and Al Barakaat v. Council and Commission*, ECLI:EU:C:2008:461.

[42] In the same vein, on the "transcription" of UN Security Council resolutions into Community law by means of the adoption of the decision to impose restrictive measures within the framework of the CFSP, see E. Lagrange, *La représentation institutionnelle dans l'ordre international* (Kluwer Law International 1992), 512-514.

> or more Member States on the one hand, and one or more third countries on the other, shall not be affected by the provisions of the Treaties.
>
> To the extent that such agreements are not compatible with the Treaties, the Member State or States concerned shall take all appropriate steps to eliminate the incompatibilities established. Member States shall, where necessary, assist each other to this end and shall, where appropriate, adopt a common attitude.

In his view, it would appear from the principles of good faith and non-contradiction in international law that EU Member States have an obligation under Article 351(2) TFEU to exercise their rights within the UN in such a way as to minimize the occurrence of proven incompatibilities with EU law, and more particularly from the point of view of respect for the rights of defense of individuals targeted by collective measures against terrorism. [43]

The implementation of the obligation of Members of the Union and the United Nations under Article 351(2) of the TFEU is made possible by the inherent asymmetry in the legal relations in question, which is based on the absence of a formal link between the European Union and the United Nations. Indeed, the UN Charter leaves considerable scope for Member States to implement UNSC resolutions, allowing for the addition of stricter legal conditions resulting from Union law. Consequently, the Member States of the two organizations in question play a crucial role in the material coordination of the two orders since they constitute their sole meeting point. However, the Member States are not the only institutions to be responsible for the respect of the obligations arising from the two legal systems. The *Kadi* judgment, to take just this example, is not directed against the Member States of the Union, but against the EU institutions which have designed and adopted the regulation implementing the relevant UNSC resolution. It is therefore they who must modify their normative processes in order to bring them into line with Union law. Member States, for their part, are urged to seek new normative practices within the United Nations in order to prevent the implementation of UNSC resolutions from becoming effectively incompatible with Union law.

ii. *The coordination of the Union and the UN by their common Member States*

The normative coordination of the UN and EU legal orders by their common Member States and the resulting EU influence on the UN has been analyzed elsewhere and cannot be fully explained here. [44]

It will suffice to recall that it took the form of a significant diplomatic effort on the part of Union Member States in the UNSC to set in motion a dynamic of procedural

---

[43] Opinion of AG Poiares Maduro, joined cases C-402/05 P and C-415/05 P, *Kadi and Al Barakaat v. Council and Commission*, ECLI:EU:C:2008:30.

[44] See Ch. Beaucillon, *Les mesures restrictives de l'Union européenne, supra note* 2,, 514-597.

reform. EU Member States represented fourteen and a half per cent of the Members of the United Nations – more precisely, twenty-eight (before Brexit) out of one hundred and ninety-three. However, their potential influence in the World Organization was reinforced by the fact that the United Kingdom and France are permanent members of the UNSC. The EU was thus represented through its Members by two fifths of the UNSC, and therefore had a significant weight in it. In addition to this predominant position, there is the rotation of the non-permanent members of the UNSC. Since the 2000s, eleven Members of the European Union – or related parties – have been elected non-permanent members of the UNSC. Thus, have served alongside France and the United Kingdom: the Netherlands from 1999 to 2000, Ireland and Norway[45] from 2001 to 2002, Germany and Spain from 2003 to 2004, Greece from 2005 to 2006, Belgium and Italy from 2007 to 2008, Croatia from 2008 to 2009,[46] Austria from 2009 to 2010 and finally Germany and Portugal from 2010 to 2012. This significant presence of EU Member States in the UNSC is organized by the first paragraph of Article 34 TFEU, which essentially requires Member States to coordinate within international organizations and to defend the Union's positions if not all Member States participate, which is the case in the UNSC. It is therefore not insignificant, in this context, that the Member States of the Union have begun to meet before the sessions of the UNSC on sanctions against Osama bin Laden and his associates, and before the meetings of the relevant Sanctions Committee. This practice was apparently launched under the French Presidency of the European Union, between July and December 2008, i.e. six months after the opinion of AG Poiares Maduro,[47] and just at the time of the Court's first decision in the *Kadi* case.[48]

This major diplomatic effort led to the introduction in 2009 of an administrative appeal mechanism, the Al Qaeda and other terrorist groups related sanctions regime's Ombudsperson,[49] whose mode of operation was thoroughly revised in 2011 to make it more effective.[50] However, it is not a jurisdictional mechanism. The effort of the MS has indeed been strongly supported by judicial activism on the part of the Court of Justice of the European Union. In 2013, in the so-called *Kadi 2* decision, the Court of Justice confirmed the General Court's principled position on the need to ensure effective judicial review of Union regulations implementing UNSC

---

[45] Norway is not a member of the European Union, but belongs to both the European Free Trade Association (EFTA) and the European Economic Area (EEA).

[46] Croatia was then in the process of joining the European Union.

[47] *Supra* note 43; Delivered on 23 January 2008.

[48] *Supra* note 41; of 3 September 2008.

[49] S/RES/1904(2009), *Threats to international peace and security caused by terrorist acts*, 17 December 2009.

[50] S/RES/1989(2011), *Threats to international peace and security caused by terrorist acts*, 17 June 2011.

decisions.[51] In particular, the Court recognized the need to allow the Union judge to review whether the grounds for inclusion on the Union's list of targets of restrictive measures – that is, the grounds common to the United Nations Committee – are sufficiently substantiated.[52] In other words, the Court makes the implementation of UNSC decisions by EU institutions conditional on the possibility for each person to be included on the European lists of targets of restrictive measures to verify the validity of the grounds for their inclusion by requesting the cooperation of the Al Qaeda Sanctions Committee when the implementing acts are adopted or challenged before the Union judge.

It is at the time of the challenge of the measures before the EU Court of Justice that the requirements for full control of the legality of the acts implementing the decisions of the UNSC reveal the extent of their consequences on relations between the United Nations and the European Union. Indeed, the Court considers that "the secrecy or confidentiality" of the additional information requested to carry out the control cannot be set against it.[53] The Court therefore issues a form of judicial ultimatum by announcing that insufficiently substantiated grounds cannot serve as a basis for EU restrictive measures,[54] which led it to annul in the present case the contested regulation maintaining Mr. Kadi on the list of targets of the measures.[55]

The resolution of this tension created by the lack of equivalence in the protection of fundamental rights between, on the one hand, the control carried out at UN level by the Focal Point[56] and the Ombudsperson[57] and, on the other hand, the effective judicial control required by the Court of Justice, seems to lie in the definition of an unprecedented cooperation between the World Organization and the EU. For

---

[51] Joined cases C-584/10 P, C-593/10 P and C-595/10 P, *European Commission and Others v. Kadi*, ECLI:EU:C:2013:518, para. 133.

[52] *Ibidem*, paras118-119.

[53] *Ibidem*, para. 125.

[54] *Ibidem*, para. 123.

[55] *Ibidem*, paras 151-164. It should be recalled, however, that Mr. Kadi had meanwhile been removed from the 1267 Committee's lists, and that the Court's decision is therefore of no consequence in this case for the implementation of the United Nations decision, since it no longer had any effect on Mr. Kadi at the time of the judgment of the CJEU.

[56] S/RES/1617(2005), *Threats to international peace and security caused by terrorist acts*, 20 October 2005. This mechanism was the first remediation measure adopted at the UN level to tackle the issue raised by the *Kadi* line of jurisprudence about the access by the targeted persons to an appeal mechanism against their listing on the UN anti-terrorism lists. However, unlike the Ombudsperson created in 2009 and specialized in anti-terrorism, the Focal point is more of a mailbox to which targets can address their request for delisting, which are then processed at a diplomatic level. This mechanism has then been extended to all UN sanctions regimes, except the Al Qaeda and other terrorist groups related sanctions regime, which benefits from the Ombudsperson mechanism.

[57] *Supra* notes 49 and 50.

the time being, it has been carried out exclusively on a case-by-case basis and through the diplomatic channels of the Member States of the Union and the UNSC.

10.3.2. EU restrictive measures imposing autonomous sanctions in reaction to a treaty breach: exporting human rights, democracy and the rule of law to third-country partners

The mechanism used by the European Union in its treaty relations with third parties and generally known as the "human rights" clause,[58] is in fact based on the articulation of two elements: an "essential element" clause and a "non-execution" clause. In a crude sense of the mechanism, the purpose of the "essential element" clause is to determine the elements of the agreement whose violation may give rise to a specific reaction from the parties. For example, it will refer to respect for democracy and human rights. The "non-execution" clause is intended to expressly determine the possible reactions under the *exceptio non adimpleti contractus*. Descriptive analyzes of the European Union's treaty practice with regard to human rights clauses thus generally examine the "essential element" clause and the "non-execution" clause one after the other, since the violation of the former leads to the activation of the latter. However, since the central issue here is the articulation of the European Union's exception of non-execution and restrictive measures, I will begin here with the "non-execution" clause.

The first "non-execution" clause was introduced in 1992, as part of the agreements concluded with Albania and the Baltic States. It simply stated that "the parties reserve the right to suspend with immediate effect the application of the agreement in whole or in part in the event of a serious breach of its essential provisions".[59] This "Baltic clause" had the disadvantage of being applicable only to serious breaches of the essential element clause, i.e. to impose more restrictive activation conditions than those provided for in Article 60(3)(b) of the 1969 and 1986 Vienna Conventions on the law of treaties.[60]

---

[58] On this subject, see *inter alia*: E. Fierro, 'Legal Basis and Scope of Human Rights Clauses in EC Bilateral Agreements: Is There a Place for a Positive Interpretation?' (2001) 7 *European Law Journal* 41; E. Paasivirta, 'Human Rights, Diplomacy and Sanctions: Aspects to "Human Rights Clauses" in the External Agreements of the European Union', in J. Petman, J. Klabbers (eds), *Nordic Cosmopolitanism: Essays in International Law for Martti Koskeniemmi* (Martinus Nijhoff 2003), 155-180.

[59] Article 21(3) of the Agreement between the European Economic Community and the Republic of Albania on trade and commercial and economic cooperation, Council Decision of 26 October 1992 on the conclusion of the Agreement between the European Economic Community and the Republic of Albania on trade and commercial and economic cooperation, OJ L 343/1, 25.11.1992.

[60] Vienna Convention on the Law of Treaties between States, signed on 23 May 1969 and entered into force on 27 January 1980, United Nations, *Treaty Series*, vol. 1155, 331; Vienna Convention on the Law of Treaties between States and International Organizations or between Inter-

It was replaced in 1994 by the so-called "Bulgarian clause",[61] which has since become the reference "non-execution" clause in the conventional practice of the EU, and can be found in the agreements the EU concluded with States from the Commonwealth of Independent States (CIS) and from the Euro-Mediterranean Partnership (EMP). Unlike the "Baltic clause", any breach of the agreement can trigger the adoption of appropriate measures. On the other hand, the violation of the essential elements of the agreement entails a case of special urgency within the meaning of the clause and the parties may thus adopt the measures they consider appropriate immediately, without going through the consultation phase that applies to the other violations of the agreement. Where an element within the "essential element" clause of the agreement has been violated, the parties may adopt appropriate measures without delay.

The "Bulgarian clause" has the effect of disconnecting EU treaty practice from the general mechanism provided for in Article 65 of the 1969 and 1986 Vienna Conventions on the Law of Treaties.[62] In this sense, EU agreements using this technique create a special right to organize the exception of non-performance. In particular, the "Bulgarian clause" extends the scope of possible reactions in the event of a breach of the "essential elements" clause: the measures taken include the possibility of suspending the agreement – or, in an extreme case, of denouncing it – but are not limited to it. This is how the potential assimilation of appropriate measures authorized in the event of a breach of an essential element of the agreement and the EU restrictive measures appears. This assimilation results, on the one hand, from the absence of procedural conditions for the adoption of appropriate measures, which can be taken immediately in the form of restrictive measures.[63] It also results from the extension of the material scope of the measures that may be adopted, which go beyond the suspension of the agreement.

---

national Organizations, signed on 21 March 1986 and t yet in force. Only the 1969 Vienna Convention on Treaties between States was in force at the time of the introduction of these treaty clauses. The absence of entry into force of the 1986 Vienna Convention does not affect the validity of the proper practice of the EC and then the EU, insofar as the inclusion of these "essential element" clauses, with reference to the provisions of the 1969 Vienna Convention, has been accepted by the Parties. Moreover, this section of the Vienna Conventions is generally considered as a codification of customary international law, binding on States and IOs.

[61] Article 118(1) and (2) of the European Agreement establishing an association between the European Communities and their Member States, of the one part, and the Republic of Bulgaria, of the other part, OJ L 358/1, 13.12.1994.

[62] *Supra* note 60.

[63] The adoption of restrictive measures in connection with more procedurally elaborate treaty mechanisms is possible, as illustrated by the measures against Zimbabwe in the context of the implementation of the Cotonou Agreement. It is not possible to develop this more technical case further here. Cf. Ch. Beaucillon, *Les mesures restrictives de l'Union européenne, supra note* 2, 219-288.

As for the so-called "essential element" clauses, the first was included in the agreements concluded with the Baltic States and Albania in May 1992.[64] The clause, which provides that "respect for democratic principles and human rights [...] inspires the domestic and international policies [of the Parties] and constitutes an essential element of this Agreement",[65] clearly refers to Article 60(3)(b) of the Vienna Convention on the Law of Treaties.[66] The latter provides that the substantive breach of an agreement – which opens the possibility of suspending its execution or to denounce it[67] – may result from "the violation of a provision essential for the achievement of the object or purpose of the treaty".

The question now is to examine the essential elements of the agreements binding the countries of the CIS and the EMP. The scope *ratione materiae* of the "essential element" clauses varies according to the group of countries to which the EU's treaty partner belongs and their Members.[68] However, respect for human rights is systematically established as an essential element of agreements concluded with third parties. This reference is sometimes supplemented by a reference to the 1948 UDHR, or to a regional instrument applicable to the group of countries concerned. A Commission communication from 1998 shows that the intention of the EC/EU and its Members has long been to strengthen the relevance of existing instruments. [69]

It should be noted that this technique of *renvoi* has a dual effect from the point of view of public international law. First, it confers on standards derived from instruments of a weak operational character – such as the Final Act of the Helsinki Conference – the value of treaty provisions, which are quite binding. Secondly, it affects the status of certain customary international norms, such as those enshrined in the UDHR. While some have considered that this treaty reference has the effect of confirming and strengthening the customary nature of the norms enshrined in the Universal Declaration,[70] it is also possible to question the effect of their inclu-

---

[64] *Supra* note 60.

[65] Article 1 of the Agreement between the European Economic Community and the Republic of Albania on trade and commercial and economic cooperation, *supra* note 59.

[66] *Supra* note 61.

[67] Articles 60(1) of the 1969 and 1986 Vienna Conventions on the law of treaties, *supra* note 60.

[68] For a detailed analysis of these clauses, see E. Cujo, *Les réactions décentralisées de l'Union européenne à l'illicite*, Ph.D. in International Law, defended on 16 December 2002 at the Paris X Nanterre University, unpublished, pp. 136-142; E. Fierro, *The EU's Approach to Human Rights Conditionality in Practice* (Martinus Nijhoff 2003), 110-130.

[69] Communication from the Commission to the Council and the European Parliament – Democratisation, Rule of law, respect for human rights and good governance: the challenges of the partnership between the European Union and the PCAs, COM/98/0146 final, para. 3, 5.

[70] A. Rosas, 'The European Union and International Human Rights Instruments', in V. Kronenberger (ed.), *The EU and the International Legal Order: Discord or Harmony* (T.M.C. Asser Press 2001), 61.

sion in a treaty instrument. In this sense, the reference to these various standards gives the Parties the power to interpret unilaterally what will constitute a violation of these obligations, although, like the EU, they are not necessarily bound by the instruments of reference.

In addition to the principle of respect for human rights, the various references in the "essential element" clauses should be examined according to the group of countries to which the clause is addressed. The most sober "essential element" clause is found in the association agreements concluded within the framework of the Euro-Mediterranean partnership. The first agreements, concluded with Tunisia in 1998 and Israel in 2000, only provided that democratic principles and human rights are essential elements of the agreement.[71] It is from the agreement signed with Morocco in 2000 that these agreements will systematically make an additional reference to the UDHR.[72] From the point of view of references to existing texts in public international law, it is surprising that the "essential element" clauses do not refer to the African Charter on Human Rights, in force since 1986 for some of the States participating in the EMP, and which are Members of the African Union.[73] It is possible to think that because of the participation in the EMP of African and Middle Eastern States, the reference to the UDHR was the only one likely to guarantee a coherent and uniform reference to the concept of human rights, among all partners.

The "essential element" clause binding the countries belonging to the Commonwealth of Independent States generally refers to "respect for democracy, the principles of international law and human rights [...] as well as the principles of the market economy".[74] In this specific context, the concepts of human rights and democracy refer to the Charter of the United Nations, the Helsinki Final Act, and the Charter of Paris for a New Europe. In addition, the reference to the principle of the market economy derives from the communist past of the CIS member countries. In

---

[71] Euro-Mediterranean Agreement establishing an association between the European Community and its Member States, of the one part, and the Republic of Tunisia, of the other part, OJ L 97/2, 30.3.1998; Euro-Mediterranean Agreement establishing an association between the European Communities and their Member States, of the one part, and the State of Israel, of the other part, OJ L 147/1, 21.6.2000, Articles 2 of the Agreements.

[72] Euro-Mediterranean Agreement establishing an association between the European Communities and their Member States, of the one part, and the Kingdom of Morocco, of the other part, OJ L 70/2, 18.3.2000, Article 2. The other States concerned by such a clause are Jordan, Egypt, Algeria and Lebanon.

[73] The African Charter on Human and Peoples' Rights has been binding on Algeria, Egypt and Tunisia since its entry into force in 1986. Morocco has withdrawn from the African Union because of the accession of Western Sahara to membership.

[74] For example, see Decision of the Council and the Commission of 12 May 1999 on the conclusion of the Partnership and Cooperation Agreement between the European Communities and their Member States, of the one part, and the Republic of Kazakhstan, of the other part, OJ L 196/ 1, 28.7.1999, Article 2.

the sense of the "essential element" clause which binds CIS members, the market economy refers to the principles set out at the 1990 Bonn Conference of the Organization for Security and Cooperation in Europe (OSCE).[75]

The European Union practice shows that some States belonging to the CIS or the EMP which have signed partnership agreements with the EU have also been the target of restrictive measures by the European Union. For instance, the first measures adopted against Uzbekistan date back to November 2005.[76] Their purpose is to react to the "Andijan events", i.e. the shooting by the Uzbek authorities of the crowd of demonstrators gathered in the city in May 2005 in opposition to the government. More specifically, the EU recalls that it "strongly condemned the excessive, disproportionate and indiscriminate use of force" by the Uzbek authorities, and that it "deeply regretted that the Uzbek authorities did not respond adequately to the United Nations' request for an independent international investigation".[77] These regrets regarding the refusal to open an international investigation were expressed by the Council of the European Union a first time on 23 May 2005, a second time on 13 June 2005, a third time on 18 July 2005 – the date on which the Council also mentioned that it was considering the adoption of restrictive measures against Uzbekistan – and a fourth and last time on 3 October 2005.[78] The measures adopted in November 2005 therefore follow four successive letters of formal notice from the European Union, and are intended to respond to a human rights violation by the Uzbek government against its population. Like the other CIS States, the "essential element" clause of the partnership agreement between the EC and Uzbekistan provides that:

> Respect for democracy, the principles of international law and human rights enshrined in particular in the Charter of the United Nations, the Helsinki Final Act and the Charter of Paris for a New Europe, as well as the principles of the market economy, as set out in particular in the documents of the CSCE Bonn Conference, inspires the internal and external policies of the Parties and constitutes an essential element of the partnership and this Agreement.[79]

It is thus possible to consider that the EU restrictive measures reflect the violation of an essential element of the agreement. These would therefore be immediate measures, the adoption of which is not conditional on prior consultations.

---

[75] *Ibidem.*

[76] Council Common Position 2005/792/CFSP of 14 November 2005 on restrictive measures against Uzbekistan, OJ L 299/72, 16.11.2005.

[77] *Ibidem*, recital 1 of the preamble.

[78] *Ibidem*, recitals 1-4.

[79] Partnership and Cooperation Agreement establishing a partnership between the Communities European Union and their Member States, of the one part, and the Republic of Uzbekistan, of the other part, OJ L 229/3, 31.8.1999, Article 2.

10.3.3. EU restrictive measures imposing autonomous sanctions in reaction to violations of customary international law: the case of massive human rights violations

EU practice with regard to decentralized restrictive measures reveals the existence of measures adopted in response to the alleged violation of obligations that are not owed to the European Union. The latter must therefore be considered as a non-injured organization within the meaning of the law of the responsibility of international organizations.[80] Indeed, in the cases examined here, the obligation breached is not owed "individually" to the EU.[81] Nor is it due to a group of legal subjects to which the EU belongs, and its violation does not affect the Union in a "special" way compared to the other members of the group.[82]

The various decentralized restrictive measures that the EU adopts as a non-injured organization and which fall solely under the law of international responsibility can usefully be examined in the light of the target's geopolitical situation. It is indeed possible to question the possible variation in the European Union's reasons for reacting, depending on its "proximity" – geographical but above all strategic – to the targets.

Certain regimes of restrictive measures can be approximated in that they target States bordering the territory of EU Member States and which therefore participate in the European Neighborhood Policy (ENP). The Union aims to promote respect for the territorial integrity of its States bordering the Union, or for democracy and democratic principles.

In the case of Transnistria, it is clear that the Council is responding to the serious political crisis in Moldova and the known instability of territorial claims and secession situations.[83] The EU includes Moldova among its direct geographical neighbors and, therefore, among its privileged partners.[84] However, the adoption of

---

[80] Recent doctoral research has been devoted to this question: A. Hofer, *The Beliefs and Practice of Enforcing Collective Obligations through Unilateral Sanctions*, Ph.D. thesis defended on 13 September 2019 at Ghent University, unpublished.

[81] Article 43(a) of the Draft Articles on Responsibility of International Organizations, A/66/10, "Report of the Commission to the General Assembly on the work of its sixty-sixth session" (2011) *YILC*, vol. II, Part Two, 141.

[82] Article 43(b) of the Draft Articles on the Responsibility of International Organizations. The commentary to this provision expressly refers to Article 42(b) of the Draft Articles on State Responsibility, and to the example of the coastal state specifically affected by the breach of a non-pollution obligation.

[83] Council Common Position 2003/139/CFSP of 27 February 2003 concerning restrictive measures against the leadership of the Transnistrian region (Republic of Moldova), OJ, L 053, 28.02.2003, pp. 60-61; Council Common Position 2004/622/CFSP of 26 August 2004 amending Common Position 2004/179/CFSP concerning restrictive measures against the leadership of the Transnistrian region (Republic of Moldova), OJ L 279/47, 28.8.2004.

[84] In 1993, the Republic of Moldova was already a party to the Agreement in the form of an

restrictive measures by the EU does not correspond to a reaction to the violation of an agreement between the Union and Moldova. On the contrary, these measures are intended to support the Moldovan government against the *de facto* Transnistrian regime. The measures cannot therefore be linked to the violation of the agreement with Moldova, but are in fact intended to respond to human rights violations attributed to the *de facto* regime. In this sense, the EU reacts to these violations in the interest of the international or even regional community. Indeed, the Union clearly states that it is acting to contribute to the efforts made within the framework of the OSCE. The restrictive measures that the Union adopts are therefore *a priori* additional measures, a kind of pressure adjuvant to the resolution of the political crisis in another international forum in which the Union is active. This example provides a historical perspective on the restrictive measures adopted by the European Union against Russia following the annexation of Crimea in 2014.[85]

Turning to the promotion of democracy and democratic principles, the cases of restrictive measures adopted against Belarus, then against Tunisia and Egypt will be examined in turn.

It follows from the reasons for the imposition of restrictive measures on Belarus[86] in 2004 that the European Union seeks to preserve compliance with two sets of obligations. On the one hand, these are the principles of human rights, the rule of law and democracy, which are fundamental principles of the European Union

---

Exchange of Letters between the EC and the ECSC, Armenia, Belarus, Georgia, Kazakhstan, Kyrgyzstan, Radjikistan, Turkmenistan and Ukraine, concerning the 1989 Economic Cooperation Agreement between the EC and the ECSC and the USSR: see Proposal for a Council Decision on the conclusion of the Agreements in the form of exchanges of letters with Armenia, Belarus, Georgia, Kazakhstan, Kyrgyzstan, Moldova, Tadzhikistan, Turkmenistan and Ukraine relating to the Agreement on trade and commercial and economic cooperation signed on 18 December 1989 between the European Economic Community, the European Atomic Energy Community and the Union of Soviet Socialist Republics, COM/93/101 final, OJ C 110/8, 20.4.1993, 8. Moldova also concluded a Partnership and Cooperation Agreement with the EC in 1994. On the Eastern European Partnership, see for example Ch. Hillion, *The Evolving System of European Union External Relations Evidenced in the EU Partnerships with Russia and Ukraine*, Ph.D. in EU Law, defended on 22 February 2005 at Leiden University, published online: https://www.peacepalacelibrary.nl/ebooks/files/hillion.pdf (last accessed on 17 July 2019).

[85] For the first EU reactions see: Council Decision 2014/119/CFSP of 5 March 2014 concerning restrictive measures directed against certain persons, entities and bodies in view of the situation in Ukraine, OJ L 66/26, 6.3.2014, and Council Decision 2014/145/CFSP of 5 March 2014 concerning restrictive measures in respect of actions undermining or threatening the territorial integrity, sovereignty and independence of Ukraine, OJ L 78/16, 17.3.2014. See Also on this specific case: Ch. Beaucillon, 'Crise ukrainienne et mesures restrictives de l'Union européenne: quelle contribution aux sanctions internationales à l'égard de la Russie?' (2014) *Journal of International Law (Clunet)* 787 and Ch. Beaucillon, 'Opening up the horizon: The ECJ's new take on country sanctions', *supra note* 14.

[86] Council Common Position 2004/661/CFSP of 24 September 2004 concerning restrictive measures against certain officials of Belarus, OJ L 301/67, 28.9.2004, recital 1 of the preamble.

and which are also upheld within the framework of the Council of Europe. On the other hand, the EU is directing its action towards compliance with international rules on the holding of elections – to which Belarus has in particular committed itself within the framework of the OSCE. Here again, the European Union is seeking to ensure compliance with principles generally enshrined by the international community as a whole, without having a subjective right of which Belarus would be the creditor.

The Tunisian and Egyptian cases are other illustrations of the promotion of democratic principles and human rights by the EU through the adoption of restrictive measures. Unlike Belarus, Tunisia and Egypt, in addition to their participation in the ENP, have concluded cooperation and partnership agreements with the EU.[87] These agreements, like those concluded by other States participating in the EMP, enshrine respect for human rights as an essential element of the partnership. However, the EU restrictive measures are not intended to react to the violation of an essential element of these agreements, but to support the democratic transition induced in these two States, within the framework of the Arab Spring.[88] This examination of the decentralized restrictive measures adopted by the EU as a non-injured organization shows that such measures are likely to be triggered in situations that call into question European regional stability, or the principles of the triptych "human rights, democracy, rule of law", which underpin the European Union's external action.

Other measures affect States that are further away from Europe and call into question the respect of different obligations. The following analysis will focus on three regimes of restrictive measures imposed against States not neighboring the EU. The main aim will be to compare the reasons that trigger the European Union's reaction. This comparison will make it possible, on the one hand, to determine the existence of homogeneity of the grounds for reaction against non-neighboring States and, on the other hand, to compare them with the grounds for reaction against neighboring countries. The first set of measures, affecting Myanmar, is, by its duration and exhaustiveness, one of the topical regimes put in place by the Union. The second strikes Iran and offers the example of a regime of decentralized measures being adopted against a State that is already targeted by centralized

[87] Euro-Mediterranean Agreement establishing an association between the European Community and its Member States, of the one part, and the Republic of Tunisia, of the other part, OJ L 97/2, 30.3.1998; Euro-Mediterranean Agreement establishing an association between the European Communities and their Member States, of the one part, and the Arab Republic of Egypt, of the other part, OJ L 304/39, 30.9.2004.

[88] Cf. in identical terms, the second preambular paragraph of the following decisions: Council Decision 2011/72/CFSP of 31 January 2011 concerning restrictive measures against certain persons and entities with regard to the situation in Tunisia, OJ L 28/62, 2.2.2011; Council Decision 2011/172/CFSP of 21 March 2011 concerning restrictive measures against certain persons, entities and bodies with regard to the situation in Egypt, OJ L 76/ 63, 22.3.2011.

measures decided within the framework of the United Nations. The European Union is adopting different measures here, which are not intended to help resolve the Iranian nuclear crisis, but to respond to serious human rights violations. Finally, the third regime of measures has hit Syria, in response to the military repression suffered by the population since 2011.

An examination of the various restrictive measures adopted by the EU against Myanmar in 1996, 2000, 2003 and 2010 shows that the European Union's grounds for reaction are of a completely different nature than those which trigger the adoption of restrictive measures against States neighboring the Union. Indeed, the violations that the European Union accuses the Myanmar junta of are of particular gravity.[89] Nor is it insignificant that, in the present case, decentralized measures were made necessary because of the impossibility of adopting centralized measures by the UNSC, due to the Chinese veto.

The EU's allegations involve, first, the violation of *jus cogens* standards, such as the prohibition of torture.[90] Second, they include the commission of crimes that are serious enough to constitute elements of war crimes or crimes against humanity within the meaning of the Rome Statute of the International Criminal Court.[91] In addition to torture, these include arbitrary summary executions, forced labor, forced displacement of populations, specific violations against women, and political arrests. Third, the Union alleges the violation of a number of civil and political rights, such as freedom of expression, movement or assembly. These rights are generally recognized in international human rights law, for example in the International Covenant on Civil and Political Rights.[92] In this perspective, the Union seeks to condemn the Myanmar regime's misuse of the democratic model, pushes it to initiate a process of national reconciliation and rewards recent progress in this area by influencing its measures.

Turning to the second example, the EU has imposed two separate sets of restrictive measures on Iran. The first corresponds to measures to implement the decisions of the UNSC, adopted on the basis of Chapter VII of the Charter. It therefore falls

---

[89] See in particular: Council Common Position 96/635/CFSP of 28 October 1996 on Burma/Myanmar, OJ 1996, L287/1 8.11.1996; Council Common Position 2003/297/CFSP of 23 April 2003 on Burma/Myanmar, OJ L 106/36, 29.4.2003.

[90] The prohibition of torture was established as belonging to *jus cogens* by the following decisions: International Criminal Tribunal for the Former Yugoslavia, Case IT-95-17/1-T, *Prosecutor v. Anto Furundzija*, Trial Chamber II, Judgment, 10 December 1998, para. 2, main features of the prohibition of torture under international law; CCPR/C/21/Rev.1/Add.11, General Comment No 29, States of Emergency (Art. 4), 24 July 2001, 1950th session, para. 7, 4 and para. 11, 6; ECtHR, *Al-Adsani v. United Kingdom*, App. No 35763/97, 21 November 2001, paras 60-61.

[91] Articles 5, 7 and 8 of the Statute of the International Criminal Court, adopted in Rome on 17 July 1998, which entered into force on 1 July 2002.

[92] See respectively Articles 19, 12 and 21 of the International Covenant on Civil and Political Rights, A/RES/2200 A (XXI) of 16 December 1966, which entered into force on 23 March 1976.

outside the scope of the decentralized reaction mechanisms studied here.

The second set of restrictive measures imposed on Iran dates from 2011. The purpose of the Council is to respond to certain serious human rights violations in Iran. On the one hand, these violations would be illustrated by an increase in executions – including by public stoning – and by an increase in the repression, persecution and arrest of Iranian citizens exercising their freedom of expression and assembly. On the other hand, they would be characterized by the use of torture or other inhuman or degrading treatment.[93] The reasons for the implementation of this regime of restrictive measures are unambiguous. As in the case of Myanmar, the EU is responding to human rights violations, some of which constitute violations of mandatory rules of international law. This is the case for instances of torture or inhuman treatment.[94] In this respect, it can be deduced from the terms of the European Union's decision that the conditions for carrying out the death penalty – public, in particular by stoning – are treated by the EU as cases of torture or inhuman or degrading treatment.[95] Moreover, as in the case of Myanmar, the Union intends to defend respect for certain civil and political rights, such as freedom of expression and assembly.

Unlike the Iranian case, the restrictive measures adopted against Syria do not "double" a UN centralized regime of measures. On the contrary, like Myanmar, the restrictive measures against Syria were adopted in a context of deep UNSC blockage. The European Union's restrictive measures against Syria were thus initiated in April 2011.[96]

It must be noted that the wording of the EU's reasons for reaction is much more sober and less detailed than in the examples previously examined. However, this sobriety refers to a factual situation widely condemned by the international community. Indeed, UN General Assembly resolution 66/253 adopted in February 2012 condemns the massive and systematic violations of human rights by the Syrian authorities.[97] Similarly, in March 2012, the UN Human Rights Council adopted a

---

[93] Council Decision 2011/235/CFSP of 12 April 2011 concerning restrictive measures against certain persons and entities with regard to the situation in Iran, OJ 2011, L 100/ 51, recital 2 of the preamble.

[94] See *supra* note 90.

[95] Such a position is also confirmed by the European Union's guidelines on human rights and humanitarian law. See *EU Guidelines, Human Rights and International Humanitarian Law, Council of the European Union*, March 2009, available at: https://eeas.europa.eu/sites/eeas/files/guide lines_en.pdf (last accessed July 2019), 13, where the prohibition of torture is interpreted as imposing restrictions on the use of the death penalty.

[96] Council Decision 2011/273/CFSP of 9 May 2001 concerning restrictive measures against Syria, OJ L 121/11, 10.5.2011.

[97] A/RES/66/253, 17 February 2012, *The situation in the Syrian Arab Republic.* Adopted with 137 votes in favor, 12 against and 17 abstentions.

resolution under the unambiguous title: "widespread and systematic violations of human rights and fundamental freedoms by the Syrian authorities".[98] It follows from the above that the EU restrictive measures respond to particularly serious violations of human rights and humanitarian law by the Syrian Government, and that, despite the blocking of the UNSC, these violations are met with widespread condemnation within the international community.

Analysis of the grounds for imposing restrictive measures on States that are not neighbors of the European Union shows that they are measures in response to the commission of particularly serious internationally wrongful acts, involving violations of peremptory norms of public international law or other massive human rights violations. The European Union's reasons for reacting thus differ from those it puts forward when targeting states participating in the neighborhood policy. The closer the relationship with the target, the lower the tolerance threshold for human rights violations seems to be. The further away the target is, the more the measures respond to violations of particular gravity.

10.4. Conclusions

As I recalled in the introduction and in some of the developments of this chapter, the European Union's direct power to impose sanctions is generally analyzed through the case law of its courts. In the perspective of an analysis of power, this casuistic approach emphasizes the way power is exercised at a determined time, rather than analyzing its basis.

The recent case law of the Court of Justice on restrictive measures has already been the object of in depth analysis, which can be quickly recalled.[99] To date, this issue is twofold, and can be dealt with in terms of both 'lisbonization' and refinement of the jurisprudence on restrictive measures. First, the Court's case law has evolved as a result of the entry into force of the Lisbon Treaty and the systematization of the Union's competences. From the point of view of the competence of the Court of Justice of the European Union, the preliminary ruling in the *Roseneft* case[100] undoubtedly opens up new prospects as to the possibility of challenging the validity of decisions to impose restrictive measures adopted by the Union in the context of the CFSP. This contentious route, which had long been considered im-

---

[98] Resolution of 1 March 2012, adopted with 37 votes in favor, 3 against and 4 abstentions (of 47 members).

[99] See Ch. Beaucillon, 'Opening up the horizon: The ECJ's new take on country sanctions', *supra note* 14.

[100] Case C-72/15, *PJSC Rosneft Oil Company v. Her Majesty's Treasury*, ECLI:EU: C:2017:236. See in more detail, S. Poli, 'The Common Foreign Security Policy after Rosneft: Still imperfect but gradually subject to the rule of law', (2017) 54 *Common Market Law Review* 1799.

possible, could, if the conditions were met, complement the existing case law, which until now has been limited to the examination of the corresponding regulations. In this respect, the dispute over the legal basis for the regulations implementing the Union's restrictive measures has also evolved: the Court has in fact endorsed the emergence of a second possible legal basis alongside Article 215 TFEU. Article 291(2) TFEU may thus be used as a legal basis, when only the Council is in possession of the information necessary to update the lists of targets concerned.

Second, it should be stressed that recent case law focuses on unilateral restrictive measures. In this context, the Union judicature has had to develop a complex set of criteria to assess the real link between the State targeted by the restrictive measures and the private persons actually affected by them. Similarly, the Court has opened up, under quite exceptional conditions, new prospects for compensation for the prejudice suffered as a result of the restrictive measures. [101]

While the interest of the above line of analysis is not to be denied, questioning the very basis of the EU's direct sanctioning power in the field of restrictive measures is a less common exercise, and makes it possible to go beyond the more familiar framework of prudential analysis.

Going off the beaten tracks allowed explaining in detail how the EU sanctions the respect of its values and interests by States and persons outside its territory, by imposing restrictive measures on them. I have shown by which legal instruments and mechanisms the EU exports values that seem universal, but only after reinterpreting them according to its own legal order. Moreover, I have shown by the extent of the examples used that this complex and protean practice has been built over the long term, and its analysis provides legal support for the political argument that the EU is a normative power.

The last question is to know for which purpose the EU wishes to use this normative power. Let us take again our introductory distinction between the unilateralist export method and the concerted export method. On the one hand, the massive use of restrictive measures corresponding to *decentralized* reactions to wrongfulness contributes to a more general phenomenon of unilateral, sometimes even extraterritorial, international sanctions such as those imposed by the United States. The intensification of this practice could have the effect of leading other States with flourishing economies to use the same instruments of non-military coercion, and could eventually lead to clashes between powers that intend to impose their own interpretation of (international) law on other members of the world community.[102] The gen-

---

[101] This paragraph is a very schematic summary of the systematic analysis of over 100 decisions by the EU judicature between 2014 and 2018. See Ch. Beaucillon, 'Opening up the horizon: The ECJ's new take on country sanctions', supra note 14.

[102] This could for instance be the case of China: See C. Cai, *China's position and practice with regard to unilateral/extraterritorial sanctions*, paper presented at the *Unilateral/Extraterritorial Sanctions* conference, Paris, Panthéon-Sorbonne University, 12-13 December 2019.

eralization of unilateral international sanctions has also been reported as having a negative impact on the enjoyment of human rights, the respect of which is, as exposed above, paradoxically one of the objectives of the EU when adopting such measures.[103] On the other hand, the political conditionality of partnership agreements, illustrated by the human rights clauses I have analyzed above, has led some of the Union's partners, and in particular countries of the Asia-Caribbean-Pacific group, to prefer partnerships with China, which are less intrusive on the issue of human rights. This could for instance explain some of the difficulties encountered in renegotiating the Cotonou Agreement, which must be completed before the end of 2020.[104]

These latter considerations are not intended to challenge the seemingly noble goals pursued by the European Union when it imposes restrictive measures. The question that finally arises is whether these instruments, especially when used unilaterally, will also produce, in a broader political and legal perspective, effects other than those intended; and where the Union should strike a balance between the various objectives of its external action.

[103] Suffice it to mention here the work of the UN Special Rapporteur on the negative impact of coercive measures on the enjoyment of human rights, appointed following the Human Rights Council resolution of 3 October 2014 (A/HRC/RES/27/21).

[104] The renegotiations of the Cotonou Agreement should have been concluded before February 2020, the date on which the Agreement should have terminated. This deadline has been extended in view of the difficulties for stakeholders to reach an agreement in a context where the tariff preferences previously granted to the ACP are being removed.

Chapter 11

ENTERING THE BUFFER ZONE BETWEEN LEGALITY AND ILLEGALITY: EU AUTONOMOUS SANCTIONS UNDER INTERNATIONAL LAW

Andrea Spagnolo *

ABSTRACT: *The present Chapter offers an international law perspective on the sanctioning power of the EU, analysing the autonomous sanctions' regime. In particular, the Chapter tries to answer to the main research question that arises from an overview of EU autonomous sanctions: their legality under international law. Building on the current status of international law concerning the law of sanctions, the Chapter develops the argument that to defend the legality of autonomous sanctions one could rely on the theory of third-party countermeasures, which, however, is not firmly established in international law.*

KEYWORDS: *EU autonomous sanctions – countermeasures – non-intervention – economic measures – non-injured parties – third-party countermeasures – WTO*

11.1. Introduction: research question and structure of the chapter

In a recent article, the consistency with international law of sanctions adopted by States or regional organisations, such as the EU, irrespective of any United Nations (UN) Security Council Resolution, was defined as an "unfinished business". [1]

Diverging views on the legality of these tools are still the subject of heated debate between the most powerful States that adopt sanctions to induce compliance with international rules, and the targeted countries, which believe that such measures have only political purposes. [2] It is not surprising that Iran and Venezuela recently challenged

---

* Assistant Professor of International Law, Department of Law, University of Turin.

[1] D. Hovell, 'Unfinished Business of International Law: The Questionable Legality of Autonomous Sanctions' (2019) 113 *American Journal of International Law Unbound* 140, 140.

[2] See J. Farrall, 'Sanctions', in Jacob Katz Cogan, Ian Hurd, Ian Johnstone (eds.), *The Oxford Handbook of International Organizations* (OUP 2016) 617.

the United States' unilateral and autonomous sanctions respectively before the International Court of Justice (ICJ)[3] and the World Trade Organisation (WTO).[4]

There are no pending cases on the legality of EU sanctions[5] and EU Courts have only had the opportunity to clarify the perimeter of action of the EU from the perspective of human rights protection;[6] however, many doubts remain on the legality of EU autonomous sanctions from the point of view of international law. Indeed, as such measures inevitably affect the relationship between the EU and non-member countries, this begs the question as to which legal regime is applicable and, accordingly, which limits it imposes. In particular, one may wonder whether and to what extent international law is applicable to this relationship. A country affected by EU sanctions, in fact, might reasonably raise a similar question to challenge their legitimacy or to react to what it deems to be a wrongful act.

In this perspective, this Chapter aims to offer a purely international law perspective on EU autonomous sanctions, with a view to clarifying and analysing the conditions under which such measures may be considered legal or illegal.

For this purpose, the Chapter is structured as follows. Firstly, it will be explained why EU autonomous sanctions represent a buffer zone between legality and illegality in international law. In particular, it will be demonstrated that the "law of sanctions" in international law presents some grey areas in which we find sanctions adopted by the EU autonomously. Secondly, the practice of EU autonomous sanctions will be illustrated. It will then be shown that EU sanctioning regimes might either be lawful measures under international law or unlawful measures under certain special regimes (in particular, the principle of non-intervention and the WTO regime). Lastly, the argument that the EU might adopt third party countermeasures under general international law will be explored.

11.2. Identifying the buffer zone in the law of sanctions in international law

The term sanctions – and, more generally, the very existence of a sanctioning system in international law – has been fuelling a debate challenging the very nature of international law as a legal system.[7] In fact, although this theoretical debate will not

---

[3] *Certain Iranian Assets (Islamic Republic of Iran v. United States of America)*, Application Instituting Proceedings, filed in the Court Registry on 14 June 2016.

[4] *United States – Measures Relating to the Trade in Goods and Services*, WT/DS574/2 of 15 March 2019.

[5] In the past, Argentina challenged the sanctions imposed by European Community Member States before the GATT. See *infra*, para. 5.

[6] See the Chapter authored by N. Lazzerini, in this book.

[7] The debate has been polarised into two well-known positions. Austin, on the one hand, saw sanctions as a tool in the hand of the sovereign to enforce the law. Therefore, considering the ab-

be discussed here, it is worth highlighting that the term "sanctions" in international law is not clearly and unequivocally defined.[8]

Article 41 of the UN Charter, which represents the legal basis of what we commonly refer to as UN sanctions, does not use that term and generally makes reference to "measures not involving the use of armed force", such as the "complete or partial interruption of economic relations and of rail, sea, air, postal, telegraphic, radio, and other means of communication, and the severance of diplomatic relations".[9]

Interestingly, the term sanctions is also largely absent from the International Law Commission (ILC)'s codification of the rules on international responsibility.[10] The ILC's approach, in fact, is based upon the idea that apart from UN sanctions, other States' reactions to internationally wrongful acts should be regarded as countermeasures. The language of the Draft Articles on Responsibility of States for Internationally Wrongful Acts (DARSIWA) is clear:

> In the literature concerning countermeasures, reference is sometimes made to the application of a "sanction", or to a "reaction" to a prior internationally wrongful act; historically the more usual terminology was that of "legitimate reprisals" or, more generally, measures of "self-protection" or "self-help". The term "sanctions" has been used for measures taken in accordance with the constituent instrument of some international organisations, in particular under Chapter VII of the Charter of the United Nations – despite the fact that the Charter uses the term "measures", not "sanctions". The term "reprisals" is now no longer widely used in the present context, because of its association with the

---

sence of a superior entity in international law, he challenged its characterisation as a legal system: J. Austin, *Lecture on Jurisprudence. Or, the Philosophy of Positive Law* (John Murray 1880) X, 6 and 85. On the other hand, Hart argued that the coercive power of international law does not really depend on its (in)capacity to sanction any violations: H.L. Hart, *The Concept of Law* (OUP 2012), 48. See, recently, N.D. White, 'Autonomous and Collective Sanctions in the International Legal Order' (2018) 27 *Italian Yearbook of International Law* 3.

[8] See, accordingly, T. Ruys, 'Sanctions, retorsions and countermeasures: concepts and international legal framework', in L. van den Herik (ed.), *Research Handbook on UN Sanctions and International Law* (Edward Elgar Publishing 2017) 24. See, also, A. Tzanakopoulos, 'Sanctions Imposed Unilaterally by the European Union: Implications for the European Union's International Responsibility', in A.Z. Marossi, M.R. Bassett (eds), *Economic Sanctions under International Law. Unilateralism, Multilateralism, Legitimacy, and Consequences* (TMC Asser Press and Springer 2015) 146-147. According to White and Abass, this is one of the 'least developed area of international law': N.D. White, A. Abass, 'Sanctions and Countermeasures', in M. Evans (ed.), *International Law*, (OUP 2014) 537.

[9] UN Charter, Article 41.

[10] International Law Commission (ILC), *Draft articles on responsibility of States for internationally wrongful acts, with commentaries* (ILC Yearbook 2001) Vol. II Part Two (hereafter DARSIWA); *Draft articles on responsibility of international organizations* (ILC Yearbook 2011) Vol. II Part Two (hereafter DARIO).

> law of belligerent reprisals involving the use of force. At least since the Air Service Agreement arbitration, the term "countermeasures" has been preferred, and it has been adopted for the purposes of the present articles. [11]

The Draft Articles on Responsibility of International Organisations (DARIO) employ even clearer – and narrower – terminology on this issue, assuming that the term sanctions can only be associated with measures:

> which an organisation may be entitled to adopt against its members according to its rules, [which] are per se lawful measures and cannot be assimilated to countermeasures. [12]

According to the ILC, therefore, when we use the term sanctions in relation to the activity of an international organisation, we must only refer to the internal sanctioning mechanism existing in the relationship between the organisation and its members. [13]

It follows from the above that the term sanctions in international law is more of a scholarly creation than an autonomous legal concept. [14] It is a term that is normally associated with any reaction to a violation of international law. [15] Accordingly, the term sanctions is commonly associated with measures of constraint taken either by States or by international organisations in order to restore international legality, interrupted by the illicit conduct of an international legal entity. [16]

In this context, it is not surprising that some scholars suggest labelling as sanctions all phenomena that fit into the above description. As a consequence, measures imposed by the UN Security Council under Chapter VII of the UN Charter, countermeasures and restrictive measures adopted by other international organisations – including the EU – would be equivalent and might be labelled as sanctions. [17]

---

[11] See DARSIWA, Commentary to Article 21, para. 3.

[12] See DARIO, Commentary to Article 22, para. 3.

[13] See F. Dopagne, 'Sanctions and countermeasures by international organizations. Diverging lessons from the idea of autonomy', in R. Collins, N.D. White (eds), *International Organizations and the Idea of Autonomy. Institutional Independence in the International Legal Order* (Routledge 2011), 267 ff. For a critique on this narrow definition: Y. Kerbrat, 'Sanctions et Contre-Mesures: Risques de Confusion dans les Articles de la CDI sur la Responsabilite des Organisations Internationales', (2013) 46 *Revue belge de droit international* 103.

[14] See A. Tzanakopoulos (n 8) 146 who affirms that 'sanctions' 'is not a term of art in international law.'

[15] A. Pellet, A. Miron, 'Sanctions', *Max Planck Encyclopedia of Public International Law* (OUP, 2013) para. 4.

[16] P.-M. Dupuy, 'Observations sur la pratique récente des "sanctions" de l'illicite' (1983) 87 *Revue générale de droit international public* 505.

[17] See, again, Tzanakopoulos, *supra* note 8, 147. See, also and consistently, J. Salmon, *Dictionnaire de droit international public* (Bruylant 2001) 1017.

In contrast, some other scholars suggest that there are at least two arguments against this position, as a sharp distinction exists between UN sanctions and countermeasures. With regard to the first argument, it is said that UN sanctions and countermeasures fall under different categories as the former reflect the existence of a centralised organ in the international community competent for adopting sanctions, [18] while the latter reflect the classical form of private justice in international law. [19] According to the second argument, UN sanctions aim to restore international peace and security when the trigger mechanism set forth in Article 39 of the UN Charter is activated, while countermeasures are adopted by States unilaterally to react to the violation of international obligations owed to them or to the whole international community. [20]

The second argument fails to encompass the whole practice of the UN Security Council which, rather, seems to suggest that UN sanctions have a broader scope, namely, to ensure respect of certain international rules, particularly so-called core norms. [21] Moreover, sanctions can also represent "a tool of law enforcement aimed at ensuring the cessation of wrongful conduct and/or reparation for any injury caused". [22]

The first argument, conversely, reveals the truth when it bases the permissibility of sanctions on the mandate received by the UN from the whole international community under the UN Charter. This does not mean that the possibility for States or regional organisations to adopt unilateral measures is prohibited or excluded, as there is nothing in the UN Charter that infers this. [23] It is the UN Charter itself that envisages the possibility of making recourse to regional arrangements for enforcement purposes. According to Article 53, in fact, the Security Council can use regional organisations for enforcement action under its authority: this means that prior authorisation from the Security Council is required. [24]

In this context, the sanctioning power of the EU, envisaged by Article 215 TFEU, seems to touch a nerve. To date, more than thirty unilateral sanctions

---

[18] Pellet and Miron, *supra* note 15, para. 6.

[19] D. Alland, *Justice privée et ordre juridique international: étude théorique des contre – mesures en droit international public* (Pedone 1994) 24-26.

[20] See, again, Pellet and Miron, *supra* note 15, para. 7 and White, *supra* note 7 and 21.

[21] V. Gowlland-Debbas, 'UN Sanctions and International Law: An Overview', in V. Gowlland-Debbas (ed.), *United Nations Sanctions and International Law* (Brill 2001) 1.

[22] M. Dawidowicz, *Third-Party Countermeasures in International Law* (CUP 2017) 24.

[23] See Ruys, *supra* note 8, 41. See, also, J. Bröhmer, G. Ress, C. Walter, 'Article 53', in B. Simma *et al.* (eds), *The Charter of the United Nations* (OUP Oxford 2012) 1478.

[24] See A. Orakelashvili, 'Sanctions and Fundamental Rights of States: The Case of EU Sanctions against Iran and Syria', in M. Happold, P. Eden (eds), *Economic Sanctions and International Law* (Hart Publishing 2016) 32-33.

adopted by the EU against third countries are in force, demonstrating the vitality of the instrument and the frequency of its use. Within them, a large amount of the sanctioning regime is "autonomous", namely adopted outside – or in addition to – the framework of a UN Security Council resolution. In other words, the EU adopts sanctions without any authorisation from the UN.

11.3. An introduction to EU restrictive measures (sanctions)

The EU sanctioning regime presents interesting features which are worthy of a brief analysis. First of all, it must be clarified that the TFEU regards what scholars usually label sanctions as "restrictive measures".[25] Although the terminology may give rise to some confusion, it is clear from the Basic Principles on the use of Restrictive Measures that in EU jargon the term "restrictive measures" is clearly used to describe a sanctioning power.[26]

The institutional framework of EU sanctions appears to be twofold. Firstly, the EU has a role in implementing sanctions adopted by the UN Security Council under Chapter VII of the UN Charter. In this regard, the legal basis of the measures adopted by the EU is to be found in the combination of the provisions contained in Articles 25 and 103 of the UN Charter, which binds UN Members to obey the UN Security Council resolutions and, more generally, the duties deriving from the Charter. Secondly, the EU adopts autonomous sanctions irrespective of any prior resolution of the UN Security Council.

It should be noted that such a binary categorisation does not actually fit the reality of EU practice. In fact, the EU has proven to be capable of adopting autonomous additional sanctions also in the context of measures implementing UN Security Council resolutions. This is the case, for example, of the sanctions imposed on Iran[27] and North Korea[28] to prevent the proliferation of nuclear weapons and weapons of mass destruction.

The Basic Principles are informative on the relationship between EU sanctions and the UN Security Council, which represents one of the problems raised in the introduction. The very first paragraph of the document, indeed, clarifies that the EU is:

---

[25] Art. 215 TFEU. For a discussion, see the Chapter authored by Ch. Beaucillon in this book. See also L. Borlini, S. Siligardi, 'Defining elements and emerging legal issues of "EU sanctions"' (2018) 27 *Italian Yearbook of International Law* 33.

[26] Council of the European Union, Basic Principles on the Use of Restrictive Measures (Sanctions), PESC 450, 10198/1/04 REV 1 of 7 June 2004.

[27] Council Decision of 26 July 2010 concerning restrictive measures against Iran and repealing Common Position 2007/140/CFSP.

[28] Council Decision (CFSP) 2016/849 of 27 May 2016 concerning restrictive measures against the Democratic People's Republic of Korea and repealing Decision 2013/183/CFSP.

> [..] committed to the effective use of sanctions as an important way to maintain and restore international peace and security in accordance with the principles of the UN Charter and of our common foreign and security policy. In this context, the Council will work continuously to support the UN and fulfil our [its] obligations under the UN Charter.[29].

The same document also provides guidance on the way in which the EU defines and limits its sanctioning powers. In particular, it indicates the compatibility of autonomous sanctions with international law. In fact, according to the Basic Principles:

> If necessary, the Council will impose autonomous EU sanctions in support of efforts to fight terrorism and the proliferation of weapons of mass destruction and as a restrictive measure to uphold respect for human rights, democracy, the rule of law and good governance. We will do this in accordance with our common foreign and security policy, as set out in Article 11 TEU, and in full conformity with our obligations under international law.[30]

In reviewing EU autonomous restrictive measures in light of their purpose, it can be seen that the vast majority of regimes aim to uphold the protection of human rights. It is interesting to look closely at some of those sanctioning regimes.

As regards Belarus, the EU Council first adopted restrictive measures against certain officials on 24 September 2004.[31] In particular, the measures were imposed against persons considered to be involved in the unresolved disappearances of four well-known persons in Belarus in 1999-2000, according to the Report of a Commission appointed by the Parliamentary Assembly of the Council of Europe.[32] The measures, therefore, were adopted to encourage Belarus to respect the rights of persons to be protected from enforced disappearances and the related procedural rights.[33] The restrictive measures, which have been partially lifted, entailed an arms

---

[29] *Ibidem*, para. 1.

[30] *Ibidem*, para. 3.

[31] Council Common Position 2004/661/CFSP of 24 September 2004 concerning restrictive measures against certain officials of Belarus.

[32] Council of Europe, *Parliamentary Assembly, Disappeared Persons in Belarus, Report by the Committee on Legal Affairs and Human Rights, Rapporteur: Mr Christos Pourgourides, Cyprus, Group of the European People's Party*, 4 February 2004, Doc. 10062, available at: https://www.refworld.org/docid/4162a4654.html.

[33] Council Common Position 2004/661/CFSP, Preamble, para. 7: 'the Council, in view of the apparent obstruction of justice, has decided to implement targeted sanctions in the form of restrictions on admission aimed at those individuals who are responsible for, but failed to start, the initiation of independent investigation and prosecution of the alleged crimes and at those who are considered by the Pourgourides Report to be key actors in the disappearances and the subsequent cover-up.'

embargo, the freezing of individual assets, an entry ban with regard to certain individuals, along with the restriction on the export of equipment used for internal repression.[34]

Human rights protection is also at the core of the restrictive measures imposed against Iran due to its systematic repression of Iranian citizens who exercised their freedom of expression and right to peaceful assembly during the 2011 protests. To this end, travel restrictions and asset freezes were initially introduced with respect to "persons complicit in or responsible for directing or implementing grave human rights violations in the repression of peaceful demonstrators, journalists, human rights defenders, students or other persons who speak up in defence of their legitimate rights".[35] The measures were also imposed against those who are "complicit in or responsible for directing or implementing grave violations of the right to due process, torture, cruel, inhumane and degrading treatment, or the indiscriminate, excessive and increasing application of the death penalty, including public executions, stoning, hangings or executions of juvenile offenders in contravention of Iran's international human rights obligations".[36]

A reaction against the repression of political opponents and of independent press justified the adoption of restrictive measures against Zimbabwe, which were first introduced on 18 February 2002[37] and renewed for the first time in 2004.[38] The Council expressed serious concerns about the legislation in Zimbabwe which seriously infringed the right to freedom of speech, assembly and association, and the legislation regulating the media. The Government of Zimbabwe continued to engage in serious violations of human rights and of freedom of opinion, association and peaceful assembly. Thus, the EU Council imposed an embargo on arms and equipment which might be used for internal repression, travel restrictions and asset freezes.

The restrictive measures adopted against Zimbabwe were also designed to promote respect for democracy and the rule of law. Indeed, the sanctioning regime originally put in place in 2002 and 2004 was extended in 2010 due to "the lack of progress in the implementation of the Global Political Agreement signed in September 2008".[39] Accordingly, some of those measures were lifted when the EU

---

[34] See Council Decision 2012/642/CFSP of 15 October 2012 concerning restrictive measures against Belarus.

[35] Council Decision 2011/235/CFSP of 12 April 2011 concerning restrictive measures directed against certain persons and entities in view of the situation in Iran, Preamble, para. 4.

[36] *Ibidem.*

[37] Council Common Position of 18 February 2002 concerning restrictive measures against Zimbabwe.

[38] Council Common Position 2004/161/CFSP of 19 February 2004 renewing restrictive measures against Zimbabwe.

[39] Council Decision 2010/92/CFSP of 15 February 2010 extending restrictive measures against Zimbabwe, Preamble, para. 3.

Council concluded that a peaceful and credible constitutional referendum in Zimbabwe would represent an important milestone in the preparation of democratic elections.[40]

The case of the second set of restrictive measures adopted against Zimbabwe shows that human rights protection and the promotion of democracy and the rule of law are closely interrelated objectives.

The restrictive measures adopted against Myanmar/Burma represent another example. They were initially adopted in 1996 "in view of the absence of progress towards democratisation and of the violation of human rights"[41] and aimed at "promoting progress towards democratisation and securing the immediate and unconditional release of detained political prisoners".[42] Such measures included an arms embargo, travel restrictions and the suspension of high-level bilateral governmental visits to Myanmar/Burma. Interestingly, in response to the positive developments, the EU has lifted all restrictive measures against Myanmar/Burma except for the arms embargo and the embargo on equipment which might be used for internal repression.[43] However, in reaction to the systematic human rights abuses perpetrated by Myanmar/Burma military and security forces, particularly in the Kachin, Rakhine and Shan States, the Council adopted, in 2018, additional measures that included extending the embargo on arms and equipment which might be used for internal repression, as well as targeted restrictive measures against senior military officers of the Myanmar armed forces.[44]

Interestingly, the EU has also adopted restrictive measures on individuals who have undermined democracy by misappropriating State funds. This is the case of the sanctioning regimes imposed against persons in Egypt,[45] Tunisia[46] and Ukraine.[47] These restrictive measures aim to support the peaceful and orderly transition to a civilian and democratic government in the countries involved, by freezing

---

[40] See Annex II of Council Decision 2011/101/CFSP of 15 February 2011 concerning restrictive measures against Zimbabwe.

[41] 96/635/CFSP: Common Position of 28 October 1996 defined by the Council on the basis of Article J.2 of the Treaty on the European Union, on Burma/Myanmar.

[42] *Ibidem.*

[43] Council Decision 2012/225/CFSP of 26 April 2012 amending Decision 2010/232/CFSP renewing restrictive measures against Burma/Myanmar.

[44] Council Decision (CFSP) 2018/655 of 26 April 2018 amending Decision 2013/184/CFSP concerning restrictive measures against Myanmar/Burma.

[45] Council Decision 2011/172/CFSP of 21 March 2011 concerning restrictive measures directed against certain persons, entities and bodies in view of the situation in Egypt.

[46] Council Decision 2011/72/CFSP of 31 January 2011 concerning restrictive measures directed against certain persons and entities in view of the situation in Tunisia.

[47] Council Decision 2014/119/CFSP of 5 March 2014 concerning restrictive measures directed against certain persons, entities and bodies in view of the situation in Ukraine.

the assets of the individuals responsible for the misappropriation of State funds.

In some cases, restrictive measures have been adopted for the sole purpose of contributing to the peaceful settlement of internal crises or conflicts.

An interesting case regards the conflict in the Transnistrian region, in Moldova. While restrictive measures were initially imposed to target "those members of the Transnistrian leadership considered to be responsible for the lack of cooperation to promote a political settlement of the conflict",[48] they were extended to a second group of persons, namely those who were responsible for the design and implementation of the intimidation and closure campaign against Latin-script Moldovan schools in the Transnistrian region.[49] Such a reason is interesting as it proves the extreme variety of situations that might be considered by the EU in order to promote a political settlement of an internal dispute.

The peaceful settlement of an internal crisis or conflict is an objective that is sometimes difficult to differentiate from human rights protection and the promotion of democracy. This is evidenced by the restrictive measures adopted by the EU against those individuals undermining democracy or obstructing the search for a political solution in Burundi.[50]

The final category of sanctioning regimes worthy of attention concerns violations of international law. We will briefly discuss these restrictive measures as the Basic Principles do not mention violations of international law as possible grounds for imposing sanctions.

However, violations of international law have always been considered as justification for imposing certain economic restrictive measures. One example is represented by the restriction on imports of goods from Argentina decided by the then European Economic Community (EEC) as a response to the invasion of the Falkland Islands.[51]

With regard to current practice, two cases are worth mentioning: the measures imposed on Russia for the violation of Crimea's territorial integrity and those imposed on Turkey.

As is known, the measures adopted against Russia are the result of the outbreak of violence in Crimea, which led, in 2014, to the illegal secession of that region from

[48] Council Common Position 2003/139/CFSP of 27 February 2003 concerning restrictive measures against the leadership of the Transnistrian region of the Moldovan Republic, Preamble, para. 3.

[49] Council Common Position 2004/622/CFSP of 26 August 2004 amending Common Position 2004/179/CFSP concerning restrictive measures against the leadership of the Transnistrian region of the Moldovan Republic.

[50] Council Decision (CFSP) 2015/1763 of 1 October 2015 concerning restrictive measures in view of the situation in Burundi.

[51] Council Regulation (EEC) no. 877/82 of 16 April 1982 suspending imports of all products originating in Argentina.

Ukraine. According to a joint statement of the Heads of State or Government of the EU Members States, this was the result of "the unprovoked violation of Ukrainian sovereignty and territorial integrity by the Russian Federation"[52] due to the massive influence that the latter State had on the armed groups which engaged the Ukrainian Government. Accordingly, the EU firstly imposed travel restrictions on individuals responsible for violating Ukraine's territorial integrity[53] then imposed an arms embargo and other restrictive measures on financial transactions with Russia[54], to force that State to terminate its destabilising influence in Ukraine. The restrictive measures were broadened in scope after the conclusion of the Minsk Agreement, with a view to fostering its implementation.

The restrictive measures imposed on Turkey are also of great interest. They were adopted to react to "Turkey's continued illegal actions in the Eastern Mediterranean and the Aegean Sea", undermining Greek and Cypriot sovereignty rights on natural resources.[55] In particular, the EU challenged the drilling activities performed by Turkey in the Eastern Mediterranean, within the territorial waters of Cyprus. More specifically:

> drilling activities infringe the sovereignty or sovereign rights and jurisdiction of the Republic of Cyprus in its territorial sea, exclusive economic zone and continental shelf and, when such activities are carried out in areas where the exclusive economic zone and continental shelf have not been delimited under international law with a State having an opposite coast, they jeopardise or hamper the reaching of a delimitation agreement. These actions are contrary to the principles of the United Nations Charter, including the peaceful resolution of disputes, and pose a threat to the interests and security of the Union.[56]

This passage is interesting because, on the one hand, it reiterates that the restrictive measures – which consist of asset freezes and restrictions on admissions – are due to the violation of the duty to cooperate in the definition of competence in the EEZ (exclusive economic zone). On the other hand, it is worth noting that the EU justified the measures on the grounds that Turkey's drilling activities are contrary to the UN Charter

---

[52] European Council, Statement of the Heads of State or Government on Ukraine of 6 March 2014, para. 2.

[53] Council Decision 2014/145/CFSP of 17 March 2014 concerning restrictive measures in respect of actions undermining or threatening the territorial integrity, sovereignty and independence of Ukraine.

[54] Council Decision 2014/512/CFSP of 31 July 2014 concerning restrictive measures in view of Russia's actions destabilising the situation in Ukraine.

[55] See European Council Conclusions EUCO 1/18 of 23 March 2018, para. 12.

[56] Council Decision (CFSP) 2019/1894 of 11 November 2019 concerning restrictive measures in view of Turkey's unauthorised drilling activities in the Eastern Mediterranean, Preamble, para. 9.

and pose a threat to the EU itself. The two justifications are parallel but appear to share the common aim of preventing a threat to international peace and security.

11.4. Exploring the buffer zone

The regimes of EU sanctions described above might well be lawful measures under international law, namely: retorsions. According to the ILC's DARSIWA, an act of retorsion is "'unfriendly' conduct which is not inconsistent with any international obligation of the State engaging in it even though it may be a response to an internationally wrongful act".[57] The ILC also provided a tentative list of acts that might fall into this category: "the prohibition of or limitations upon normal diplomatic relations or other contacts, embargoes of various kinds or withdrawal of voluntary aid programmes".[58]

Acts of retorsion share the same rationale as countermeasures: they are both measures of self-help. Like the latter, the former can also be aimed at directing the targeted States to act consistently with their international obligations.[59] However, they can be distinguished on the ground that the former do not constitute a violation of international law. Recourse to retorsions as measures of self-help is largely disappearing from State practice, due to the increasing "legalisation" of international relations and the role of sector-based and/or regional dispute settlement mechanisms.[60]

However, they are not completely vanishing, and the restrictive measures adopted by the EU might constitute evidence of their vitality. In fact, measures such as the restriction on admission to the territory of the EU, limitation of diplomatic relations or embargoes, as evidenced by the ILC quotation above, might, at a first glance, be consistent with the definition of retorsion. Accordingly, EU restrictive measures would be lawful and require no justification.[61] Nonetheless, even if it is now clear that there is no duty in international law to entertain diplomatic relations with other States[62] and that a State is free to determine the limits upon entering its

---

[57] DARSIWA, Commentary to the Introduction to Chapter II 'Countermeasures', p. 128, para. 3.

[58] *Ibidem.*

[59] See, accordingly, T. Giegerich, 'Retorsions', in *Max Planck Encyclopedia of Public International Law* (OUP 2011), para. 8. See, also, Ruys, *supra* note 8, 41. See also and generally N. Ronzitti, 'Sanctions as Instruments of Coercive Diplomacy: An International Law Perspective', in N. Ronzitti (ed), *Coercive Diplomacy, Sanctions and International Law* (Brill 2016) 1.

[60] See, accordingly, Giegerich, *supra* note 59, para. 11.

[61] A. Tzanakopoulos, 'The Right to be Free from Economic Coercion' (2015) 4 *Cambridge Journal of International and Comparative Law* 616, 626.

[62] According to Article 2 of the Vienna Convention on Diplomatic Relations the establishment, maintenance and termination of diplomatic relations takes place on a mutual consensual basis between independent sovereign States. See *ex multis* E. Denza, *Diplomatic Law. Commentary on the Vienna Convention on Diplomatic Relations* (OUP 4th ed 2012) 22.

territory,[63] the line between legality and illegality is blurred when it comes to economic measures. In fact, the imposition of economic measures may be at odds with the principle of non-intervention in the internal or external affairs of sovereign States,[64] which has undoubtedly acquired a customary status in international law in line with the 1970 Declaration on Principles of International Law concerning Friendly Relations and Co-operation among States in accordance with the Charter of the United Nations:

> No State may use or encourage the use of economic, political or any other type of measures to coerce another State in order to obtain from it the subordination of the exercise of its sovereign rights and to secure from it advantages of any kind, Also, no State shall organise, assist, foment, finance, incite or tolerate subversive, terrorist or armed activities directed towards the violent overthrow of the regime of another State, or interfere in civil strife in another State.[65]

The connection between the imposition of economic measures and the principle of non-intervention is still a matter of concern for the UN General Assembly, which, since its 38th session, every two years adopts a resolution on *Unilateral economic measures as a means of political and economic coercion against developing countries*.[66] In the last-in-time resolution of this kind, the plenary organ of the UN urged:

> the international community to adopt urgent and effective measures to eliminate the use of unilateral economic, financial or trade measures that are not authorised by relevant organs of the United Nations, that are inconsistent with the principles of international law or the Charter of the United Nations or that contravene the basic principles of the multilateral trading system and that affect, in particular, but not exclusively, developing countries.[67]

It is worth noting that the resolution was broadly supported by the General Assembly as it was adopted with 116 votes in favour and only 2 against (US and Israel), but that all EU Member States abstained along with some of the States that are candidates or potential candidates for acceding to the EU.

---

[63] See *ex multis* K. Hailbronner, J. Gogolin, 'Aliens', in *Max Planck Encyclopedia of Public International Law* (OUP, 2013), para. 14.

[64] Ruys, *supra* note 8, 45; Ronzitti, *supra* note 59, 2-3.

[65] United Nations General Assembly Resolution A/RES/2625 (XXV) of 24 October 1970. On the customary status of the principle of non-intervention, there is broad consensus. See *Military and Paramilitary Activities in and against Nicaragua (Nicaragua v. United States of America)* (Merits) [1986] ICJ Rep 14, 191.

[66] United Nations General Assembly Resolution A/RES/38/197 of 20 December 1983.

[67] United Nations General Assembly Revised Draft Resolution A/C.2/74/L.5/Rev.1 of 13 November 2019, para. 2.

The explanations provided by the States are quite informative on the different positions that emerged upon voting. They are clearly summarised in the Report prepared bi-annually by the UN Secretary General on the basis of the previous UN General Assembly Resolution on *Unilateral Economic Measures.* [68]

The States affected by EU restrictive measures took a clear position on their legality and on the consequences of their imposition. By way of example, the delegation of Burundi affirmed that:

> The unilateral economic sanctions that the European Union has imposed on Burundi unjustly have direct consequences on the implementation of sustainable development goals in general and the lives of vulnerable groups such as women, children, sick people in hospitals and unemployed youth, among others. [69]

In a similar vein, the Sudanese delegation stated that:

> Sudan rejects all unilateral measures since they are inconsistent with the principles of international law as set forth in the Charter of the United Nations and contravene the basic principles of the multilateral trading system. The Sudan considers that these measures directly violate the sovereignty of developing countries and that they hinder the achievement of sustainable development and inclusive economic growth. [70]

More generally, the Russian delegation concluded that:

> The Russian Federation has always maintained that the unilateral imposition of restrictive economic measures as a means of exerting pressure on other countries is inadmissible. [71]

In the same Report, the EU claimed that its restrictive measures were fully compliant with international law and condemned the unilateral recourse to coercive economic measures. [72] It is interesting to quote the European External Action Service's justification of the abstention by the EU Member States in the voting procedure at the General Assembly:

> The European Union and its Member States consider that such unilateral economic measures are admissible in certain circumstances in particular when necessary in order to fight terrorism and the proliferation of weapons of mass

---

[68] The last-in-time UN Secretary General Report is the following: UN Doc. A/74/264 of 31 July 2019, prepared pursuant to United Nations General Assembly Resolution A/RES/72/201 of 17 January 2018, para. 5.

[69] UN Doc. A/74/264, Annex, p. 5.

[70] *Ibidem*, p. 13. See, also, the comments sent by the Representatives of Syria (*ibidem*, p. 15).

[71] *Ibidem*, p. 11.

[72] *Ibidem*, p. 20.

> destruction, or to uphold respect for human rights, democracy, the rule of law and good governance. The European Union and its Member States are committed to using sanctions as part of an integrated, comprehensive policy approach, which should include political dialogue, incentives, conditionality and could even involve, as a last resort, the use of coercive measures in accordance with the United Nations Charter.[73]

It appears from the above quotations that, on the one hand, States suffering from the imposition of EU restrictive measures regard them as unjust measures of economic coercion. On the other hand, the EU does not consider them as "coercive", but as political tools. It seems, therefore, that the EU does not qualify its restrictive measures as being in violation of international law and in particular of the principle of non-intervention.

Indeed, it is doubtful whether economic sanctions or restrictive measures are, as such, prohibited by the principle of non-intervention. According to a 1983 Note of the UN Secretary General:

> [t]here is no clear consensus in international law as to when coercive economic measures are improper, despite relevant treaties, declarations and resolutions adopted in international organisations which try to develop norms limiting the use of such measures.[74]

This position finds support in the relevant literature,[75] though it is partially mitigated by the coercive nature of the economic measure involved, which should be assessed "according to [its] nature".[76] It is clearly difficult to draw a line that excludes *prima facie* the illegality of an economic measure on the ground of respect of the principle of non-intervention. As has been argued, it might also depend on how far the targeted State is reliant on economic support or on the economic relationship it entertains with the EU.[77]

The Basic Principles on EU restrictive measures contain no specific indications, apart from the very generic limit of the non-violation of international law. The Sanctions Guidelines contain no reference either to the principle of non-intervention or to the coercive nature of the measures adopted. They simply prevent the EU from

---

[73] EU Explanation of Vote: United Nations 2nd Committee: Resolution on Unilateral economic measures as a means of political and economic coercion against developing countries, 21 November 2019, available at https://eeas.europa.eu/delegations/un-new-york/71332/eu-explanation-vote-united-nations-2nd-committee-resolution-unilateral-economic-measures-means_en.

[74] UN Doc. A/48/535 of 25 October 1983, para. 2, letter a).

[75] See, for example, Tzanakapoulous, *supra* note 61, 627. See, also, O.Y. Elagab, *The Legality of Non-forcible Counter-measures in International Law* (*Oxford* Clarendon Press 1988) 212-213.

[76] UN Doc. A/48/535, para. 2, letter b). See, also, Giegerich, *supra* note 59, paras 24-25.

[77] Ruys, *supra* note 8, 27.

imposing extraterritorial sanctions as they would be "in breach of international law".[78]

The possible violation of the principle of non-intervention, however, does not constitute the only issue of concern when EU restrictive measures are imposed. Leaving aside, for the purpose of this Chapter, all possible violations of the rights of the targeted individuals,[79] it may be the case that economic restrictive measures violate rules emanating from the WTO regime.

In this regard, it is interesting to recall the already mentioned sanctions imposed on Argentina by the EEC Members in reaction to the invasion of the Falkland Islands; in particular, the measures adopted by them consisted of the suspension of goods imports of products originating from Argentina.[80] The Organization of American States (OAS) promptly affirmed that such measures were "incompatible with the Charter of the United Nations and of the OAS and the General Agreement on Tariffs and Trade (GATT)".[81] Argentina then lodged a complaint before the GATT Council of Representatives in which it denounced several violations of the agreement: the clause of most-favoured nation treatment; the ban on import prohibitions and restrictions, and the prohibition on non-discrimination, amongst others.[82]

The EEC Member States, along with all States that adopted sanctions against Argentina, argued before the GATT that they had decided to suspend the import of goods for "security reasons" according to Article XXI of the Agreement, which allows States to take "any action which it considers necessary for the protection of its essential security interests".[83]

A similar argument, based upon Article XXI, was raised before GATT by the EEC Member States to justify measures imposed on the then Socialist Federal Republic of Yugoslavia (SFRY).[84] The SFRY, in line with Argentina's position, claimed that Article XXI could not be invoked by the EEC Member States as the measures imposed had not been authorised by the UN.[85] Interestingly, the GATT Council decided to establish a Panel to deal with this issue[86] but, regrettably, the Panel did not have the chance to discuss it as the Council did not recognise the

[78] Sanctions guidelines-Update, EU Doc. 5664/18 of 4 May 2018, para. 52.

[79] See, in this regard, the Chapter authored by N. Lazzerini.

[80] Council Regulation (EEC) no. 877/82 of 16 April 1982 suspending imports of all products originating in Argentina.

[81] OAS Doc. 28/82 rev. 3, Resolution I of 28 April 1982, para. 6.

[82] GATT, *Trade Restrictions Affecting Argentina Applied for Non-Economic Reasons*, L/5317 of 30 April 1982.

[83] GATT, Article XXI, letter b).

[84] GATT, *Trade Measures Taken by the European Community against the Socialist Federal Republic of Yugoslavia*, L/6948 of 2 December 1991.

[85] GATT, doc. DS27/2 of 10 February 1992.

[86] GATT, doc. C/M/255 of 10 April 1992, p. 18.

Former Republic of Yugoslavia as the legitimate successor of the SFRY.[87]

Despite this, the argument raised by the SFRY is worthy of attention. In fact, the absence of any UN authorisation to impose sanctions excludes the most precise line of justification present in Article XXI, namely that indicated in letter c), according to which "any action in pursuance of [Contracting Party] obligations under the United Nations Charter for the maintenance of international peace and security" can constitute an exception.[88] As EU autonomous sanctions are not backed by UN authorisation, the only possible ground for justifying them under the GATT is the aforementioned "essential security interests" clause, contained in letter b) of Article XXI. However, doubts remain as to whether such a justification can succeed, for at least two reasons. Firstly, it is not entirely clear that Article XXI, letter b) is a self-judging clause. This interpretation was criticised by the Appellate Body in the *US-Nicaragua* dispute, although the final report in that case was never adopted.[89] While there are no specific GATT/WTO reports dealing with the relationship between economic sanctions and Article XXI letter b), it is reasonable to maintain that the sanctioning State only enjoys a margin of appreciation in the imposition of such measures, but not full *carte blanche*.[90]

As to the second reason, it is doubtful whether the interpretation of the "essential security interests" clause can be stretched to encompass the protection of interests that are not entirely related to the protection of the security of the sanctioning States. This is proven by the GATT Member States' reaction to Sweden's invocation of the clause to justify measures to protect its industries. In fact, on that occasion, Sweden was criticised as the reasons put forward[91] were not accepted as being related to a "security interest".[92] While there are no other cases to be cited, it is reasonable to believe, as some authors do, that the clause should be interpreted narrowly.[93]

Against this background, it seems that EU restrictive measures qualify either as measures of retorsion, thus being lawful under international law, or as violations of

---

[87] GATT, doc. C/M/264 of 14 July 1993, p. 3, para. 1.

[88] GATT, Article XXI, letter c).

[89] GATT, *US-Nicaragua Trade*, doc. L/6053 of 13 October 1986, para. 5.17: 'If it were accepted that the interpretation of Article XXI was reserved entirely to the contracting party invoking it, how could the Contracting Parties ensure that this general exception to all obligations under the General Agreement is not invoked excessively or for purposes other than those set out in this provision?'.

[90] See, accordingly, A.D. Mitchell, 'Sanctions and the World Trade Organisation', in van den Herik, *supra* note 8, 298.

[91] GATT, doc. L/4250 of 17 November 1965, p. 3: 'Such a capacity is indispensable in order to secure the provision of essential products necessary to meet basic needs in case of war or other emergency in international relations.'

[92] GATT, doc. C/M/109 of 10 November 1965, p. 8-9.

[93] See, again, Ruys, *supra* note 8, 30-31 and Mitchell, *supra* note 90, 300.

certain international rules, namely the principle of non-intervention and some rules stemming from the WTO regime, particularly when they consist of embargoes or other economic measures. In the latter case, this paragraph has shown that it is not entirely clear on which grounds the EU can claim the lawfulness of such measures, particularly when they are said to be adopted in violation of the GATT.

11.5. EU restrictive measures as third-party countermeasures adopted by non-injured entities

In light of the considerations presented at the end of the previous paragraph, it is reasonable to seek elsewhere the justification for adopting autonomous restrictive measures. It is the EU itself which suggests a possible solution. Going back to the founding documents and to EU practice related to the imposition of autonomous sanctions, it appears that the EU refers broadly to their compatibility with international law. [94]

Interestingly, the Sanctions Guidelines contain the following instruction:

> [w]hen the adoption of restrictive measures in the framework of UN is not possible, the European Union should encourage broader support of the international community for its autonomous measures. [95]

According to some commentators, the above guideline indicates the willingness of the EU not to act in isolation. [96] To put it another way, it seems that the EU allows itself to adopt autonomous sanctions only when there is broad international consensus to avoid disputes on the grounds of their legality. This gives rise to two considerations.

Firstly, it seems that the action by the EU – and, in some cases, by other States or international organisations – operates as a sort of substitute of the Security Council, particularly when this body is blocked by vetoes. The second consideration relates to the reasons that incite the EU to adopt autonomous sanctions. On one hand, the constant search for broad consensus suggests that the EU deems it necessary to act autonomously to protect the general interests of the international community; namely, interests that are shared by a vast majority of States. [97] In fact, the

---

[94] See M. Gestri, 'Sanctions imposed by the EU: Legal and institutional aspects', in N. Ronzitti (ed.), *Coercive Diplomacy, Sanctions and International Law* (Brill 2016) 73.

[95] Council of the European Union, Guidelines on implementation and evaluation of restrictive measures (sanctions) in the framework of the EU Common foreign and security policy, CFSP/PESC 68 of 4 May 2018, para. 3.

[96] See, again, Gestri, *supra* note 94, 74.

[97] See, on this, P. Palchetti, 'Reaction of the European Union to Breaches of *Erga omnes* obligations', in E. Cannizzaro (ed.), *The European Union as an Actor in International Relations* (Kluwer Law International 2002) 219, 221-222.

term "general interest" has been used precisely to identify interests in the international community which are not confined to bilateral relationships, but which affect a group of, if not all, States.[98]

The notion of general interest inevitably recalls that of *erga omnes* obligations, elaborated by the International Court of Justice (ICJ) in its famous *dictum* in the Barcelona Traction case:

> an essential distinction should be drawn between the obligations of a State towards the international community as a whole, and those arising vis-à-vis another State in the field of diplomatic protection. By their very nature the former are the concern of all States. In view of the importance of the rights involved, all States can be held to have a legal interest in their protection; they are obligations *erga omnes*.[99]

Against this background, one may argue that the EU adopts autonomous restrictive measures, or sanctions, to protect the general interests of the international community (*erga omnes* obligations) or of a collective group of States/entities (*erga omnes partes* obligations).[100] However, the Basic Principles quoted above contain a final clause according to which the EU acts in full conformity with international law.[101] Therefore, the following doubt may arise: does international law entitle the EU to adopt and enact restrictive measures to bring to an end to violations of *erga omnes* obligations? In order to answer this question, we must introduce and summarise the heated scholarly debate on the admissibility of third-party countermeasures, namely countermeasures adopted by non-injured States or international organisations.

The debate is polarised between two opposing views. On one hand, such reactions seem pernicious, as they undermine inter-State relations, allowing the most powerful States to act unilaterally according to their own policies.[102] On the other hand, third-party countermeasures appear to be the only way to guarantee respect of the *erga omnes* obligation and, more generally, to allow international law to protect the community interests.[103]

The polarisation of the debate led the ILC to discard the idea of including, in the final version of the DARSIWA, a specific provision allowing States to adopt

---

[98] See G. Gaja, 'The Protection of General Interests in the International Community', 364 *Collected Courses of the Hague Academy of International Law* 21.

[99] *Case concerning the Barcelona Traction, Light and Power Company, Limited (Belgium v. Spain)* (Merits) [1970] ICJ Rep 3, para. 33.

[100] See, again, Gestri, *supra* note 94, 99. See, also, N.D. White, *supra* note 7, 16.

[101] See *supra* para. 3.

[102] See, in particular, I. Brownlie, *Principles of Public International Law* (OUP 2008, 7th ed.) 515; J. Crawford, *Brownlie's Principles of Public International Law* (OUP 2012) 603.

[103] Such a position is summarised by Gaja, *supra* note 98, 9. For an overview of all scholarly positions, see, again, M. Dawidowicz, *supra* note 22, 11.

countermeasures for defending general interests.[104] Accordingly, the ILC adopted a neutral position toward such a possibility. In fact, according to Article 54 of the DARSIWA:

> This chapter does not prejudice the right of any State, entitled under article 48, paragraph 1, to invoke the responsibility of another State, to take lawful measures against that State to ensure cessation of the breach and reparation in the interest of the injured State or of the beneficiaries of the obligation breached.

Article 48, para. 1, of the DARSIWA, which represents the legal ground for non-injured States for invoking the responsibility of another State, indeed makes reference to the violation of the *erga omnes* or *erga omnes partes* obligation.[105]

It is important to note that Article 54 of the DARSIWA applies both to States and international organisations. To this end, it is worth recalling that, according to Article 22 of the DARIO:

> [...] the wrongfulness of an act of an international organisation not in conformity with an international obligation towards a State or another international organisation is precluded if and to the extent that the act constitutes a countermeasure taken in accordance with the substantive and procedural conditions required by international law.

The Commentary to Article 22 of the DARIO clarifies that the requirements under international law are by analogy "the conditions that are set out for countermeasures taken by a State against another State in articles 49 to 54 on the responsibility of States for internationally wrongful acts".

Aside from the disagreement between its Members, the ILC justified the absence of any reference to so-called third-party countermeasures in the DARSIWA with a lack of practice:

> the current state of international law on countermeasures taken in the general or collective interest is uncertain. State practice is sparse and involves a limited number of States. At present, there appears to be no clearly recognised entitlement of States referred to in article 48 to take countermeasures in the collective interest.[106]

---

[104] For a review of the debate within the ILC, see D. Alland, 'Countermeasures of General Interest' (2012) 13 *European Journal of International Law* 1221.

[105] 'Any State other than an injured State is entitled to invoke the responsibility of another State in accordance with paragraph 2 if: (a) the obligation breached is owed to a group of States including that State, and is established for the protection of a collective interest of the group; or (b) the obligation breached is owed to the international community as a whole'.

[106] DARSIWA, Commentary to Article 54, p. 139, para. 6.

The ILC also highlighted the difference between "lawful measures" and "countermeasures", the former being the only accepted form of reaction by non-injured States or international organisations.[107]

The position of the ILC is far from being able to draw a precise line on the permissibility of third-party countermeasures in international law. Scholars criticise the way in which Article 54 was drafted on two grounds. Firstly, it is argued that reference to "lawful measures" does not make any sense in international law, since, if the measure is lawful – namely: a retorsion –, there is no need to specify that it is a lawful reaction to an internationally wrongful act.[108] Secondly, several authors have demonstrated that the practice on third-party countermeasures is not at all limited to some sparse cases but, rather, represents the recourse to such measures firmly rooted in international law.[109]

The International Law Institute (*Institut de Droit International*) took the position that:

> Should a widely acknowledged grave breach of an *erga omnes* obligation occur, all the States to which the obligation is owed: [...] (c) are entitled to take non-forcible counter-measures under conditions analogous to those applying to a State specially affected by the breach.[110]

At this point it is difficult to establish if the *Institut*'s resolution reflects a rule of customary international law that specifies the content of Article 54 of the DARSIWA. What is clear here is that EU practice can represent evidence of a growing practice in support of the above position.[111]

However, such a conclusion needs to be handled with care. In fact, the EU, in the Basic Principles on the adoption of sanctions, does not mention the generic term "general interests" and it does not refer to *erga omnes* obligations. Rather, it lists a number of objectives that the autonomous sanctions shall pursue: the fight against

---

107 *Ibidem*, para. 7.

108 See Alland, *supra* note 104, 1233.

109 See, again, Dawidowicz, *supra* note 22, 111-238; the same Author develops his argument here: 'Third party countermeasures: A progressive development of international law?' (2016) 29 *QIL-QDI Zoom In* 3. See, also, Pellet and Miron, *supra* note 15, paras 58-59. See, *contra,* C. Focarelli, 'International law and third-party countermeasures in the age of global instant communication' (2016) 29 *QIL-QDI Zoom In* 17.

110 Institut de Droit International, *Obligations* erga omnes *in international law*, Resolution, Krakow Session, 2005, Article 5.

111 This is the opinion of Gestri, *supra* note 94, 99: 'EU can be regarded as a trailblazer by the advocates of the controversial doctrine of collective countermeasures in reaction to *erga omnes* obligations, having on numerous occasions adopted sanctions without being individually affected by the breach of international law allegedly committed by the target state.' The opinion is shared by N.D. White, *supra* note 7, 17 and Dawidowicz, *supra* note 22, 144.

terrorism and WMD, the protection of human rights, democracy and the rule of law and good governance.[112] While the first three appear to be in line with the most widely recognised "list of general interests" in the international community, doubts remain as to whether the protection of democracy, rule of law and good governance fall within that category. In fact, while the ILC's Commentary to Article 48 refused to list the *erga omnes* obligations,[113] some indications can be drawn from the ICJ's practice. The above mentioned judgment in *Barcelona Traction* contains a possible example of what the ICJ deems to be *erga omnes* obligations:

> Such obligations derive, for example, in contemporary international law, from the outlawing of acts of aggression, and of genocide, as also from the principles and rules concerning the basic rights of the human person, including protection from slavery and racial discrimination.[114]

In its judgment in the *East Timor* case, the ICJ added the right of self-determination of peoples to this list.[115] According to the most progressive literature, the following can be considered "community interests": the maintenance of international peace and security, the solidarity between developed and under-developed countries, the protection of the environment, the protection of common heritage, and the protection of human rights.[116]

More generally, the permissibility of countermeasures is necessarily based upon the commission of an internationally wrongful act on the part of the sanctioned States.[117] More specifically, the permissibility of countermeasures in reaction to violations of *erga omnes* obligations should be accepted only for grave breaches, as also required by the resolution of the *Institut de Droit International.*[118]

When looking at EU restrictive measures as described in paragraph 2 of this Chapter against the background of this construction, it appears that some of them hardly fit even the most progressive "list" of *erga omnes* obligations, namely all

---

[112] See, *supra,* paragraph 2.

[113] DARSIWA, Commentary to Article 48, p. 127, para. 9.

[114] *Case concerning the Barcelona Traction, Light and Power Company, Limited (Belgium v. Spain)*, para. 34.

[115] *East Timor (Portugal* v. *Australia)* (Merits) [1995] ICJ Rep 90, 102, para. 29.

[116] See, for example, B. Simma, 'From Bilateralism to Community Interests', 250 *Collected Courses of the Hague Academy of International Law* 235-243.

[117] DARSIWA, Article 49.

[118] See, accordingly, F. Dopagne, 'Countermeasures by International Organizations: The Decentralised Society in the Heart of the Institutionalised Society', in H. Ruiz-Fabri, R. Wolfrum, J. Gogolin (eds), *Select Proceedings of the European Society of International Law* (Hart Publishing 2008) 210-211; P. Klein, *La responsabilité des organisations internationales dans les ordres juridiques internes et en droit des gens* (Bruylant 1998) 401-402.

those measures imposed on States for the purposes of enhancing democracy, good governance and respect for the rule of law, especially when they are not connected with grave human rights violations. [119]

A more complex scenario is triggered when the EU reacts to violations of international law, as demonstrated by the measures against Turkey and Russia. Concerning the former, the EU justified the imposition of measures on the grounds that Turkey's action constituted a threat to peace and international security under the UN Charter. Be that as it may, one might ask whether the EU is entitled to qualify a situation as a threat to international peace and security. It is therefore more convincing to argue that the EU adopted the countermeasures on behalf of its Member States whose rights had been violated by Turkey, namely Greece and Cyprus. [120] With regard to the sanctions imposed on Russia, the matters are more complicated. In fact, it is not at all clear that the violation of the sovereignty rights of another State – in this case, Ukraine – can be considered as an *erga omnes* obligation or as a "community interest". [121] Curiously, if the EU had qualified the situation in Crimea as an act of aggression committed by Russia against Ukraine, it would have been easier to qualify the reaction as a countermeasure against a *grave* breach. [122]

The necessary consequence of classifying EU autonomous restrictive measures as third-party countermeasures will be that the EU is obliged to respect some substantial and procedural standards set forth in the DARSIWA. In particular, two important requirements might be considered: proportionality and the conditions for resorting to countermeasures.

As regards respect of the proportionality requirement, it must be acknowledged that the Sanctions Guidelines duly mention the respect for proportionality; however, nothing more is said other than "the measures must be proportionate to their objectives". [123]

Therefore, it is worth seeking the content of the principle in general international law, in particular, in Article 51 of the DARSIWA, which imposes on the reacting States the duty to adopt countermeasures "commensurate with the injury suffered, taking into account the gravity of the internationally wrongful act and the rights in question". According to the ILC Commentary to the Article, "[t]he reference to

---

[119] On the broader scope of EU sanction see Borlini and Siligardi, *supra* note 25, 40-42.

[120] On the capacity of the EU to act on behalf of its Member States see Palchetti, *supra* note 97, 223.

[121] On the difficult categorisation of EU restrictive measures against Russia, see Ch. Beaucillon, 'Crise ukrainienne et mesures restrictives de l'Union européenne: quelle contribution aux sanctions internationales à l'égard de la Russie?' (2014) *Journal de Droit International (Clunet)* 787.

[122] See, accordingly, P. De Sena, L. Gradoni, 'Crimea: le ragioni del torto (russo) e il torto delle ragioni (occidentali)' (2014) 1 *Quaderni di SIDIBlog* 5, 18.

[123] Sanction Guidelines, para. 9.

'the rights in question' has a broad meaning, and includes not only the effect of a wrongful act on the injured State but also on the rights of the responsible State".[124]

The broad interpretation of the term "rights in question" suggested by the ILC suggests that due attention should be paid when sanctions are imposed on less developed countries. In this regard, one should again read the comments sent by targeted countries to the UN for the purposes of drafting the resolution on *Unilateral Economic Measures*. Some of the comments – particularly the ones presented by Burundi and Sudan – highlight the impact that EU economic measures have on the economy of the targeted States.[125] Therefore, it is reasonable to opine that the EU, when imposing certain restrictive measures, must respect the principle of proportionality as defined by the ILC.

Turning to the procedural conditions, immediate reference should be made to Article 52 of the DARSIWA, which reads as follows:

> 1. Before taking countermeasures, an injured State shall: (*a*) call upon the responsible State, in accordance with article 43, to fulfil its obligations under Part Two; (*b*) notify the responsible State of any decision to take countermeasures and offer to negotiate with that State. 2. Notwithstanding paragraph 1 (*b*), the injured State may take such urgent countermeasures as are necessary to preserve its rights. 3. Countermeasures may not be taken, and if already taken must be suspended without undue delay if: (*a*) the internationally wrongful act has ceased; and (*b*) the dispute is pending before a court or tribunal which has the authority to make decisions binding on the parties. 4. Paragraph 3 does not apply if the responsible State fails to implement the dispute settlement procedures in good faith.

Article 52 is a complex one as it imposes several duties on the entities that adopt countermeasures. In addition, the interpretation of some of those duties is still open to debate. In particular, it is not clear whether Article 52 demands a prior exhaustion of means of dispute settlement.[126] However, it is clear that, insofar as such dispute settlement mechanisms exist, they shall be explored by the entity invoking the right to adopt countermeasures, without prejudice to its right to act with urgency.[127] What is less doubtful is the duty of the EU to notify the targeted State of its intention to impose restrictive measures. In the Sanctions Guidelines, a notification procedure is described only when the decision to adopt sanctions is already taken.[128]

---

[124] DARSIWA, Commentary to Article 51, p. 135, para. 6.

[125] See, *supra*, para. 3.

[126] DARSIWA, Commentary to Article 52, p. 136, para. 2. The necessity of prior exhaustion of means of dispute settlement was advanced by Special Rapporteur Arangio-Ruiz, in the Fourth Report on State Responsibility (p. 22).

[127] *Ibidem*.

[128] Sanction Guidelines, para. 18 ff.

11.6. Concluding remarks

The autonomous sanctioning regimes adopted by the EU represent a stress-test for various special regimes in international law and for the general rules on the responsibility of States and international organisations.

On one hand, the EU seems to regard its restrictive measures as lawful, but it does not provide any explicit justification under international law. On the other hand, some targeted States have complained of the unlawfulness of the sanctions imposed as being violations of the principle of non-intervention or of the GATT.

From an international law perspective, the principle of non-intervention and the WTO rules still represent obstacles to the imposition of certain economic measures and it is not at all clear whether the exceptions provided in those special regimes can provide a solid legal basis for the EU to prevent any contestation.

One possibility is to consider the EU as being allowed to adopt third-party countermeasures in reaction against violations of *erga omnes* obligations. This solution appears promising and seems to incorporate some of the features of EU autonomous sanctions: in particular, some of the purposes can be regarded as *erga omnes* obligations and the search for a broad consensus in the international community appears to be evidence that the EU is acting to pursue general interests.

However, the adoption of third-party countermeasures by non-injured States or international organisations is far from being firmly established in international law. As demonstrated in this Chapter, it is reasonable to opine that EU practice might help in contributing to develop a customary rule that permits recourse to third-party countermeasures. In such a scenario, recourse to autonomous sanctions should not be allowed without restrictions, as the procedural and substantial conditions imposed by the law on international responsibility would inevitably also apply to the EU.

Chapter 12
SANCTIONS IN EU COMPETITION LAW: ENSURING DETERRENCE WITHIN THE DECENTRALISED ENFORCEMENT SYSTEM OF ARTICLES 101 AND 102 TFEU

Luca Calzolari *

ABSTRACT: *The chapter focuses on the use of sanctions in the competition law field. The analysis discusses the theoretical foundation of antitrust sanctions, showing the close relation between sanctioning powers and the much-debated issue of the goals of competition law. Moreover, it looks at the "modernized" system of enforcement of Articles 101 and 102 TFEU, where sanctioning powers are shared between the Commission and the National Competition Authorities and, on a more practical note, the methodology to quantify sanctions. Lastly, the chapter deals with two recent developments characterizing the antitrust enforcement system that challenge the centrality of public sanctions, namely the ever-increasing diffusion of negotiated remedies and the call for criminalisation of antitrust offences.*

KEYWORDS: *competition law – antitrust – articles 101 and 102 TFEU – deterrence – public enforcement – fining guidelines*

12.1. Preliminary remarks

The primary goal of the EU competition law enforcement system is to ensure that Articles 101 and 102 TFEU are not infringed. Compliance with any set of rules may occur only if the concerned persons are provided with sufficient incentives to avoid violation. The main incentive to ensure compliance is that the expected costs of an infringement exceed the expected benefits for the prospective wrongdoer. Ever

* Assistant Professor of EU Law, University of Turin.

since it has been devised, EU competition law has been enforced almost exclusively through the public enforcement channel. Fines imposed on undertakings by the Commission have therefore represented the most important instrument to ensure the deterrent effect of antitrust rules. This prominence is confirmed, if only by the fact that the application of enormously large fines is probably the main reason that makes competition law known to the general public.

In the context of the transformation of EU competition law inaugurated by Regulation (EC) No 1/2003,[1] the centrality of public fines within the enforcement system has been lessened over time. This process has caused a significant evolution of the modalities by which the sanctioning powers are exercised in the antitrust realm. The traditional powers of the Commission have been improved and coupled with new enforcement tools, both within and outside the public enforcement pillar.

Given the above, section 2 discusses the theoretical foundation of antitrust sanctions, showing the close relation between sanctioning powers and the much-debated issue of the goals of competition law. Focusing on the developments brought by Directive (EU) No 2019/1 ("*ECN+ Directive*"),[2] section 3 describes the "modernized" system of enforcement of Articles 101 and 102 TFEU, where sanctioning powers are shared between the Commission and the National Competition Authorities ("*NCAs*"). Section 4 deals with the Commission's and NCAs' discretion in setting fines and with the consequent issue of the standard of judicial review. On a more practical note, section 5 analyses the methodology to quantify sanctions codified in the 1998 and 2006 Commission's Fining Guidelines.[3] Section 6 focuses on two of the most controversial issues related to the Commission's sanctioning powers, *i.e.* the limited role played by intent and imputability in the antitrust realm. By way of conclusion, sections 7 discusses two recent developments characterizing the antitrust enforcement system that challenge the centrality of public sanctions, namely the ever-increasing diffusion of negotiated remedies and the call for criminalisation of antitrust offences.

12.2. The optimal level of antitrust sanctions: a quest for the soul of competition policy

As in many other domains, the EU competition law enforcement system has three main purposes. Firstly, it sets substantive rules to enshrine given shared values. Sec-

[1] Council Regulation (EC) No 1/2003 of 16 December 2002 on the implementation of the rules on competition laid down in Articles 81 and 82 of the Treaty, OJ 2003, L 1/1.

[2] Directive (EU) No 2019/1 of the European Parliament and of the Council of 11 December 2018 to empower the competition authorities of the Member States to be more effective enforcers and to ensure the proper functioning of the internal market, OJ 2019, L 11/3.

[3] Guidelines on the method of setting fines imposed pursuant to Article 15(2) of Regulation No 17 and Article 65(5) of the ECSC Treaty, OJ 1998, C 9/3 and Guidelines on the method of setting fines imposed pursuant to Article 23(2)(a) of Regulation No 1/2003, OJ 2006, C 210/2.

ondly, it secures compliance with such rules by deterring potential violations. Thirdly, being impossible to prevent all violations, it handles the consequences of unavoidable infringements: adequate mechanisms shall be established to punish wrongdoers and compensate the aggrieved parties.[4] Sanctions are paramount for the last two purposes, playing a decisive role to deter and punish violations.

The primary goal of the enforcement system is to ensure that Articles 101 and 102 TFEU are not violated, so that the anticompetitive effects that they aim to prevent are actually avoided. Unless an *ex ante* authorization system applies (as it was under Regulation (EEC) 17/62 for Article 101(3) TFUE, and as it is for concentrations),[5] compliance may occur only if sufficient incentives to avoid violations are provided to the rules' addressees. Economists suggest that the most effective incentive to comply is that the expected costs exceed the expected benefits of the violation. Public fines (and civil damages,[6] which however are better suited to compensate the aggrieved parties)[7] attach a potential cost to anticompetitive behaviours, making them less attractive.

Public fines, therefore, not only aim at punishing wrongdoers but also – and mainly – at deterring other undertakings from engaging in anticompetitive behaviours. In essence, deterrence is a function of two variables: the level of the expected costs and the probability of detection of the infringement. If either the amount of the sanction or the rate of detection of the violations increase,[8] the deterrent effect of – any provision, including – competition rules increases too.[9]

Setting the optimal level of deterrence of Articles 101 and 102 TFEU is an operation that cannot be performed without addressing the much-debated issue of the goals of competition law: setting fines is actually a quest for the soul of competition law. Due to their social and political implications and their connection to economic concepts,[10] competition rules contain only generally worded standards,

---

[4] F. Denozza and L. Toffoletti, 'Le funzioni delle azioni private nel libro bianco sul risarcimento del danno antitrust: compensazione, deterrenza e coordinamento con l'azione pubblica', in F. Rossi Dal Pozzo and B. Nascimbene (eds), *Il private enforcement delle norme sulla concorrenza* (Giuffré, 2009) 101.

[5] Council Regulation (EEC) No 17 of 6 February 1962 First Regulation implementing Articles 85 and 86 of the Treaty, OJ 1962, 13/204; Council Regulation (EC) No 139/2004 of 20 January 2004 on the control of concentrations between undertakings, OJ 2004, L 24/1.

[6] *Infra* Section 3.

[7] *Infra* Section 7.

[8] *E.g.*, because the powers of the competition authorities are strengthened or because individuals bring more damages actions before civil courts.

[9] A. Heimler and K. Mehta 'Violations of Antitrust Provisions: The Optimal Level of Fines for Achieving Deterrence' (2012) 35 *World Competition* 103.

[10] A. Pera, 'Changing Views of Competition, Economic Analysis and EC Antitrust Law' (2008) 4 *ECJ* 127, 129-131.

leaving considerable room for their interpretation. [11] The lack of clear legal definitions of the concepts mentioned by competition law provisions has allowed their content to evolve over time, following the development of economic, political and legal opinions. [12]

Space limitations prevent a comprehensive presentation of theories on the aims of competition law. Suffice it to recall that even today the two oldest and leadings antitrust jurisdictions – the US and the EU – are inspired by diverging principles and pursue different goals: while EU competition law is based on the so-called formalistic approach to antitrust rules inspired by the Freiburg School, [13] the welfarist approach has been the standard applied in the US ever since the Chicago School became prominent in the 1980s. [14]

The main difference is that US antitrust rules are intended solely to enhance allocative efficiency (*i.e.*, to promote consumer welfare), while EU competition policy aims mainly at protecting the market structure and the competitive process. EU competition law serves broader – and also non-economic – purposes connected to the protection of individual – economic and political – freedoms and to the creation and the preservation of the internal market.

Far from being a mere academic question, the antitrust divide across the Atlantic often resulted in similar conducts being differently assessed by US and EU authorities. [15] The fact that some behaviours are allowed in one jurisdiction and prohibited in the other cannot but be reflected in a different approach to the instrument used to ensure compliance with substantive rules, *i.e.* deterrence through sanctions.

One of the corollaries of the welfarist thinking is indeed the "internalisation approach", according to which expected costs of antitrust infringements shall be higher than the harm caused to third parties multiplied by the inverse of the probability of detection. [16] Only behaviours that reduce efficiency are deterred. Anticompetitive conducts creating efficiency gains (*i.e.* creating larger surplus than the damages caused to third parties) are permitted. [17]

---

[11] C.D. Ehlermann, 'The modernization of EC Antitrust Policy: a Legal and Cultural Revolution' (2000) 37 *Common Market Law Review* 537, 537-538.

[12] W.P.J. Wils, 'The Relationship between Public Antitrust Enforcement and Private Actions for Damages' (2007) *Concurrences* 1, 3.

[13] T-325/16, *České dráhy*, ECLI:EU:T:2018:368, para 173; C-52/09, *Telia-Sonera*, ECLI:EU:C:2011:83, paras 22-24; see also C-413/14 P, *Intel*, ECLI:EU:C:2017:632.

[14] The welfarist approach became prominent at the expenses of the Harvard School. According to the Structure-Conduct-Performance paradigm proposed by the latter, the market structure determines the undertakings' behaviours on the market which, in turn, determines how markets perform.

[15] D.D Sokol, 'Troubled Waters Between U.S. and European Antitrust' (2017) 115 *Michigan Law Review* 955.

[16] G.S. Becker, 'Crime and Punishment: An Economic Approach' (1968) 76 *JPE* 169; G.J. Stigler, 'The Optimum Enforcement of Laws' (1970) 78 *JPE* 526.

[17] W.P.J. Wils, *Efficiency and Justice in European Antitrust Enforcement* (Hart, 2008) 57.

By contrast, according to the "deterrence approach", expected costs of antitrust violations shall be higher than the expected profits, again multiplied by the inverse of the probability of detection. Since in this perspective competition rules pursue wider purposes than merely achieving efficiency, all potential anticompetitive conducts are deterred, regardless of their economic effects. [18]

12.3. Sanctioning powers within the context of the "modernized" system of enforcement of Articles 101 and 102 TFEU

In this context, it is not surprising that Article 87(2)(a) EEC already envisaged the adoption of secondary legislation empowering the Commission to fine undertakings that, *inter alia*, infringed competition rules. Without sanctioning powers *vis-à-vis* individuals, the effectiveness of the new policy (then) enshrined in Articles 85 and 86 EEC would have been seriously hampered.

The power was conferred on the Commission by Article 15 of Regulation (EEC) No 17/62. The first sanction was imposed in 1969 in the *Quinine* cartel case for 500.000 Units of Account. [19] The level of sanctions remained relatively low for around a decade, when competition policy was still developing within the EU. The situation began to change in 1983, when the Commission acknowledged the deterrent purpose of antitrust sanctions. [20] Deterrence has ever since remained the main goal of public enforcement: [21] the level of sanctions has therefore significantly increased, recently breaching the four billion Euro's threshold for a single undertaking. [22]

The "modernization" of EU competition law envisaged by Regulation (EC) No 1/2003 – enhanced the efficiency but also – increased the level of complexity of the enforcement system. The decentralized application of Articles 101 and 102 TFEU entails that the Commission is no longer the only authority having the power to "punish" antitrust offences. Firstly, public sanctions are imposed also at the national level by the NCAs, grouped in the ECN. [23] Secondly, following the envisaged development of private enforcement, civil actions are increasingly brought before na-

---

[18] *Ibidem.*

[19] Commission decision of 16 July 1969, IV/26.623 – *Quinine cartel.* C. Harding, 'The use of fines as a sanction in E.E.C. competition law' (1979) 16 *Common Market Law Review* 591.

[20] The Commission clarified that fines aim, *inter alia*, to "prevent a repetition of the offence, and to make the prohibition in the Treaty more effective" (XIIIth Report on Competition Policy (Commission, 1983), para. 62).

[21] Indeed, "deterrence is an objective of the fine and a reference point for the Commission throughout the calculation of the fine" (T-56/09 and T-73/09, *Saint-Gobain*, ECLI:EU:T:2014:160, para. 380)

[22] Commission Decision of 18 July 2018, AT.40099 – *Google Android.*

[23] Commission Notice on cooperation within the Network of Competition Authorities, OJ 2004, C 101/43.

tional courts by individuals damaged by anticompetitive behaviours.

From a theoretical perspective, the modernized system of application of EU competition law makes it even clearer that it is actually impossible to achieve the optimal level of expected costs: regardless of whether they are set considering the harm caused or the profit made by the infringer, expected costs nowadays originate from several independent sources and are no longer predictable let alone determinable *ex ante.*[24] On a more practical note, problems arose because the same substantive rules were applied within the context of different enforcement frameworks: in the lack of EU legislation, it was for Member States to regulate both the NCAs' enforcement activities and damages actions, leading to uneven public and private enforcement of Articles 101 and 102 TFEU.

Aiming at ensuring a more level playing field, the EU legislator tackled both issues: while Directive No 2014/104/EU harmonises certain procedural rules on antitrust damages actions,[25] the ECN+ Directive deals with the institutional role of ANCs and their enforcement and decision-making powers. There is no room here to discuss the significant and much debated innovations brought by Directive No 2014/104/EU; yet, the binding effect on national courts of decisions adopted by the domestic NCA and the value as *prima facie* evidence of decisions issued by foreign NCAs[26] deserve at least to be mentioned, just as the harmonized regime for the disclosure and use of evidence in civil proceedings (including documents contained in the NCAs' files).[27]

Dealing with one of the two fundamental pillars of the decentralised system of public enforcement (*i.e.* the NCAs' activities), the ECN+ Directive is more relevant for this paper's purposes. In essence,[28] the ECN+ Directive models the powers that Member States shall confer to the NCAs upon those already granted to the Commission by Regulation (EC) No 1/2003. Although innovative aspects are therefore limited, this approach is coherent with the main purposes pursued by the EU legislator, *i.e.* to improve competition enforcement and to foster convergence. The harmonization of national rules is an effective means to reduce the risk that public enforcement proceedings reach different outcomes (especially in terms of sanctions) depending on the Member State where the infringement is committed. Reliance on a well-established framework as the one enshrined in Regulation (EC) No 1/2003 is

---

[24] M.J. Frese, 'Fines and Damages under EU Competition Law: Implications of the Accumulation of Liability' (2011) 34 *World Competition* 397.

[25] Directive No 2014/104/EU of the European Parliament and of the Council of 26 November 2014 on certain rules governing actions for damages under national law for infringements of the competition law provisions of the Member States and of the European Union, OJ 2014, L 349/1. See F. Munari and C. Cellerino (eds), *L'impatto della nuova direttiva 104/2014 sul private antitrust enforcement* (Aracne, 2016).

[26] Article 9 Directive No 2014/104/EU.

[27] Articles 5 to 7 Directive No 2014/104/EU.

[28] On the ECN+ Directive, L. Calzolari, *Il sistema di enforcement delle regole di concorrenza dell'Unione europea* (Giappichelli, 2019) 112 ff.

also appropriate, considered that in some Member States NCAs actually lacked basic enforcement and sanctioning powers: too innovative solutions were unlikely to be profitably transposed at the national level.

The ECN+ Directive covers many different profiles to ensure that NCAs can apply competition rules effectively. For example, Member States shall grant adequate financial and human resources to the NCAs and ensure their independence from other public institutions [29]. As far as enforcement powers are concerned, NCAs shall be able to perform inspections (both at business and private premises) and to conduct interview and request information, [30] including digital ones. [31] Implementing Article 5(2) Regulation (EC) No 1/2003, [32] the harmonization of the catalogue of decisions that can be adopted by the NCAs has been completed too. Similar to the Commission, NCAs shall be able to impose interim measures and to adopt commitment decisions. [33] If an antitrust offence is ascertained, NCAs shall have the power to order that it is brought to an end and to impose structural and behavioural remedies on the infringers.

As it was easily predictable, particular attention has been paid to NCAs' sanctioning powers. Due to significant differences in national legislations, the level – and even the mere application – of sanctions was one of the elements that varied the most between Member States. The impact on deterrence was paramount: in some jurisdictions, antitrust violations entailed virtually no expected costs. One of the crucial issues was that a number of NCAs lacked the power to impose sanctions and, to this purpose, had to apply to national criminal court, where criminal procedural guarantees applied. Showing a clear preference for the effectiveness of competition rules over the infringers' procedural rights, the ECN+ Directive establishes that effective, proportionate and dissuasive sanctions for procedural [34] and substantive violations shall be capable of being imposed directly by the NCAs or, at least, by a court in non-criminal judicial proceedings. [35]

Articles 14 and 15 of the ECN+ Directive further clarify the modalities pursuant to which the NCAs shall quantify sanctions. To ensure the level playing field, the basic principle is that the same criteria already applied by the Commission and cod-

---

[29] Article 4 ECN+ Directive.

[30] Articles 6 to 9 ECN+ Directive.

[31] Article 6(1)(b) and Recital 30 ECN+ Directive.

[32] Pursuant to such disposition, Member States already had to confer to NCAs the power to "requir[e] that an infringement be brought to an end", "order[...] interim measures", "accepting commitments", and "impos[e] fines, periodic penalty payments or any other penalty provided for in their national law".

[33] Articles 11 and 12 ECN+ Directive. On commitments, see Section 7.

[34] *E.g.*, failure to comply with investigative measures ordered by the NCAs.

[35] Article 13(1) ECN+ Directive.

ified in the mentioned Fining Guidelines[36] shall guide also the NCAs. Before analysing such criteria,[37] it is worth noting that the ECN+ Directive establishes that also the approach to the concepts of intent and imputability developed at the EU level shall be applied by the NCAs: the latter shall interpret the notions of intent and negligence coherently with the case law of the ECJ on competition rules[38] and should therefore disregard the – likely different – interpretations of these notions developed in national – criminal or administrative – proceedings; Member States shall ensure that the notion of undertaking developed by the ECJ applies also at the national level.[39] The relevance of these two fundamental principles inherent to the EU competition law system will be briefly discussed in section 6.

While there is no room to discuss the rules on leniency provided by the ECN+ Directive to foster convergence between national regimes[40] and enhance coordination between the activities of the Commission and the NCAs,[41] it is worth concluding by noting that also the phase following the adoption of NCAs' decisions is regulated by the ECN+ Directive. Firstly, codifying the case law, it has been clarified that NCAs shall be able to defend their decisions before national courts.[42] Secondly, a mechanism of mutual assistance has been established to enhance cooperation between NCAs with regard to, *inter alia*, the enforcement of sanctioning decisions in Member States other than that of issuance.[43]

Mutual assistance enhances the deterrent effect of competition rules and, coupled with the mentioned privileged evidentiary value of foreign NCAs' decisions in civil proceedings[44], completes the free movement of antitrust decisions.[45]

---

[36] *Supra* note 3.

[37] See section 5.

[38] Recital 42 ECN+ Directive.

[39] Article 13(5) ECN+ Directive.

[40] The ECN+ Directive requires Member States to establish a national leniency program for cartels and seeks the harmonization of national rules on general conditions for leniency and of the criteria according to which NCAs can grant immunity or reduce sanctions (Articles 17 to 19 ECN+ Directive).

[41] Attempting (with limited success) to address some of the issues arose in the *DHL* case (C-428/14, *DHL Express*, ECLI:EU:C:2016:27), the ENC+ directive, *inter alia*, requires Member State to ensure that a national system of summary applications and markers for immunity is available (Articles 22 and 21 ECN+ Directive).

[42] Article 30 ECN+ Directive, codifying C-439/08, *VEBIC*, ECLI:EU:C:2010:739.

[43] Articles 24 and ff. ECN+ Directive.

[44] Article 9(2) Directive No 2014/104/EU.

[45] There are some similarities with the well-established system of circulation of judgments disciplined by Regulation (EU) No 1215/2012 of the European Parliament and of the Council of 12 December 2012 on jurisdiction and the recognition and enforcement of judgments in civil and commercial matters, OJ 2012, L 351/1.

12.4. The margin of discretion conferred to the Commission (and NCAs): the standard of judicial review in competition cases

The Commission's discretion and the perceived lack of transparency with regard to the methodology used to calculate sanctions were often questioned. To address such problems, the Commission adopted the mentioned Fining Guidelines in 1998 and in 2006.[46] Despite the Commission's efforts, this development did not overcome the criticism. The lack of formal legislation on the matter led many to argue that the degree of discretion enjoyed by the Commission is still inappropriate for such a sensitive matter.

Accordingly, many believe that the system does not fully comply with several general principles of EU law (*e.g.* legal certainty, protection of legitimate expectations and sound administration) and may even violate undertakings' fundamental rights,[47] enshrined also in the EU Charter of Fundamental Rights. This line of criticism is reinforced by the fact that the mentioned levels reached by antitrust sanctions raise doubts on their legal nature.[48] As recognized by the ECtHR,[49] antitrust hefty fines may indeed be qualified as criminal penalties under the three well-known *Engel* criteria,[50] on a case-by-case basis.

However, the EU competition enforcement system is expressly qualified as administrative in nature by Article 23(5) of Regulation (EC) No 1/2003. Such explicit qualification was recently restated by Article 13 of the ECN+ Directive, confirming the intent of the EU legislator. The ECJ always avoided taking a definite stance on the point.[51] Although the case law seems to exclude the criminal nature of antitrust proceedings and sanctions,[52] such exclusion does not entail that criminal procedural guarantees are *per se* inapplicable to competition proceedings. Even if competition law is not part of the core area of criminal law, the two sectors have a similar

---

[46] *Supra* note 3.

[47] R. Nazzini, 'Administrative Enforcement, Judicial Review and Fundamental Rights in EU Competition Law: A Comparative Contextual-Functionalist Perspective' (2012) 49 *Common Market Law Review*. 971; A. Andreangeli, *EU Competition Enforcement and Human Rights* (Edward Elgar, 2008); G. Di Federico, *La riforma del procedimento antitrust e diritti della difesa* (Editoriale scientifica, 2008).

[48] Editorial, 'Towards a more judicial approach? EU antitrust fines under the scrutiny of fundamental rights' (2011) 48 *Common Market Law Review*. 1405; W. P.J. Wils, 'The Increased Level of EU Antitrust Fines, Judicial Review and the ECHR' (2010) 33 *World Competition* 5

[49] ECtHR, n. 43509/08, *Menarini Diagnostics*.

[50] Namely, the offences' qualification under domestic law, the nature of the offence, and the nature and severity of sanctions, *i.e.* their deterrent and punitive nature (cf. ECtHR, n. 5100/71 e al., *Engel*).

[51] T-279/02, *Degussa*, ECLI:EU:T:2006:103, para 71.

[52] 374/87, *Orkem*, ECLI:EU:C:1989:387, para 29; T-433/16, *Pometon*, ECLI:EU:T:2019:201.

character: the fundamental principles stemming from criminal law are therefore capable of influencing also competition proceedings.[53]

In other words, the relation between criminal and competition law is not a matter of "if", but of "how much": namely, how much protection should be ensured to undertakings involved in competition proceedings compared to the full catalogue of criminal procedural guarantees. The ECN+ Directive confirmed that the appropriate level of protection should be set by balancing two divergent interests: the protection of undertakings' fundamental rights and the need to ensure that Articles 101 and 102 TFEU are effectively enforced.[54]

The need to protect the effectiveness of competition rules stems also from the EU courts' approach to the Commission's margin of appreciation with regard to the quantification of sanctions. The fact that undertakings cannot anticipate the exact amount of the sanction related to a given antitrust offence does not question the legality of Article 23(2) Regulation (EC) No 1/2003.[55] Moreover, while Fining Guidelines can be derogated by the Commission if necessary to ensure the deterrent effect of antitrust rules,[56] the case law also clarifies that they can be applied retroactively without infringing either the principle of legal certainty or the principle that sanctions must have a proper legal basis.[57]

One of the consequences of the Commission's discretion is that the General Court (GC) has unlimited jurisdiction in actions brought against sanctioning decisions.[58] As an exception to the general standard of review applicable under Article 263 TFEU, the GC can therefore examine the merit of the case (including the Commission's assessment of the infringement's gravity) for the purposes of sanctions. The full jurisdiction entails the possibility for – and the obligation of – the GC to perform "*an in-depth review both of the legality of the contested decision and of whether the amount of the fine set out in that decision was appropriate*",[59] includ-

---

[53] Opinion of AG Kokott, C-681/11, *Schenker*, ECLI:EU:C:2013:126, paras 40 ff.

[54] Recital 14 ECN+ Directive.

[55] C-90/15 P, *Hansen & Rosenthal*, ECLI:EU:C:2017:123.

[56] 2006 Guidelines (*supra* note 3) para 37. Indeed, "[t]he proper application of the [EU] competition rules in fact requires that the Commission may at any time adjust the level of fines to the needs of that policy" (T-701/14, *Niche Generics*, ECLI:EU:T:2018:921, para. 445). However, the Commission's discretion is not unlimited: the Commission shall express the factual and legal reasons that led it to decide to derogate the guidelines and shall communicate said reasons to the undertakings before the decision is issued and not only in the following judicial proceeding (T-58/14, *Stührk Delikatessen Import*, ECLI:EU:T:2018:474).

[57] This holds true as long as undertakings can reasonably expect sanctions (C-490/15 P and C-505/15 P, *Ori Martin*, ECLI:EU:C:2016:678).

[58] Article 31 Regulation (EC) No 1/2003. Another consequence is that the Commission cannot impose fines without precisely explaining the methodology it uses to determine and calculate fines (T-105/17, *HSBC Holdings*, ECLI:EU:T:2019:675).

[59] C-411/15 P, *Timab*, ECLI:EU:C:2017:11 para. 109.

ing if the complaint relates to "*considerations of fairness*".[60]

In addition to the review of the sanction's legality, the GC is therefore empowered to recalculate the sanction's amount initially determined by the Commission.[61] The same standard of review applies also in the context of leniency proceedings: the Commission's discretion does not prevent the GC from assessing the sufficiency of the evidence submitted by the applicants to meet the relevant threshold for immunity or for the sanctions' reduction.[62]

However, EU courts cannot substitute their own reasoning to the assessment made by the author of the challenged act without overstepping the latter's competences; therefore, they cannot establish antitrust liability (let alone impose sanctions) in the Commission's place.[63] Moreover, although they shall motivate their judgements, the duty to state reasons does not require EU Courts to justify the approach followed in one case against the approach taken in another case, even if the two cases concern the very same Commission's decision.[64]

The ECJ's judicial review powers are less intense than those of the GC. The ECJ can only verify whether the GC considered all the essential factors to assess the infringement gravity and whether it provided convincing arguments to dismiss the appeal[65]. The ECJ, therefore, cannot evaluate the fairness and reasonableness of the amount of sanction imposed by the GC according to the latter's unlimited jurisdiction.[66] Consequently, an error in law by the GC can be found only in exceptional circumstances, such as when the sanction's level determined by the GC is so excessive to breach the proportionality principle.[67]

---

[60] T-486/11, *Orange Polska*, ECLI:EU:T:2015:1002, para. 68.

[61] The GC can therefore "cancel, reduce or increase the fine or periodic penalty payment imposed" (C-617/13 P, *Repsol*, ECLI:EU:C:2016:416, para. 84).

[62] T-251/12, *EGL*, ECLI:EU:T:2016:114; T-265/12, *Schenker*, ECLI:EU:T:2016:111.

[63] C-603/13 P, *Galp Energía España*, ECLI:EU:C:2016:38.

[64] C-644/13 P, *Villeroy & Boch*, ECLI:EU:C:2017:59, para. 38.

[65] In particular, the GC shall address all the arguments raised by the applicant if the latter requested the GC to exercise its unlimited jurisdiction (cf. C-99/17 P, *Infineon Technologies*, ECLI:EU:C:2018:773, para. 192).

[66] *Inter alia*, the requirements of reasonableness and fairness demand that the level of the sanction is "consistent with the requirements of individualisation and progressiveness of the 'penalty' – two principles of cardinal importance in any punitive system, both in the criminal and the administrative spheres"; a goal which is not fully achieved when "some of the calculation operations are essentially formal and abstract in character and therefore do not have concrete repercussions on the final amount of the fine" (cf. opinion of AG Tizzano, C-189/02 P, C-202/02 P, C-205/02 P to C-208/02 P and C-213/02 P, *Dansk Rørindustri*, ECLI:EU:C:2004:415, para. 130.

[67] Cf. C-619/13 P, *Mamoli Robinetteria*, ECLI:EU:C:2017:50; C-487/16 P, *Telefónica*, ECLI:EU:C:2017:961.

12.5. Setting sanctions in practice: the 2006 Fining Guidelines

On a more practical note, the mentioned Fining Guidelines[68] set a three-step procedure for the calculation of sanctions. Firstly, the basic amount of the fine is determined. Secondly, the basic amount is adjusted following an overall assessment of the relevant circumstances. Lastly, the legitimacy of the amount is verified against the so-called turnover cap.

Although each of these three steps will be described below, greater attention will be paid to the first phase.[69]

a) *The first phase: Setting the basic amount of the sanction*

Also the fine's basic amount is determined by the Commission through a three-step procedure.

The first step is the calculation of the "value of sales" ("*VoS*") directly or indirectly related to the infringement. A percentage up to 30% is then applied to the VoS to reflect the infringement's gravity. Lastly, the VoS, already adjusted to reflect the infringement's gravity, is multiplied by the number of years of infringement.

The rationale behind relying on the VoS affected by the infringement is that such value is considered the most adequate proxy to assess the economic relevance of the infringement and, in case of collusive practices, also a good parameter to reveal the role of each participant in the infringement.[70] The scope of application of the notion shall be analysed from a temporal, geographic and material perspective.

As per the temporal criterion, the Guidelines prescribe that sales made during the last business year of participation in the infringement shall be taken into account. If appropriate[71], this rule can be derogated and the Commission may for example refer to the average of the yearly sales during the whole infringement or to the sales made in years other than the last one: this may result necessary, *inter alia*, if concerned markets experienced unusual volatility[72] or if extraordinary transactions occurred (such as

---

[68] *Supra* note 3.

[69] For further references, E. Barbier de La Serre and E. Lagathu, 'The Law on Fines Imposed in EU Competition Proceedings: The Ever-Increasing Reach of Settlements' (2019) 10 *Journal of European Competition Law and Practice* 505; Id., 'The Law on Fines Imposed in EU Competition Proceedings: Converging Towards Hazier Lines' (2018) 9 *Journal of European Competition Law and Practice* 459; Id., 'The Law on Fines Imposed in EU Competition Proceedings: Time for a Refresh of the Fining Guidelines?' (2017) 8 *Journal of European Competition Law and Practice* 409.

[70] *Contra* V. Bageri, Y. Katsoulacos and G. Spagnolo, The distortive effects of antitrust fines based on revenue (2013) 123 *Ec. Journal* F545.

[71] The applicants' request was recently rejected in T-827/14, *Deutsche Telekom*, ECLI:EU:T:2018:930; T-851/14, *Slovak Telekom*, ECLI:EU:T:2019:182.

[72] C-95/15 P, *H&R ChemPharm*, ECLI:EU:C:2017:125; T-540/08, *Esso* ECLI:EU:T:2014:630; Commission Decision 21 February 2018, AT.39920 – *Braking Systems*, paras 93-95.

concentrations or divestitures),[73] which may lessen the connection between the infringement's economic relevance and the last business year's sale.

A certain flexibility applies also with regard to the geographic dimension. The general rule is that all sales made within the European Economic Area (EEA) on the relevant geographic market affected by the infringement are taken into account. However, if the geographic scope of the infringement extends beyond the EEA, sales made within the EEA may no longer be the adequate proxy to determine the role of each undertaking. The exemplary case is that of worldwide market-sharing agreements where some of the cartelists refrain from selling within the EEA precisely to cartelize the market. Since the lack of sales within the EEA would prevent the possibility to set the sanction's basic amount, the Commission is allowed to follow a different approach: firstly, the total VoS affected by the global cartel on the worldwide market is set; secondly, the share of the sales of each undertaking on the worldwide market is determined; lastly, the share of each undertaking on the worldwide market is applied to the aggregate sales affected by the cartel within the EEA.[74]

Sales made within a specific area of the EEA can be considered for sanctioning purposes only if the Commission proves that the infringement actually affected such area.[75] By contrast, the Commission is not requested to prove that specific sales made within the area affected by the infringement were actually affected by the infringement.[76] A presumption of relevance applies: undertakings may rebut it by providing specific evidence demonstrating that some of the sales were performed at market conditions despite they occurred in an area covered by the infringement.[77] Therefore, two different standards of proof apply to the establishment of an antitrust infringement and to its sanctioning.[78]

As per the material aspects, the practice identified different categories of sales. The main distinction is between direct and indirect sales. Direct sales concern both the product affected by the infringement and any transformed product incorporat-

---

[73] T-471/13, *Xellia Pharmaceuticals*, ECLI:EU:T:2016:460.

[74] C-373/14 P, *Toshiba*, ECLI:EU:C:2016:26.

[75] Indeed, only sales falling – directly or indirectly – within the scope of the infringement shall be considered (C-444/11 P, *Team Relocations*, ECLI:EU:C:2013:464).

[76] C-263/16 P, *Schenker*, ECLI:EU:C:2018:58; C-264/16 P, *Deutsche Bahn*, ECLI:EU:C:2018:60; C-231/14 P, *InnoLux*, ECLI:EU:C:2015:451; T-104/13, *Toshiba*, ECLI:EU:T:2015:610; T-92/13, *Philips*, ECLI:EU:T:2015:605.

[77] The Commission must examine all the arguments submitted to rebut the presumption (*Schenker, supra* note 62).

[78] For example, the Commission is not requested to assess whether services covered by a non-compete agreement are in competition among them to establish a violation of Article 101 TFEU; however, this assessment is necessary to include their sales in the amount of the fine (T-216/13, *Telefònica*, ECLI:EU:T:2016:369; T-208/13, *Portugal Telecom*, ECLI:EU:T:2016:368).

ing the former, even if the infringers manufactured the final product outside the EEA. The opposite solution would harm the goals pursued by Article 23(2) of Regulation (EC) No 1/2003, reducing the effectiveness of Articles 101 and 102 TFEU.[79] Indirect sales are instead not relevant for sanctioning purposes.[80] This term refers to sales of transformed products sold within the EEA by innocent undertakings that purchased outside the EEA – and incorporated within their transformed products – a product affected by an antitrust infringement. In these cases, the connection between the infringers' conduct and the internal market is too weak to activate the Commission's enforcement powers.

The above are only the basic principles and of course several controversial issues remain unsettled. For example, some cases suggest that the notion of direct sales includes also internal sales, *i.e.* sales between legal entities of the same group;[81] although based on the principle of effectiveness, this assumption may conflict with the notion of undertaking, which will be discussed below.[82] Another peculiar case is that of undertakings that, although involved in an antitrust offence, do not operate on the market affected by the infringement:[83] the VoS affected by the violation is not an adequate proxy to assess the relevance of their role in the infringement, simply because there are no sales. To quantify their sanctions, the Commission is therefore allowed to follow different approaches and to choose parameters other than the VoS.[84]

Another much-debated issue concerns the different impact that sanctions – due to the methodology used to calculate them – have on mono-product and diversified undertakings. Indeed, the centrality of the VoS parameter entails that fines imposed on mono-product undertakings cannot but represent a higher proportion of their total turnover if compared to diversified undertakings. The ECJ not only rejected the conclusion that this difference could conflict with the principles of proportionality and equal treatment,[85] but also clarified that diversifying the regimes would be equivalent to grant mono-product undertakings an unfair competitive advantage *vis-à-vis* diversified undertaking.[86]

---

[79] *InnoLux*, *supra* note 76 para. 55.

[80] T-91/13, *LG Electronics*, ECLI:EU:T:2015:609.

[81] C-261/16 P, *Kühne*, ECLI:EU:C:2018:56; C-580/12 P, *Guardian Industries*, ECLI:EU:C:2014:2363.

[82] *Infra* Section 6. Internal sales should be reconciled with one of the implications of the single economic entity doctrine, according to which intra-group agreements cannot breach Article 101 TFEU because undertakings are free to organize themselves even if composed by several legal persons (C-73/95 P, *Viho Europe*, ECLI:EU:C:1996:405).

[83] This can include Hub&Spoke cartels or services provided by consulting firms to the parties of a cartel that facilitate its management.

[84] C-194/14 P, *AC-Treuhand*, ECLI:EU:C:2015:717.

[85] *H&R ChemPharm*, *supra* note 72.

[86] C-101/15 P, *Pilkington Group*, ECLI:EU:C:2016:631. The practice, however, suggests that the

Once the VoS is determined, the procedure to set the sanction's basic amount continues with the assessment of the infringement's gravity. This assessment is performed on a case-by-case basis: all the relevant circumstances are evaluated, such as the nature of the infringement, the infringers' combined market share, the infringement's geographic scope and the intensity of its management and implementation. As said, a percentage up to 30% of the VoS can be applied.[87] The Commission may – but is not obliged to[88] – take into account the actual impact of the infringement on the market to decide whether the value of the percentage should be set at the lower or at the higher end of the mentioned range.[89] Groups of undertakings to which different gravity percentages are applied can be created.[90] A so-called "entry-fee" can be applied to increase deterrence against the most serious antitrust infringements: the aim is to render unattractive for prospective infringers even the very first steps of collusive behaviours; the amount may vary between 15% and 25% of the VoS.

b) *The second phase: The fine-tuning of the basic amount*

As anticipated, during the second step of the procedure for the calculation of sanctions, the basic amount is adjusted through an overall assessment of the relevant circumstances, including aggravating and mitigating ones.[91] While aggravating circumstances (*e.g.*, refusal to cooperate with the Commission,[92] persisting with the infringement, recidivism or the undertaking's leading role)[93] may cause an increase of the sanction up to 100% of the basic amount, the percentage of the reduction for mitigating circumstances (*e.g.*, cooperation,[94] or negligence rather than intent)[95] is

---

Commission could be keen to evaluate whether such high proportion could be qualified as a peculiarity of the case allowing to depart from the Guidelines pursuant to their para 37. On this topic, see also T-95/15, *Printeos*, ECLI:EU:T:2016:722 and T-466/17, *Printeos*, ECLI: EU:T:2019:671.

[87] 2006 Guidelines paras 19-26. For example, "in the case of secret horizontal price-fixing and market-sharing agreements [...] the rate should, at the very least, be above 15%" (T-451/14, *Fujikura*, ECLI:EU:T:2018:452, para. 144).

[88] T-406/09, *Donau Chemie*, ECLI:EU:T:2014:254 para. 71.

[89] *Orange Polska*, *supra* note 60. Recent case-law, however, seems to suggest that the limited potential effect on competition of the infringement "forms part of those circumstances that the Commission is required to take account of in the assessment of mitigating circumstances [...] and not in the assessment of the gravity of the infringement itself" (T-447/14, *NKT Verwaltungs*, ECLI:EU:T:2018:443, para. 303).

[90] T-413/10 and T-414/10, *Socitrel*, ECLI:EU:T:2015:500

[91] 2006 Guidelines paras 27 ff.

[92] This includes the supply of misleading information to the Commission (T-66/99, *Minoan Lines*, ECLI:EU:T:2003:337).

[93] T-146/09 RENV, *Parker-Hannifin*, ECLI:EU:T:2016:411.

[94] To be eligible as a mitigating circumstance, cooperation shall occur outside the leniency

not specified. It is not clear whether the limited involvement in the infringement does constitute a mitigating circumstance.[96]

The Commission actually enjoys a broad margin of discretion not only with regard to the amount of the reduction but also on the reduction as such. Submitting evidence supporting the existence of one of the mitigating circumstances listed by paragraph 29 of the Fining Guidelines does not secure a reduction; even if the undertaking meets the burden of proving the presence of one of those circumstances, the Commission is still free to assess the appropriateness of the request on the basis of all relevant circumstances.[97]

Deterrence plays a significant role also in this phase. The Commission shall not reduce sanctions if the reduction could hamper their deterrent effect and undermine the effectiveness of competition rules.[98] Moreover, sanctions can be increased,[99] *inter alia*, if imposed on undertakings having particularly large turnovers or to exceed the profit made or the harm caused by the infringers.[100] Reference to these concepts reflects the mentioned distinction between the deterrence and the internalisation approach.

c) *The third phase: The application of the turnover cap*

The last phase of the procedure for the calculation of sanctions is the easiest to describe. Pursuant to Article 23(2) of Regulation (EC) No 1/2003, antitrust sanctions cannot exceed 10% of the total global turnover of the undertaking in the previous business year.

---

programme (*EGL, supra* note 62). Proposing commitments is not a mitigating circumstance (Commission decision of 27 June 2017, COMP/AT.39740 – *Google Search (Shopping)*).

[95] Cf. Section 6.

[96] Reductions between 5% and 10% have been granted to cartelists due to their passive role or limited involvement in the infringement (Commission Decisions of 16 June 2017, COMP/AT.39780 – *Envelopes*; 17 March 2017, COMP/AT.39258 – *Airfreight*; 8 February 2017, COMP/AT.40018 – *Car battery recycling*). However, since said circumstances – which were qualified as mitigating circumstances by the 1998 Guidelines (*supra* note 3) – are no longer listed within the 2006 Guidelines (*supra* note 3), recent cases suggest that the passive role or limited involvement in the infringement no longer represent a mitigating circumstance (T-450/14, *Sumitomo Electric*, ECLI:EU:T:2018:455; T-448/14, *Hitachi Metals*, ECLI:EU:T:2018:442).

[97] T-472/13, *Lundbeck*, ECLI:EU:T:2016:449 para 841; C-447/11, *Caffaro*, EU:C:2013:797, para 103.

[98] *Toshiba, supra* note76

[99] The Commission shall make the undertakings aware of its intention to increase sanctions for deterrence purposes (T-404/12 *Toshiba*, ECLI:EU:T:2016:18).

[100] The ECJ confirmed that the harm caused and the profit made by the infringers are both relevant to quantify sanctions and should be evaluated to assess the gravity of the infringement or the existence of mitigating or aggravating circumstances (T-270/12, *Panalpina*, ECLI:EU:T:2016:109).

As mentioned, the turnover cap is actually the only certain element of the sanctioning process: except for it, undertakings can hardly anticipate the level of sanctions that they risk if breaching competition rules. The turnover cap, however, conceals one of the most debated issues concerning the Commission's fining policy, namely the regime of corporate group liability, which will be discussed below.

12.6. The limited role played by intent and imputability in the antitrust realm

From a theoretical viewpoint, intent and imputability are two of the most controversial concepts related to Commission's and NCAs' sanctioning powers. As mentioned, the ECN+ Directive has recently requested NCAs to follow the same approach to these notions developed at the EU level. [101]

EU competition rules do not mention intention as a necessary element to ascertain antitrust infringements. [102] The case law contains virtually no reference to the role of intent for the application of Articles 101 and – particularly – 102 TFEU. [103] By affirming that "*the intention of the parties is not an essential factor in determining whether a concerted practice is restrictive*" [104] nor "*a necessary factor in determining whether an agreement is restrictive*" [105], the ECJ essentially confirmed that a quasi-strict liability regime applies to antitrust offences. [106]

After all, competition is not about morality but about efficiency and the market structure's preservation: just as dreaming about monopolies is not a competitive issue but rather fuels economic growth, [107] so a collusive scenario achieved without the undertakings having planned it represents a competitive problem. [108]

---

[101] Cf. section 3.

[102] P. Akman, 'The Role of Intent in the EU Case Law on Abuse of Dominance' (2014) 39 *European Law Review* 316; M.E. Stucke, 'Is Intent Relevant?' (2012) 8 *Journal of Law, Economics and Policy* 801; P.L. Parcu, 'Considerazioni sulla rilevanza del movente nella valutazione delle violazioni antitrust', in A. Raffaelli (ed.), *Antitrust Between EU and National Law IX* (Bruylant, 2011) 289; A. Bavasso, 'The Role of Intent under Article 82: From Fishing the Turkeys to Spotting Lioness in Regent's Park' (2005) 26 *European Competition Law Review* 616.

[103] S. Bastianon, *Il risarcimento del danno antitrust tra esigenze di giustizia e problemi di efficienza. Prime riflessioni sul Libro verde della Commissione* (2006) 8 *Mercato, Concorrenza e Regole* 321, 336.

[104] C-8/08, *T-Mobile Netherlands*, ECLI:EU:C:2009:343, para. 27.

[105] C-32/11, *Allianz Hungària*, ECLI:EU:C:2013:160, para. 37.

[106] M. Hazelhorst, 'Private Enforcement of EU Competition Law: Why Punitive Damages Are a Step Too Far' (2010) 18 *European Review of Private Law* 757, 763.

[107] P.L. Parcu, M.L. Stasi, 'The Role of Intent in the Assessment of Conduct under Article 102 TFEU', in P.L. Parcu, G. Monti, M. Botta (eds), *Abuse of Dominance in EU Competition Law* (Edward Elgar, 2017) 12.

[108] The limited role of intent in competition cases may be relevant also to ascribe to undertak-

While intent is not a constitutive element of antitrust offences, it may be relevant to impose and quantify sanctions. According to Article 23 of Regulation (EC) No 1/2003 and Article 13 of the ECN+ Directive, sanctions can be imposed "*on undertakings* [...] *where, either intentionally or negligently they infringe*" competition rules. Once again, therefore, divergent standards of proof apply to the establishment and the sanctioning of antitrust offences.

Actual perception of being breaching competition rules is not requested [109] and the condition is satisfied if infringers could not be unaware of the practice's anticompetitive nature. The degree of foreseeability of the practice's anticompetitive nature should be assessed to quantify the sanction and, particularly, to reduce it as a mitigating circumstance. [110] While the need to receive legal advice to evaluate the anticompetitive risks of a given conduct cannot exclude the foreseeability of its anticompetitive nature, [111] the case law suggests that the novelty of the infringement or the uncertain anticompetitive nature of the conduct may lead to significant reductions of the sanction. [112]

From a different viewpoint, the limited relevance of intent is also connected to the fact that parent companies are jointly and severally liable for antitrust infringements committed by their subsidiaries. The legal regime for corporate group liability is grounded in the concept of "undertaking", [113] in turn rooted in the single economic entity doctrine. [114] Although undertakings are the addresses of Articles 101 and 102 TFEU, the concept is not defined in the Treaties or in secondary legislation. According to the case law, the term should reflect the economic reality rather than the legal one. [115] Separate legal persons are a single "undertaking" for the purposes of competition law if they are connected from an economic and managerial perspective. [116]

---

ings the decisions autonomously taken by algorithms (L. Calzolari, 'La collusione fra algoritmi nell'era dei big data: l'imputabilità alle imprese delle "intese 4.0" ai sensi dell'art. 101 TFUE' (2018) *Medialaw* 219).

[109] C-681/11, *Schenker*, ECLI:EU:C:2013:404.

[110] T-460/13, *Sun Pharmaceutical*, ECLI:EU:T:2016:453.

[111] T-470/13, *Merck*, ECLI:EU:T:2016:452.

[112] C-62/86, *AKZO Chemie*, ECLI:EU:C:1991:286 with regard to an abuse of a dominant position as a result of the application of "predatory prices".

[113] See A. Jones, 'The Boundaries of an Undertaking in EU Competition Law' (2012) 8 *Eur. Comp.J* 301; O. Odudu, 'The Meaning of Undertaking within Article 101' (2005) 7 *CYELS* 209; W.P.J. Wils, 'The Undertakings as Subject of E.C. Competition Law and the Imputation of Infringements to Natural or Legal Person' (2000) 25 *European Law Review* 99.

[114] O. Odudu and D. Bailey, 'The Single Economic Entity Doctrine in EU Competition Law' (2014) 51 *Common Market Law Review* 1721.

[115] 170/83, *Mario Andreoli*, ECLI:EU:C:1984:271, para. 11.

[116] The "authors of the Treaties chose to use the concept of an 'undertaking' to designate the

If they do not determine their own conducts on the market, subsidiaries surely form a single economic entity with the holding company. Just as a company is the only entity liable for antitrust offences committed by each of its departments, so too an "undertaking" is the only entity liable for the infringements committed by each of the legal persons by which it is composed. However, corporate group liability is controversial mainly because the Commission can hold parent companies liable even without proving that they were aware of – let alone involved in – the infringement planned or committed by their subsidiaries. Especially if parent companies hold nearly the entire capital of their subsidiaries,[117] an almost irrebuttable presumption that they influence their subsidiaries applies.[118] In theory, parent companies may rebut the presumption by submitting evidence that the subsidiaries act autonomously of, and receive no instructions from, the parent companies. Such requirement of proof, however, amounts to a so-called *probatio diabolica*: demonstrating the independence of a subsidiary means refuting an abstract possibility, direct evidence of its autonomy on the market being impossible to submit.[119]

Unsurprisingly, there are virtually no cases where parent companies succeeded in arguing that they did not influence a wholly owned subsidiary.[120] The liability of purely financial investors (such as private equity firms) under the presumption at stake exemplarily demonstrates the rigidity of the approach.[121] Indeed, even the fact that the only economic activity performed by a company was that of acquiring distressed companies to restructure and sell them out has been considered by the ECJ as a circumstance supporting – rather than denying – the exercise of decisive influence over the target by the acquiring company.[122] The very same approach is applied also when subsidiaries disregard the explicit instructions received by their parent companies "*not to participate in any anticompetitive practices in a given market*".[123]

Although controversial, the regime of corporate group liability has been devised to prevent undertakings from escaping antitrust liability by setting up subsidiaries

---

perpetrator of an infringement of competition law [...] and not other concepts such as that of 'companies or firms' or 'legal persons', used in particular in Article [54 TFEU]" (C-231/11 P to C-233/11 P, *Siemens AG*, ECLI:EU:C:2014:256, para. 41).

[117] T-299/08, *Elf-Aquitaine*, ECLI:EU:T:2011:217; C-508/11 P, *Eni*, ECLI:EU:C:2013:289.

[118] C- 97/08 P, *Akzo-Nobel*, ECLI:EU:C:2009:536 para. 60.

[119] This critics, however, has been dismissed by the case-law (T-168/05, *Arkema*, ECLI:EU: T:2009:367 para. 82).

[120] One of the few exceptions is T-24/05, *Alliance One International*, ECLI:EU:T:2010:453.

[121] Commission Decision of 2 April 2014, AT.39610 – *Power Cables*.

[122] T-395/09, *Gigaset*, ECLI:EU:T:2014:23.

[123] Indeed, "the existence of an express instruction [...] not to participate in any anticompetitive practices [...] can be a strong indication of the actual exercise of decisive influence by the parent over the subsidiary" (C-155/14 P, *Evonik Degussa*, ECLI:EU: C:2016:446 para. 40).

to which they "assign the task" to breach competition rules in the interest of the group.[124] With regard to sanctions, moreover, the Commission's ability of recovering is enhanced: parent companies are liable even if the subsidiary becomes insolvent or is liquidated.[125] The Commission is also able to impose higher sanctions increasing the deterrent effect of Articles 101 and 102 TFEU: the 10% turnover cap is applied to the overall turnover of the group rather than to the lower turnover of the single subsidiary.[126]

The single economic entity doctrine has many other implications.[127] For example, the risk of incurring in the aggravating circumstance of – indirect – recidivism significantly increases. Since antitrust infringements committed by any entity of the group are ascribed to the parent company, the latter qualifies as a repeat offender even if the relevant offences were committed solely by two (or more) of its subsidiaries and no finding of infringement was made against the holding.[128]

Strictly related to such theory is also the possibility to apply EU competition law extraterritorially[129] and fine foreign companies if they breach Articles 101 and 102 TFEU. Even when parent companies are based abroad, the fact that a subsidiary is established in a Member State is enough for the Commission to assert its jurisdiction and to sanction the foreign holdings.[130]

---

[124] This can include the task to manage the whole group's sales with the aim that the subsidiary enters into a cartel with the parent company's competitors.

[125] The ECJ recently extended the scope of application of this principle to private enforcement, clarifying that damages can be claimed against successors of undertakings (C-724/17, *Skanska*, ECLI:EU:C:2019:204).

[126] Such possibility has been only partially limited by the recent case law of the ECJ, according to which "where the liability of a parent company is purely derivative of that of its subsidiary and in which no other factor individually reflects the conduct for which the parent company is held liable, the liability of that parent company cannot exceed that of its subsidiary" (C-597/13 P, *Total*, ECLI:EU:C:2015:613, para 38; C-286/11 P, *Tomkins*, ECLI:EU:C:2013:29 para. 43).

[127] *E.g.*, since joint liability applies to undertakings, the Commission cannot determine the internal division of the sanction between the legal entities composing the undertaking (C-625/13 P, *Villeroy & Boch*, ECLI:EU:C:2017:52; C- 247/11 P and C-253/11 P, *Areva*, ECLI:EU:C:2014:257).

[128] C-93/13 P and C-123/13 P, *Versalis*, ECLI:EU:C:2015:150.

[129] 48/69, *Imperial Chemical*, ECLI:EU:C:1972:70.

[130] F. Munari, 'Sui limiti internazionali all'applicazione extraterritoriale del diritto europeo della concorrenza' (2016) *RDI* 32; L. Calzolari, M.G. Buonanno, 'The Relations between the European Union and the Swiss Confederation in the Antitrust Field: between Extraterritoriality and the Recent Agreement Concerning Cooperation on the Application of their Competition Laws', in V. Salvatore (ed.), *The Free Movement of Persons between Switzerland and the European Union* (Giappichelli, 2016) 55; J. Scott, 'The New EU "Extraterritoriality"' (2014) 51 *Common Market Law Review* 1343; M.M. Dabbah, *International and Comparative Competition Law* (Cambridge University Press, 2010); E. Elhauge and D. Geradin, *Global antitrust law and economics* (Foundation Press, 2007).

12.7. Negotiated remedies *vis-à-vis* individual sanctions: diverging trends?

As discussed above, the main instrument of enforcement of EU competition law has always been public enforcement. Fines imposed by the Commission have therefore represented the most important instrument to ensure the deterrent effect of Articles 101 and 102 TFEU and to punish wrongdoers. Following the modernization process, Commission's sanctions have been coupled with those of the NCAs.

By way of conclusion, it is worth noting that recent developments seem to challenge the centrality of public sanctions in the context of the antitrust enforcement system. For example, private enforcement is likely to increase thanks to Directive No 2014/104/EU. Civil damages will therefore reinforce their role *vis-à-vis* public fines. While it also serves deterrence purposes by increasing the expected costs of antitrust offences, private enforcement is however mainly aimed at compensating those who suffered from such offences.[131] Private enforcement is therefore more closely related to corrective justice purposes than to the aim of deterring antitrust offences and punishing wrongdoers. Subject to limited and well-known exceptions,[132] no conflicts may arise between public and private enforcement since the two pillars complement and reinforce each other in pursuing their specific goals: the more decisions are issued by the Commission, the more follow-on actions are brought, ensuring the effectiveness of the right to damages; in turn, more damages actions means higher costs for prospective infringers, increasing the deterrent effect of competition rules.

Other developments have occurred within the sphere of public enforcement. For example, new kinds of remedies not focused on imposing sanctions have been established, *i.e.* commitment and settlement decisions. If undertakings submit commitments that meet the Commission's or NCAs' competitive concerns, the latter can make such commitments binding for the proposing undertakings.[133] While

---

[131] R. Pardolesi, 'Complementarietà irrisolte: presidio (pubblico) del mercato e azioni (private) di danno' (2011) 13 *Mercato, Concorrenza e Regole* 463.

[132] Conflicts almost exclusively arise on access to leniency documents: the latter would help prospective claimants to prove their case in civil proceedings but at the same time their disclosure would hamper the attractiveness of leniency programs (*i.e.* the Commission's most effective investigative tool against secret cartel); indeed, the cartelists' incentives to reveal the cartel are reduced if cooperation may lead to damages actions. Here, a balance between the protection of public enforcement and the need to ensure the effectiveness of private enforcement shall be struck (C-360/09, *Pfleiderer*, ECLI:EU:C:2011:389; C-536/11, *Donau Chemie*, ECLI:EU:C:2013:366).

[133] Article 9 Regulation (EC) No 1/2003; Article 12 ECN+ Directive. *Inter alia*, N. Dunne, 'Commitment decisions in EU competition law' (2014) 10 *Journal of Competition Law and Economics* 399; A. Giannaccari and C. Landi, 'Antitrust? Grazie, abbiamo altri impegni!' (2012) 14 *Mercato, Concorrenza e Regole* 231; J. Temple Lang, 'Commitment decisions under Regulation 1/2003: legal aspects of a new kind of competition decision' (2003) 24 *European Competition Law Review* 347.

they close the proceeding establishing that there are no longer grounds for action, commitment decisions do not ascertain the infringement, let alone impose a sanction. Although for this reason this remedy is declared inappropriate when the Commission intends to impose a fine,[134] commitments are actually much diffused within the Commission's practice[135] and have been adopted also in respect of conducts that, if proved, would have represented serious antitrust offences.[136]

Introduced by Regulation (EC) No 622/2008,[137] cartel settlements aim at increasing the effectiveness of Article 101 TFEU. By simplifying procedures and reducing the number of appeals,[138] they attempt to increase the number of cases handled by the Commission with the same resources. Unlike leniency programs, cartel settlements are not an investigative instrument but an alternative to the ordinary adversarial procedure.[139] Undertakings are not requested to confess their participation in an unknown cartel: rather, when it already holds incriminating evidence, the Commission may grant a 10% reduction on the sanction otherwise applicable under the standard procedure if undertakings admit their participation in the cartel and waive some of their procedural rights. Settlements are largely diffused too[140] and also their scope of application has been interpreted extensively.[141]

---

[134] Recital 13 Regulation (EC) No 1/2003; Recital 39 ECN+ Directive apparently offers a wider leeway since it mentions "secret cartels" as the only offence toward which "[i]n principle [...] commitment decisions are not appropriate".

[135] Apart from cartels, around 60% of the decisions issued since the adoption of Regulation (EC) No 1/2003 are based commitments proposed by undertakings (http://ec.europa.eu/competition/elojade/isef/index.cfm?clear=1&policy_area_id=1).

[136] Commission Decisions 7 July 2016, AT.39850 – *Container Shipping*; 12 December 2012, COMP/39.847 – *E-books*).

[137] Commission Regulation (EC) No 622/2008 of 30 June 2008 amending Regulation (EC) No 773/2004, as regards the conduct of settlement procedures in cartel cases, OJ 2008, L 171/3; see also Commission Notice on the conduct of settlement procedures in view of the adoption of Decisions pursuant to Article 7 and Article 23 of Council Regulation (EC) No 1/2003 in cartel cases, OJ 2008, C 167/1. *Inter alia* F. Laina and E. Laurinen, 'The EU Cartel Settlement Procedure: Current Status and Challenges' (2013) 4 *Journal of European Competition Law and Practice* 302; A. Ortega Gonzalez, 'The Cartel Settlement Procedure in Practice' (2011) 32 *European Competition Law Review* 170.

[138] T-456/10, *Timab*, ECLI:EU:T:2015:296, para. 60, but see *infra* note 145.

[139] *Timab*, *supra* note 59, para. 136.

[140] From the analysis of all the decisions published on the Commission's website it emerges that settlements account for around the 60% of Commission's decisions adopted in cartel cases since 2010.

[141] Using para 37 of the 2006 Guidelines (*supra* note 3) as legal basis, the Commission "settled" firstly an Article 102 TFEU case, granting a 30% reduction of the fine because the undertaking admitted the infringement (Commission Decision 20 September 2016, AT.39759 – *ARA Foreclosure*) and, then, five non-cartel cases concerning vertical restraints, granting reductions ranging from 40% to 50% (Commission Decisions of 24 July 2018, AT.40465 – *Asus*; AT. 40469

Commitments and settlements are based on negotiations between undertakings and the Commission (or the competent NCA) and reduce the expected costs of antitrust infringements. Their diffusion causes a shift from traditional adversarial competition law enforcement [142] and undertakings may have the impression that they can get away with antitrust offences without serious consequence, simply by negotiating their way out.

Unless procedural savings increase the detection of (other) antitrust offences at a rate that compensates for the reduction of expected costs, commitments and settlements may affect the deterrent effect of competition rules. The reduction of expected costs arises because both public sanctions and civil damages are absent or at least decreased. The lack of public sanctions is adamant with regard to commitments; however, also the settlement's practice suggests that the reduction could sometimes exceed the 10% figure. Although the Commission always applies such legal limit, it seems keen to assess the circumstances of the case more benevolently than in ordinary procedures, probably to convince hesitant undertakings. For example, settlements are characterized by a more favourable approach to mitigating and aggravating circumstances than ordinary decisions. [143]

Moreover, during settlement talks undertakings can informally discuss with the Commission all the aspects of the case. Although not altering the quantification of the final sanction, informal negotiations may affect follow-on actions, further reducing expected costs. For example, undertakings may be keener to accept settlements imposing a higher entry-fee but referring to a smaller geographic market: in this way, the likelihood of damages actions from prospective claimants of the "excluded area" is reduced. Since the market definition is not subject to judicial review, [144] the Commission may use the above as a bargaining chip.

– *Denon & Marantz*; AT. 40181 – *Philips*; AT. 40182 – *Pioneer*; and Commission Decision 17 December 2018, AT.40428 – *Guess*).

[142] Indeed, one of the most significant characteristics of commitment decision is that they are proactive in nature: also due to a peculiar interpretation of the proportionality principle (C-441/07 P, *Alrosa*, ECLI:EU:C:2010:377) they aim at shaping the (future) market structure rather than punishing past behaviours.

[143] A.L. Hinds, 'All settled? Some six years of cartel settlement' (2014) 35 *European Competition Law Review* 292. Aggravating circumstances have been applied only in one settlement decision (Commission Decision 27 January 2016, AT.40028 – *Alternators and starters*, para. 107-108). By contrast, mitigating circumstance are often applied (*inter alia* Commission Decisions of 19 May 2010, COMP/38.511 – *DRAMs*, paras 109-110; 19 October 2011, COMP/39.605 – *CRT Glass*, paras 89-91; 7 December 2011, COMP/39.600 – *Refrigeration compressors*, paras 83-85; 4 December 2013, AT.39.861 – *Yen Interest Rate Derivatives*; 19 March 2014, AT.39922 – *Bearings* paras 94-95).

[144] In principle undertakings have no incentive to challenge settlement and commitment decisions, having agreed on their content – but see *Timab*, *supra* note 59 and *Printeos*, *supra* note 86. With regard to settlements, however, the envisaged reduction of the appeals could be seriously hindered by the case law (based on a much questionable interpretation of the principle of *res iudi-*

While the prejudice to private enforcement is obviously even stronger with regard to commitment decisions (since no infringement is ascertained), [145] what matters here is that the diffusion of negotiated remedies (and the consequent feeling that antitrust infringements entail less and less frequently the imposition of a public sanction) is somehow at odd with another development of competition law, namely the increasing interest for the "criminalization" of the most serious antitrust offences, such as hard-core cartels. [146]

If under EU law only undertakings can be fined for antitrust offences, in some Member States also individuals (*e.g.* directors and managers) can be subject to criminal and administrative sanctions in relation to their personal involvement in antitrust infringements. A few Member – and former Member – States adopted specific rules to "criminalize" competition law creating antirust criminal offences. [147] Other Member States introduced criminal sanctions for procedural offences in antitrust procedures. [148] In yet other Member States, [149] involvement of individuals in anticompetitive behaviours may be covered by wider criminal provisions, unrelated to competition law: for example, cartel behaviours can be qualified as fraud or bid rigging.

Putting aside the fact that the antitrust realm is *per se* unfit for criminal law, [150] the criminalisation of competition law would entail a significant shift from a system where public fines (explicitly qualified as administrative in nature) [151] are imposed

---

cata) according to which cartel decisions become final *vis-à-vis* the undertakings that do not challenge them even if fellow cartelists obtain their annulment (*e.g.* T-185/18, *Lucchini SpA*, ECLI:EU:T:2019:298). At the national level, a similar (and unconvincing) approach has been applied even in a case where the NCA's decision (not challenged by one of the leniency applicants) has been annulled because the competent court established that the concerned undertakings did not enter in a cartel agreement (cf. TAR Lazio 29 March 2017 n. 4010).

[145] Follow-on actions are nevertheless allowed (C-547/16, *Gasorba*, ECLI:EU:C:2017:891).

[146] W.P.J. Wils, 'Is Criminalization of EU Competition Law the Answer?' (2005) 28 *World Competition* 117.

[147] Individuals involved in cartels can be criminally prosecuted in Ireland, Denmark, France, Sweden and the UK. For further references see J. Keith and H. Farin, 'Criminal Sanctions: An overview of EU and national case law' (2015) *E-Competitions* No 64713.

[148] The improper use of information obtained in antitrust investigations is criminally sanctioned in Belgium and failure to pay antitrust fines is a criminal offence for the undertakings' directors in Malta.

[149] The list includes Italy, Germany, Austria and Hungary.

[150] Outside the area of cartels, the economic notions and generally worded standards of Articles 101 and 102 TFEU are hard to reconcile with the principle of legal certainty.

[151] A middle ground solution would be to subject not only individuals but also undertakings to criminal liability in case of violation of Articles 101 and 102 TFEU. As said, however, the administrative nature of competition sanctions has been recently reaffirmed by Article 13 of the ECN+ Directive. At least at the EU level, therefore, the introduction of criminal liability of legal persons for antitrust offences seems rather unlikely. By contrast, at the national level, conducts capable of trig-

only on undertakings to a legal regime where individuals can be directly sanctioned, imprisoned and even extradited [152] if they breach competition rules.

The two trends seem to have quite opposite effects on the enforcement system: the decreasing attention paid to sanctioning undertakings showed by the negotiability of antitrust offences' consequences is coupled with an increasing focus (so far only at the national level) on the punishment of the natural persons involved in antitrust infringements, by the call for the introduction of criminal or other sanctions (such as disqualification) [153] against individuals.

---

gering the application of Article 101 TFEU (or similar domestic provisions on the prohibition of collusive behaviours) may already fall within the scope of application of criminal dispositions (such as those on bid rigging) which in some Member States may be addressed also to legal persons.

[152] G. De Stefano, 'Meet the First Extradited Businessman on Cartel Charges' (2017) 8 *Journal of European Competition Law and Practice* 251.

[153] A. Khan 'Rethinking Sanctions for Breaching EU Competition Law: Is Director Disqualification the Answer?' (2012) 35 *World Competition* 77.

Chapter 13

PROTECTING THE ENVIRONMENT THROUGH UNION SANCTIONS: THE MANY FACETS OF THE ENFORCEMENT OF EU ENVIRONMENTAL LAW

Francesco Munari *

ABSTRACT: *This Chapter looks at the use of sanctioning powers within the EU Common Environmental Policy. The analysis shows that the EU stands out when it comes to enforcing environmental rules, when compared with the Member States and other international organisations. The Chapter initially examines the legal tools available to EU institutions, particularly the Commission and the Court of Justice, to ensure that Member States comply with EU environmental law. Thereafter, the analysis considers the EU's capacity to ensure that individuals comply with environmental law. Finally, the Chapter specifically focuses on the so-called Environmental Crimes Directive (ECD), the potential of which is still to be fully tested. In particular, it is argued that the powers entrusted to Member States to impose sanctions under their domestic legislation may not provide results that satisfy the ultimate rationale of the ECD, i.e. harmonisation.*

KEYWORDS: *EU environmental law – enforcement of EU environmental law – sanctions – enforcement on Member States – enfoircement on individuals*

---

* Full Professor of EU Law, University of Genoa.

13.1. Introduction

For many years I have argued that there is unacceptable inconsistency between the continuous global proclamations advocating the absolute need to enhance the protection and promotion of our planet [1] and the adequacy of environmental rules, as well as, more importantly, the remarkable carelessness shown in implementing and enforcing them at all levels. [2]

It is also my belief that, in this situation, the European Union stands as an exception. Over the decades, it has been able to adopt and, in particular, apply environmental rules and standards more effectively than any other State or international organisation. The EU environmental policy and law have thus been capable, in general, not only of limiting environmental degradation, but also of improving the quality of our environment. However, some areas are still lagging behind, such as that of greenhouse gas (GHG) emissions originating from the transport industry. [3]

It is therefore a fortunate opportunity to deal with sanctions and enforcement of EU law in the field of environmental policy: much can be written about the subject matter but, unsurprisingly, some grey areas are worthy of greater attention by stakeholders, including EU institutions, the bodies of the single Member States, and individuals, who are at the very core of any efficient environmental policy. Moreover, it can be said that the specific solutions adopted for the environment may well be useful in other areas of law.

This chapter will therefore be structured as follows: after providing some introductory information on the legal framework that characterises EU environmental law and policy, I will provide some data to highlight the level of enforcement of EU environmental law. The nature of the EU as a privileged institution in enforcing environmental rules and standards will then be documented; thereafter, I will pinpoint the advantages of the EU system, in which compliance with these rules and standards is secured, directly or indirectly (i.e. via the Member States), through penalties: in particular, in the first part of my analysis, I will consider the legal tools available to EU institutions, particularly the Commission and the Court of Justice (CJEU) [4], for guar-

---

[1] See, as a recent example, the IPCC Special Report, *Climate Change and Land*, released on 8 August 2019 and available at https://www.ipcc.ch/report/srccl/.

[2] F. Munari, L. Schiano di Pepe, *Tutela transnazionale dell'ambiente. Principi, regole, problemi* (Il Mulino, 2012) 1.

[3] The goals of the European Commission to achieve a reduction of emissions in the transport sector (see *A European strategy for low-emission mobility* at https://ec.europa.eu/clima/policies/transport_en) have not yet been achieved, and unless much bolder measures are adopted, they might not be achieved in the coming years (see the report by Research4Committees, *The Paris Agreement and the EU Transport Policy*, at https://research4committees.blog/2018/03/20/the-paris-agreement-and-the-eu-transport-policy/).

[4] On the role of the CJEU in the subject matter, see, inter alia, F. Jacobs, 'The Role of the Eu-

anteeing compliance with EU environmental law by the Member States. Powerful tools such as infringement procedures, sanctions and enforcement strategies will be investigated, along with the possibility of adopting interim measures and enforcing EU environmental law in specific cases upon single Member States.

The second part of the chapter looks at the capacity of the EU to guarantee that individuals comply with environmental law: this part will focus on legislative acts such as Directive 2004/35/EC on environmental liability,[5] as well as on the general obligation established by EU law for Member States to adopt 'effective, proportionate and dissuasive' penalties in their legislation with a view to securing compliance with EU rules and standards. Finally, the analysis focuses on Directive 2008/99/EC,[6] also known as the Environmental Crimes Directive (ECD), the potential of which is still to be fully tested: indeed, the powers entrusted to Member States to impose sanctions under their domestic legislation may not provide results that satisfy the ultimate rationale of the ECD, i.e. harmonisation.

13.2. The EU environmental policy and rules as crafted at primary law level: converging principles to secure compliance

The possibility for the EU legal regime to implement rigorously its environmental rules stems from some cornerstone principles purposely inserted at primary law level, particularly in the TFEU.

Firstly, a striking (and unique) feature of the EU normative framework of relevance for our purposes is the principle of integration: according to article 37 of the Charter of Fundamental Rights of the European Union,

> A high level of environmental protection and the improvement of the quality of the environment must be integrated into the policies of the Union and ensured in accordance with the principle of sustainable development.[7]

This principle is the key to understanding that environmental protection and

---

ropean Court of Justice in the Protection of the Environment' (2006) 18 *Journal of Environmental Law* 185; I.J. Koppen, 'The Role of the European Court of Justice', in A. Jordan (ed.), *Environmental Policy in the European Union. Actors, Institutions, and Processes* (Earthscan, 2002) 100.

[5] OJ 2004, L 143/56; a consolidated version of the directive was published on 26 June 2019.

[6] OJ 2008, L 328/28.

[7] This provision was modelled on the principle of integration which has been embodied in the Treaty of Rome for decades and is currently contained in article 11 TFEU. On this provision, see, generally, M. Onida, 'Art. 37 Tutela dell'ambiente', in R. Mastroianni, O. Pollicino, S. Allegrezza, F. Pappalardo and O. Razzolini (eds.) *Carta dei Diritti Fondamentali dell'Unione Europea* (Giuffrè, 2017) 692; G. Marin-Duran, E. Morgera, 'Commentary on Article 37 of the EU Charter of Fundamental Rights – Environmental Protection', in S. Peers, T. Hervey, J. Kenner, A. Ward (eds.), The EU Charter of Fundamental Rights. A Commentary (Hart, 2014).

promotion can only be achieved by taking a holistic approach that encompasses all areas of law. As such, it seems remarkably intuitive of the EU primary legislator[8]: it not only avoids environmental policies being considered as recessive with regard to the other policies and priorities of the Union,[9] but it also, and more importantly, serves as a guide for interpreting all EU policies coherently with environmental protection. The emblematic example of the importance of this intuition now consists of the Paris Climate Agreement, which requires an overall re-assessment of all human activities in order to achieve its goals and, therefore, a substantial reform of the legal framework under which these activities may (legitimately) be continued.

Another important feature of EU environmental legal principles has been set out for some time by CJEU case-law, advocating a broad definition of 'environment' under EU law. This notion includes the environment in the strictest sense of human health, as well as the exploitation of natural resources.[10] The relevance of this approach is self-explanatory, as it permits the EU to implement its environmental policy very broadly, allowing it to use extensively the shared competences enjoyed by it in this area of law. In fact, as we will see below, the EU is a more powerful 'authority' than the Member States in enforcing environmental law and applying sanctions for infringements of its provisions; this leads to a further upside in terms of the effectiveness of EU law in our subject matter. Once again,

---

[8] See B. Sjåfjell, 'The environmental integration principle: a necessary step towards policy coherence for sustainability', in F. Ippolito, M.E. Bartoloni, M. Condinanzi (eds.), *EU and the Proliferation of Integration Principles under the Lisbon Treaty*, (Routledge, 2019); J.H. Jans, 'Stop the Integration Principle?' (2011) 33 *Fordham Int'l L.J.* 1533.

[9] By contrast, this is precisely what has always happened in a similar pattern of transnational economic integration, namely the WTO system, in which any measure adopted by a contracting party to protect the environment has all too often been viewed as a sort of 'green protectionism', when protectionism was certainly not the rationale behind environmental measures aimed at restricting trade that is unsustainable from an environmental perspective. On this topic, the literature is vast: see, amongst others, and for further insights, M.W. Gehering, 'Legal Transitions to the green economy' (2016) 12 *McGill Int'l J. Sust. Dev. L. & Pol'y* 135; T.W. Dagne, 'The Debate on Environmentally Motivated Unilateral Trade Measures in the World Trade Organization: The Way Forward' (2010) 9 *Wash. U. Global Stud. L. Rev.* 427; E. Vranes, *Trade and the Environment. Fundamental Issues in International Law, WTO Law, and Legal Theory* (OUP, 2009); S. Charnovitz, 'The WTO's environmental progress' (2007) 10 *Journal of International Economic Law* 685; A. Goyal, *The WTO and International Environmental Law* (OUP, 2006); O. Perez, *Ecological Sensitivity and Global Legal Pluralism: Rethinking the Trade and Environment Debate* (Hart, 2004); E. Neumayer, *Greening Trade and Investment: Environmental Protection Without Protectionism* (Earthscan, 2001); D. Tsogtbaatar, 'Trading for the Future: Environmental Dimensions of Global Trade' (2000) 5 *International Trade and Business Law Annual* 277; M.A: Cole, "*Examining the Environmental Case Against Free Trade*' (1999) 33 *Journal of World Trade* 183; E.U. Petersmann, 'International Trade Law and International Environment Law – Prevention and Settlement of International Disputes in GATT' (1993) 27 *Journal of World Trade* 43.

[10] C-157/96, *National Farmers' Union*, ECLI:EU:C:1998:191 and T-229/04, *Paraquat*, ECLI:EU: T:2007:217.

the challenge posed by the Paris Climate Agreement to all States to achieve a complete turnaround of their societies will certainly enhance the importance of having a broad definition of environment as a legal background for law-making as well as for implementing the already existing legislation.

Finally, the pillars on which EU environmental policy is built include, notably, the standard of care for the environment that must be applied at EU level: notably, Article 191 TFEU requires 'a high level of protection'.[11] 'High' level is clearly to be interpreted in comparison to that applied within international conventions, on the matrix of which domestic – and, in our case, EU – rules are traditionally developed.

The decision to remain at the forefront of environmental protection worldwide has involved a massive effort by the EU as legislator; indeed, over 200 pieces of EU secondary legislation (mainly directives) have been adopted in this field, having clear implications on their implementation, enforcement and sanctions: the EU has created a fully-fledged legal regime to protect and promote 'any' aspect of the environment at EU level; this system is coupled with an efficient enforcement structure which is capable, *inter alia*, of imposing sanctions on Member States that do not comply with the EU rules.

Needless to say, there will be more to come and more will have to be done for the purposes of implementing the Paris Climate Agreement, but analysing the current situation certainly provides us with food for thought for the future.

13.3. The multi-faceted scenario of enforcement of EU environmental law: enforcement on Member States and sanctions for non-fulfilment of the obligation to implement EU environmental directives

As noted earlier, at EU level a remarkable amount of legislation on the environment has been adopted. The key challenge is thus to enforce existing rules and standards, and the EU legal system is apparently provided with more adequate tools to serve this purpose than both domestic and international law.[12]

On the one hand, and firstly, EU law enjoys a wider geographic scope of application than national legislation; secondly, and more importantly, EU law has a much stronger means of enforcement compared with international law. These elements lead to enhanced compliance by both Member States and individuals: the former

---

[11] On Article 191 TFEU see S. Amadeo, 'Commento all'art. 191 TFUE', in A. Tizzano (eds.), *Trattati dell'Unione europea* (Giuffrè, 2014) 1616; P.A. Pilittu, 'Commento all'art. 191 TFUE', in F. Pocar, M.C. Baruffi (eds.), *Commentario breve ai trattati dell'Unione europea* (CEDAM, 2014) 1109.

[12] On this much discussed topic, see K. Collins, D. Earnshaw, 'The Implementation and Enforcement of European Community Environmental Legislation' (1992) 1 *Environmental Politics* p. 213; R. Macrory, 'The Enforcement of Community Environmental Laws: Some Critical Issues' (1992) 29 *Common Market Law Review* 347.

permits the adoption and implementation of much more ambitious goals than could be imagined by a single Member State while the latter actually allows these goals to be pursued.

As far as enforcement against Member States is concerned, both public enforcement through infringement procedures, and – at least prospectively – private enforcement through damages actions brought by individuals against Member States are available.

On the other hand, enforcement on individuals occurs through (i) the environmental liability directive (ELD) as well as other directives requiring Member States to introduce specific liability for individuals who infringe the relevant EU environmental rules and standards, and (ii) the ECD.

I shall now examine the 'public enforcement' side in relation to Member States that do not comply with their duty to implement and apply the EU's environmental rules.

This area involves the general remedy established by the Treaties if a Member State fails to fulfil its obligations under EU law, i.e. the infringement procedure set out by Articles 258-260 TFEU.

More precisely, with regard to sanctions, when the Commission refers Member States to the CJEU for having infringed EU law, the Court may impose financial sanctions if the Member State in question has (i) not yet complied with an earlier judgment ruling on the infringement;[13] or (ii) failed to fulfil its obligation to notify measures transposing a directive adopted under a legislative procedure.[14] According to the latest version of Article 260(3), second paragraph, the sanction may encompass both a lump sum payment, to punish the existence of the infringement itself, and/or a daily penalty payment, to deter any continuation of the infringement after the CJEU judgment.

The CJEU case-law has shaped the general regime set out by the treaty provision mentioned above. In particular, in order to establish some level of certainty, the CJEU has clarified that:

> the basic criteria which must be taken into consideration in order to ensure that that payment has coercive effect and that EU law is applied uniformly and effectively are, in principle, the seriousness of the infringement, its duration and the ability to pay of the Member State in question. In applying those criteria, regard must be had, in particular, to the effects on public and private interests of the failure to comply and to how urgent it is for the Member State concerned to be induced to fulfil its obligations.[15]

[13] Article 260(2) TFEU

[14] Article 260(3) TFEU.

[15] C-251/17, *Commission v Italy*, ECLI:EU:C:2018:358, para 71. See also C-93/17, *Commission*

Moreover, the sanctions should reflect the 'degree of persuasion needed in order for the Member State which has failed to comply with a judgment establishing a breach of obligations to alter its conduct and bring to an end the infringement established' and, as far as the penalty payment is concerned, it should be set 'so that it is both appropriate to the circumstances and proportionate to the infringement established and the ability to pay of the Member State'.[16] The CJEU enjoys broad discretion in establishing the amount of the lump sum payment: the relevant factors considered by the Court consist of the need to dissuade the Member State involved from repeating similar infringements in future, the appropriateness of the payment to the circumstances, its proportionality to the infringement, the seriousness of the infringement and the length of time for which the infringement continued after the judgment establishing it was delivered.[17] Based upon this reasoning, the CJEU rejected the 'N' factor which had rigidly been established by the Commission to establish *ex ante* the amount of penalty payments,[18] and the Commission subsequently adopted new criteria to allow for a foreseeable calculation of the penalties.[19]

Moving from general to specific, the available statistics show that 333 infringement procedures were pending before DG ENV at the end of 2018, 53 of which involved the application of Article 260 TFEU.[20] This figure is high and reveals the close attention paid by the Commission in its role of watchdog concerning compliance with EU environmental law. Those same statistics reveal further elements, *i.e.* that the 2018 figures are significantly lower than those of previous years (e.g. in 2007-2008 an average of 480 procedures was pending); this implies that – against a clear delay at national level in enforcing EU environmental instruments – substantial work has been done to improve compliance.[21]

Sanctions in environmental infringement procedures also have a remarkably longstanding track record: their initial application dates back almost 30 years, when

---

v Greece, ECLI:EU:C:2018:903; C-196/13, *Commission v Italy*, ECLI:EU:C:2014:2407; C-328/16, *Commission v Greece*, ECLI:EU: C:2018:98.

[16] Quotations from *Commission v. Italy*, *supra* note 15, paras 68-69.

[17] *Commission v. Italy*, *supra* note 15, paras 99-100.

[18] *Commission v Greece*, *supra* note 15. The 'N' factor took as evidence the gross domestic product (GDP) of that Member State and the number of votes it had in the Council.

[19] See Modification of the calculation method for lump sum payments and daily penalty payments proposed by the Commission in infringement proceedings before the Court of Justice of the European Union (2019/C 70/01), OJ C70/1).

[20] See http://ec.europa.eu/environment/legal/law/statistics.htm. On the relationship between the infringement procedure mechanism and the protection of the environment, see, inter alia, Di L. Borzsák, *The Impact of Environmental Concerns on the Public Enforcement Mechanism* (Wolters Kluver, 2011).

[21] As to the sectors involved, the most heavily affected are those of water, waste and air protection. Spain (32), Greece (23), Italy, and France (19) are the Member States having the highest number of open procedures.

the CJEU ordered Greece to pay a penalty of €20,000 for each day of delay in implementing measures that had been demanded in a previous judgment on waste and toxic waste.[22] In addition, the first case in which both a penalty payment and a lump sum were applied simultaneously also involved the environment, namely in an infringement procedure against France on fisheries conservation.[23]

Sanctions have been used intensively to secure deterrence and compliance against a failure to adopt the necessary measures to comply with previous CJEU judgments that had ascertained a breach of environmental directives. Member States have been sanctioned, inter alia, for failing in their obligations to implement properly (a) Directives 75/442/EEC, 91/689/EEC and 1999/31/EC on waste management;[24] (b) Directive 1999/31/EC on existing landfill sites and failure to close a landfill site operating without a site-conditioning plan;[25] (c) Directive 2008/1/EC on integrated pollution prevention and control;[26] Directive 91/271/EEC on urban waste-water treatment.[27]

The frequency of infringement procedures in this subject matter and the Court's severity in applying sanctions have generally prevented Member States from falling foul of their obligations to adopt the relevant EU environmental standards, thereby also avoiding any regulatory competition between Member States based upon their national laws.[28]

Indeed, there is no doubt that, with powers being granted to the EC (and now the EU) in this subject matter, the adoption of environmental rules or programmes at EU level has generally been coupled with a strong enforcement policy in order to secure their implementation by the Member States. As this approach is also likely to be maintained (and possibly strengthened) in future, it may be the case that a strict enforcement stance – with adequate sanctions – will also characterise the implemen-

---

[22] C-45/91, *Commission v. Greece*, ECLI:EU:C:1992:164. The previous judgment which Greece had not implemented is C-387/97, ECLI:EU:C:2000:356.

[23] C-304/02, *Commission v France*, ECLI:EU:C:2005:444.

[24] C-584-14, *Commission* v. *Greece*, ECLI:EU:C:2016:636; C-653-13, *Commission* v. *Italy*, ECLI:EU:C: 2015:478; *Commission* v. *Italy* (note 11); C-374-11, *Commission* v. *Ireland*, ECLI:EU:C: 2012:827.

[25] C-626-16, *Commission* v. *Slovakia*, ECLI:EU:C:2018:525.

[26] C-243-13, *Commission* v. *Sweden*, ECLI:EU:C: 2014:2413.

[27] C-251-17, *Commission* v. *Italy*, ECLI:EU:C:2018:358; C-205-17, *Commission* v. *Spain*, ECLI:EU:C: 2018:606; *Commission* v. *Greece* (note 11); C-167-14, *Commission* v. *Greece*, ECLI:EU:C: 2015:684; C-576-11, *Commission* v. *Luxembourg*, ECLI:EU:C: 2013:773; C-533-11, *Commission* v. *Belgium*, ECLI:EU:C: 2013:659.

[28] On this topic, see F. Munari, 'Do Environmental Rules and Standards Affect Firms' Competitive Ability?' (2019) 4 *European Papers* 207; V. Heyvaert. 'Regulatory Competition. Accounting For the Transnational Dimension of Environmental Regulation' (2013) 25 *Journal of Environmental Law* 1.

tation of the EU's ambitious policies following the Paris Climate Agreement, which are likely to affect substantially the application of Directive 2008/50/EC:[29] I refer to the '2020 Climate & Energy Package', as confirmed by the Europe 2020 Strategy, aiming at reducing GHG emissions by 23% on the 2016 figures; the '2030 Climate & Energy Framework', and the '2050 Low-Carbon Roadmap'.[30]

This is all confirmed by the fact that these initiatives are strengthened by an enforcement strategy under Article 260 TFEU, the aim of which is to sanction those Member States that fail to control their levels of air pollution, thus infringing Directive 2008/50/EC on ambient air quality and cleaner air for Europe: infringement cases are ongoing against Austria, Belgium, Czech Republic, Denmark, France, Germany, Hungary,[31] Italy, Poland, Portugal, Spain, and Romania.[32]

13.4. Interim measures and sanctions to protect the environment

Within the ample toolbox provided by the infringement procedure,[33] interim measures to ensure rapid compliance are one of the most crucial instruments. For some time, the CJEU has clarified that, in the above procedure, it has the power to prescribe any such measure that it considers necessary to preserve the *effet utile* of the final decision issued under art. 260 TFEU.

Needless to say, interim measures are particularly relevant in infringement cases concerning environmental law, also in specific application of the precautionary and preventive action principles, so as to avoid irreparable damage being caused to the environment.[34]

Interim measures would, however, be futile in the absence of sanctions against Member States that were unwilling to apply them. Hence, in a major environmental

---

[29] OJ 2008, L 152/1. A consolidated version of the Directive was published on 18 September 2015.

[30] These packages imply *inter alia* the modification of EU legislation on the emission trading system (ETS), i.e. in particular, Directive 2003/87/EC as amended (OJ 2003, L275/32, a consolidated version was published on 8 April 2018), Directive 2009/28/EC on renewable energy (OJ 2009, L 140/16, a consolidated version was published on 5 October 2015), and the introduction of new EU governance of the energy union and climate action according to Regulation 2018/1999 (OJ 2018, L 328/1). For more information and for references seehttps://ec.europa.eu/clima/policies/strategies_en.

[31] C-637/18, *Commission v Hungary*.

[32] C-638/18, *Commission v Romania*.

[33] For more details on this topic see the chapter by Luca Prete.

[34] C-76/08, *Commission v. Malta*, ECLI:EU:C:2008:252, when the President of the CJEU ordered Malta to refrain from adopting any measure applying the (hunting) derogation provided by Article 9 of the Wild Birds Directive (2009/147/EC). See, inter alia, M. Hedemann-Robinson, 'Enforcement of EU Environmental Law and the Role of Interim Relief Measures' (2010) 19 *European Energy and Environmental Law Review* 204.

case, the Court imposed sanctions against Poland in an infringement procedure for its alleged failure to comply with the *Habitat* and *Wild Bird* Directives,[35] for which interim measures had simultaneously been adopted. Responding to the Member State concerned, the Court clarified that

> the prospect of a periodic penalty payment being imposed in such a situation encourages the relevant Member State to comply with the interim measures ordered, it enhances the effectiveness of those measures and guarantees the full effectiveness of the final decision, thus falling entirely within the ambit of the objective of Article 279 TFEU.[36]

Conclusively, it can be said that, with regard to enforcement and sanctions on Member States for their failure to comply with obligations stemming from EU environmental rules, the picture seems quite clear and satisfactory, as deterrence is established and the criteria for assessing the amount of sanctions also respect the general principles of law as clarified by the CJEU.

13.5. Damages actions by individuals against Member States for breach of EU environmental law?

In antitrust jargon, the situation described above would be classified as 'public enforcement' of EU environmental law. It is interesting to consider whether, as in competition law, it may also be possible for there to be 'private enforcement', i.e. if, under the *Francovich* doctrine,[37] individuals can claim compensation from Member States for damages suffered as a consequence of their failure to comply with EU environmental law[38].

While the answer, in principle, is a resounding "yes", to my knowledge there is no evidence of this sort of enforcement having taken place yet. One reason for this may be the difficulty in itself of establishing a causal link between damage occurring to an individual and the breach of EU environmental law by a Member State: the very nature of the environment – i.e. a 'good' which is common to all – makes the

---

[35] Respectively, Directive 92/43/EEC (OJ 1992, L 206/7) and Directive 2009/147/EC (OJ 2010 L 20/7), both amended by Directive 2013/17/EU (OJ 2013 L 158/193).

[36] C-441/17 R, *Commission v Poland*, ECLI:EU:C:2017:877, para 105. See P. Wenneras, 'Saving a Forest and the Rule of Law: Commission v. Poland' (2019) 56 *Common Market Law Review* 541.

[37] C-6/90 and C-9/90, *Francovich and Bonifaci v Italy*, ECLI:EU:C:1991:428.

[38] On this topic, see P. Wennerås, 'State Liability for Decisions of Courts of Last Instance in Environmental Cases' (2004) 16 *Journal of Environmental Law* 329; H. Somsen, 'Francovich and its application to EC environmental law' in H. Somsen (ed.), *Protecting the European Environment: Enforcing EC Environmental Law* (Blackstone, 1996) 135; G. Slynn, 'The European Community and the environment' (1993) 5 JEL261.

apportionment of individual environmental rights infrequent, with the ascertainment of any breach of such rights being similarly rare.

However, in general, this possibility cannot be ruled out: after all, the European Court of Human Rights has assessed that, under certain conditions, a group of citizens who had suffered damages due to the failure of their State adequately to apply and enforce rules on waste could validly claim a right to damages.[39] These rules are clearly of EU origin, stemming from the relevant directives on waste.

The point I would like to make in this paragraph is that, unlike any other legal system, at EU level, lawsuits may be brought (either individually or collectively) to claim damages from Member States found to be in breach of the relevant EU environmental rules. Like the antitrust regime, it is also possible to imagine (and foresee) follow-on cases after a Tribunal or a CJEU judgement as a result of a decision by the Commission establishing that a Member State has infringed EU environmental law under Article 258 TFEU.

From this additional 'bottom up' approach, the combination of infringement procedures and the *Francovich* doctrine can provide further deterrence for the stricter enforcement of EU environmental law, coupled with 'sanctions' that, even if disguised as damages claims, would provide additional weaponry for stronger protection and promotion of our environment. Although, legally speaking, damages actions are different from 'sanctions', it goes without saying that, for the Member State concerned, they have the same deterrent impact and negative economic effect.

In this vein, the growing importance of class actions and of general actions for damages having a 'widespread nature' in modern legal systems, as advocated, in particular, by 'classical' scholars engaged in economic analyses of law,[40] may serve not only the need to safeguard the 'rights' of claimants, but may eventually also have positive global effects on the quality of our environment.

13.6. Enforcement on individuals: Directive 2004/35/EC on environmental liability (and related sanctions under Member States' national laws)

Protection and promotion of the environment is not only a top-down matter; indeed, I believe it is much more of a bottom-up process. Thus, it requires proactive actions by all individuals, who cannot expect institutions to deal with the problem alone.

---

[39] See 30765/08, *Di Sarno et al. v. Italy*; 59909/00, *Giacomelli v. Italy*.

[40] P. Trimarchi, *Rischio e responsabilità oggettiva* (Giuffrè, 1961); P. Trimarchi, *La responsabilità civile: atti illeciti, rischio, danno*, (Giuffrè, 2017); F. James, 'Accident Liability Reconsidered', (1948) 57 *Yale Law Journal*, 549; G. Calabresi, *The Cost of Accidents: A Legal and Economic Analysis* (Yale University Press, 1977); R. A. Posner, *Economic Analysis of Law*, 8th ed. (Aspen Publishers, 2011); M. Atiyah, *Accidents, Compensation and the Law*, 9th ed. (Cambridge University Press, 2018).

Consistently with the above, the EU legal system has for some time offered another tool to ensure that environmental damages caused by individuals are subject to liability and are eventually sanctioned. As we are dealing with EU directives, this obviously requires a two-stage process: the first stage is the duty of Member States to enact domestic legislation implementing the relevant pieces of EU secondary law.

In this regard, the most relevant example is perhaps the one offered by the already mentioned ELD,[41] which defines environmental damage as a

> measurable adverse change in a natural resource or measurable impairment of a natural resource service which may occur directly or indirectly.[42]

The ELD establishes an administrative law regime requiring public authorities to ensure that the "polluter pays" principle for environmental damages is respected and it outlines two regimes depending on the activities concerned: (i) a strict liability regime applying to the activities listed in Annex III, such as offshore oil and gas operations or the management of extractive waste; (ii) a fault-based liability regime applying to other activities.

By implementing the "polluter pays" principle, the aim is to prevent environmental damages and pollution in the first place, and to do so consistently with well-known schemes in environmental, legal and economic discourse, i.e. the reduction of environmental externalities.

The CJEU adopted a proactive and multifaceted approach under the ELD in order to enhance its enforcement.

Firstly, its temporal scope of application has been extended: even though the ELD applies to damages caused by an emission, event or incident that took place on or after 30 April 2007 (i.e. the end of the implementation period), the ELD has been con-

---

[41] There is vast literature on the ELD; see, generally, L. Bergkamp, B. Goldsmith (eds.), *The EU Environmental Liability Directive: A Commentary* (OUP, 2013); S. Cassotta, *Environmental damage and liability problems in a multilevel context: the case of the environmental liability directive* (Kluwer Law International, 2012); M. Petersen, 'The Environmental Liability Directive – Extending Nature Protection in Europe' (2009) 11 *Environmental Law Review* 5; M. Hinteregger, *Environmental liability and ecological damage in European law* (Cambridge University Press, 2008); G. Winter, J.H. Jans, R. Macrory and L. Krämer, 'Weighing up the EC Environmental Liability Directive' (2008) 20 *Journal of Environmental Law* 163; G. Betlem and E.H.P. Brans (eds.), *Environmental Liability in the EU – The 2004 Directive compared with US and Member States Law* (CMP, 2006).

[42] Article 2.2 ELD. Note, however, that environmental damage in the ELD is reserved only to specific kinds of damage as defined in Article 2.1. On the definition and assessment of environmental damages, see J. Lipton, E. Özdemiroğlu, D. Chapman, J. Peers, *Equivalency Methods for Environmental Liability Assessing Damage and Compensation Under the European Environmental Liability Directive* (Springer, 2018); L. De La Fayette, 'The Concept of Environmental Damage in International Liability Regimes', in M. Bowman, A. Boyle (eds.), *Environmental Damage in International and Comparative Law – Problems of Definition and Valuation* (OUP, 2002)149.

sidered, quite rightly, to apply to activities that took place before that date, but were not yet brought to completion.[43]

Secondly, even though Articles 6 and 7 ELD generally place the burden of implementing remedial measures to restore the quality of the environment upon the person responsible, in order to have them approved by the competent Member States' authorities, the CJEU has not imposed a strict interpretation of this principle. Thus, the Court has avoided to deprive the Member States of their task of monitoring the effectiveness of the relevant remedial measures even after their approval. In this sense, it has been clarified that national authorities can substantially alter environmental damage remedial measures that have been chosen after consulting with the operators concerned and that have already been implemented or begun to be put into effect as long as they (a) give those operators the opportunity to be heard, except where the urgency of the environmental situation requires immediate action on the part of the competent authority, (b) invite the owner of the land on which those measures are to be carried out to submit its observations, and (c) state in its decisions the grounds on which the choice is based.[44]

Thirdly, and again in line with the proactive approach that encourages the effectiveness of the remedies and the strict implementation of the duties on the individuals concerned to remove pollution (or be held liable if they refuse to do so), the *ERG* judgment[45] further establishes that, in some circumstances, the ELD can restrict the property rights of the individuals concerned, and in particular the use of land that has already been decontaminated, if any further use of this land may give rise to more contamination. In other words, the CJEU considers the ELD applicable by Member States also to 'innocent' individuals, as a tool to prevent environmental pollution, when the use of the property by such individuals would potentially be harmful; after all, as stated by the Court in reference to its landmark judgments on this topic,

> while the right to property forms part of the general principles of EU law, it is not an absolute right and must be viewed in relation to its social function. Consequently, its exercise may be restricted, provided that those restrictions in fact correspond to objectives of general interest pursued by the European Union and do not constitute disproportionate and intolerable interference, impairing the very substance of the rights guaranteed.[46]

---

[43] C-379/08 and C-380/08, *ERG et al.*, ECLI:EU:C:2010:127; C-534/13, *Fipa Group*, ECLI:EU:C:2015:140; C-529/15, *Gert Folk*, ECLI:EU:C:2017:419.

[44] *ERG et al.*, *supra* note 43, paras 46 ff.

[45] *ERG et al.*, *supra* note 43, paras 72 ff.

[46] *ERG et al.*, *supra* note 43, para. 80. See 44/79, *Hauer*, ECLI:EU:C:1979:290, para. 23; Case 265/87, *Schräder HS Kraftfutter*, ECLI:EU:C:1989:303, para. 15; Case C-293/97, *Standley and Others*, ECLI:EU:C:1999:215, para. 54; and C-402/05 P and C-415/05 P, *Kadi and Al Barakaat International Foundation* v *Council and Commission*, ECLI:EU:C:2008:461, para. 355.

Well, there has been no doubt since *ADBHU* that environmental protection is one of the objectives of general interest that can limit the exercise of property rights.[47]

Fourthly, the ELD prevents Member States from granting 'immunity' from liability to the individuals concerned merely because their activity was authorised by the competent authorities: hence, it

> preclud[es] a provision of national law which excludes, generally and automatically, that damage which has a significant adverse effect on the ecological, chemical or quantitative status or ecological potential of [a site] categorized as 'environmental damage', due to the mere fact that it is covered by an authorization granted under that law.[48]

Fifthly, and by the same token, the harmonisation required by the ELD prohibits Member States from excluding persons affected or likely to be affected by environmental damage, as per Article 12(1)(a), from being entrusted with the protection afforded by the ELD:[49] Member States therefore have no power to limit the *locus standi* of specific categories of 'natural or legal persons' (a) to submit to the competent authority any observations relating to instances of environmental damage or an imminent threat of such damage of which they are aware, (b) to ask the competent authority to take action under the ELD, and (c) as the case may be under relevant national legislation, to claim for damages when their rights are impaired.[50]

Sixthly, in line with Article 193 TFEU, which does not require, for its application, any specific notification by the Member States to the Commission,[51] the Court has clarified that the core of the ELD is the "polluter pays" principle, whose scope of application is limited to those cases in which a causal link is established between the environmental damage and the 'operator' (i.e. the person causing it)[52]. Consequently, the Member States are entitled to enforce more stringent protective measures outside the scope of application of the ELD. For instance, this occurs when the 'polluter' cannot be identified or held liable coherently with the above; in the *Fipa Group* case it was held that the ELD did not rule out domestic legislation requiring the innocent landowner to reimburse the site cleaning costs undertaken

---

[47] Case 240/83, *ADBHU*, ECLI:EU:C:1985:59, para. 13; see also 302/86, *Commission* v *Denmark*, ECLI:EU:C:1988:421, para 8; C-213/96, *Outokumpu*, ECLI:EU:C:1998:155, para. 32.

[48] *Gert Folk*, *supra* note 43, para. 34.

[49] *Gert Folk*, *supra* note 43, paras 41 ff.

[50] Article 3.3 ELD does not attribute directly to 'private parties a right of compensation as a consequence of environmental damage or of an imminent threat of such damage'. However, this right is normally protected by national legislation on tort liability.

[51] See, inter alia, C-2/10, *Azienda Agro-Zootecnica Franchini and Eolica di Altamura*, ECLI:EU:C:2011:502, para. 53.

[52] *Fipa Group*, *supra* note 43, para. 59.

by the competent authority within its market value when it was impossible to identify the polluter of the land, or to require that person to adopt remedial measures. Along the same line of reasoning, in the more recent case *Túrkevei Tejtermelő Kft*, national legislations imposing joint liability and even sanctions upon landowners have been considered legitimate, provided that (a) they are appropriate for the purpose of contributing to achieving the objective of more stringent protection, (b) the methods for determining the amount of the fine do not go beyond what is necessary to achieve that objective, and (c) the landowner can escape liability if he/she demonstrates beyond reasonable doubt that he/she has not caused environmental damage[53].

Even though in the above cases (and especially in *Fipa Group*) the notion of 'sanctions' tends to become blurred with that of liability, there is no doubt that the ELD can also be seen as a tool for encouraging Member States to apply a regime on environmental protection beyond the scope of application of the ELD itself: in particular, the potential liability (and related sanctions, or the duty to make good and adopt remedial activities) that is indirectly placed onto natural or legal persons adjacent to the 'operator', i.e. individuals having contacts or relationships between themselves, is worth noting. If (additional) liability is imposed on these persons, an additional dissuasive effect is established, so that behaviours potentially likely to generate environmental damages are deterred: the overall benefit from this for society as a whole is self-evident.

13.7. The duty of Member States to enforce effective, proportionate and dissuasive penalties in the event of an infringement of EU environmental law as a general principle of EU law: detailed sanctions for breaches of the ETS regime and relevant CJEU case-law

As already noted, the ELD is seen as the most prominent piece of legislation obliging Member States to adopt a specific regime to transform the "polluter pays" principle into a set of hard and fast rules applicable to the persons responsible, thus also encouraging the enactment of sanctions against the offenders;[54] that said, EU environmental law includes many other pieces of secondary legislation actually obliging Member States to establish effective, proportionate and dissuasive penalties and sanctions for any infringements, and to take all measures necessary to ensure that those penalties are implemented.

Examples of this kind are manifold; this is not by chance, the earliest of them date back to the same period in which the ELD was adopted, and thereafter this so-

[53] C-129/16, *Túrkevei Tejtermelő Kft*, ECLI:EU:C:2017:547.

[54] See *supra*, note 50.

lution gradually expanded and now applies to most of the environmental rules originating at EU level.

More precisely, under relevant pieces of EU legislation, the Member States are subject to a three-fold obligation: (a) to lay down rules on penalties applicable to infringements of the national provisions adopted pursuant to the relevant EU regulations or (more frequently) directives, and to enact them in such a way that they are 'effective, proportionate and dissuasive'; (b) to take all necessary steps to ensure that these measures are implemented; (c) to notify the relevant penalties (as well as any subsequent amendment thereof) to the Commission, in order to guarantee proper and punctual sharing of information on this topic between EU States and institutions, as well as compliance with the duties set out above.[55]

In this vein, and aside from the other pieces of legislation mentioned below, it is worth citing (a) Article 16 of the already quoted ETS Directive 2003/87,[56] containing the same obligations referred to above, plus a detailed series of sanctions which will be discussed below; (b) Article 60 of Directive 2006/88/EC on animal health requirements for aquaculture animals and products thereof, and on the prevention and control of certain diseases in aquatic animals;[57] (c) Article 50 of Regulation (EC) no. 1013/2006 on shipments of waste;[58] (d) Article 126 of Regulation 1907/2006/EC establishing the so-called REACH regime, i.e. one of the most ambitious and all-encompassing pieces of legislation worldwide based on the precautionary principle and aimed at securing *inter alia* 'a high level of protection of human health and the environment';[59] (e) Article 34 of Directive 2013/30/EU on safety of offshore oil and gas operations.[60]

Almost invariably, the relevant EU legislative acts impose on Member States the requirement to enact 'effective, proportionate and dissuasive penalties'; the CJEU has often guided Member States in focusing on the above parameters. In particular, in the *Total Waste Recycling* case,[61] the Court clarified that national courts are re-

---

[55] Whereas non-compliance can immediately be sanctioned under the infringement procedures referred to in previous paragraphs 3 and 4.

[56] See *supra* note 30.

[57] OJ 2006, L 328/14. A consolidated version of this Directive, which has been repeatedly amended, was published on 6 March 2014.

[58] OJ 2006, L 190/1. A consolidated version of this Regulation, which has been repeatedly amended, was published on 1 January 2018.

[59] OJ 2006, L 396/1. A consolidated version of the REACH Regulation was published on 2 July 2019. The quotations in the text are drawn from Article 1 of the REACH Regulation. The REACH system works through 'the promotion of alternative methods for assessment of hazards of substances', as well as at establishing 'the principle that it is for manufacturers, importers and downstream users to ensure that they manufacture, place on the market or use such substances that do not adversely affect human health or the environment'.

[60] OJ 2013, L 178/66.

[61] C-487/14, *SC Total Waste Recycling SRL*, ECLI:EU:C:2015:780, para. 55.

quired, when reviewing the proportionality of such penalties, to take particular account of the risks for the environment or human health that may be caused by the infringement.

However, when deemed opportune, the notion of 'effective, proportionate and dissuasive penalties' is further specified by referring to parameters that can certainly provide useful guidance in general. This is true, for instance, of Directive (EU) 2016/802 relating to a reduction in the sulphur content of certain liquid fuels[62]: in implementing at EU level the corresponding requirement set forth by the MARPOL Convention, and in particular its Article 4(4),[63] Article 18 of the Directive establishes that penalties

> may include fines calculated [...] as to ensure that the fines at least deprive those responsible of the economic benefits derived from the infringement [...] and that those fines gradually increase for repeated infringements.

Even more specific is the regime set forth by Regulation (EU) 995/2010 laying down obligations for operators that market timber and timber products,[64] whose Article 19 establishes that penalties may include

> fines proportionate to the environmental damage, the value of the timber or timber products concerned and the tax losses and economic detriment resulting from the infringement, calculating the level of such fines in such way as to make sure that they effectively deprive those responsible of the economic benefits derived from their serious infringements, without prejudice to the legitimate right to exercise a profession, and gradually increasing the level of such fines for repeated serious infringements; seizure of the timber and timber products concerned, immediate suspension of authorisation to trade.

The panorama of sanctions that EU law requires Member States to implement also contains interesting variations. In line with the growing importance of publicising the failure by the persons involved to fulfil their environmental obligations, in some cases EU law establishes that the sanctions to be applied include ensuring publication of the names of the offenders. This is the case contemplated by Article 16(2) of the ETS Directive,[65] requiring the disclosure of the names of those 'opera-

---

[62] OJ 2016, L 132/58.

[63] Stating that 'The penalties specified under the law of a Party pursuant to the present article shall be adequate in severity to discourage violations of the present Convention and shall be equally severe irrespective of where the violations occur'. The text of the MARPOL Convention can be found at http://www.mar.ist.utl.pt/mventura/Projecto-Navios-I/IMO-Conventions%20(copies)/MARPOL.pdf.

[64] OJ 2010, L 295/23.

[65] See *supra* note 30.

tors or aircraft operators' that do not surrender sufficient allowances.

The complexity of the ETS regime on allowances has forced the EU to couple the general principle concerning effective, proportionate and dissuasive measures with a set of precise sanctions that are to be applied in specific cases, over which the Member States do not enjoy any discretion. More precisely, Article 16(3) of the ETS Directive envisages the liability rule and the related sanctions as follows:

> any operator who does not surrender sufficient allowances by 30 April of each year to cover its emissions during the preceding year shall be held liable for the payment of an excess emissions penalty. The excess emissions penalty shall be EUR 100 for each tonne of carbon dioxide equivalent emitted by that installation for which the operator has not surrendered allowances.

It is worth noting that, since the ETS Directive is based on measurement mechanisms concerning allowances that are verified by independent persons, sanctions are applied only in the case of omitted communication of allowances and not where the communication is incorrect. Otherwise, this would amount to a violation of the principle of proportionality of sanctions. Member States, however, remain free to establish stricter domestic regimes and, therefore, to sanction operators for submitting erroneous communications; these sanctions established directly by Member States shall comply with the general principles of effectiveness, proportionality and dissuasiveness. [66]

The sanctioning obligations set out by EU law in the case of infringement of the relevant environmental provisions is generally based on a regime of strict liability: given the need to protect the environment as such and, to this end, to establish standards and rules that must be applied in order to achieve the environmental goals set out by the EU legislator, quite rightly the Court has stated that, unless the specific EU provisions establish that the infringement must be of fraudulent nature, the offender's intention to harm the environment is irrelevant. [67]

---

[66] C-148/14 *Germany v Nordzucker*, ECLI:EU:C:2015:287, paras 42-45.

[67] C-69/15, *Nutrivet*, ECLI:EU:C:2016:425, paras 42 ff. The case refers to exports of waste, but the principles stated in the judgement can certainly be extended to other areas of environmental law. On the other hand, this is fully consistent with the classical contents on environmental rules, whose rationale is invariably that of modifying human behaviours that were, in the past, considered legitimate in order to change past behavioural patterns into (more) sustainable ones (see, for more general reflections on this topic, F. Munari, L. Schiano di Pepe, *supra* note 2, 52 ff.

13.8. Directive 2008/99/EC on the protection of the environment through criminal law: a point of arrival for sanctions in EU sectoral law or rules still to be fine-tuned?

As in many other areas of environmental law, the EU enacted its specific legislation on criminal sanctions for severe damages to the environment following the adoption of an international convention on the same topic. This is also the case for the ECD provisions which are intended to implement and enhance the contents of the 1998 Strasbourg Convention on the protection of the environment through criminal law adopted by the Council of Europe.[68]

At that time, i.e. prior to the Lisbon Treaty, the competences conferred to the Union under criminal law fell within the so-called third pillar. For this reason, the EU legislator opted to implement the contents of the Strasbourg Convention by means of a Framework Decision under Articles 29, 31(e) and 34(2)(b) EU,[69] rather than through a Directive, whose legal basis would have been Article 175 EC (now Article 191 TFEU).

This 'cautious' approach was, however, struck down by the CJEU in the famous *Protection of the environment through criminal penalties* case:[70] once again, the Court demonstrated a proactive approach in having the EU environmental policy and law strongly implemented, and declared that, even though, as a general rule, neither criminal law nor the rules of criminal procedure fell within the Community's competence, this

> does not prevent the Community legislature, when the application of effective, proportionate and dissuasive criminal penalties by the competent national authori-

---

[68] The text and information on the convention (which has been ratified by many, but not all, Member States) can be found at https://www.coe.int/en/web/conventions/full-list/-/conventions/treaty/172. On the ECD and its application see, *inter alia,* M.G. Faure, The Revolution in Environmental Criminal Law in Europe (2017) 35 *Virginia Environmental Law Journal* 321; G.F. Perilongo and E. Corn, 'The ecocrime directive and its translation into legal practice: EU green offences and their impact at national level according to the results of a recent survey' (2017) 8 *New Journal of European Criminal Law* 236; G.M. Vagliasindi, 'The European Harmonisation in the Sector of Protection of the Environment through Criminal Law: The Results Achieved and Further Needs for Intervention' (2012) 3 *New Journal of European Criminal Law* 320; M.G. Faure, 'The implementation of the Environmental Crimes Directives in Europe' in J Gerardu, D Grabiel, MR Koparova, K Markowitz and D Zaelke (eds), *9th International Conference on Environmental Compliance and Enforcement* (INECE, 2011) 360; H.E. Zeitler, 'Happy end of a long saga – Agreement on the Directive for the Protection of the Environment through Criminal Law' (2008) 5 *Journal for European Environmental & Planning Law* 281.

[69] More precisely, Framework Decision 2003/80/JHA (OJ 2003 L 29/55).

[70] C-176/03, *Commission v. Council*, ECLI:EU:C:2005:542. See, inter alia, M, Wasmeier, and N, Twaites, 'The "battle of the pillars": does the European Community have the power to approximate national criminal laws?' (2004) 29 *ELRev.* 613; F. Comte, 'Criminal environmental law and Community competence' (2003) 12 *European Environmental Law Review* 147.

ties is an essential measure for combating serious environmental offences, from taking measures which relate to the criminal law of the Member States which it considers necessary in order to ensure that the rules which it lays down on environmental protection are fully effective.[71]

The above judgment was the origin of the ECD, whose main features can be summarised as follows.

The introduction of criminal penalties 'demonstrate[s] a social disapproval of a qualitatively different nature compared to administrative penalties or a compensation mechanism under civil law'.[72] Along this line of reasoning, the objective of the ECD is to introduce nine behaviours that are classified as criminal offences when they are committed intentionally or at least with serious negligence in breach of EU law or national measures implementing EU law.[73]

The ECD further sanctions with criminal penalties the behaviours of inciting, aiding and abetting the nine environmental crimes.[74] In order to complete the picture with sanctioning schemes, a system of criminal liability for legal persons is also envisaged, which Member States are bound to introduce in their national legisla-

---

[71] *Commission v. Council*, *supra* note 64, para. 48.

[72] See recital 3 ECD.

[73] Article 3 ECD envisages the following environmental crimes: (a) the discharge, emission or introduction of a quantity of materials or ionising radiation into air, soil or water, which causes or is likely to cause death or serious injury to any person or substantial damage to the quality of air, the quality of soil or the quality of water, or to animals or plants; (b) the collection, transport, recovery or disposal of waste, including the supervision of such operations and the after-care of disposal sites, and including action taken as a dealer or a broker (waste management), which causes or is likely to cause death or serious injury to any person or substantial damage to the quality of air, the quality of soil or the quality of water, or to animals or plants; (c) the shipment of waste, where this activity falls within the scope of Article 2(35) of Regulation (EC) No 1013/2006 of the European Parliament and of the Council of 14 June 2006 on shipments of waste and is undertaken in a non-negligible quantity, whether executed in a single shipment or in several shipments which appear to be linked; (d) the operation of a plant in which a dangerous activity is carried out or in which dangerous substances or preparations are stored or used and which, outside the plant, causes or is likely to cause death or serious injury to any person or substantial damage to the quality of air, the quality of soil or the quality of water, or to animals or plants; (e) the production, processing, handling, use, holding, storage, transport, import, export or disposal of nuclear materials or other hazardous radioactive substances which causes or is likely to cause death or serious injury to any person or substantial damage to the quality of air, the quality of soil or the quality of water, or to animals or plants; (f) the killing, destruction, possession or taking of specimens of protected wild fauna or flora species, except for cases where the conduct concerns a negligible quantity of such specimens and has a negligible impact on the conservation status of the species; (g) trading in specimens of protected wild fauna or flora species or parts or derivatives thereof, except for cases where the conduct concerns a negligible quantity of such specimens and has a negligible impact on the conservation status of the species; (h) any conduct which causes the significant deterioration of a habitat within a protected site; (i) the production, importation, exportation, placing on the market or use of ozone-depleting substances.

[74] Article 4 ECD.

tions.[75] This latest provision is very important, given that environmental crimes are not infrequently carried out in the interest of firms: if the latter are also likely to suffer negative consequences from crimes committed by their managers, it goes without saying that the deterrent effect of the ECD also operates in relation to their shareholders and in general the stakeholders of the firms involved.

Despite the criminal offences being clearly listed, the ECD lacks precision in determining the sanctions that Member States are bound to introduce into their criminal laws. This does not come as a surprise as the ECD was enacted before the Lisbon Treaty, i.e. when the EU did not yet have truly enforceable power in establishing criminal sanctioning provisions. In such a situation, the ECD is construed in the same terms as the model adopted for the directives referred to in the previous paragraphs;[76] consequently, it neither specifies the typology nor establishes directly specific criminal sanctions; rather, it only requires Member States to introduce 'effective, proportionate and dissuasive' criminal penalties.[77]

Unfortunately, the Member States have displayed very different interpretations of the notion of effective, proportionate and dissuasive penalties; this has occurred from several viewpoints.

Firstly, as regards criminal penalties by typology, some Member States have sanctioned (with differing degrees of severity depending on the crime concerned) the offences listed in Article 3 ECD with imprisonment, with imprisonment and fines, with imprisonment or fines, or simply with fines.[78]

Secondly, as far as some serious offences are concerned, i.e. those listed in Article 3, letters a), d) e) and i) ELD,[79] the period of imprisonment varies from a one-month jail sentence to life imprisonment; the same is true for the offences listed in Article 3, letters b) and c), where the sanctions vary from a 6-month prison sentence to, again, life imprisonment.[80] Even given the fact that we are talking about six different behaviours, it seems self-evident that the range of severity chosen by Member States appears to be far from harmonised.

In such a situation, it hardly seems debatable that the aim of the ELD to achieve

---

[75] Article 6 ECD.

[76] See paras 6 and 7.

[77] See Articles 5 and 7 ECD.

[78] See the 2016 ENEC Study on the implementation of Directive 2008/99/EC on the Protection of the Environment Through Criminal Law, available at http://www.lawyersfornature.eu/wp-content/uploads/2016/05/Study-on-the-implementation-of-Directive-2008_99_ENEC_SEO_BirdLife_May2016.pdf. The information below is all drawn from this ENEC study.

[79] See *supra* note 73.

[80] Generally, the study mentioned in note 78 indicates that sanctions are much less severe in Luxembourg, whereas Austria, Malta and the Netherlands have chosen an opposite approach as to the severity of punishment.

the implementation of homogeneous criminal sanctions at EU level has not been achieved. This might have prospective negative consequences on overall ELD enforcement throughout the EU: in particular, in those instances where an act might have negative effects for the environment affecting more than one Member State, the remarkable differences in sanctioning that act might risk jeopardising the achievement of the goal of implementing a high level of environmental protection, and having a harmonised system of penalties applicable to offenders.

It is perhaps too early to assess whether the concerns expressed above are well-founded, and whether in the EU there will, therefore, be diverging sanctioning policies at domestic level for the same EU environmental crimes. If this were the case, however, after the Lisbon Treaty a remedy might be envisaged.

Reference is made to Article 83(1) TFEU. This provision lists ten 'Euro crimes' ('*particularly serious crime with a cross-border dimension*'), which, nevertheless, have a tenuous connection with environmental protection. Yet, the same provision empowers the Council '*[o]n the basis of developments in crime... [to] adopt a decision identifying other areas of crime*'.

However, even more than Article 83(1), the contents of Article 83(2) TFEU may serve the purpose of filling the gaps that currently characterise the sanctioning side of the ECD. Under this provision,

> If the approximation of criminal laws and regulations of the Member States proves essential to ensure the effective implementation of a Union policy in an area which has been subject to harmonization measures, directives may establish minimum rules with regard to the definition of criminal offences and sanctions in the area concerned.

Undoubtedly, Article 83(2) TFEU could become the legal basis for further enforcement of the ECD as far as its sanctioning side is concerned. Hopefully, there will be no need to complete the ECD with the adoption of a directive establishing sanctions for eco-crimes. That said, once again, EU law demonstrates its capability to implement serious rules and sanctions for the protection and promotion of the environment.

13.9. Concluding remarks

While this article focuses on sanctions to secure the implementation of EU environmental law, a final *caveat* is warranted in order to avoid missing out on the real objective of environmental protection and promotion.

Tellingly, sanctions are important from any legal perspective: any breach of obligations or prohibitions established statutorily cannot go unpunished. However, when it comes to protecting the environment, a legal reasoning based solely on sanctions would clearly be limited and misleading: the preservation and promotion of the environment requires a radical change in the behavioural patterns of individuals on earth, in general, and within the EU more specifically. In particular, it requires a totally new approach to how people enforce their existing 'rights' (to consume, to eat, to move, to procreate, and so on), with a view to limiting the enjoyment of these 'rights' for the benefit of the earth and of future generations, whose 'rights' cannot yet be invoked (or enforced), but must be considered before they are substantially nullified.[81]

This entails an extraordinary need to build capacity on the existing world population as well as immense educational efforts at all levels to change well-rooted cultural ideas and to understand that life as we know it on our planet is likely to be destroyed by humans, unless they voluntarily and convincingly decide to change their way of living. Evidence of the above is contained in the Paris Climate Agreement, and specifically in its Article 11, but is valid throughout all legal systems.

Institutions can help with this necessary turnaround, and the EU will probably remain at the forefront of the most active decision-making entities in this respect. However, sanctions will probably only be a single course on the menu… and not even the main one.

[81] I had already suggested this necessary approach which now, fortunately, appears to be seen at the forefront of any environmental discourse in my book with Lorenzo Schiano di Pepe, *supra* note 2, see, in particular, at 113 et seq.

Chapter 14

EU SANCTIONING POWERS AND DATA PROTECTION: NEW TOOLS FOR ENSURING THE EFFECTIVENESS OF THE GDPR IN THE SPIRIT OF COOPERATIVE FEDERALISM

Paul De Hert *

ABSTRACT: *The Chapter deals with the use of sanctioning powers in the context of EU data protection law and reflects on the thorny relationship between different typologies of sanctions (criminal and administrative) in the light of the new administrative sanctioning powers of the Data Protection Authorities. The analysis starts form short historical presentation of the EU (secondary) laws dealing with data protection and, then it looks at changes to EU primary law brought about by the Treaty of Lisbon with an explicit imperative to improve EU data protection. The core of the analysis discusses the system of remedies in the GDPR and some examples of recent sanctioning practices by the national DPAs. The analysis is followed by three more reflective sections about supervisory convergence without creating new EU institutions, the administrative enforcement fray and defence rights and the role of criminal law in EU data protection law. The chapter also offers some guidance observations about the operationalisation of the threefold system of enforcement set up by EU data protection law.*

KEYWORDS: *sanctions – administrative law – criminal law – data protection – GDPR – supervisory authority*

---

* Professor at the Vrije Universiteit Brussels (VUB-LSTS). Associated-Professor at Tilburg University (TILT). Coordinator of the EU project Supporting Training Activities on the Data Protection Reform" (STAR), http://www.project-star.eu/ The author would like to thank Sara Roda for her help.

14.1. Introduction: the enforcement of EU data protection relies on a criminal justice model, a civil justice model, and an enforcement agency model

Very much like EU equality and non-discrimination law,[1] EU data protection law proposes a mixture of remedies provided by civil, administrative or criminal law. In 2013, under the regime of the 1995 Data Protection Directive (*below*), the European Union Fundamental Rights Agency (FRA) found with regard to data protection that "in almost all member states criminal sanctions can be imposed, in the form of a fine or imprisonment."[2] Some states (e.g. the UK and the Netherlands) only criminalized some data protection wrongs and mainly used civil law or administrative sanctions, others opted for an extensive set of data protection crimes. Some countries like Belgium in that period exclusively opted for criminal law.[3]

The 1995 Directive left the choice of the enforcement regime to the discretion of the Member States. This explains why in Italy the remedial system relies mainly on administrative sanctions, while the criminal path was favoured in Belgium. This also explains why most, but not all Member States, on the basis of the Directive mandated national agencies ('Data Protection Authorities') to sanction data protection violations with administrative fines and entrusted them with investigatory powers.

Most Member State laws, again like most non-discrimination laws, emphasized in one way or another the use of civil remedies. Civil court procedures are not as much about the erosion of the social fabric, but deal with the dignity of the victim, and are aimed at bringing data protection violations to an end, restoring the *status quo antes* and ensuring compensation and damages for harm incurred as well as for future loss of earnings.[4]

---

[1] R. Iordache, I. Ionescu, 'Discrimination and its Sanctions - Symbolic vs. Effective Remedies in European Anti-discrimination Law', (2014) 19 *European Anti-discrimination Law Review*, 11; A. Galetta, P. De Hert, 'The Proceduralisation of Data Protection Remedies under EU Data Protection Law: Towards a More Effective and Data Subject-Oriented Remedial System?', (2015) 8 *Review of European Administrative Law (REALaw)* 125, 132-134.

[2] European Union Agency for Fundamental Rights, Access to data protection remedies in EU member states, Publications Office of the European Union, Luxembourg, 2013, 7. http://fra.europa.eu/en/publication/2014/access-data-protection-remedies-eu-member-states; the FRA added that "[s]anctions that data protection authorities are empowered to impose differ between member states. [...] The duration of a sentence and the amount of a fine also vary across member states" (*Ibidem*, p. 7).

[3] If a country opts for criminal law sanctions, these are almost always to be found in the respective data protection acts, with the exception of France. A 1992 French law moved the sanctions of the 1978 general data protection law to the criminal code, more particularly to a section on "Des atteintes aux droits de la personne résultant des fichiers ou des traitements informatiques".

[4] Compare Iordache, Ionescu, *supra* note 1, 12 & 14.

In the past years the EU, based on the Lisbon *acquis*, has implemented an impressive reform of its data protection laws. It has amended the foregoing enforcement system, without fundamentally altering its three building blocks: a criminal justice model, a civil justice model, and an enforcement agency model. Citizens can still have some of their data protection complaints treated under criminal law. They can still bring cases before civil law courts or rely on what McCrudden calls the enforcement agency model – individual grievances are remedied with the assistance of a specialised body that has investigatory powers in assisting victims of data protection infringements.[5] New is the requirement in EU law that all Member States equally empower their Data Protection Authorities to impose administrative fines.

In the following we will mainly deal with the use of sanctioning powers in the context of EU data protection law and reflect on the thorny relationship between different typologies of sanctions (criminal and administrative) in the light of the new administrative sanctioning powers of the Data Protection Authorities. Rather than a conceptualization of the authorities as such, we intend to offer a conceptualization of the exercise of sanctioning powers by these authorities.

After a short historical presentation of the EU (secondary) laws dealing with data protection (section 1), we look at changes to EU primary law brought about by the Treaty of Lisbon with an explicit imperative to improve EU data protection (section 2). Both the EU Charter and the Treaty on the Functioning of the European Union require the presence of independent and effective data protection authorities (DPAs). We look at the relevant provision on these requirements in the 2016 General Data Protection Regulation or GDPR (section 3), followed by brief discussion of the responsibilities, tasks and powers of DPAs (section 4), their duties to cooperate at the European and international level (one-stop-shop and EDPB) (section 5).

We then turn to the core of the analysis, discussing the system of remedies in the GDPR (section 6) and some examples of recent sanctioning practices by the national DPAs (section 7). The analysis is followed by three more reflective sections about supervisory convergence without creating new EU institutions (section 8), the administrative enforcement fray and defence rights (section 9) and the role of criminal law in EU data protection law (section 10). The chapter is followed by conclusions and some guidance observations about the operationalisation of the threefold system of enforcement set up by EU data protection law.

14.2. EU secondary laws on data protection

Data protection is an EU law field that has undergone substantial, if not ground-

---

[5] C. McCrudden, 'National Legal Remedies for Racial Inequality', in S. Fredman, P. Alstone (eds) *Discrimination and Human Rights: The Case of Racism* (Oxford University Press, 2001), 253-259. Compare L. Farkas, 'Collective actions under European anti-discrimination law', (2014) 19 *European Anti-discrimination Law Review*, 25.

breaking, change over the past years. In early 2012, the European Commission presented its proposals for the EU data protection reform package. This "package" comprised a proposal for a Regulation, the General Data Protection Regulation [6] (intended to replace the 1995 EU Data Protection Directive) [7] and a proposal for a Directive, the Law Enforcement Directive [8] (intended to replace Framework Decision 2008/977/JHA on the protection of personal data processed in the framework of police and judicial cooperation in criminal matters). [9] In April 2016, a five-year law-making process finally came to an end, with the formal adoption of the General Data Protection Regulation (Regulation (EU) 2016/679, GDPR) [10] and the Law Enforcement Directive (Directive (EU) 680/2016, LED). [11]

The GDPR is applicable to processing activities of personal data by all public and private actors in EU Member States, with the exception of law enforcement authorities (see *below*). It is an ambitious text aimed not only at replacing the 1995 EU Data Protection Directive, and hence resolve harmonization issues across the EU, but also at bringing EU data protection law in line with modern personal data processing. To this end, a series of changes have been suggested by the European Commission (and accepted by the co-legislators) aimed at serving this double role: detailed data protection provisions intend to exclude or limit the need for any national legislative intervention, while new data protection tools and novelties (e.g. impact assessments and a

---

[6] European Commission, Proposal for a Regulation of the European Parliament and of the Council on the protection of individuals with regard to the processing of personal data and on the free movement of such data (General Data Protection Regulation), COM(2012) 11 final, 25 January 2012.

[7] Directive 95/46/EC of the European Parliament and of the Council of 24 October 1995 on the protection of individuals with regard to the processing of personal data and on the free movement of such data, OJ 1995, L 281/31-50.

[8] European Commission, Proposal for a Directive of the European Parliament and of the Council on the protection of individuals with regard to the processing of personal data by competent authorities for the purposes of prevention, investigation, detection or prosecution of criminal offences or the execution of criminal penalties, and the free movement of such data, COM(2012) 10 final, 25 January 2012 .

[9] Adopted 27 November 2008 and published in Official Journal 30 December 2008. Implementation deadline was 27 November 2010.

[10] Regulation (EU) 2016/679 of the European Parliament and of the Council of 27 April 2016 on the protection of natural persons with regard to the processing of personal data and on the free movement of such data, and repealing Directive 95/46/EC (General Data Protection Regulation), OJ 2016, L119/1–88. See for a short discussion, C. Burton, L. De Boel, C. Kuner, A. Pateraki, S. Cadiot, S. Hoffman, 'The Final European Union General Data Protection Regulation', (2016) *Privacy and Security Law Report*, 14.

[11] Directive (EU) 2016/680 of the European Parliament and of the Council of 27 April 2016 on the protection of natural persons with regard to the processing of personal data by competent authorities for the purposes of the prevention, investigation, detection or prosecution of criminal offences or the execution of criminal penalties, and on the free movement of such data, and repealing Council Framework Decision 2008/977/JHA, OJ 2016, L 119/89-131.

risk-based approach, recognition of accountability, privacy by design, notification breach, the right to be forgotten, data portability, etc.) aim at bringing the EU data protection view into the new era.

The LED had to be transposed by EU Member States by May 2018. It has two main objectives: to increase the level of fundamental rights' protection in the area of police and criminal justice matters within the EU, and to facilitate data-sharing between law enforcement authorities in EU Member States, as their co-operation is based on mutual recognition of each other's national data protection rules. The Directive replaced the 2008 Data Protection Framework Decision primarily to resolve its basic limitation in scope: the new Directive regulates personal data processing by Member States competent authorities that are responsible for the execution of criminal penalties or for the prevention, investigation, detection or prosecution of crimes (understood broadly, including the safeguarding against and the prevention of threats to public security), and not only inter-Member States exchanges of data, as was the case under the Framework Decision. The Directive also addresses several shortcomings in applying the basic data protection principles brought forward by the 2008 Data Protection Framework Decision.

The 2012 package did not deal with all EU existing data protection laws. Two other instruments remained to be adapted: the e-Privacy Directive regulating rules and safeguards for citizen in the area of telecommunications,[12] and Regulation 45/2001 containing data protection and communication rules for (most) EU institutions. Accordingly, on 10th January 2017 the European Commission published a proposal for a new Regulation on data protection for Union institutions, bodies, offices and agencies (EUIB Regulation), together with the proposal for a new e-Privacy Regulation.

The discussion on the new e-Privacy Regulation is still far from finished but is said to be finalised by 2020. The future Regulation aims to achieve the establishment of a new privacy framework by complementing and particularizing the GDPR but this time in the area of electronic communications data. The proposed Regulation takes account of the important technological and economic developments in the sector of electronic communications and will modernize existing principles according to new practices. It aims to promote a high level of protection of confidentiality in communications regardless of the technology used.

The new EUIB Regulation was published in November 2018 after a short legislative process completed in 18 months, with intense discussions and around 100 amendments.[13] Like its predecessor (Regulation 45/2001), the new Regulation lays

---

[12] Directive 2002/58/EC of the European Parliament and of the Council of 12 July 2002 concerning the processing of personal data and the protection of privacy in the electronic communications sector (Directive on privacy and electronic communications), OJ 2002, L 201/37.

[13] Regulation (EU) 2018/1725 of the European Parliament and of the Council of 23 October 2018 on the protection of natural persons with regard to the processing of personal data by the

down data protection obligations for the EU institutions and bodies when they process personal data and develop new policies. These obligations are taken mostly from the GDPR, but also include obligations taken from the most recent version of the proposal for a new e-Privacy Regulation. The Regulation further sets out the duties of the EDPS, in particular its role as an independent supervisory authority of the EU institutions and bodies when they process personal data, as an advisor on policies and legislation that affect privacy and cooperating with similar authorities to ensure consistent data protection.

14.3. EU primary law provisions on data protection and the imperative to improve EU data protection

The foregoing shows an intense regulatory activity in the past years. Data Protection was gradually working itself up to the short list of EU top priorities. The first important step in that development was the Charter of Fundamental Rights of the European Union (Charter), proclaimed as soft law instrument on 7 December 2000 and turned into a binding legal instrument with the Treaty of Lisbon, which entered into force on 1 December 2009. [14] Significant and deviating from the 1950 European Convention on Human Rights (ECHR) was the distinction made in the Charter between the right to respect for private life, which included protection of communications (Article 7 Charter) and the right to the protection of personal data (Article 8 Charter), [15] spotlighting the growing importance of data protection in the constitutional assemblage of current society.

The Treaty of Lisbon has contributed to this success of data protection law. In particular, Article 16 of the Treaty on the Functioning of the European Union (TFEU) constitutes a central provision in the EU data protection field since it recognizes (again) an independent individual right to data protection, separate from any other right. [16] It is essentially this specific Article that triggered the EU

Union institutions, bodies, offices and agencies and on the free movement of such data, and repealing Regulation (EC) No 45/2001 and Decision No 1247/2002/EC, OJ 2018, L 295/39-98.

[14] Charter of Fundamental Rights of the European Union, OJ 2012, C326/391.

[15] Article 8 Charter (Protection of personal data): "1. Everyone has the right to the protection of personal data concerning him or her. 2. Such data must be processed fairly for specified purposes and on the basis of the consent of the person concerned or some other legitimate basis laid down by law. Everyone has the right of access to data which has been collected concerning him or her, and the right to have it rectified. 3. Compliance with these rules shall be subject to control by an independent authority."

[16] Article 16 TFEU: "1. Everyone has the right to the protection of personal data concerning them. 2. The European Parliament and the Council, acting in accordance with the ordinary legislative procedure, shall lay down the rules relating to the protection of individuals with regard to the processing of personal data by Union institutions, bodies, offices and agencies, and by the

data protection overhaul discussed in the foregoing.

While an analysis of Article 16 TFEU and its requirements for EU data protection exceeds the purposes of this analysis,[17] here it is enough to make three observations.

Firstly, Article 16 TFEU allows law-makers to approach data protection not in terms of the EU internal market or the old pillar system or any other similar limitations, but in terms of an independent, separate, cross-sector individual right that needs to be respected in all the EU competence areas. The limit is no longer EU secondary law, but EU primary law. In other words, it is no longer necessary to consider EU secondary data protection laws such as the 1995 EU Data Protection Directive[18] as the data protection standard-setting texts, against which all level of data protection both in and out of the EU ought to be assessed. Article 16 TFEU makes this exercise superficial and mandates the EU co-legislators to regulate both data processing by EU institutions and data processing by (all) actors in Member States when carrying out activities which fall within the scope of Union law (see also our third point *below*). Our feeling is that Article 16 TFEU intentionally draws the attention away from the normal subsidiarity principle exercise ('powers are in hands of Member States, unless the Union can do better') and draws the data protection policy agenda to the Brussels levels, based on an implicit understanding that this area is *supra* national. As we will see *below* the current enforcement system defined by the GDPR and the LED still relies on the intervention of national supervisory authorities. When this turns out to be inadequate it is conceivable one day, based on Article 16 TFEU, to replace this with an enforcement system that relies more on an EU supervisory body.

Secondly, Article 16 TFEU asks for effective, independent oversight. While "*independent*" oversight is most likely external, 'effective oversight' may well be a combination of internal and external mechanisms. To this end, existing pre-Lisbon data protection oversight mechanisms were not necessarily need to be replaced under the new EU data protection environment, but a fresh look at those mechanisms, in place at the time of the Lisbon Treaty, in light of Article 16 TFEU, is nevertheless warranted by the TFEU.

Thirdly, Article 16 TFEU asks for simple and straightforward individual access to

---

Member States when carrying out activities which fall within the scope of Union law, and the rules relating to the free movement of such data. Compliance with these rules shall be subject to the control of independent authorities".

[17] See for instance the relevant analysis in H. Hijmans, A. Scirocco, 'Shortcomings in EU Data Protection in the Third and the Second Pillars. Can the Lisbon Treaty be expected to help?', (2009) 46 *Common Market Law Review*, 1494. See also P. De Hert, 'The Right to Protection of Personal Data. Incapable of Autonomous Standing in the Basic EU Constituting Documents?', (2015) 31 *Utrecht Journal of International and European Law*, 1.

[18] Directive 95/46/EC.

justice. This in turn requires clear and direct replies to the basic questions of legal standing (who can sue data controllers and in which court?), scope of judicial review (what can the judge assess?), available remedies (monetary indemnity) and cost of the whole process. These answers need to be clear and accessible to individuals across the EU, regardless of the legal instruments they are based on or the type of processing they refer to.

Of equal importance is Declaration 21 attached to the Treaty.[19] This provision demonstrates that in EU law the criminal justice and law enforcement area is distinguished from other personal data processing activities and awarded with the possibility (but not obligation) to benefit from specific rules, fitted to its particular needs and purposes.[20] It explains the continued presence of a specific general instrument for this area (the LED Directive) and specific data protection provisions in the EU laws on law enforcement related agencies (like Europol, Eurojust, European Public Prosecutor Office) and databases (like Schengen and Eurodac), with specific provisions on data subject rights (such as the access to their data) and supervision.[21]

It is interesting to observe what the drafters have summarized and mentioned both in the Charter and in the TFEU. Data Protection law is in fact a complex bundle of principles, rules, ideas, obligations and powers, a bundle that grows over time, with new ideas and sensibilities (such as about a right to be forgotten). Both primary texts only 'pick' some of these elements, and consequently do not mention

---

[19] "The Conference acknowledges that specific rules on the protection of personal data and the free movement of such data in the fields of judicial cooperation in criminal matters and police cooperation based on Article 16 of the Treaty on the Functioning of the European Union may prove necessary because of the specific nature of these fields".

[20] See P. De Hert, V. Papakonstantinou, 'The Data Protection Framework Decision of 27 November 2008 Regarding Police and Judicial Cooperation in Criminal Matters - A Modest Achievement However Not the Improvement Some Have Hoped for', (2009) 26 *Computer Law & Security Review* 403. These are well-identified by now and need only be mentioned here in brief: the need for security agencies to, among others, use hints and hearsay as well as to constantly correlate and re-examine information within their systems in order to effectively execute their tasks makes a level of flexibility as regards individual data protection imperative. Declaration 21 carries therefore concrete consequences for the EU criminal justice and law enforcement area both in terms of architecture, whereby specialized data protection legislation is permitted, if not encouraged, and in terms of substantial law, whereby such specialized legislation may include different data protection provisions than those applying to all other, general personal data processing.

[21] P. De Hert, J. Sajfert, 'Police, privacy and data protection from a comparative legal perspective', in M. den Boer (ed.), *Comparative Policing from a Legal Perspective* (Edward Elgar, 2018), 306; P. De Hert, V. Papakonstantinou, 'Data protection policies in EU Justice and Home Affairs. A multi-layered and yet unexplored territory for legal research' in A. Ripoll Servent, F. Trauner (eds), *Routledge Handbook of Justice and Home Affairs Research* (Routledge, 2018), 169; P. De Hert, V. Papakonstantinou, 'Data protection: the EU institutions' battle over data processing vs individual rights', in F. Trauner, A. Ripoll Servent (eds), *Policy change in the Area of Freedom, Security and Justice. How EU Institutions Matter* (Routledge, 2015), 178.

others (like the principle of data minimization). Striking pick in both texts is the right to have independent authorities controlling on processing activities.[22]

Hijmans emphasizes the importance of this anchor for data protection authorities (DPAs) in EU primary law: "control by these authorities is not only an essential part of enforcement, it is even qualified as "an essential component of the protection" itself. In other words, EU law does not only provide for institutions with a specific responsibility for the protection, but it gives the right to data protection an institutional dimension. DPAs as independent public authorities for data protection are a unique phenomenon in EU law. This specific position is, in the first place, the result of the constitutional foundation of the role of the DPAs in primary law".[23]

Primary law does not only anchor the existence of supervisory authorities, but also requires them to be independent. Hijmans identifies a plurality of more or less self-explanatory reasons for this,[24] but does not mention the identity building aspect behind this institutional requirement vis-à-vis the outside world. Many third countries, with the US as the most striking example, have no independent supervision as an essential component of data protection,[25] and in a connected world with international transfers, the EU is using its basic documents to defend its vision on effective enforcement of privacy and data protection, with independent agencies as a major building block. [26]

---

[22] Comp. Article 8(3) Charter: 'Compliance with these rules shall be subject to control by an independent authority' and Article 16(2) *in fine* TFEU: 'Compliance with these rules shall be subject to the control of independent authorities'.

[23] H. Hijmans, *The European Union as Guardian of Internet Privacy* (Springer, 2016), 564.

[24] See on six reasons for independence of DPA's, Hijmans, *supra* note 23, 330-333.

[25] Hijmans, *supra* note 23, 339-340.

[26] I share the skepticism of Neudorf about creating a big fuzz about independence (as opposed to effectiveness), especially in a global context. We recall that Article 13 ECHR requires 'effective' remedies and keeps silence about the 'independence' of the authorities empowered to discuss the rights infringements. Independence is only one of the formulae to enhance impartiality, as opposed to the realization of a particular political arrangement or a proxy for substantive views about fundamental rights protection. There is no magic checklist to produce impartially. Courts are social institutions bound up with their culture and context that build their legitimacy over the course of time. Promoting high substantive and formal standards of independence, without taken into consideration local history and the important role played by informal constraints in judicial institutions and oversight mechanism. Compare L. Neudorf, 'Promoting Independent Justice in a Changing World', (2012) 12 *Human Rights Law Review*, 107; A. Jori, 'Shaping vs applying data protection law: two core functions of data protection authorities', (2015) 5 *International Data Privacy Law* 133. This author identifies hesitations within the EU and its Member States between DPAs adding political advocacy to their basic roles as mediators and enforcers, and DPAs reducing themselves or being reduced by politics to the more technical roles of mediators and enforcers checking compliance with the law and no more. The author develops the thesis that countries with 'grand' DPAs that dare to stand up against governments are probably those that meet all criteria of the rule of law and vice versa (135).

Now, what are these intriguing controlling bodies? What does independent mean? and Why is their independent supervision of such an importance to have it anchored in EU primary law?[27] The following offers a conceptualization of the exercise of sanctioning powers by these authorities rather than a conceptualization of the authorities as such. We refer to the excellent book of Hielke Hijmans for more in-depth conceptualizations of these authorities.[28]

14.4. Independent and effective data protection authorities (DPAs) and the GDPR

The GDPR is a long legal act (173 recitals and 99 articles and almost half of it focusses on the independence, collaboration duties, tasks and powers of the data protection authorities. What are they?

Chapter VI (Articles 51-59) and Chapter VII (Articles 60-76) discuss respectively the general job-description of DPA's and their collaborations in the EU context.

In the line of EU primary law provisions discussed *above*, the GDPR requires that each Member State shall provide for one or more independent public authorities to be responsible for monitoring the application of those rules to protect the fundamental rights and freedoms of natural persons in relation to processing and to facilitate the free flow of personal data within the Union (Article 51(1) GDPR). These authorities, – DPAs – are independent public authorities that supervise the application of the data protection law in the Member States. Each supervisory authority shall contribute to the consistent application of the GDPR. In order to exercise their power in an effective way they have investigative and corrective powers. Where more than one authority is established in a State, this state shall designate the lead supervisory authority (Article 51(3) GDPR).

The GDPR distinguishes between the "members" and the staff working within these agencies. A DPA can be directed by one, two or more "members" and be tailored taking into account legal and organization culture of a given Member State. Required is proper 'staffing' and members with the qualifications, experience and skills required to make a DPA work. Choice and design of the DPA is left rather open in the GDPR and is partly a non-legal matter. Law has a lot to say on "inde-

---

[27] Compare with the right to non-discrimination. This right is also one of the selected Charter rights that has made it explicitly into the TFEU, but there is no mentioning of the presence of a specific oversight mechanism.

[28] Hijmans's analysis is very rich and productive and is based on a comparison between DPA's and EU agencies in other areas of law and on literature on expert bodies. The most fundamental claim in his book is that DPAs –and certain other expert bodies– qualify as a new branch of government complementing the traditional separation of powers. See Hijmans, *supra* note 23, 341-353.

pendence of DPAs" (see *below*), but there is so far little case law on design and effectiveness of DPAs.[29]

Article 52 GDPR defines the idea of independence and should be read together with other related GDPR-provisions that complement the main idea. Needed is "complete independence" in performing tasks and exercising powers (Article 52(1) GDPR), which requires remaining free from external influence, whether directly or indirectly, and not seeking or taking instructions from anybody (Article 52(2) GDPR); self-restraint from the DPAs' members ("refraining from actions incompatible with their duties and incompatible occupations") (Article 52(3) GDPR); proper resources, with financial control that does not affect its independence, and proper staffing, with a staff that needs to be self-appointed (Article 52(4-6) GDPR). Article 53 GDPR adds further with, more or less, traditional requirements about how to appoint members of DPA's, what conditions (integrity, experience and skills) they need to fulfill to be eligible, and what kind of legal basis is needed to organize dismissals and retirements.

All these elements read as a handbook chapter on protecting these agencies against authoritarian political interventions. For that the GDPR-drafters were able to fall back on important Court of Justice of the European Union (CJEU) judgements that defined and clarified the notion of independence already incorporated in the 1995 Directive.[30] With political developments towards more authoritarian types of governance within Europe, these provisions nicely anticipate all kinds of tricks to tame supervision and to reduce supervisory authorities to mere enforcers, cutting of their more political advocacy tasks.[31]

As we observed above there is a lack of legal clarification of effectiveness of DPAs. There is abundant case law by the CJEU on the notion of independence, but there is less on the more complex notion of effectiveness. This will be a challenge

---

[29] On the importance of the design of supervisory authorities in the area of data protection law, see K.A. Bamberger, D.K. Mulligan, 'Privacy on the Books and on the Ground', (2010) 63 *Stanford Law Review* 247.

[30] See C-518/07 *Commission v. Germany*, ECLI:EU:C:2010:125 (violation of the requirement of independence by making the authorities responsible for monitoring personal data processing outside the public sector in the different *Lander* subject to State oversight); C-614/10 *Commission v. Austria*, ECLI:EU:C:2012:631 (violation of the requirement of independence by integrating the DPA within the departments of the Federal Chancellery, and placing DPA staff under the authority of the Federal Chancellery and subject to its supervision); C-288/12 *Commission v. Hungary*, ECLI:EU:C:2014:237 (violation of the requirement of independence by prematurely ending the term of a member of the DPA); C-362/14 *Schrems v. Data Protection Commissioner*, ECLI: EU:C:2015:650 (adequacy decisions by the Commission bind Member States but cannot eliminate or reduce the powers of the DPAs accorded by Article 8(3) of the CFR). For a short discussion see L. Laudati, *Summaries of EU Court Decisions Relating to Data Protection 2000-2015* (Olaf Publishing, 2016) 51-53, 59; Hijmans, *supra* note 23, pp. 354-360; Jori, *supra* note 26, 137-139; Galetta, De Hert, *supra* note 1, 132-134.

[31] Galetta, De Hert, *supra* note 1, 133-143.

for the legal apparatus, but not an impossible one. We remind that both Article 13 ECHR and Article 47 Charter provide for a right to an effective (and not "independent") remedy.[32] From a human rights perspective, effectiveness is the key target of a remedy. Independence can contribute to effectiveness but does not equal it. American observers are critical of the many differences that persist in the organization of DPAs within Europe and rightly argue for more research on European privacy practices "on the ground" to learn from what works and what does not work within Europe.[33] This kind of literature is now being produced within Europe,[34] and will undoubtedly benefit from case law on the matter and self-reporting by DPAs about their performance.

Vranaki emphasizes the complex nature of some of the investigations and controls by DPAs that often involve different co-operative relationships between various actors.[35] She opposes an understanding of the regulatory roles of EU DPAs solely in terms of a "top-down" exercise of authority by the EU DPAs over the data controller. A dominant focus on the enforcement powers of DPAs, blinds us from seeing broader, multifaceted, and non-normative roles played by DPAs. Looking at concrete relationships between DPAs and other actors with a broad understanding of possible compliance attitudes and regulatory enforcement styles (beyond "punish" or "persuade" categories), Vranaki points at different co-operative relationships between all the various actors, with the DPAs' mixing deterrence and persua-

---

[32] See for an analysis of the *Schrems* and *Leander* judgements, and a short reflection about Article 13 ECHR, P. De Hert, J. Sajfert, 'The role of the data protection authorities in supervising police and criminal justice authorities processing personal data', in C. Brière, A. Weyembergh (eds), *The Needed Balances in EU Criminal Law: Past, Present and Future* (Hart, 2018), 243-255, 252-253.

[33] K.A. Bamberger, D.K. Mulligan, 'Privacy in Europe: Initial Data on Governance Choices and Corporate Practices', (2013) 81 *George Washington Law Review*, 1529.

[34] See C. Raab, I. Szekely, 'Data Protection Authorities and Information Technology', (2017) 33 *Computer Law & Security Review*, 421-433; F. Bieker, 'Enforcing Data Protection Law – the Role of the Supervisory Authorities in Theory and Practice', in A. Lehmann, D. Whitehouse, S. Fischer-Hübner, L. Fritsch, C. Raab (eds.), *Privacy and Identity Management: Facing up to Next Steps* (Springer, 2017), 125–139; D. Barnard-Wills, 'The Technology Foresight Activities of European Union Data Protection Authorities', (2017) *Technological Forecasting and Societal Change* 116; A. Vranaki, 'Social Networking Site Regulation: Facebook, Online Behavioral Advertising, Power and Data Protection Laws', (2017) 43 *Rutgers Computer & Technology Law Journal* 169; A. Vranaki, 'Learning Lessons from Cloud Investigations in Europe: Bargaining Enforcement and Multiple Centers of Regulation in Data Protection', (2016) 2 *Journal of Law, Technology and Policy* 245-275; A. Vranaki, 'Cloud Investigations by European Data Protection Authorities: An Empirical Account' in J.A. Rothchild (ed.), *Research Handbook on Electronic Commerce Law* (Edward Elgar, 2016), 518-544; P- De Hert, D. Kloza, P. Makowski (eds) *Enforcing Privacy: Lessons from Current Implementations and Perspectives for the Future* (Wydawnictwo Sejmowe, 2015), 146.

[35] Vranaki, *Cloud Investigations*, *supra* note 34.

sion depending on factors such as compliance attitude and technological complexities to carry out the investigation. These entanglements and the interactivity observed in the practice of data protection law enforcement explain why actors are required to talkwith each other or discuss actions and controls together, and why the picture of top-down DPA enforcement is far from accurate.[36] The GDPR is in fact a product of this development and proposes not only sanctions, but also facilitative instruments and foresees interactions between diverse stakeholders, such as lawmakers, EU DPAs, European Data Protection Board (EDPB), European Commission, data controllers, data processors, and quasi-regulators (e.g. third-party certification bodies).[37] For Asma Vranaki effective enforcement will depend on the regulatory relationship management of the parties involved, with the DPA's picking the right enforcement style and with the firms working harder on their relationships with the EU DPAs.[38]

Hijmans develops a framework for understanding the effectiveness of DPAs.[39] He acknowledges that no cases have been brought before the CJEU focusing on this requirement and labels effectiveness as "not an obligation that, under current law, can easily be quantified or challenged in legal proceedings",[40] not only because DPAs are free to set their own agendas, but also because it is for the Member States, not the EU, to foresee that they are provided with adequate resources, and also accountability requirements about their effectiveness which might endanger their independence in the long run. Overall Hijmans' tone is optimistic. The GDPR is designed to streamline these authorities and a main element is to allocate more effective sanctioning powers.[41] These new powers, together with the detailed GDPR provisions on for instance proper staffing and activity reports (Article 59 GDPR),[42] will make some European controls (and possible case law) on the effectiveness of national DPAs possible. Moreover, various soft tools could enhance the effectiveness of DPAs without prejudice to their independence,

---

[36] See on horizontal style of supervision, focusing on cooperation with the supervisee and the risks that engaging in a dialogue with the private sector may complicate enforcement in the event of a later – alleged – breach of data protection law, Hijmans, *supra* note 23, 337-338 with ref. to A. Ottow, *Market & Competition Authorities, Good Agency Principles* (Oxford, 2015), 164.

[37] A. Vranaki, 'Smart Regulation and the General Data Protection Regulation', (2016) *Computers & Law*, 9-11.

[38] *Ibidem*, 11.

[39] Hijmans, *supra* note 23, 365-374.

[40] *Ibidem*, 370.

[41] See section 7.

[42] About the very positive image the UK DPA was able to present via its activity report, see 'ICO Publishes First Annual Report Since GDPR's Implementation', posted on 18 July 2019, https://www.huntonprivacyblog.com/2019/07/18/ico-publishes-first-annual-report-since-gdprs-implementation/#more-17750.

Hijmans concludes, and gives the following examples: peer reviews, impact assessments or engaging with external experts.[43]

In a next section we will discuss the long list of tasks for DPAs. Compared to the 1995 Directive this list has grown considerably (including more stringent 'European tasks'), a fact that provoked a comment by the Belgian DPA whether overtasking could affect the desired effectiveness of the national authorities.[44] The comment is straightforward and easy to understand. If we expect a DPA to deal with every single complaint of 'its' citizen, and thus identify with its role as ombudsperson (=complaints handling), other roles and tasks might be jeopardized. Lack of clear choices *or*, on the contrary, clear choices against, for example, the ombudsperson-role (in order to concentrate on other tasks, such as shaping policy), might fire back negatively in the face of a DPA in the public eye perception.[45]

14.5. Responsibilities, tasks and powers of DPAs (Articles 57-58-59 GDPR)

DPAs are independent from governments. They are responsible for enforcing data protection laws at a national level and providing guidance on the interpretation of those laws (Recital 117, Article 51 GDPR). Each Member State is required to appoint one or more DPAs to implement the GDPR and protect the rights and freedoms of individuals (Recital 117, Article 51 GDPR).

The GDPR makes a complicated distinction between competences (Article 55 GDPR), tasks (Article 57 GDPR) and powers (Article 58 GDPR). The two latter provisions identify no less than 22 tasks and 26 powers, with Article 57 ironically adding "fulfilling any other tasks related to the protection of personal data" to the list of tasks as item 22.

In literature, several classifications are proposed to understand the tasking of DPAs.[46] In our understanding of the ambitious list of tasks contained in Article 57

---

[43] Hijmans, *supra* note 23.

[44] Belgian DPA, Opinion no. 35/2012 of 21 November 2012 on the draft regulation of the European Parliament and of the Council on the protection of individuals with regard to the processing of personal data and on the free movement of such data, para. 143, via https://www.dataprotectionautho rity.be/sites/privacycommission/files/documents/opinion_35_2012.pdf. Compare Raab, Szekely, *supra* note 34, 430 (smaller DPA are lacking ICT-expertise for technology foresight).

[45] See the harsh, in our view not always fair, comments on 30 years of functioning of the Dutch DPA in the press, in B. Heilbron, E. Koopman, 'De Autoriteit Persoonsgegevens is nog altijd onvolwassen. De tragedie van het Privacytoezicht' (2019) 3 *De Groene Amsterdammer*, available at https://www.groene.nl/artikel/de-tragedie-van-het-privacytoezicht.

[46] For a short discussion, Raab, Szekely, *supra* note 34, 421-422; Jori, *supra* note 26, 134. Both refer to the groundbreaking role of Canadian political scientist Colin J. Bennett who differentiates between the roles of DPAs as ombudsmen, as auditors, as consultants, as educators, as policy advisers, as negotiators, as enforcers, and as international ambassadors.

GDPR, these can be bundled around the following seven addressees and themes: 1) public institutions and bodies (advise on legislative and administrative measures relating to the protection of natural persons' rights and freedoms with regard to processing); 2) the GDPR (monitor and enforce the application of the GDPR; promote awareness of controllers and processors of their obligations under the GDPR; conduct investigations on the application of the GDPR); 3) data subjects (promote public awareness and understanding of the risks, rules, safeguards and rights in relation to processing; upon request, provide information concerning the exercise of their rights under the GDPR; handle complaints); 4) controllers and processors (encourage the drawing up of codes of conduct and carry out a periodic review of certifications; authorize contractual clauses and provisions; approve binding corporate rules; establish and maintain a list in relation to the requirement for data protection impact assessment; give advice on the processing operations); 5) other supervisory authorities (cooperation; sharing information and provide mutual assistance); 6) international cooperation (contribute to the activities of the EDPB); monitor relevant developments, insofar as they have an impact on the protection of personal data); and 7) any other tasks related to the protection of personal data.

The 26 powers of the DPAs identified in Article 58 GDPR are about: 1) investigative powers (DPAs have the authority to intervene in all organizations and business activities, insofar as personal data is processed and carry out investigations and review certifications; obtain access to all personal data and to all information necessary for the performance of its tasks; obtain access to any premises of the controller and the processor, including to any data processing equipment and means); 2) corrective powers (issue warnings and reprimands for the controller; order the controller or the processor to comply with the data subject's requests to exercise his or her rights pursuant to the GDPR; communicate a personal data breach to the data subject; impose an administrative fines); 3) authorization of processing activities and advisory powers; and 4) authorization of model clauses and binding corporate rules.[47]

14.6. European and trans-border tasks and cooperation between DPAs (one-stop-shop and EDPB)

Many GDPR-provisions deal with the trans-border aspects of the DPA's work. In principle, their jurisdiction and enforcement powers are largely restricted to the territory of their own Member State (Recital 124, Articles 51, 55, 56 GDPR), but the reality of the digital society and the goal of the EU to facilitate the free flow of per-

---

[47] For a comparison with the reduced list of tasks and powers provided for in the LED, De Hert, Sajfert, *supra* note 32, 250-252.

sonal data between Member States without compromising the protection of personal data explains the importance of these provisions on the extra- and trans-border aspects of their work. DPAs are not only required to cooperate and provide each other with mutual assistance (Recitals 135-138 and Articles 4(23), 56 and 63-67; Articles 68-76 GDPR), but are also asked to accept a one-stop-shop mechanism as a derogation from the territorial jurisdiction principle in certain cases (Recitals 124-128, Articles 55-56; Article 29 Data Protection Working Party (WP29) Lead DPA Guidelines).[48]

This mechanism applies to and should benefit organizations operating across Member States and thus processing personal data of data subjects in different Member States. It allows these organizations to deal with only one DPA (as opposed to up to 27 DPAs). Hence, a single "lead DPA" can be chosen when different authorities are responsible for the processing operations, performed by the same entity, but affecting rights of data subjects in different Member States.

How does it work? If a data controller conducts cross-border data processing in the EU, according to the GDPR the supervisory authority is the one based in the Member State where the data controller has its main establishment. If the data controller's activity concerns citizens of another Member State, the local DPA of that state may hand over the case to the DPA of the main establishment (lead supervisory authority) or can handle the case locally in co-operation with the latter.

A DPA that wishes to take action must consult with the other affected DPAs to ensure consistency of the GDPR (consistency mechanism). In particular, it shall inform the lead supervisory authority without delay and the latter shall decide within three weeks whether or not it will handle the case in accordance with the procedure provided in Article 60 GDPR.[49]

The foregoing is the provisional outcome of a power struggle between several stakeholders. As said, the one-stop-shop mechanism must be understood as a derogation from the jurisdiction principle of territority (states enforce norms within their territory). 'Proximity' was one of the arguments by opponents of this derogation. In their view, proximity required that individuals were entitled to protection by the DPA in the Member State where they reside.[50] The opposition against one-stop-shop mechanisms was partly fuelled by a lack of trust in the effectiveness of DPAs in other countries.[51]

---

[48] WP29, Guidelines for identifying a controller or processor's lead supervisory authority, WP 244, adopted on 13 December 2016.

[49] If the lead supervisory authority decides to handle the case, then Article 60 GDPR applies. If the lead supervisory authority decides not to handle the case, then the supervisory authority which informed the lead supervisory authority shall handle it according to Articles 61 and 62 GDPR.

[50] See on this discussion, Hijmans, *supra* note 23, p. 371.

[51] For a comparison with the more modest European tasks of DPAs and the lack of GDPR-

Essential in the success of the GDPR will be the functioning of the EDPB, made up of representatives of DPAs from each Member State and the European Data Protection Supervisor (EDPS). The European Commission takes part in the meetings of the EDPB without voting rights (Articles 68-76 GDPR). This organ – successor to WP29 under the 1995 Directive – functions as an advisory and appellate body to the national DPAs and is the central guarantor of the so-called GDPR consistency mechanism, supplementing the cooperation rules discussed above, to ensure an harmonious application of the GDPR across the different EU Member States.[52] One aspect of competence is to solve disagreements between DPAs faced with tasks to cooperate or between a lead DPA and other DPAs in one-stop-shop scenarios.

The EDPB will take binding decisions by two-thirds majority (a simple majority is sufficient for non-binding opinions) in case of disagreement about decisions to be taken in the cooperation procedure; in case of disagreements in one-stop-shop scenarios about the DPA that will be the lead DPA; in case the DPA does not consult the EDPB where required or does not follow an EDPB opinion (Article 65 GDPR). The advisory tasks contained in Article 64 GDPR ('Opinion of the Board') and Article 70 GDPR ('Tasks of the Board') are also important. The EDPB can be asked to express itself (via opinions, guidelines, recommendations, and other soft law instruments) both on practical matters or problems, and on more general policy-related matters, such as new upcoming legislation and clarification of GDPR provisions. The EDPB is now at the centre of the new data protection landscape in the EU. Every month new guidance is proposed and made available on its website on issues of all levels of importance, from vulgar and technical to fundamental for the interpretation of core concepts of the GDPR.

This GDPR framework seems to suit the national authorities, who are reported to come to the EDPB enthusiastically with all kinds of ideas and materials to be transformed and elaborated in EDPB instruments and opinions.[53] Based on the observations of the author, the new framework, including the power to rule by binding decisions on disputes regarding cross-border processing, has the potential to en-

---

cooperation tools in the LED (e.g. one-stop-shop, consistency mechanism, dispute resolution by the EDPB and joint operations of the supervisory authorities), see De Hert, Sajfert, *supra* note 32, 253-254. The argument of proximity has had an impact in the sense that Member States were keen to keep this part of the supervisory actions as much as possible within the remit of their jurisdiction.

[52] For a short description, see Burton, De Boel, Kuner, Pateraki, Cadiot, Hoffman, *supra* note 10, 11.

[53] See the website of the EDPB, https://edpb.europa.eu/edpb_en. A good flavour of the work tempo is given by the foregoing footnote and by the Annual Report 2018 (https://edpb.europa.eu/sites/edpb/files/files/file1/edpb_annual_report_2018_summary_-_digital_-_final_1507.pdf) proudly summing up an impressive number of guidelines, consistency opinions, binding decisions, opinions about legal acts and letters drafted and produced between 25 May (date of the first plenary meeting) and 31 December 2018.

sure a uniform application of EU data protection rules by a network of national authorities (see *below*).

14.7. Remedies

One of the 22 tasks of the DPAs discussed *above* concerns complaint handling: the complaint can be lodged either by an individual data subject, or by a representative organization or association (in accordance with Article 80 GDPR) and needs to be followed up by a procedure of investigation and feedback within a reasonable period, "in particular if further investigation or coordination with another supervisory authority is necessary" (Article 57(1)(f) GDPR). The right is further elaborated in Chapter VIII of the GDPR "Remedies, liabilities and penalties", Articles 77-84 GDPR) "without any prejudice to any other administrative or judicial remedy". This right to complain can be exercised either before the DPA of the data subject's or representative organization or association's country of residence, or before the DPA of the Member State where the alleged infringement occurred (Recital 141, Article 77 GDPR; possible conflict with one-stop-shop concept, see *above*). It is noteworthy that the remedy before a DPA is not exclusive. [54] Articles 78 and 79 GDPR foresee an additional right to an effective judicial remedy for all natural and legal persons (individual or via a representative organization) against decisions of a DPA concerning them; failures by a DPA to deal with a complaint within three months; and, for data subjects, against any unlawful processing of their personal data by a controller or processor (Recital 143, Articles 78-79 GDPR).[55]

Hence, data protection might go to court, and in fact it does go to all kinds of courts (labour courts, criminal courts, administrative courts, civil courts…), but the onus of GDPR in terms of length, detail and insistence is on the administrative enforcement system controlled by the DPA.[56] This also explains the long provisions on the possible administrative sanctions in the GDPR.

Before the GDPR, under the 1995 Directive, discretion was left to Member States in their choice of sanctions: criminal, administrative, or other (civil or tort

[54] See Hijmans, *supra* note 23, 335; Galetta, De Hert, *supra* note 1.

[55] The GDPR also sets out rules on jurisdiction allowing the data subject to bring a private enforcement action in the Member State where the offending controller or processor has its establishment, or alternatively in the Member State where the data subject has his or her habitual residence. See on these novelties in the context of private international law, L. Lundstedt, 'International Jurisdiction over Crossborder Private Enforcement Actions under the GDPR', 2018, Faculty of Law, Stockholm University Research Paper No. 57, 45. Available at SSRN: https://ssrn.com/abstract=3159854 or http://dx.doi.org/10.2139/ssrn.3159854.

[56] Critically on the lack of attention for the data protection three layered-remedy system other than the administrative remedies before DPAs and with reference to best practices in Member States that were ignored by the GDPR legislator, see Galetta, De Hert, *supra* note 1, 125-151.

law) or a mix. Considering that the 1995 Directive left the choice of the enforcement regime to the discretion of Member States, the use of criminal sanctions varies from one country to another. Whereas some states only criminalized some data protection wrongs and mainly used civil law or administrative sanctions, others opted for an extensive set of data protection crimes or (e.g. Belgium) relied exclusively on criminal law. Most data protection acts entail mixed approaches with both provisions on penal and on administrative sanctions (e.g. Austria).[57] This example is now followed in the GDPR that, contrary to the 1995 Directive, explicitly distinguishes criminal and administrative sanctions, with one very general provision on criminal sanctions (Article 84 GDPR),[58] and one long, very detailed provision on administrative sanctions (Article 83 GDPR). Article 83(1) opens with a duty for states to arm their DPAs with administrative sanctions. The text partly restricts the discretion of Member States under the 1995 Directive to choose between types of sanctions, by setting out guidelines for administrative sanctions that Member States can introduce. The Article reads as a criminal code with provisions about how administrative sanctions should be determined and a list of 'administrative wrongs' grouped in paragraphs (Article 83(3) to (6) GDPR) with the amounts of fines going up in relation to the increasing seriousness of the wrong. A quick count of the provisions that are related to fines gives a list of almost 50 administrative data protection wrongs.

Articles 83(4) and 83(5) GDPR introduce two levels of fines: (1) up to 10 million or 2% of the undertaking's global annual turnover, whichever is higher, for certain infringements, mostly with regard to the obligations of the controller and the processor pursuant to Articles 8, 11, 25 to 39 and 42 and 43 GDPR and (2) up to 20 million or 4% of the undertaking's global annual turnover, for (more severe) infringements of the basic data protection principles for processing, the data subjects' rights, international transfers and non-compliance with an order or a temporary or definitive limitation on processing or the suspension of data flows by the supervisory authority. These fines are generally considered to be "high", especially in the light of the fines initially proposed by the European Commission and are said to add real "teeth" to data protection enforcement in the EU.[59]

---

[57] More in detail, see P. De Hert, G. Boulet, 'The Co-existence of Administrative and Criminal Law Approaches to Data Protection Wrongs', in D. Wright, P. De Hert (eds), *Enforcing Privacy. Regulatory, Legal and Technological Approaches* (Springer, 2016), 357-394; P. De Hert, 'The EU Data Protection Reform and the (Forgotten) Use of Criminal Sanctions', (2014) 4 *International Data Privacy Law*, 262.

[58] Article 84 GDPR (Penalties): "1. Member States shall lay down the rules on other penalties applicable to infringements of this Regulation in particular for infringements which are not subject to administrative fines pursuant to Article 83, and shall take all measures necessary to ensure that they are implemented. Such penalties shall be effective, proportionate and dissuasive. 2. Each Member State shall notify to the Commission the provisions of its law which it adopts pursuant to paragraph 1 (...)".

[59] Compare Burton, De Boel, Kuner, Pateraki, Cadiot, Hoffman, *supra* note 10, 12.

Read together with a number of other sanctions and measures, such as warnings, periodic review, data protection audits, one has the feeling of completeness: the proposed administrative enforcement system is detailed and seems well prepared. Powers of DPAs are thought through, controllers and processors can no longer process data in an unchecked manner, but have to work transparently creating an environment where proof of good behaviour can always be given immediately; and actors and mechanisms, such as certification bodies, data protection officers and binding corporate rules, are organized with precise instructions to add value, rather than to serve as window dressing.

14.8. Overview of recent sanctioning practices

The annual reports of the DPAs, together with the binding decisions from the EDPB with regard to all trans-border cases (in and out the EU), will help us understand how the fining powers in the GDPR work in practice. Although these administrative sanctions already existed in most countries, some countries did not have them and were interested in having them. Also, not all DPAs in these counties without administrative sanctions were interested in adding administrative fining to their enforcement policies. Article 83(9) GDPR had to resolve problems with Estonia and other countries unfamiliar with the systems of fining by administrations. Where a Member State's legal system does not provide for administrative fines, fines may be initiated by the DPA and imposed by national courts (Article 83(9) GDPR).[60]

Belgium had to create a system of administrative sanctioning within its data protection law by setting up a Litigation Chamber within the DPA and imposed its first (modest) administrative fine on May 28, 2019 in a case against a local authority.[61] The message spread, in particular amongst public servants: under the new GDPR nobody will escape punishment in case of abuse!

Other legal systems that already applied administrative sanctions updated their sanctions and continued their enforcement policies. On 26 March, the President of

---

[60] See also Recital 151 GDPR: "The legal systems of Denmark and Estonia do not allow for administrative fines as set out in this Regulation. The rules on administrative fines may be applied in such a manner that in Denmark the fine is imposed by competent national courts as a criminal penalty and in Estonia the fine is imposed by the supervisory authority in the framework of a misdemeanour procedure, provided that such an application of the rules in those Member States has an equivalent effect to administrative fines imposed by supervisory authorities. Therefore, the competent national courts should take into account the recommendation by the supervisory authority initiating the fine. In any event, the fines imposed should be effective, proportionate and dissuasive".

[61] See 'First Fine Imposed by the Belgian DPA Since GDPR', posted on June 4, 2019, https://www.huntonprivacyblog.com/2019/06/04/first-fine-imposed-by-the-belgian-dpa-since-gdpr/#more-17559.

the Polish Personal Data Protection Office (UODO) announced the first administrative fine under the GDPR of 230,000 Euro. The fine was imposed on a data broker for not providing approximately 6.6 million sole traders with its privacy notice. The broker had only given notice to those persons in public files with an email address, but had not informed others mentioned in public databases (but only with a postal address) because of cost concerns. The case is bad news for data brokers, data aggregators, banks, recruitment agencies and their clients and any other data controllers that collect data from public sources. An appeal to an administrative court is announced.[62]

In 2018, the Information Commissioner's Office (ICO) – the UK DPA – imposed 22 fines under the UK Data Protection Act 2018, including fines against Equifax, Facebook, Uber, the Crown Prosecution Service and Yahoo. Since the infringements in question took place before the GDPR came into force, the maximum fine for a single violation was £ 500,000.[63] The maximum fine was given to Facebook for serious breaches of data protection law with regard to the use of data analytics for political purposes in the Cambridge Analytica case. The penalty was imposed in connection with the app developed by Dr Aleksandr Kogan. The app collected data which was subsequently passed to a parent company of Cambridge Analytica. The penalty was imposed for breach of the first data protection principle (fair processing) and breach of duty to have appropriate technical and organizational measures in place.[64] In GDPR terms, these would equate to Articles 5(1)(a) and 5(1)(f) punishable according to 83(5) GDPR. Elizabeth Denham, Information Commissioner, commented that the "fine would inevitably have been significantly higher under the GDPR".[65]

Another event revealing the ICO strong policy stance against the disregard of personal data provisions concerned the Vote Leave case in March 2019.[66] Vote Leave Limited (the UK's official Brexit campaign) was fined £40,000 for sending almost 200,000 unsolicited texts promoting the aims of the campaign. The ICO car-

---

[62] I. Kowalczuk-Pakula, 'A million PLN fine for GDPR' posted 26 March 2019, https://www.twobirds.com/en/news/articles/2019/poland/a-million-pln-fine-for-gdpr.

[63] 'ICO Publishes First Annual Report Since GDPR's Implementation', posted on July 18, 2019, https://www.huntonprivacyblog.com/2019/07/18/ico-publishes-first-annual-report-since-gdprs-implementation/#more-17750.

[64] R. Boardman, 'Facebook - Cambridge Analytica monetary penalty' posted October 2018, via https://www.twobirds.com/en/news/articles/2018/global/facebook-cambridge-analytica-monetary-penalty.

[65] ICO, 'ICO issues maximum £500,000 fine to Facebook for failing to protect users' personal information', posted October 25, 2018, https://ico.org.uk/about-the-ico/news-and-events/news-and-blogs/2018/10/facebook-issued-with-maximum-500-000-fine/.

[66] 'UK ICO Fines Vote Leave £40,000 for Unsolicited Texts' posted on 22 March 2019, https://www.huntonprivacyblog.com/2019/03/22/uk-ico-fines-vote-leave-40000-for-unsolicited-texts/.

ried out searches and found nuisance calls, spam texts and unsolicited direct marketing as 'areas of significant public concern' (see on this concept *below*).

In January 2019, the French CNIL found Google lacking in transparency when it comes to how it collects and handles user data in the name of serving up personalized ads. A very high fine (50 million Euro) – the largest yet issued under the EU's new data privacy law – was imposed because the infringements observed deprived users of essential guarantees, such as transparency and informed consent and were not incidental, one-off, time-limited but continuous and ongoing breaches. The case is expected to profoundly change the way an American company, such as Google's subsidiary DoubleClick, profiles and targets ads to internet users in the EU based on information gleaned from websites, account registrations, social media, advertising and marketing efforts, newsletters and list rentals, data brokerages, public sources of information and more. [67]

14.9. Creating supervisory convergence without creating new EU institutions (reflection 1)

Data processing today is often a trans-border activity. Territoriality concepts and proximity of 'your' DPA are pleasant consumer-friendly features, but they cannot hide the trans-border reality behind data flows and e-commerce. The GDPR serves not only fundamental rights protection, but also "the accomplishment of an economic union, convergence of the economies within the internal market, and free flow of personal data between Member States" (Recitals 2 and 3 GDPR). With this in mind, the proposal from the Belgian DPA to create a single European Data Protection Authority that would handle trans-/international issues at European level without interfering with the work and internal organization of the DPAs in Member States, makes some sense and is respectful of the principle of subsidiarity: "multinational and transnational" data processing operations (data processing operations that are carried out in a similar manner across borders of Member States or carried out by a single controller in different Member States) can be isolated and deserve a harmonized European set of rules at the highest level. [68]

The proposal did not find much support and does not fit the more general trends within the EU regarding sanctioning administrative law. The trend is currently towards a system of rather detailed EU laws imposing administrative sanctions to be enforced by Member States with the purpose of levelling the "playing field" amongst national authorities and fostering supervisory convergence without

[67] T. Seals, 'Google Fined $57M in Largest GDPR Slap Yet', posted on 22 January 2019, https://threatpost.com/google-fine-privacy-gdpr/141055/.

[68] Belgian DPA, Opinion no. 35/2012 of 21 November 2012 on the draft regulation, paras 8-9.

creating new institutions.[69] This trend first occurred in sectors with a strong global urgency. Mateo highlights sectors such as financial markets and securities market after the 2008 bank-crisis, but also mentions in a footnote the GDPR,[70] that was partly the outcome of the Snowden surveillance revelations.

In both areas, a policy was gradualy developed with more harmonization of sanctions but with a reliance on national authorities to enforce them. This experimentally developed system of "cooperative federalism" could be rolled out further in the future if it proves its value. If not, further centralization, "neither possible nor desirable at this stage", could be expected in future years with a sort of single supervisory mechanism at the European level.[71]

Note that, in principle, several different supervisory models can be selected at European level,[72] but in the case of data protection this will require some gymnastics around Article 16 TFEU and Article 8 of the Charter, which both impose national authorities and, hence, seem to anchor firmly the supervisory model of a network of supervisors.[73]

The current success of cooperative federalism and its network idea of this governance model has also to do with its avoidance of more centralization. It needs to be understood in the light of struggles between "Brussels" and the Member States and has the capacity of addressing irritations from Eurosceptics. Moreover, there are technical and pragmatic reasons for its success. Creating independent EU structures might be contrary to the *Meroni* and *Romano* case-law, restricting the delegation of powers to avoid a weakening of the European Commission's powers.[74] This is avoided by setting up in different areas of EU law networks of supervisors, made up of different independent national authorities, coordinated by a Union body, also endowed with a statute of independence.[75]

---

[69] F. Pascua Mateo, 'Harmonising National Sanctioning Administrative law: An Alternative to a Single Capital-Markets Supervisor', (2018) 24 *European Law Journal* 321-348.

[70] *Ibidem*.

[71] *Ibidem*.

[72] M. Scholten, A. Ottow, 'Institutional Design of Enforcement in the EU: The Case of Financial Markets', (2014) 10 *Utrecht Law Review* 80.

[73] For a broader analysis of obstacles in EU primary law for creating a single EU supervisory system, see Pascua Mateo, *supra* note 69, 334.

[74] More in detail, Pascua Mateo, *supra* note 69, 326. However, the Court of Justice interpreted the *Meroni* conditions very generously in the ESMA case (C-270/12). The issue is dealt with in Jacopo Alberti's chapter in this book.

[75] *Ibidem*, 326-327 ("In this way, the Union has been able to exercise an increasing intervention in the markets, whilst national supervisors have reinforced their role by reducing the regulatory arbitrage that entails the coordination of supervisory practices, as well as being double-hatted as internal supervisors and also enforcing EU laws in direct interaction with the European Commission. An additional advantage is the spread of knowledge about the different national situations that this governance by networks model provides for"). See also Pascua Mateo, *supra* note

This flexible model of network supervisors (from the perspective of the delicate political power balances between EU and Member States) has one obvious weakness: "it may give rise to significant differences in the transposing provisions among Member States, so as to create genuine inequality in identical substantive community laws, for which disciplinary measures play an instrumental role".[76] Mateo rightly emphasizes how this confrontation with inequalities triggered a development towards stronger harmonization (even unification) of sanctioning systems. This will be discussed in a next section.

14.10. The administrative enforcement fray and defence rights (reflection 2)

In a previous section we discussed some recent cases of administrative fining by DPAs, one of them being a French case by the CNIL against Google.[77] One observer, Tara Seals, warns that Google is the largest fish yet to be caught in the GDPR net, but it surely will not be the last, and points at a GDPR development of DPAs in various countries to "leap into the enforcement fray".[78] Although several examples are given of DPA actions that have not carried fines, but ended with warnings and negotiations, Seals still detects a risk of drastic administrative enforcement. This author hightlights the complexity of EU data protection law and sees "several areas of uncertainty that will only play out and become clarified over time".[79] Other voices step in on this point and oppose drastic administrative enforcement. With regard to the Polish case reported *above*, Chivot and Castro observe that such sanction "cuts through expectations that DPAs will play a constructive role of both regulators and advisors under the GDPR. The Polish case can also serve as an illustration of the need to clarify the European privacy law is ever more urgent".[80]

Inappropriateness of DPAs in combining enforcement with advisory tasks and legal certainty problems with vague concepts determining administrative wrongs,

---

69, 334-335 for three additional arguments against centralization through setting up European authorities.

[76] Pascua Mateo, *supra* note 69, 327-328.

[77] *Supra*, section 14.8.

[78] T. Seals, 'Google Fined $57M in Largest GDPR Slap Yet', posted on 22 January 2019, https://threatpost.com/google-fine-privacy-gdpr/141055/.

[79] See also T. Seals, 'GDPR: A Compliance Quagmire, for Now', posted on 7 June 2018, https://threatpost.com/gdpr-a-compliance-quagmire-for-now/132644/.

[80] E. Chivot, D. Castro, 'GDPR Penalties Prove Why Compliance isn't Enough. And Why Companies Need Clarity', 8 May 2019, https://www.techdirt.com/articles/20190506/10401242147/gdpr-penalties-prove-why-compliance-isnt-enoughand-why-companies-need-clarity.shtml.

were central to the critical message against the EU data protection reform ideas on enforcement voiced by the Belgian DPA. Already in 2011-2012, this DPA advocated against an EU imposed fining system for DPAs with several arguments, some more convincing than others. A first argument takes a constitutionalist point of view. In this light, the Belgian DPA observes, sanctioning cannot be entrusted to an authority like a DPA, since "only the judiciary is authorized to check compliance with the law and to punish non-compliance".[81] The argument, coming then from an authority with no mandate to impose fines, surrounded by colleagues in Member States that *had* and *have* such a mandate,[82] did not convince of course.

A second argument of the Belgian DPA against the main ideas of the GDPR reform relied on legal certainty. The many administrative wrongs identified by the EU in Article 83 GDPR (then Article 79 of the Commission proposal) are too vague from a *lex certa*-perspective, in particular the very general reference in Article 83(5) GDPR to "infringements of the basic principles".[83]

A third, probably the least serious, argument has an undertone of "freedom in diversity": "the CPP has serious doubts about the usefulness of a uniform system of administrative sanctions to be executed by the Data Protection Authorities. The CPP wonders why this is proposed today, because it does not perceive the current situation as problematic. As an example, the CPP refers to the Google Street View case and the illegal obtention of data from internet connections (Wi-Fi), where the involved Data Protection Authorities applied, according to their own policy and legislation, the control system and the available penalty system when, if any, without any difficulties: the Dutch Data Protection Authority punished Google with a penalty payment, the French CNIL imposed a fine and the CPP referred the file to the public prosecutor who proposed an amicable settlement of 150,000 Euros to Google".[84]

---

[81] Belgian DPA, Opinion no. 35/2012 of 21 November 2012 on the draft regulation, para. 154.

[82] See for instance, U. Sieber, 'Administrative Sanction Law in Germany', in M. Dyson, B. Vogel (eds), *The Limits of Criminal Law. Anglo-German Concepts and Principles* (Intersentia, 2018), 301.

[83] Belgian DPA, *supra* note 81, para. 162: "The CPP also points out that according to the rule of law violations can only be penalised when they have been sufficiently defined, regardless of whether criminal or administrative penalties are imposed. The CPP has observed that many violations (…) are a repetition of general obligations and are described in general or even vague terms that leave controllers at least a significant margin of discretion. What about predictability in this context? The CPP would like to mention article 5(a) (lawful, fair and transparent processing), article 5(e) (inexcessive retention period based on achievement of purposes), article 5(f) (processing under the responsibility and liability of the controller, who ensures compliance for each processing operation), article 6(e) (processing necessary for the performance of a task carried out in the public interest) and article 6(f) (legitimate interest of the controller which does not prevail over the interests or fundamental rights and freedoms of data subjects)".

[84] Belgian DPA, Opinion no. 35/2012 of 21 November 2012 on the draft regulation, para. 156.

We will come back later to this Google Street View example, that we find particularly problematic, but would like to defend the option taken in the GDPR. We saw already that administrative appeal against the sanction of the Polish DPA is pending and that Article 78 GDPR recognizes the right for controllers and processors to seek an effective judicial remedy against DPA decisions. In terms of constitutionalism, that makes a difference. Moreover, the GDPR does have an eye for defence rights and insists in Article 83(2) GDPR on proportional use of sanctions,[85] while at the same time it creates alternative measures that do not imply fining, such as warnings. Recitals to the GDPR echo these concerns, pointing at the possibility of using reprimands for minor infringements and at the need to respect appropriate procedural safeguards, including effective judicial protection and due process.[86] At the level of EU primary law, it is important to recall several Charter-provisions that strengthen the understanding of the proportionality principle as guarantee against excessive punishment and to observe a growing willingness of the Court of Justice to control the proportionality of sanctions.[87]

Regardless of the foregoing, we do see half work in the GDPR with the administrative sanctioning system proposed. Aspects of procedural safeguards, effective judicial protection and due process are taken care of, but the matter is, together with other aspects not dealt with in the GDPR, further left to the discretion of Member States.[88] We therefore welcome initiatives such as the one of the Dutch DPA to up-

---

[85] In imposing a fine, DPAs have to consider eleven factors spelled out in Article. 83(2) GDPR: the nature, gravity and duration of the infringement; the number of data subjects affected and the level of harm suffered by them; the intentional or negligent character of the infringement; any action taken by the controller or processor to mitigate the harm; any relevant previous infringements by the controller or processor; the degree of co-operation with the relevant DPA; whether the infringement was self-reported by the controller or processor and any other aggravating or mitigating factors.

[86] Recital 148 GDPR: "In order to strengthen the enforcement of the rules of this Regulation, penalties including administrative fines should be imposed for any infringement of this Regulation, in addition to, or instead of appropriate measures imposed by the supervisory authority pursuant to this Regulation. In a case of a minor infringement or if the fine likely to be imposed would constitute a disproportionate burden to a natural person, a reprimand may be issued instead of a fine. Due regard should however be given to the nature, gravity and duration of the infringement, the intentional character of the infringement, actions taken to mitigate the damage suffered, degree of responsibility or any relevant previous infringements, the manner in which the infringement became known to the supervisory authority, compliance with measures ordered against the controller or processor, adherence to a code of conduct and any other aggravating or mitigating factor. The imposition of penalties including administrative fines should be subject to appropriate procedural safeguards in accordance with the general principles of Union law and the Charter, including effective judicial protection and due process". Considerations for proportionality are also interwoven in Recital 150 GDPR.

[87] See for a discussion of the Charter and the case law of the Court of Justice, A. Miranda Rodrigues, 'Fundamental Rights and Punishment: Is There an EU Perspective?', (2019) 10 *New Journal of European Criminal Law* 2019, 17-27.

[88] Recital 152 GDPR: "Where this Regulation does not harmonise administrative penalties or

date its administrative fining policy to take away as much as uncertainty for calculating administrative fines.[89] But will other Member States follow up and produce similar results? Perhaps the EDPB takes up a role here by serving as a discussion forum and by producing guidelines to foster uniformity.

Troubling in the GDPR is the lack of any attention to possible negative transborder consequences of administrative enforcement frays. Google services are offered worldwide. What happens if other DPAs follow the CNIL and start fining Google for infringements harming their citizen? There is a reference to the principle of *ne bis in idem* in one of the recitals, but this only in the context of the relationship between administrative and criminal enforcement in a given country.[90] On the contrary, Recital 150 insists on a hands-free policy (a decision by one DPA does not affect the discretion of other DPAs) and expresses confidence in the consistency mechanism to promote a consistent application of administrative fines.[91]

There is, indeed, some protective value in the consistency procedure. We reacall

---

where necessary in other cases, for example in cases of serious infringements of this Regulation, Member States should implement a system which provides for effective, proportionate and dissuasive penalties. The nature of such penalties, criminal or administrative, should be determined by Member State law". See also Recital 150 GDPR: "(…) It should be for the Member States to determine whether and to which extent public authorities should be subject to administrative fines (…)".

[89] 'Dutch DPA Updates Policy on Administrative Fines', posted on 26 March 2019, via https://www.huntonprivacyblog.com/2019/03/26/dutch-dpa-updates-policy-on-administrative-fines/.

[90] Recital 149 GDPR: "Member States should be able to lay down the rules on criminal penalties for infringements of this Regulation, including for infringements of national rules adopted pursuant to and within the limits of this Regulation. Those criminal penalties may also allow for the deprivation of the profits obtained through infringements of this Regulation. However, the imposition of criminal penalties for infringements of such national rules and of administrative penalties should not lead to a breach of the principle of *ne bis in idem*, as interpreted by the Court of Justice".

[91] Recital 150 GDPR: "In order to strengthen and harmonise administrative penalties for infringements of this Regulation, each supervisory authority should have the power to impose administrative fines. This Regulation should indicate infringements and the upper limit and criteria for setting the related administrative fines, which should be determined by the competent supervisory authority in each individual case, taking into account all relevant circumstances of the specific situation, with due regard in particular to the nature, gravity and duration of the infringement and of its consequences and the measures taken to ensure compliance with the obligations under this Regulation and to prevent or mitigate the consequences of the infringement. (…) Where administrative fines are imposed on persons that are not an undertaking, the supervisory authority should take account of the general level of income in the Member State as well as the economic situation of the person in considering the appropriate amount of the fine. The consistency mechanism may also be used to promote a consistent application of administrative fines. It should be for the Member States to determine whether and to which extent public authorities should be subject to administrative fines. Imposing an administrative fine or giving a warning does not affect the application of other powers of the supervisory authorities or of other penalties under this Regulation".

that a DPA that wishes to take action must consult with the other affected DPAs to ensure consistency of the GDPR. Also, it can be expected that the EDBP's power to rule by binding decisions on disputes regarding cross-border processing has the potential to ensure a uniform application of EU data protection rules, avoiding the same case being potentially dealt differently across various jurisdictions, but whether this safeguard can be compared to a safeguard that is drawn explicitly from the principle of *ne bis in idem* remains to be seen. In the drafting process of the GDPR, the LIBE Committee and the European Parliament proposed a broader safeguard that unfortunately did not make it in the final version.[92] What we miss in the Google Street View case mentioned *supra* is a concern for multiple administrative convictions for the same facts and inequality in the sanctions imposed. An undertone of "freedom in diversity" is inappropriate here.[93]

To understand the foregoing, we need to draw the bigger picture about EU competences to introduce administrative sanctions and enforcement systems, again relying on Mateo. After a first period where the understanding was that there were no such competences, a consensus developed: Union law *can* establish material rules on what behaviour is legitimate or not, but it is for Member States to further regulate the applicable enforcement system.[94] In the twenty-first century, that consensus was revised in two areas, financial markets regulation and data protection law. Two global catastrophes – respectively the 2008 banking crisis and the 2013 Snowden revelations on surveillance – have allowed the EU to move to more harmonization of the respective enforcement systems and to guarantee more coherent supervision. Without creating new EU institutions, the foundations were laid of what Mateo calls a *Common Sanctioning Law System*. Most experimentation was done in the area of financial market regulation, with its plurality of regulations and directives (on insider trading, banking, insurance, etc.). Between 2012-2016, a learning process started in this area, triggered by a 2010 Commission Communication. More detail and harmonization were obtained by adding items to the list of nuclear elements of a sanctioning law common to all Member States.[95] Gradually, an *acquis* was built up that contained common minimum standards for national disciplinary regimes, namely: nature of sanctions applica-

---

[92] The proposal was to insert in a recital (then Recital 119a) the following: "in applying penalties, Member States should show full respect for appropriate procedural safeguards, including the right to an effective judicial remedy, due process, and the principle of *ne bis in idem*".

[93] On our proposal to make decisions made by DPAs binding in all Member States and to conceive more mechanism to coordinate data sharing of cases and complaints at EU level, see Galetta, De Hert, *supra* note 1.

[94] Pascua Mateo, *supra* note 69, 321.

[95] *Ibidem*, 326-238 with reference to European Commission Communication 'Frequently Asked Questions: Communication on reinforcing sanctioning regimes in the financial services sector: More rigorous disciplinary regimes in the financial services sector' of 8 December 2010, COM(2010) 716 final.

ble, including where appropriate criminal sanctions; the typology of sanctions, issues such as the liability of legal persons, criteria to calculate the amount of fines, and the publication of sanctions.

Data Protection law is the second area where the EU was able to develop more momentum in streamlining the enforcement systems. The learning curve (2012-2016) discussed in the previous paragraph explains the growing number of amendments with regard to the sanctioning provisions in the draft GDPR and also the final outcome, a fairly complete regime of administrative sanctions and safeguards resembling the *acquis* described above. Mateo compares this regime with the requirements of the case law of the European Court of Human Rights (ECtHR) and the CJEU,[96] and concludes positively, with a strong reservation regarding the *ne bis in idem* protection, partly because the latter Court in cases such as *Akerberg Fransson* and *Prokurator Generalny v. Lukasz M. Bonda* accepts "unreservedly the legality of double jeopardy with the sole exception of two criminal penalties" and rejects the criminal nature of administrative sanctions in terms of Article 6 ECHR and its fair trial requirements.[97]

There is no reason to put administrative and criminal law enforcement on the same footing, but when the consequences of fines are considerable, different standards in terms of due process and defence rights do not seem legitimate.[98] Data protection law can learn from current EU criminal law,[99] even though in that area the EU has still not developed a mature *ne bis in idem* policy that overcomes the lack of foreseeability for natural persons and companies, due to the parallel applicability of criminal law provisions of multiple states, and has done only very little to eliminate the leeway for arbitrary considerations of the executive (forum shopping by prosecutors).[100] A comprehensive regulation regarding jurisdiction overlaps is needed for the Union. Being prosecuted or punished twice or more within the EU for the same facts, be it via criminal law or administrative law, is no longer acceptable.

---

[96] Pascua Mateo, 339-348.

[97] *Ibidem*, 340. See also A. Andreangeli, 'Ne Bis in Idem and Administrative Sanctions: Bonda', (2013) 50 *Common Market Law Review*, 1827.

[98] E. Herlin-Karnell, 'Is Administrative Law still Relevant? How the Battle of Sanctions has Shaped EU Criminal Law', in V. Mitsilegas, M. Bergström, T. Konstadinides (eds), *Research Handbook on EU Criminal Law* (Edward Elgar, 2016), 233.

[99] P. De Hert, A. Willems, 'Dealing with Overlapping Jurisdictions and Requests for Mutual Legal Assistance, while Respecting Individual Rights. What Can Data Protection Law Learn from Cooperation in Criminal Justice Matters?', in De Hert, Kloza, Makowski (eds) *supra* note 34, 49.

[100] N.I. Thorhauer, *Jurisdiktionskonflikte im Rahmen transnationaler Kriminalität. Zur Koordination der Strafgewalten über natürliche Personen und Unternehmen in der Europäischen Union* (Nomos, 2019), 853.

14.11. The role of criminal law in EU data protection law (reflection 3)

Let us return to criminal law and the short provision on data protection crimes. Is Article 84 GDPR and its compactness the result of negligence? In the past we emphasized that the objective of the Regulation (to take away differences between Member States) is not served by the open nature of the said provision. [101] A more complete implementation survey is needed to take stock about possible divergences in this regard. Why has the GDPR accepted a double regime, one harmonized (Article 83 GDPR), and another open (Article 84 GDPR)? One reason is the organization of EU criminal law. A *regulation* can impose on Member States to introduce criminal sanctions in generic terms, but the details have to be spelled out in a *directive*. [102]

Yet this does not explain the sloppy legal basis for the use of criminal law in the GDPR. What does Article 84 mean when it states that "Member States shall lay down the rules on other penalties applicable to infringements of this Regulation in particular for infringements which are not subject to administrative fines pursuant to Article 83"? Considering the long list of administrative infringements targeted in Article 83 GDPR, what is left over for criminalization? Recital 149 GDPR hardly adds more clarification, but comes up with pragmatic arguments to use criminal law (now and then): if criminal law is applied, an extra law enforcement toolbox is opened with far-reaching enforcement powers in the area of money laundering and asset confiscation and of course the possibility of full reliance on the police apparatus. [103]

These pragmatic reasons to rely on criminal law are well-known but have caused many conflicts of principle for thecriminal law system which encompasses the most severe instrument at a state's disposal in times of peace and is therefore designed to

---

101 De Hert, *supra* note 57, 262-268

102 Article 83(2) TFEU requires that minimum standards related to criminal penalties have to be adopted by using a directive (and not a regulation). See R. Sicurella, 'EU Competence in Criminal Matters', in Mitsilegas, Bergström, Konstadinides (eds), *supra* note 98, 49-77. Comp. Belgian DPA, Opinion no. 35/2012 of 21 November 2012 on the draft regulation, para. 158.

103 Recital 149 GDPR: "Member States should be able to lay down the rules on criminal penalties for infringements of this Regulation, including for infringements of national rules adopted pursuant to and within the limits of this Regulation. Those criminal penalties may also allow for the deprivation of the profits obtained through infringements of this Regulation. However, the imposition of criminal penalties for infringements of such national rules and of administrative penalties should not lead to a breach of the principle of *ne bis in idem*, as interpreted by the Court of Justice". Article 84 does not seem to prohibit criminalisation of acts that are mentioned in Article 83, but encourages states that want to use criminal law 'in particular' for other kinds of acts. For example, the Portuguese law that implements the GDPR – Law 59/2019 – specifies certain conducts related to undue access to data which result in a criminal sanction up to one or two years of prison, or a criminal fine/pecuniary penalty. See Section III of the Law, Articles 46-52, https://dre.pt/web/guest/pesquisa/-/search/123815982/details/maximized.

be a last resort enforcement system. Encouraging use of criminal law for pragmatic reasons ("you can have the police for free") is in part neglecting these foundations for opportunistic motives, a development that has led worldwide to overuse of criminal law systems in Western states that are supposed to prioritise liberty by avoiding too much criminal law.[104] The EU contributes to overuse by poorly guiding Member States in their use of criminal sanctions, combined or not with administrative sanctions.

Mitsilegas and Vavoula question the effectiveness of current EU sanctioning practices by pointing at EU anti-money laundering law, also poor in its guidance about the use of criminal law.[105] It is questionable, both authors observe, whether this lack of harmonization contributes towards the effectiveness of EU law in the field. If the choice of the EU legislator has sanctioned an infringement administratively, then the choices of Member States to "goldplate" implementation by imposing criminal sanctions should be limited by the requirement to ensure the effectiveness of EU law.[106] In the name of effectiveness de-criminalization, rather than over-criminalization could be the outcome![107]

The Belgian Data Protection Authority was already referred to several times in this contribution for its stubborn resistance against the administrative sanctioning logic in the GDPR (*supra*). Its opinion from 2012 also contains two interesting arguments in favour of *not* using administrative law but relying on criminal law. Firstly, there is a more principled or substantive argument: in particular the serious administrative infringements in Article 83(5) GDPR (fines up to 20 million or 4% of the turnover) are too serious to be labelled administrative wrongs and should be regarded as criminal law offences.[108] Secondly, the authority points at technical prob-

---

[104] See P. Hein van Kempen, M. Jendly (eds), *Overuse in the Criminal Justice System. On Criminalization, Prosecution and Imprisonment*, (Intersentia, 2019), 635.; W. Wohlers, 'Criminal Law as a Regulatory Tool', in M. Dyson, B. Vogel (eds), *The Limits of Criminal Law. Anglo-German Concepts and Principles* (Intersentia, 2018), 235 (about criminal law as *ultima ratio* as a fairytale); M. Dyson, B. Vogel, 'Crime and Regulation Compared: The Limits of Criminalisation', *ibidem*, 263.

[105] They link their critical observation to the phenomenon of 'goldplating' in EU implementation laws (the practice of national legislators exceeding the terms of EU-directives when implementing them into national law).

[106] V. Mitsilegas, N. Vavoula, 'The Evolving EU Anti-Money Laundering Regime. Challenges for Fundamental Rights and the Rule of Law' (2016) 23 *Maastricht Journal of European and Comparative Law* 261, 272.

[107] *Ibidem*.

[108] Belgian DPA, Opinion no. 35/2012 of 21 November 2012 on the draft regulation, para. 159: "The CPP also has serious doubts about the qualification of the sanctions established by article 79. Although these sanctions are explicitly described as "administrative sanctions", the CPP is of the opinion that they are criminal sanctions and having regard to the case law of the European Court of Human Rights and the EU policy. The importance of determining whether criminal sanctions are concerned, essentially relates to the fact that article 6 of the European Convention

lems with administrative enforcement of data protection wrongs: criminal offences mostly consist of several infringements and contrary to normal courts, DPAs cannot deal with the facts in a global manner.[109]

The first substantive argument of the Belgian authority – serious wrongs should be dealt with by criminal law, not administrative law – is underdeveloped in our opinion. In 2016 we looked at current sanctioning systems, at the reasons to rely on administrative sanctions as opposed to criminal sanctions, at why states often prefer to develop both sanctioning systems in parallel, [110] at the need to keep the both sanctioning systems separate and to identify a proper role for them, amongst others based on a last-resort role of criminal penalties.[111] What the Belgian authority is doing (proposing to transform half of the list of administrative data protection wrongs into crimes) is not the outcome of our exercise done in 2016. We reached a different result, more in favour of the use of administrative sanctions, but without closing the door for a possible use of criminal law, although this should preferably be dealt with in a new directive complementing the GDPR.

The second, more technical, argument of the Belgian authority is particularly strong. A global approach to *wrongs* is in some cases best not left to a specialized administrative authority.[112] If in data protection enforcement there are "areas of significant public concern" (term coined by the ICO in the 2019 Vote Leave case *above*), a society as a whole should be alerted and reflect about its responses. In particular, fraud with a huge impact on political institutions (like the fraud reported in the Vote Leave and Cambridge Analytica cases) merits a more global response and scrutiny by the criminal law system. If criminal law should serve for something, should it not be this?

---

on Human Rights and article 6 of the Treaty on the European Union stipulate that in such a context sufficient legal safeguards must be provided (for example the possibility to appeal to an independent judge). The text of the draft regulation does not mention this at all".

[109] *Ibidem*, para. 156: "[It] is rather rare that the facts of constituting a violation of the regulation are solely related to data protection: criminal offences mostly consist of several infringements of which one aspect is related to "data protection". In those cases, the scope of the Data Protection Authority will prevent the latter from dealing with the facts in a global manner. They will be limited to the aspect "data protection", because the (authority) at its level cannot appeal to the concurrence of offences technique, according to which the maximum penalty is applied to facts under dispute. Only courts and tribunals may rely on this technique and handle criminal offences as a whole".

[110] Herlin-Karnell, *supra* note 98. Ost and Van De Kerchove speak about *networks of sanctions* (*réseaux de santions*) that exist next to each other, each having fuzzy limits and all having uncertain articulations from one to each other (F. Ost, M. van de Kerchove, *De la pyramide au réseau? Pour une théorie dialectique du droit* (Publications des Facultés universitaires Saint-Louis, 2002), 243.

[111] De Hert, Boulet, *supra* note 57.

[112] See more in detail, *ibidem*.

14.12. Conclusion: boost in administrative enforcement partly on cooperative federalist arrangements with open questions about how the GDPR will be put into practice

An important change from the 1995 Data Protection Directive is that the GDPR harmonizes data protection enforcement in the EU. No doubt this development has been propelled by the Snowden revelations about massive non-transparent surveillance by states in partnership with large IT firms and by a strong mandate to develop data protection law at EU level in Article 16 TFEU.

Not discussed in this contribution are novel features regarding participation: there is a bigger role for citizens in the framework of the new duty to carry out data protection impact assessments in certain cases (Article 35 GDPR) and citizens have now a right to mandate not-for-profit bodies to lodge complaints on their behalf (Article 80(1) GDPR). Member States can even go one step further and recognize such a right independently of a data subject's mandate (Article 80(2) GDPR).[113] In terms of the threefold disctinction proposed by McCrudden between an individual justice model, a group justice model and a participation model,[114] we might speak of some advances with regard to the two last models, to complement the still dominant individualistic enforcement model (with its criminal, civil and agency components) that the GDPR took over from older data protection laws. Small improvements were made to the civil justice component, but none were made to the criminal justice component, although the very goal of the Regulation – to harmonize data protection law in the Union – would have implied such an agenda. Most energy went to the improvement of the enforcement agency component within the individual justice model, ensuring that individual data protection related grievances are remedied with the assistance of a specialised body that has investigatory and fining powers. The GDPR strengthens these investigatory powers and creates a legal obligation for all Member States to entrust these agencies (DPAs) with powers to impose administrative sanctions.

A single European agency or supervisory structure was argued for by Belgian DPA, but the idea of governance by networks relying on national agencies won. In fact, data protection was one of the first European areas where cooperative federalism was tested. The GDPR indeed tasks national supervisory authorities with the role of enforcing the GDPR in their domestic legal order, while at the same time spelling out a European dimension of enforcement imposing on the DPAs duties to cooperate and introduces a one-stop-shop mechanism with a lead DPA and a consistency mechanism supervised by the EDBP.

The DPAs are given guarantees in terms of effectiveness and independence and

---

[113] It would be useful to further analyze this provision within the doctrinal framework on collective actions proposed by Farkas, *supra* note 5.

[114] See our introduction.

strong administrative sanctioning powers, that are regulated in quite some detail (level of fines, how to determine a fine, judicial review), with some uncertainty about the *ne bis in idem* guarantee in cases where several DPAs impose administrative fines on a data controller.

The use of criminal sanctions is not harmonized, and it can be expected that Member States will continue to implement the GDPR in a non-harmonized way, either opting for no criminal law, some criminal law or a lot of criminal law.

In this contribution we have highlighted the context-dependency of the GDPR. The provisions on administrative sanctions and their limits were developed at a moment where the EU was organically perfecting its *Common Sanctioning Law System* (Pascua Mateo). Most fundamental rights objections against a sanctioning system that provides *less* guarantees compared to the criminal law system are addressed in the GDPR, including the need for respecting proportionality in sanctioning, although the *ne bis in idem* guarantee (proposed during the drafting phase) is only mentioned in the non-binding Recital 149 GDPR. Whether the consistency mechanism can help avoiding multiple sanctioning of the same acts by single data controllers and by different data protection authorities remains to be seen. The same mechanism will also determine whether the initial choice not to work with a single supervisory structure, but to strengthen the European roles and interdependencies of national supervisory authorities will stand the test of practice.[115]

A second concern addressed in this contribution is about the risk that DPAs will leap into an enforcement fray. How appropriate will these authorities combine enforcement tasks with advisory tasks in the light of the many vague concepts in data protection law? DPAs are more than "cops" but have broader, multifaceted, and non-normative roles. Data protection with its open norms and uncertainties (when precisely is an impact assessment needed?, when is new consent required for new uses of data?, what technologies have what impact?, ...) relies heavily on dialogue and persuasion. Effective enforcement will depend on the regulatory relationship management of the parties involved, with the DPA's picking the right enforcement style and with the firms working harder on their relationships with these enforcement agencies.[116]

---

[115] Comp. H. Hijmans, 'The DPAs and Their Cooperation: How Far Are We in Making Enforcement of Data Protection Law More European?' (2016) 2 *European Data Protection Law Review* 362.

[116] Vranaki, *supra* note 37, 9-11.

INDEX

For Product Safety Concerns and Information please contact our EU representative GPSR@taylorandfrancis.com
Taylor & Francis Verlag GmbH, Kaufingerstraße 24, 80331 München, Germany

www.ingramcontent.com/pod-product-compliance
Ingram Content Group UK Ltd.
Pitfield, Milton Keynes, MK11 3LW, UK
UKHW020019200926
475702UK00014B/1971
9780367765668